IRON MAN 2.0

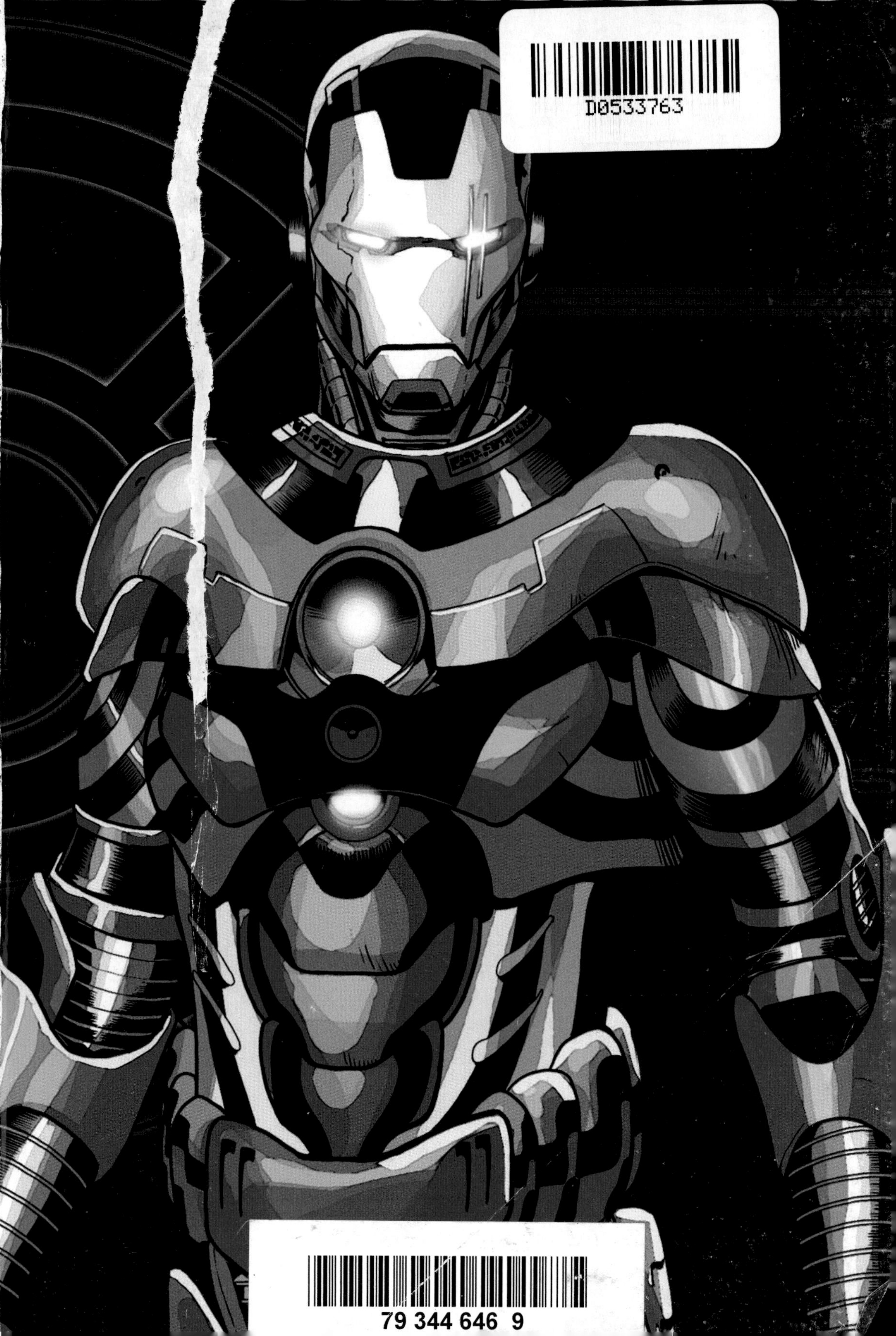

IRON MAN 2.0
PALMER ADDLEY IS DEAD

WRITER: **NICK SPENCER**

PROLOGUE (FROM *INVINCIBLE IRON MAN #500*)

ARTIST: **BARRY KITSON**
COLORIST: **MATTHEW WILSON**

ISSUES #1-3

ARTISTS: **BARRY KITSON, KANO &
CARMINE DI GIANDOMENICO**
COLORISTS: **MATTHEW WILSON, KANO
& FRANK MARTIN**

ISSUES #4-7

ARTIST: **ARIEL OLIVETTI**
PROLOGUE & EPILOGUE ARTIST, #6-7: **CARMINE DI GIANDOMENICO**
PROLOGUE & EPILOGUE COLORIST, #6-7: **MATTHEW WILSON**

COVER ART: **SALVADOR LARROCA & FRANK D'ARMATA** (#1-6)
AND **ARIEL OLIVETTI** (#7)
LETTERER: **VC'S JOE CARAMAGNA**
EDITOR: **ALEJANDRO ARBONA**
SENIOR EDITOR: **STEPHEN WACKER**

COLLECTION EDITOR: **JENNIFER GRÜNWALD**
EDITORIAL ASSISTANTS: **JAMES EMMETT & JOE HOCHSTEIN**
ASSISTANT EDITORS: **ALEX STARBUCK & NELSON RIBEIRO**
EDITOR, SPECIAL PROJECTS: **MARK D. BEAZLEY**
SENIOR EDITOR, SPECIAL PROJECTS: **JEFF YOUNGQUIST**
SENIOR VICE PRESIDENT OF SALES: **DAVID GABRIEL**
SVP OF BRAND PLANNING & COMMUNICATIONS: **MICHAEL PASCIULLO**

EDITOR IN CHIEF: **AXEL ALONSO**
CHIEF CREATIVE OFFICER: **JOE QUESADA**
PUBLISHER: **DAN BUCKLEY**
EXECUTIVE PRODUCER: **ALAN FINE**

IRON MAN 2.0 VOL. 1: PALMER ADDLEY IS DEAD. Contains material originally published in magazine form as IRON MAN 2.0 #1-7 and INVINCIBLE IRON MAN #500. First printing 2011. ISBN# 978-0-7851-4749-7. Published by MARVEL WORLDWIDE, INC., a subsidiary of MARVEL ENTERTAINMENT, LLC. OFFICE OF PUBLICATION: 135 West 50th Street, New York, NY 10020. Copyright © 2010 and 2011 Marvel Characters, Inc. All rights reserved. $16.99 per copy in the U.S. and $18.99 in Canada (GST #R127032852); Canadian Agreement #40668537. All characters featured in this issue and the distinctive names and likenesses thereof, and all related indicia are trademarks of Marvel Characters, Inc. No similarity between any of the names, characters, persons, and/or institutions in this magazine with those of any living or dead person or institution is intended, and any such similarity which may exist is purely coincidental. **Printed in the U.S.A.** ALAN FINE, EVP - Office of the President, Marvel Worldwide, Inc. and EVP & CMO Marvel Characters B.V.; DAN BUCKLEY, Publisher & President - Print, Animation & Digital Divisions; JOE QUESADA, Chief Creative Officer; JIM SOKOLOWSKI, Chief Operating Officer; DAVID BOGART, SVP of Business Affairs & Talent Management; TOM BREVOORT, SVP of Publishing; C.B. CEBULSKI, SVP of Creator & Content Development; DAVID GABRIEL, SVP of Publishing Sales & Circulation; MICHAEL PASCIULLO, SVP of Brand Planning & Communications; JIM O'KEEFE, VP of Operations & Logistics; DAN CARR, Executive Director of Publishing Technology; SUSAN CRESPI, Editorial Operations Manager; ALEX MORALES, Publishing Operations Manager; STAN LEE, Chairman Emeritus. For information regarding advertising in Marvel Comics or on Marvel.com, please contact John Dokes, SVP Integrated Sales and Marketing, at jdokes@marvel.com. For Marvel subscription inquiries, please call 800-217-9158. Manufactured between 8/25/2011 and 9/13/2011 by QUAD/GRAPHICS, DUBUQUE, IA, USA.

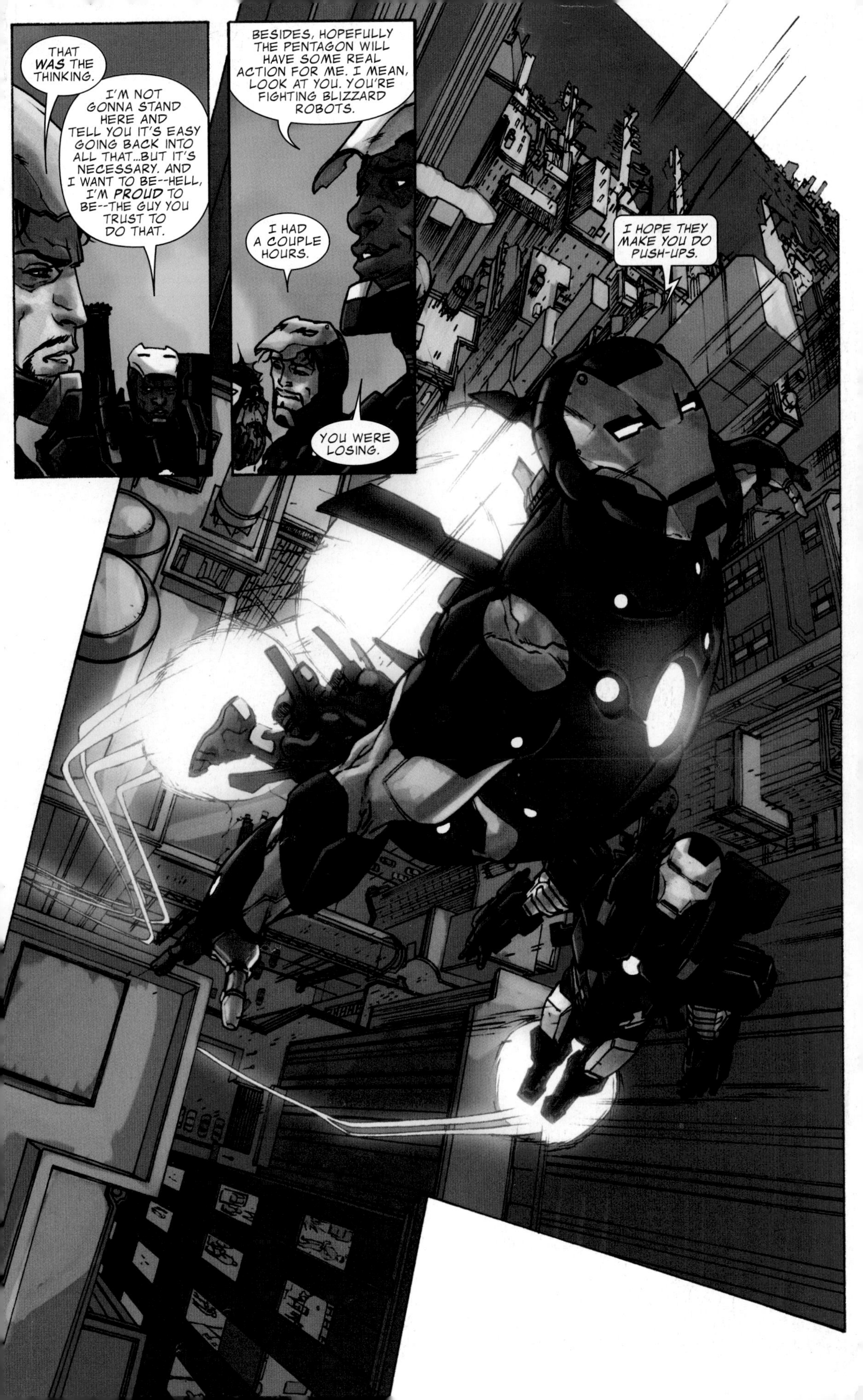
THAT *WAS* THE THINKING.
I'M NOT GONNA STAND HERE AND TELL YOU IT'S EASY GOING BACK INTO ALL THAT...BUT IT'S NECESSARY. AND I WANT TO BE--HELL, I'M *PROUD* TO BE--THE GUY YOU TRUST TO DO THAT.
BESIDES, HOPEFULLY THE PENTAGON WILL HAVE SOME REAL ACTION FOR ME. I MEAN, LOOK AT YOU. YOU'RE FIGHTING BLIZZARD ROBOTS.
I HAD A COUPLE HOURS.
YOU WERE LOSING.
I HOPE THEY MAKE YOU DO PUSH-UPS.

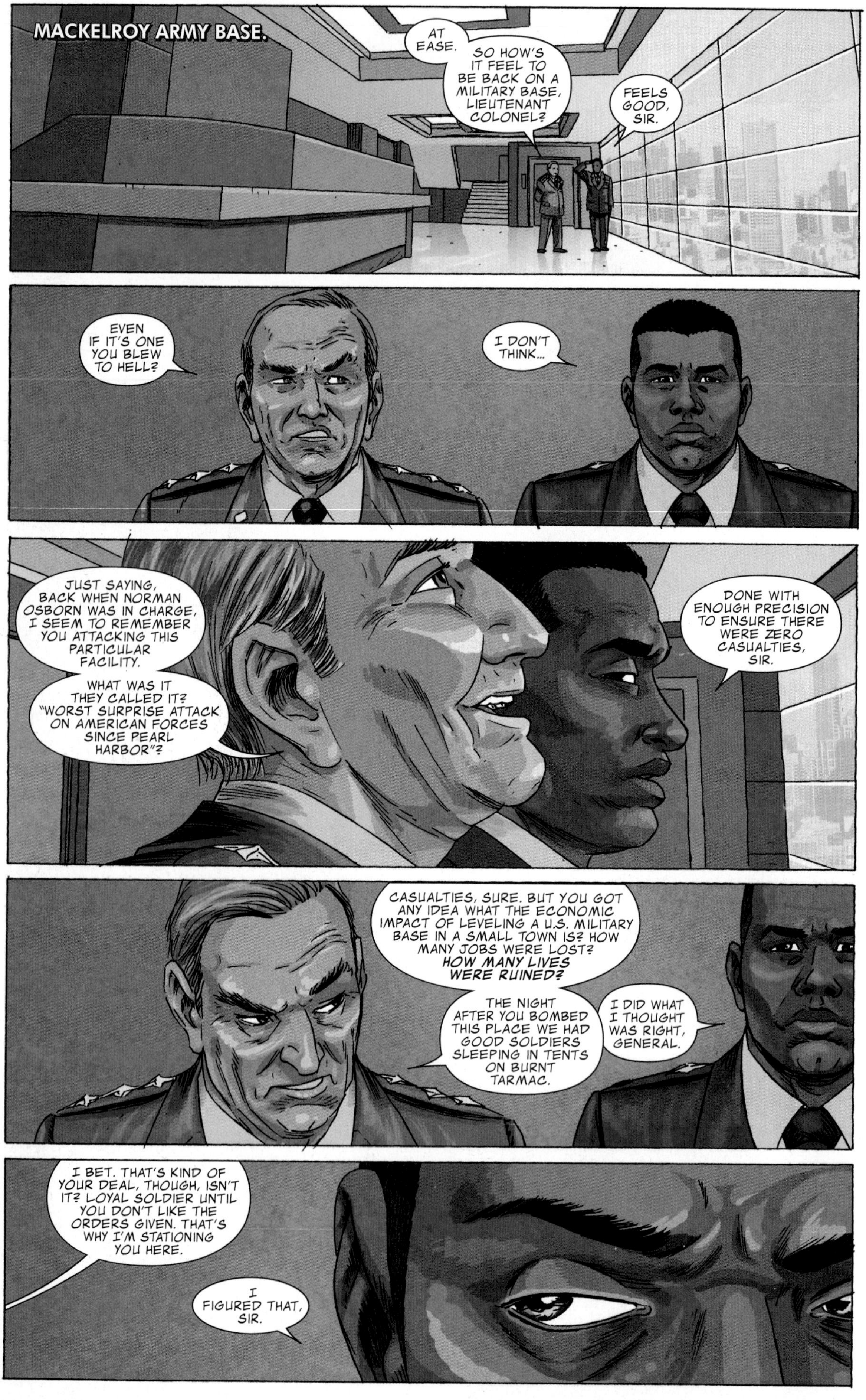
MACKELROY ARMY BASE.
AT EASE.
SO HOW'S IT FEEL TO BE BACK ON A MILITARY BASE, LIEUTENANT COLONEL?
FEELS GOOD, SIR.
EVEN IF IT'S ONE YOU BLEW TO HELL?
I DON'T THINK...
JUST SAYING, BACK WHEN NORMAN OSBORN WAS IN CHARGE, I SEEM TO REMEMBER YOU ATTACKING THIS PARTICULAR FACILITY.
WHAT WAS IT THEY CALLED IT? "WORST SURPRISE ATTACK ON AMERICAN FORCES SINCE PEARL HARBOR"?
DONE WITH ENOUGH PRECISION TO ENSURE THERE WERE ZERO CASUALTIES, SIR.
CASUALTIES, SURE. BUT YOU GOT ANY IDEA WHAT THE ECONOMIC IMPACT OF LEVELING A U.S. MILITARY BASE IN A SMALL TOWN IS? HOW MANY JOBS WERE LOST? *HOW MANY LIVES WERE RUINED?*
THE NIGHT AFTER YOU BOMBED THIS PLACE WE HAD GOOD SOLDIERS SLEEPING IN TENTS ON BURNT TARMAC.
I DID WHAT I THOUGHT WAS RIGHT, GENERAL.
I BET. THAT'S KIND OF YOUR DEAL, THOUGH, ISN'T IT? LOYAL SOLDIER UNTIL YOU DON'T LIKE THE ORDERS GIVEN. THAT'S WHY I'M STATIONING YOU HERE.
I FIGURED THAT, SIR.

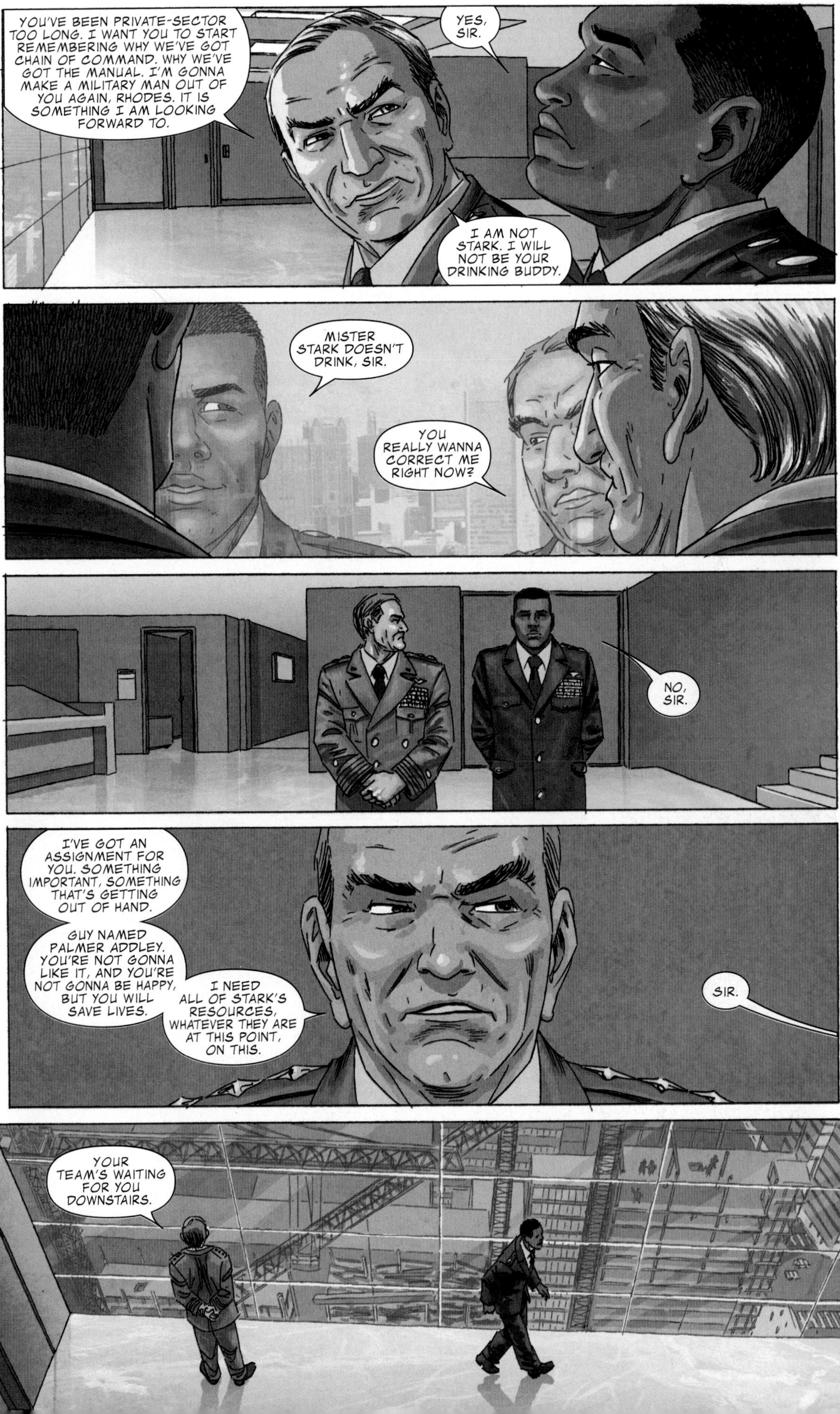
YOU'VE BEEN PRIVATE-SECTOR TOO LONG. I WANT YOU TO START REMEMBERING WHY WE'VE GOT CHAIN OF COMMAND. WHY WE'VE GOT THE MANUAL. I'M GONNA MAKE A MILITARY MAN OUT OF YOU AGAIN, RHODES. IT IS SOMETHING I AM LOOKING FORWARD TO.
YES, SIR.
I AM NOT STARK. I WILL NOT BE YOUR DRINKING BUDDY.
MISTER STARK DOESN'T DRINK, SIR.
YOU REALLY WANNA CORRECT ME RIGHT NOW?
NO, SIR.
I'VE GOT AN ASSIGNMENT FOR YOU. SOMETHING IMPORTANT, SOMETHING THAT'S GETTING OUT OF HAND.
GUY NAMED PALMER ADDLEY. YOU'RE NOT GONNA LIKE IT, AND YOU'RE NOT GONNA BE HAPPY, BUT YOU WILL SAVE LIVES.
I NEED ALL OF STARK'S RESOURCES, WHATEVER THEY ARE AT THIS POINT, ON THIS.
SIR.
YOUR TEAM'S WAITING FOR YOU DOWNSTAIRS.

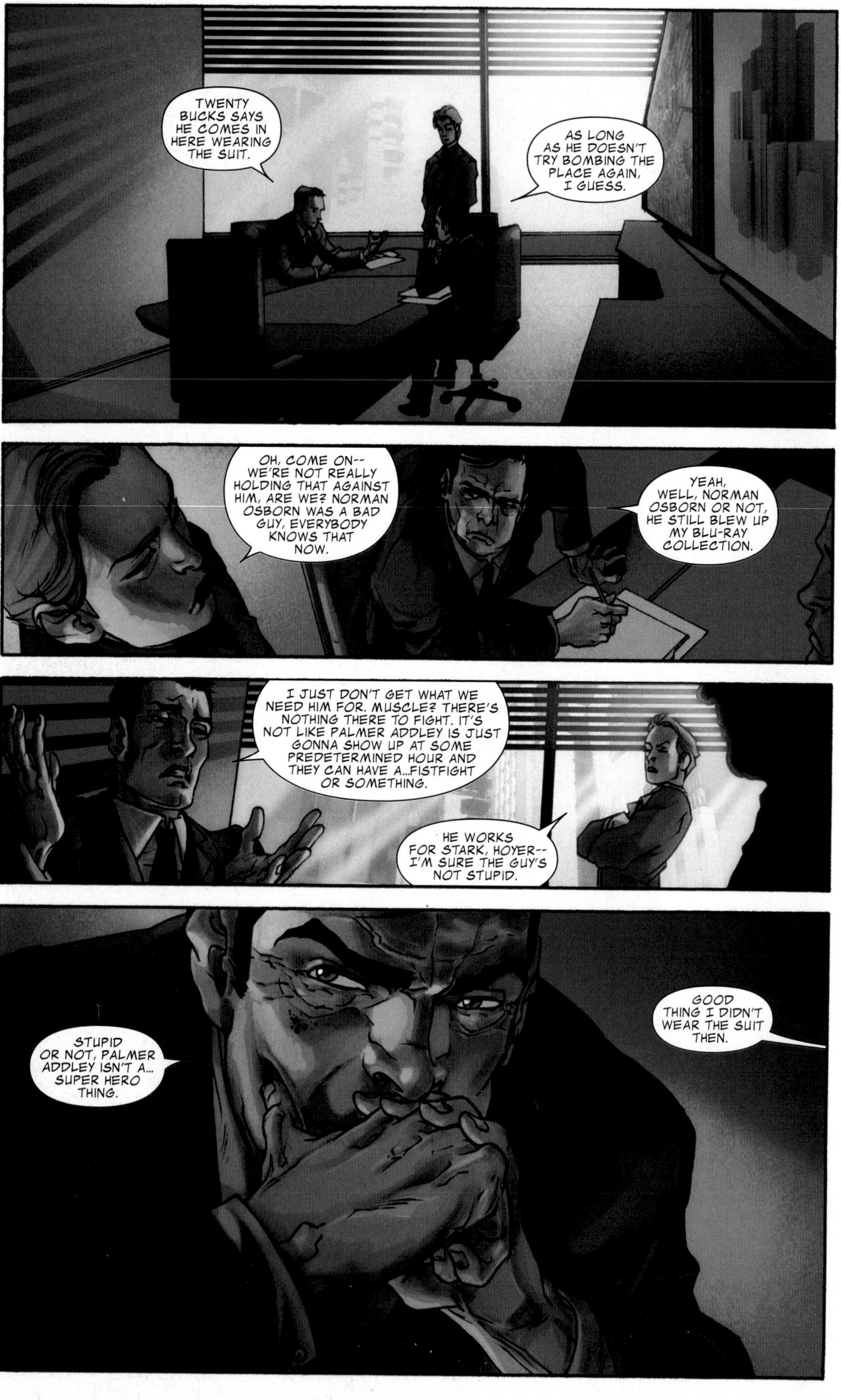
TWENTY BUCKS SAYS HE COMES IN HERE WEARING THE SUIT.
AS LONG AS HE DOESN'T TRY BOMBING THE PLACE AGAIN, I GUESS.
OH, COME ON-- WE'RE NOT REALLY HOLDING THAT AGAINST HIM, ARE WE? NORMAN OSBORN WAS A BAD GUY, EVERYBODY KNOWS THAT NOW.
YEAH, WELL, NORMAN OSBORN OR NOT, HE STILL BLEW UP MY BLU-RAY COLLECTION.
I JUST DON'T GET WHAT WE NEED HIM FOR. MUSCLE? THERE'S NOTHING THERE TO FIGHT. IT'S NOT LIKE PALMER ADDLEY IS JUST GONNA SHOW UP AT SOME PREDETERMINED HOUR AND THEY CAN HAVE A...FISTFIGHT OR SOMETHING.
HE WORKS FOR STARK, HOYER-- I'M SURE THE GUY'S NOT STUPID.
STUPID OR NOT, PALMER ADDLEY ISN'T A... SUPER HERO THING.
GOOD THING I DIDN'T WEAR THE SUIT THEN.

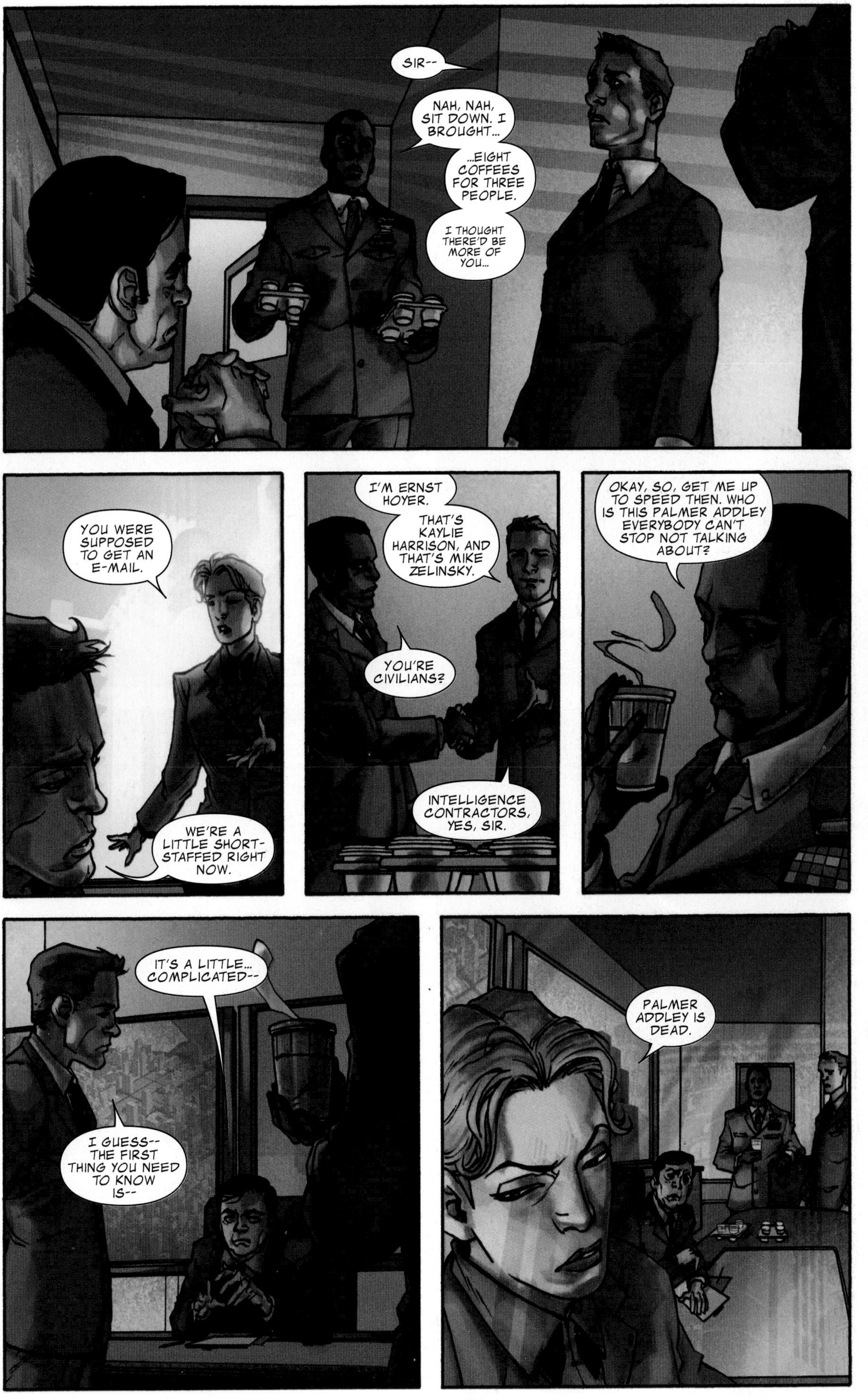
SIR--
NAH, NAH, SIT DOWN. I BROUGHT...
...EIGHT COFFEES FOR THREE PEOPLE.
I THOUGHT THERE'D BE MORE OF YOU...
YOU WERE SUPPOSED TO GET AN E-MAIL.
WE'RE A LITTLE SHORT-STAFFED RIGHT NOW.
I'M ERNST HOYER.
THAT'S KAYLIE HARRISON, AND THAT'S MIKE ZELINSKY.
YOU'RE CIVILIANS?
INTELLIGENCE CONTRACTORS, YES, SIR.
OKAY, SO, GET ME UP TO SPEED THEN. WHO IS THIS PALMER ADDLEY EVERYBODY CAN'T STOP NOT TALKING ABOUT?
IT'S A LITTLE... COMPLICATED--
I GUESS-- THE FIRST THING YOU NEED TO KNOW IS--
PALMER ADDLEY IS DEAD.

"HE WAS PART OF A DARPA DEEP IMMERSION PROGRAM RUN OUT OF THE STRATEGIC TECHNOLOGY OFFICE.

"AND WHEN I SAY DEEP IMMERSION, I MEAN *DEEP* DEEP. RESEARCHERS LIVE ON-SITE, NO OUTSIDE COMMUNICATION, SECURITY FILTERS ON *EVERYTHING*--

"THESE GUYS DON'T HAVE TELEVISIONS FOR FEAR THEY CAN FIGURE OUT HOW TO SEND SOMETHING OVER THE CABLE LINES.

"HE SPECIALIZED IN NANOTECH, ROBOTIC SYSTEMS, HIGH PRODUCTIVITY COMPUTING, SURVEILLANCE TECHNOLOGY, BIOSCIENCES...WELL, HE SPECIALIZED IN EVERYTHING, REALLY. HE WAS PRETTY MUCH THE BEST BRAIN THEY HAD.

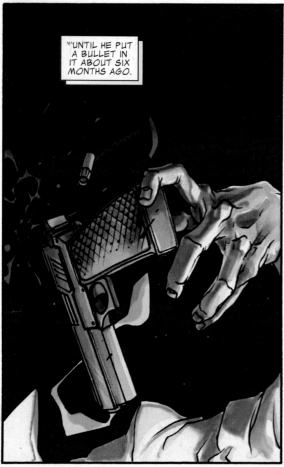

"'UNTIL HE PUT A BULLET IN IT ABOUT SIX MONTHS AGO.

"NOW THIS IS OBVIOUSLY A BIG LOSS FOR D.O.D., BUT HEY, NOT REALLY UNUSUAL--WHAT'S THE SUICIDE RATE FOR GENIUS I.Q.S? THREE TIMES THE NATIONAL AVERAGE? YOU CAN IMAGINE WHAT THAT DOES TO R&D PAYROLLS.

"ASIDE FROM THAT, THOUGH. EVERYTHING IS GOING ALONG FINE AFTER THAT FOR ABOUT TWO MONTHS.

"BUT THEN-- WELL, ALL OF ADDLEY'S BIG INITIATIVES--"

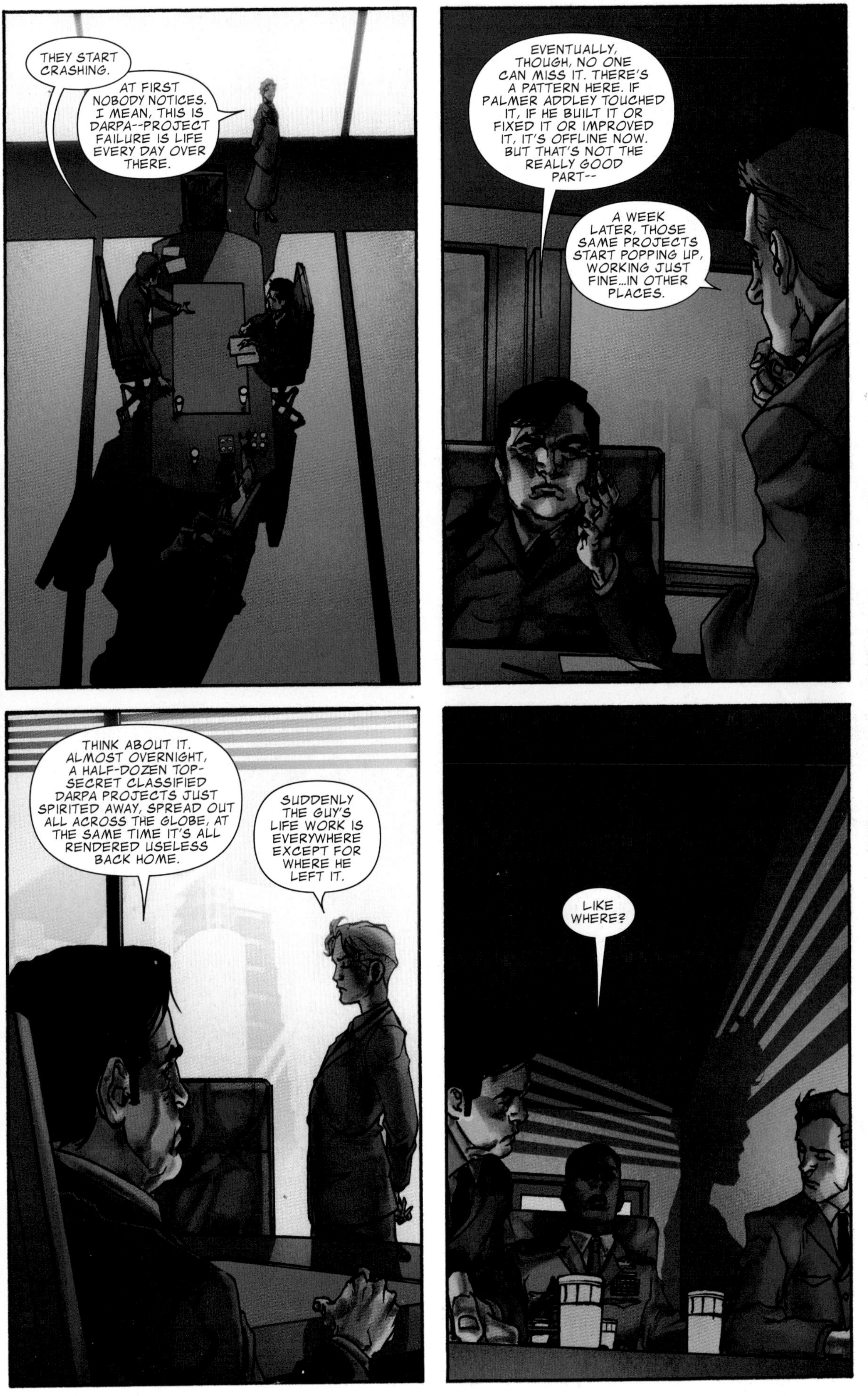
THEY START CRASHING.
AT FIRST NOBODY NOTICES. I MEAN, THIS IS DARPA--PROJECT FAILURE IS LIFE EVERY DAY OVER THERE.
EVENTUALLY, THOUGH, NO ONE CAN MISS IT. THERE'S A PATTERN HERE. IF PALMER ADDLEY TOUCHED IT, IF HE BUILT IT OR FIXED IT OR IMPROVED IT, IT'S OFFLINE NOW. BUT THAT'S NOT THE REALLY GOOD PART--
A WEEK LATER, THOSE SAME PROJECTS START POPPING UP, WORKING JUST FINE...IN OTHER PLACES.
THINK ABOUT IT. ALMOST OVERNIGHT, A HALF-DOZEN TOP-SECRET CLASSIFIED DARPA PROJECTS JUST SPIRITED AWAY, SPREAD OUT ALL ACROSS THE GLOBE, AT THE SAME TIME IT'S ALL RENDERED USELESS BACK HOME.
SUDDENLY THE GUY'S LIFE WORK IS EVERYWHERE EXCEPT FOR WHERE HE LEFT IT.
LIKE WHERE?

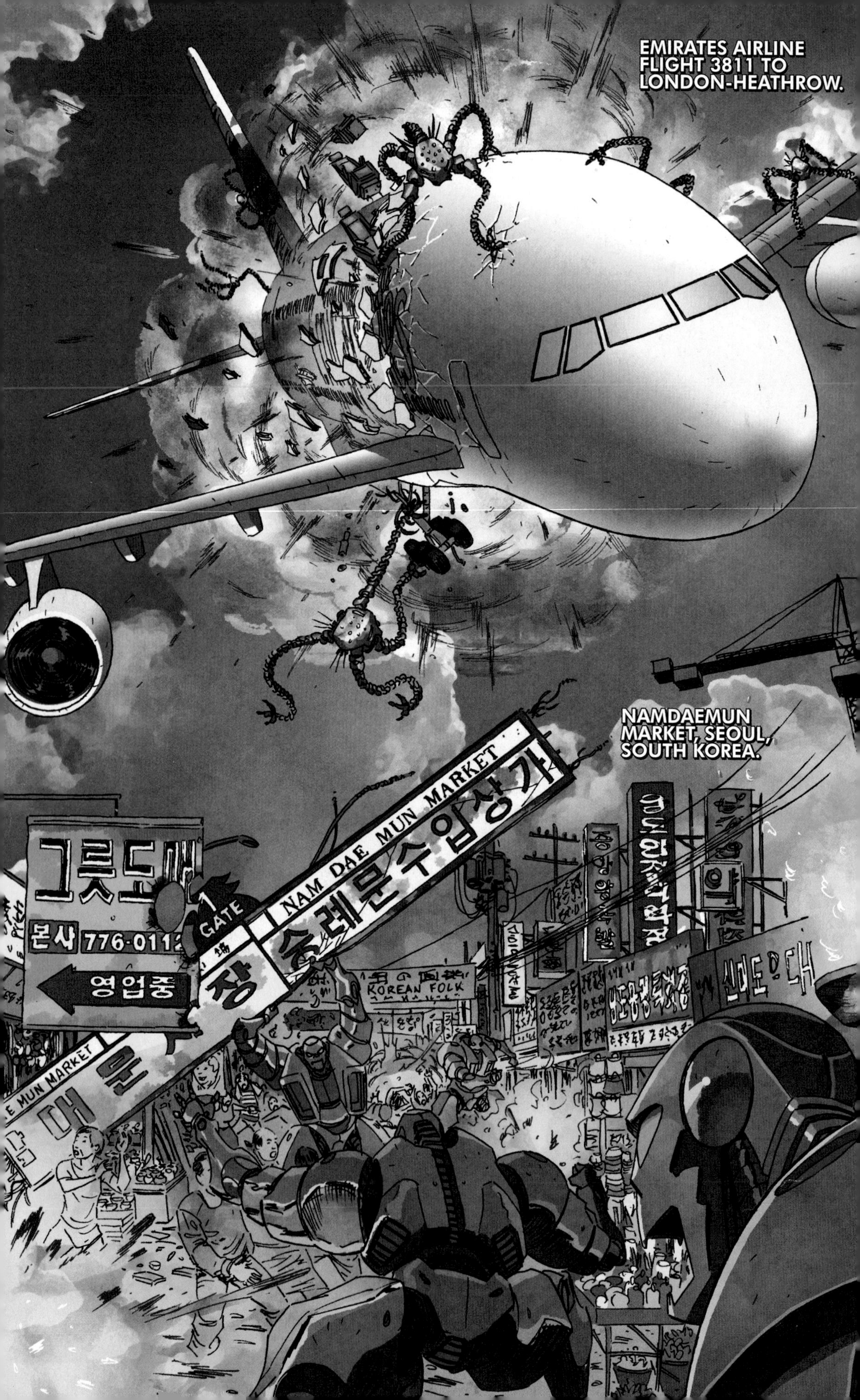
EMIRATES AIRLINE FLIGHT 3811 TO LONDON-HEATHROW.
NAMDAEMUN MARKET, SEOUL, SOUTH KOREA.
NAM DAE MUN MARKET
숭례문수입상가
GATE
영업중
KOREAN FOLK

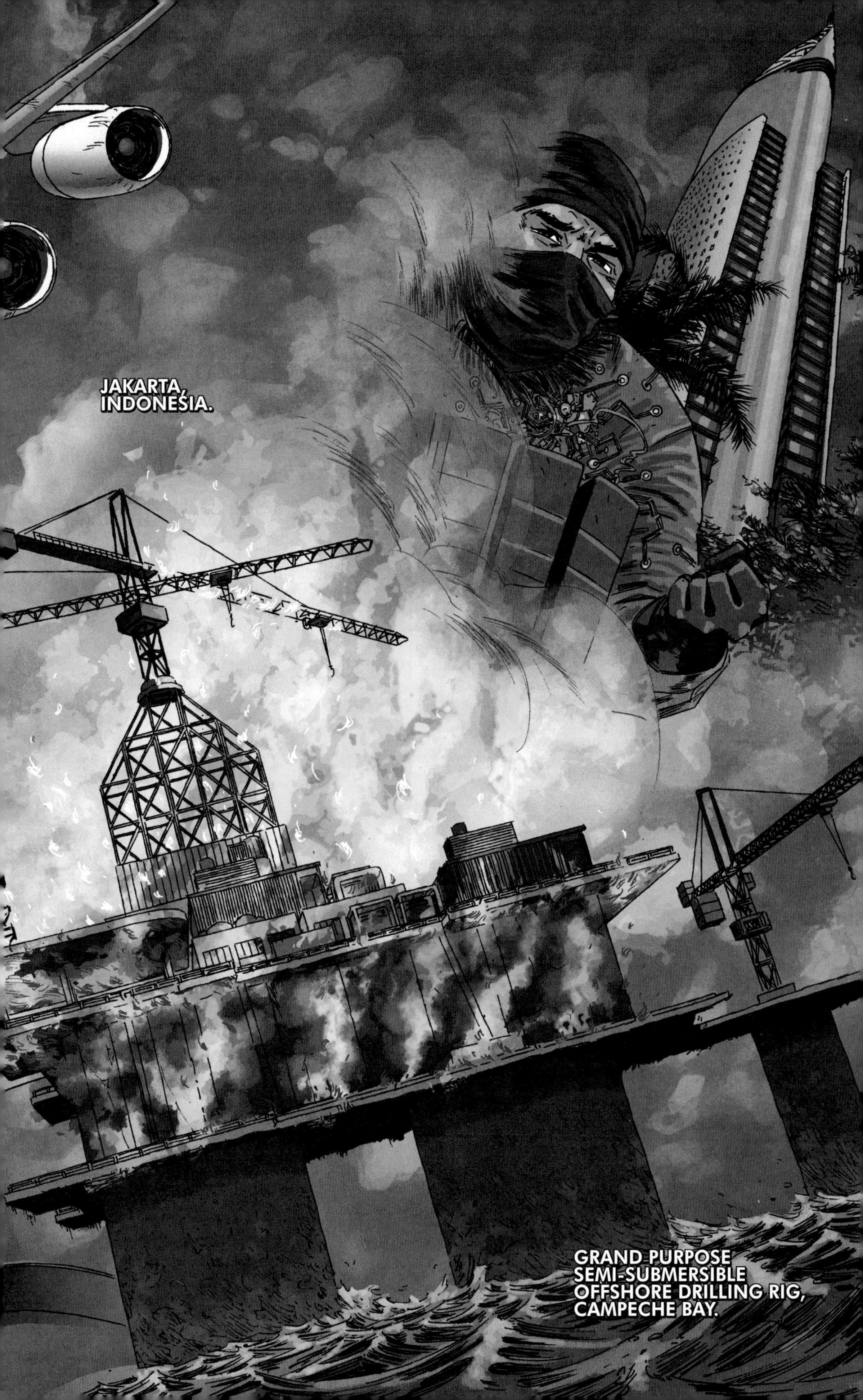
JAKARTA, INDONESIA.
GRAND PURPOSE SEMI-SUBMERSIBLE OFFSHORE DRILLING RIG, CAMPECHE BAY.

I KNOW ABOUT THESE. THESE ARE BIG-TIME TERRORIST ATTACKS. BUT I NEVER HEARD OF THIS GUY.

SELLING THE STUFF. SO HOW DO WE KNOW IT'S REALLY HIM?

AND THAT'S THE CONNECTION. IN EVERY SINGLE INSTANCE, SOMEONE ELSE TAKES CREDIT.

"BECAUSE...HE KEEPS LEAVING US MESSAGES."

OKAY, SO, HE'S NOT REALLY DEAD.

OH, HE'S DEAD. WE'VE SEEN THE BODY. IT'S HERE, ACTUALLY.

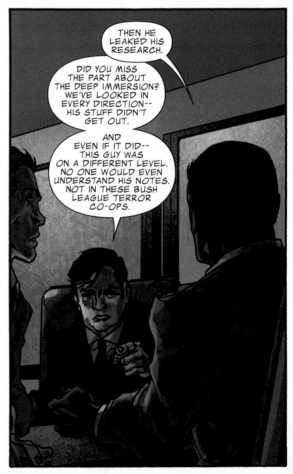

THEN HE LEAKED HIS RESEARCH.

DID YOU MISS THE PART ABOUT THE DEEP IMMERSION? WE'VE LOOKED IN EVERY DIRECTION-- HIS STUFF DIDN'T GET OUT.

AND EVEN IF IT DID-- THIS GUY WAS ON A DIFFERENT LEVEL. NO ONE WOULD EVEN UNDERSTAND HIS NOTES. NOT IN THESE BUSH LEAGUE TERROR CO-OPS.

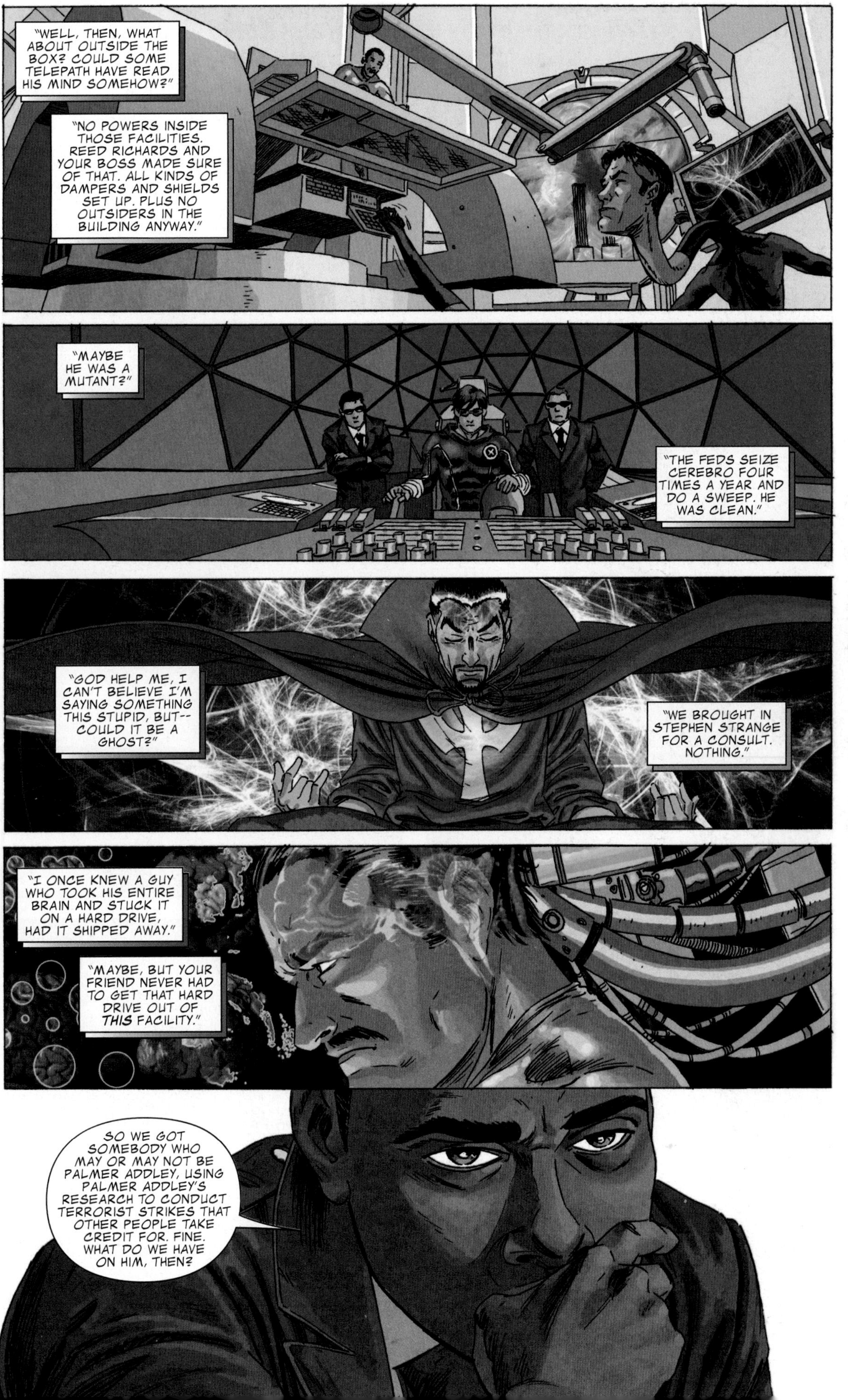
"WELL, THEN, WHAT ABOUT OUTSIDE THE BOX? COULD SOME TELEPATH HAVE READ HIS MIND SOMEHOW?"
"NO POWERS INSIDE THOSE FACILITIES. REED RICHARDS AND YOUR BOSS MADE SURE OF THAT. ALL KINDS OF DAMPERS AND SHIELDS SET UP. PLUS NO OUTSIDERS IN THE BUILDING ANYWAY."
"MAYBE HE WAS A MUTANT?"
"THE FEDS SEIZE CEREBRO FOUR TIMES A YEAR AND DO A SWEEP. HE WAS CLEAN."
"GOD HELP ME, I CAN'T BELIEVE I'M SAYING SOMETHING THIS STUPID, BUT-- COULD IT BE A GHOST?"
"WE BROUGHT IN STEPHEN STRANGE FOR A CONSULT. NOTHING."
"I ONCE KNEW A GUY WHO TOOK HIS ENTIRE BRAIN AND STUCK IT ON A HARD DRIVE, HAD IT SHIPPED AWAY."
"MAYBE, BUT YOUR FRIEND NEVER HAD TO GET THAT HARD DRIVE OUT OF *THIS* FACILITY."
SO WE GOT SOMEBODY WHO MAY OR MAY NOT BE PALMER ADDLEY, USING PALMER ADDLEY'S RESEARCH TO CONDUCT TERRORIST STRIKES THAT OTHER PEOPLE TAKE CREDIT FOR. FINE. WHAT DO WE HAVE ON HIM, THEN?

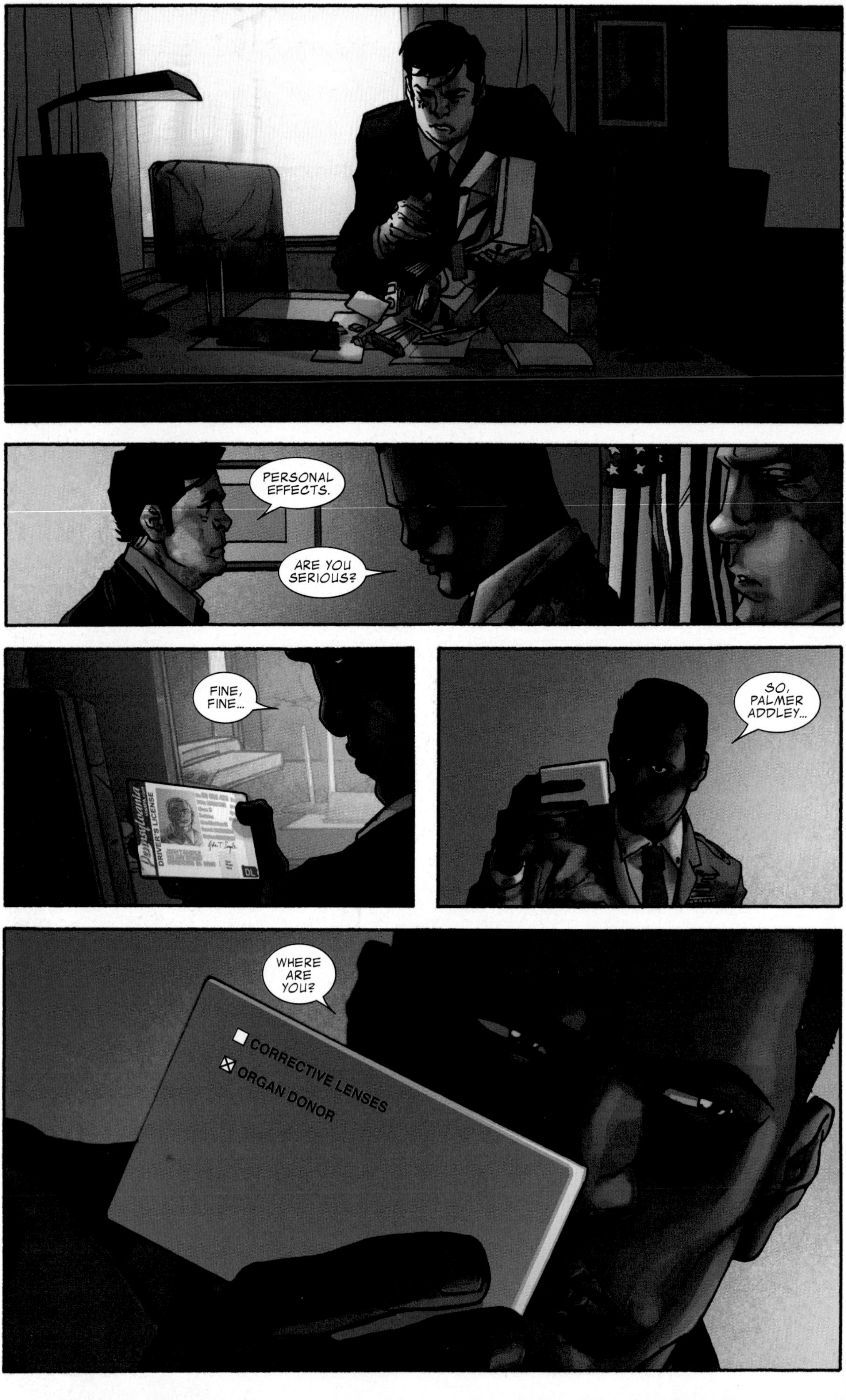
PERSONAL EFFECTS.
ARE YOU SERIOUS?
FINE, FINE...
DRIVER'S LICENSE
DL
SO, PALMER ADDLEY...
WHERE ARE YOU?
CORRECTIVE LENSES
ORGAN DONOR

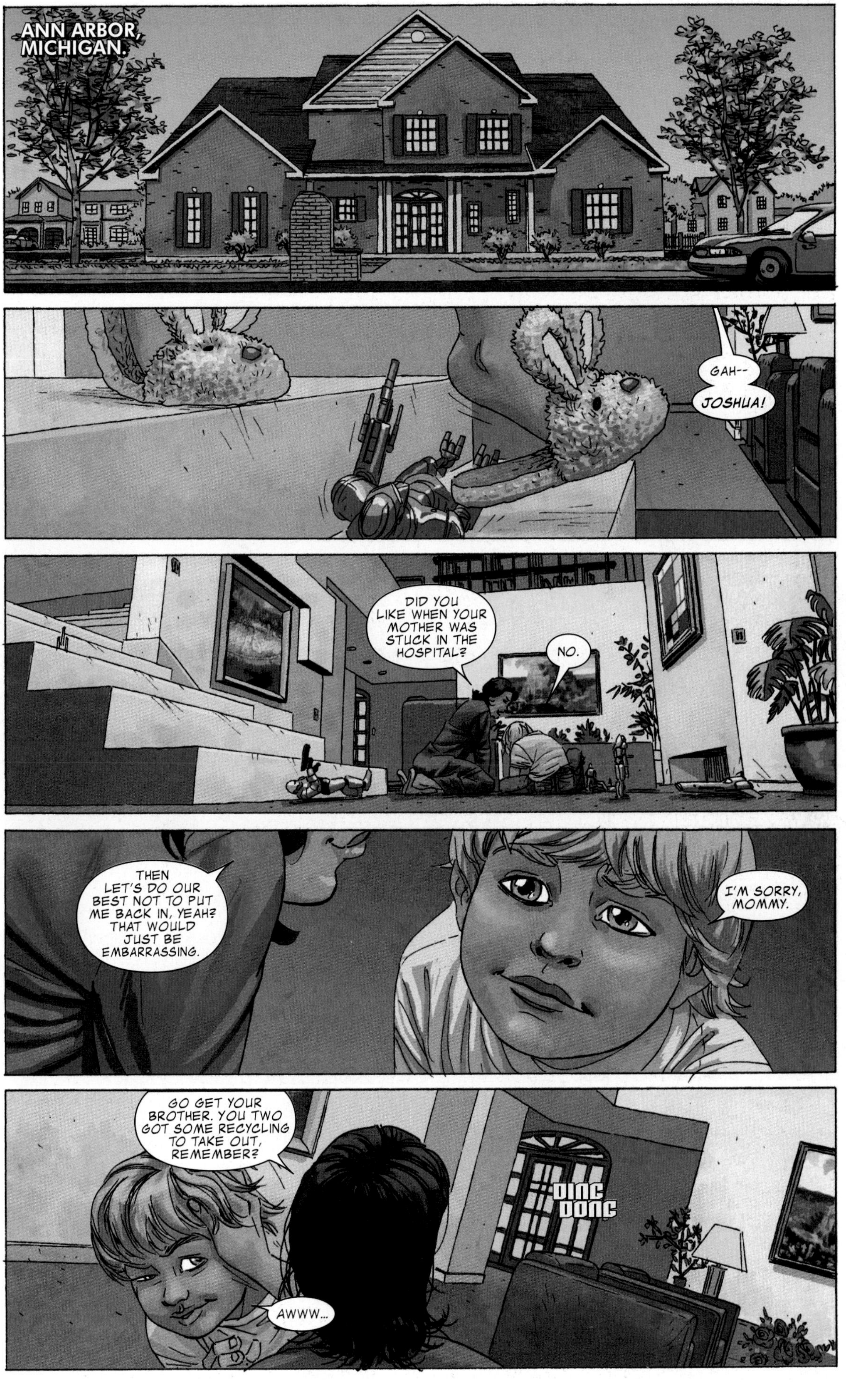
ANN ARBOR, MICHIGAN.
GAH--
JOSHUA!
DID YOU LIKE WHEN YOUR MOTHER WAS STUCK IN THE HOSPITAL?
NO.
THEN LET'S DO OUR BEST NOT TO PUT ME BACK IN, YEAH? THAT WOULD JUST BE EMBARRASSING.
I'M SORRY, MOMMY.
GO GET YOUR BROTHER. YOU TWO GOT SOME RECYCLING TO TAKE OUT, REMEMBER?
DING DONG
AWWW...

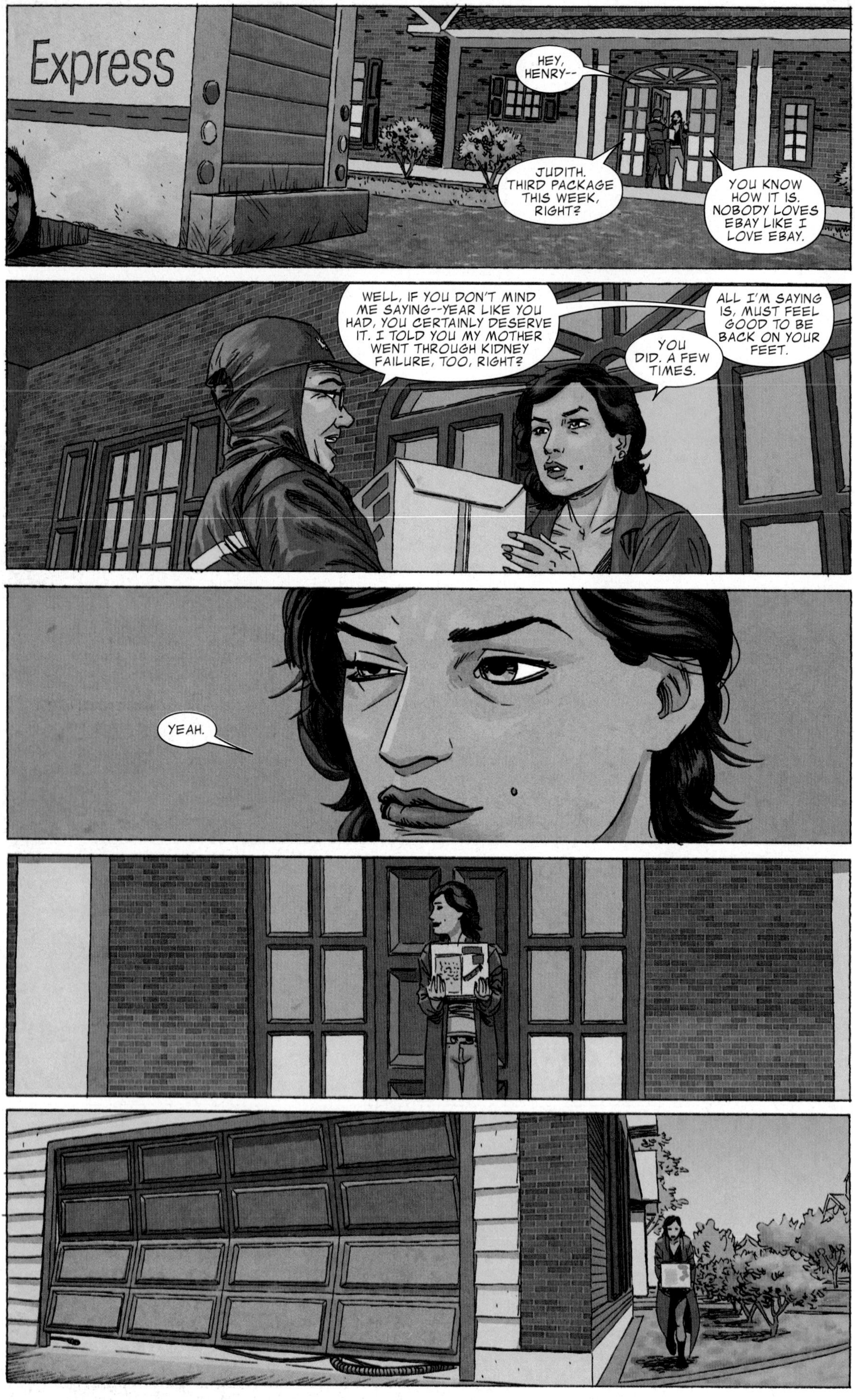
Express
HEY, HENRY--
JUDITH. THIRD PACKAGE THIS WEEK, RIGHT?
YOU KNOW HOW IT IS. NOBODY LOVES EBAY LIKE I LOVE EBAY.
WELL, IF YOU DON'T MIND ME SAYING--YEAR LIKE YOU HAD, YOU CERTAINLY DESERVE IT. I TOLD YOU MY MOTHER WENT THROUGH KIDNEY FAILURE, TOO, RIGHT?
YOU DID. A FEW TIMES.
ALL I'M SAYING IS, MUST FEEL GOOD TO BE BACK ON YOUR FEET.
YEAH.

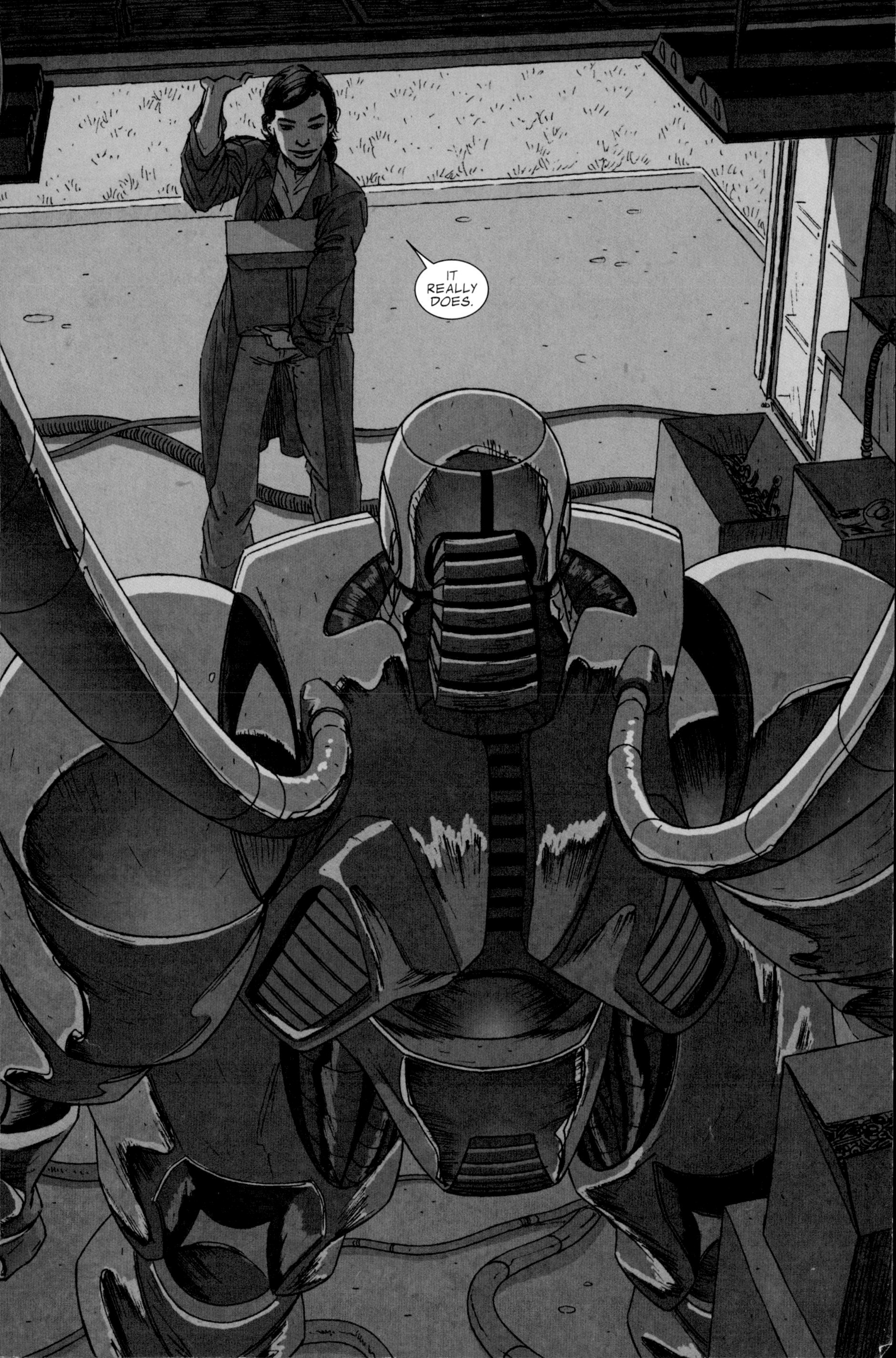
IT REALLY DOES.

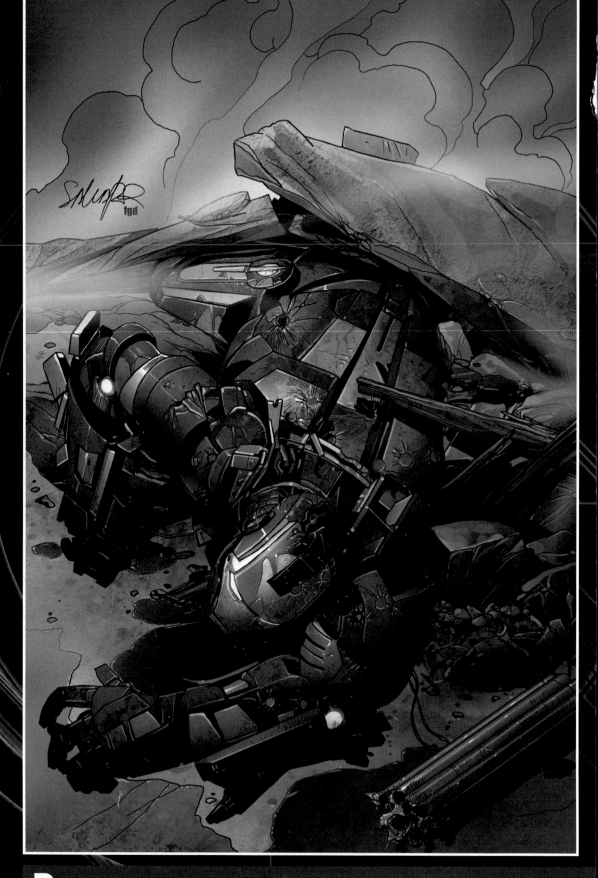

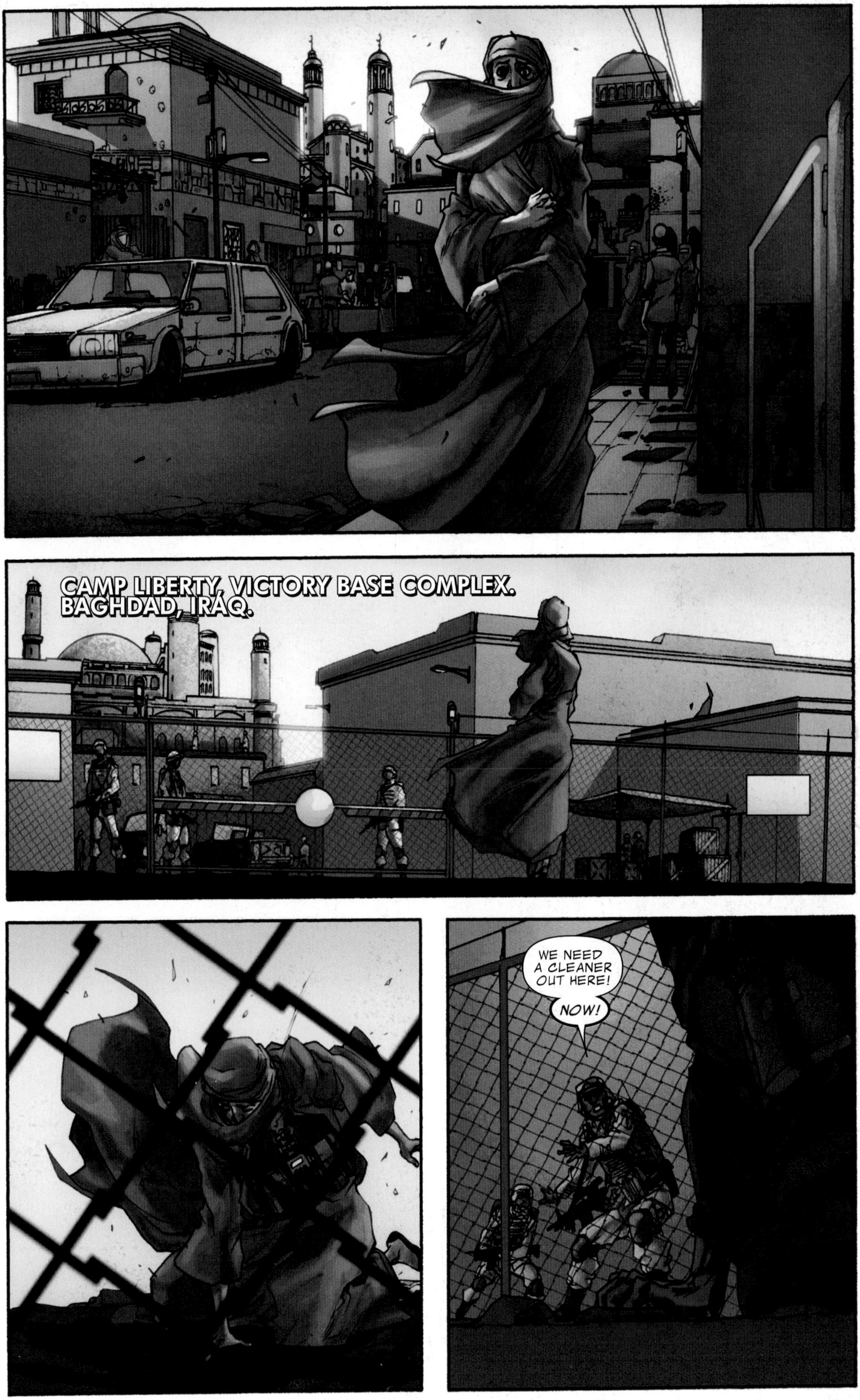
CAMP LIBERTY, VICTORY BASE COMPLEX.
BAGHDAD, IRAQ.
WE NEED A CLEANER OUT HERE!
NOW!

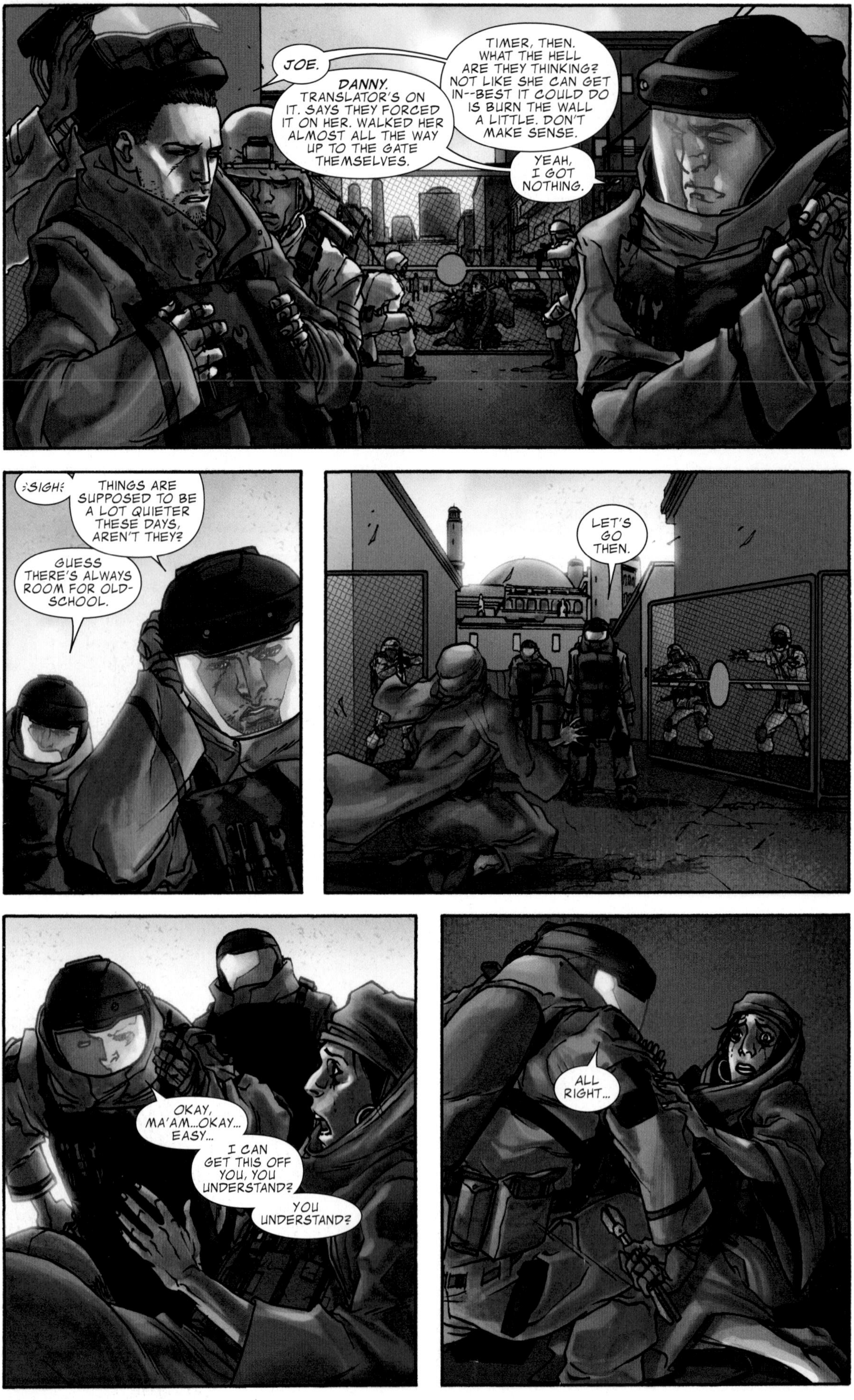
JOE.
DANNY. TRANSLATOR'S ON IT. SAYS THEY FORCED IT ON HER. WALKED HER ALMOST ALL THE WAY UP TO THE GATE THEMSELVES.
TIMER, THEN. WHAT THE HELL ARE THEY THINKING? NOT LIKE SHE CAN GET IN--BEST IT COULD DO IS BURN THE WALL A LITTLE. DON'T MAKE SENSE.
YEAH, I GOT NOTHING.
SIGH
THINGS ARE SUPPOSED TO BE A LOT QUIETER THESE DAYS, AREN'T THEY?
GUESS THERE'S ALWAYS ROOM FOR OLD-SCHOOL.
LET'S GO THEN.
OKAY, MA'AM...OKAY... EASY...
I CAN GET THIS OFF YOU, YOU UNDERSTAND?
YOU UNDERSTAND?
ALL RIGHT...

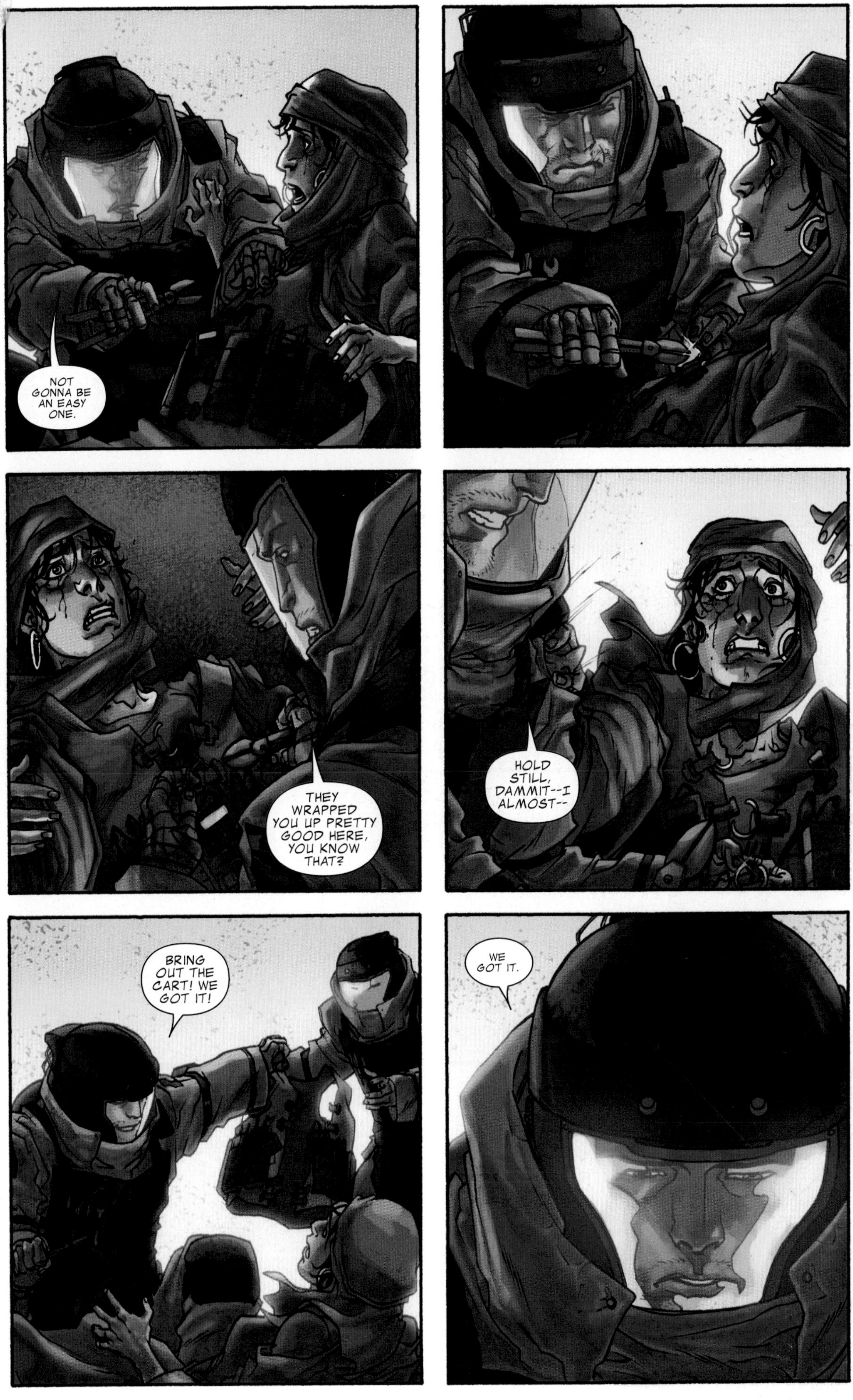
NOT GONNA BE AN EASY ONE.
THEY WRAPPED YOU UP PRETTY GOOD HERE, YOU KNOW THAT?
HOLD STILL, DAMMIT--I ALMOST--
BRING OUT THE CART! WE GOT IT!
WE GOT IT.

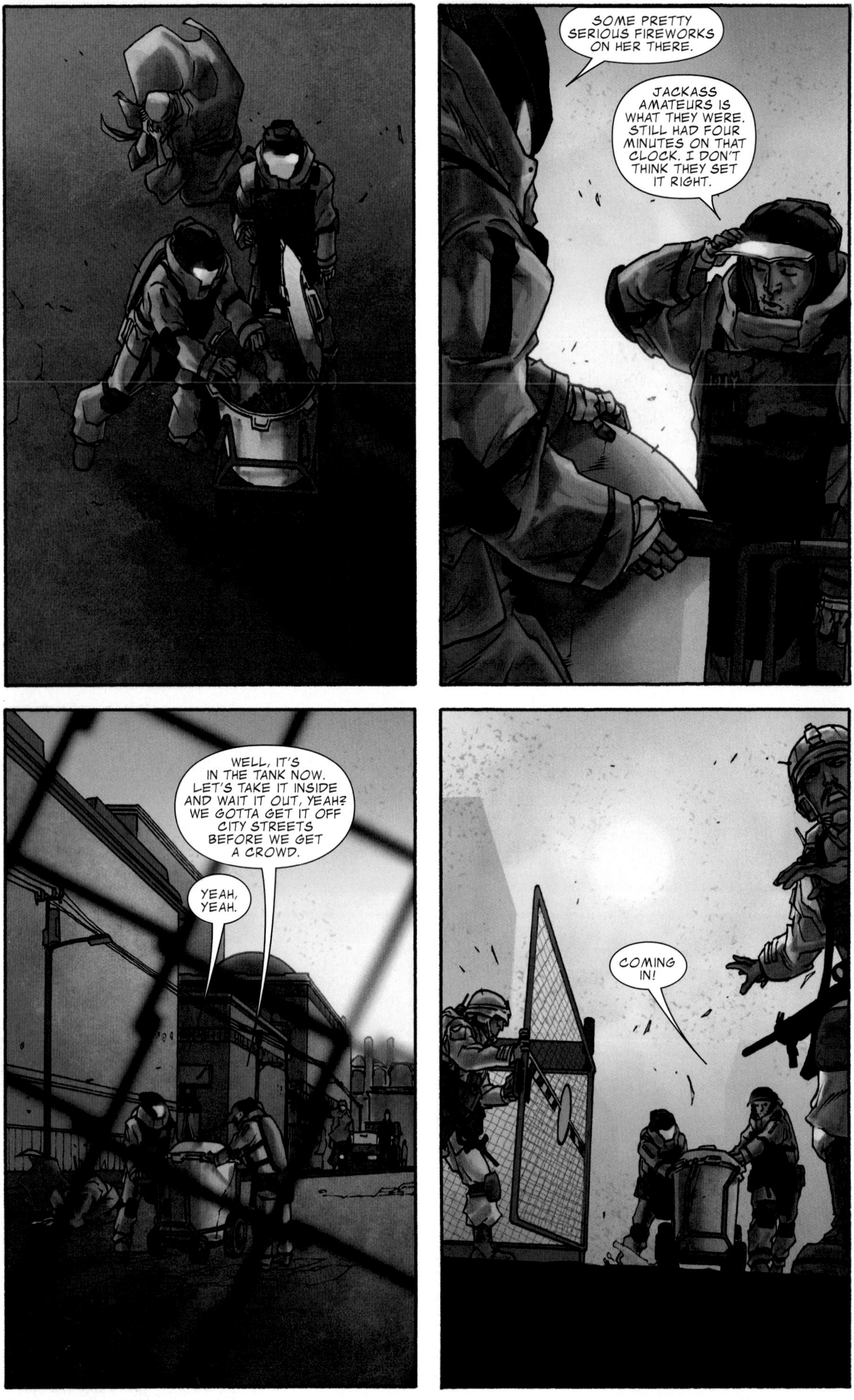
SOME PRETTY SERIOUS FIREWORKS ON HER THERE.
JACKASS AMATEURS IS WHAT THEY WERE. STILL HAD FOUR MINUTES ON THAT CLOCK. I DON'T THINK THEY SET IT RIGHT.
WELL, IT'S IN THE TANK NOW. LET'S TAKE IT INSIDE AND WAIT IT OUT, YEAH? WE GOTTA GET IT OFF CITY STREETS BEFORE WE GET A CROWD.
YEAH, YEAH.
COMING IN!

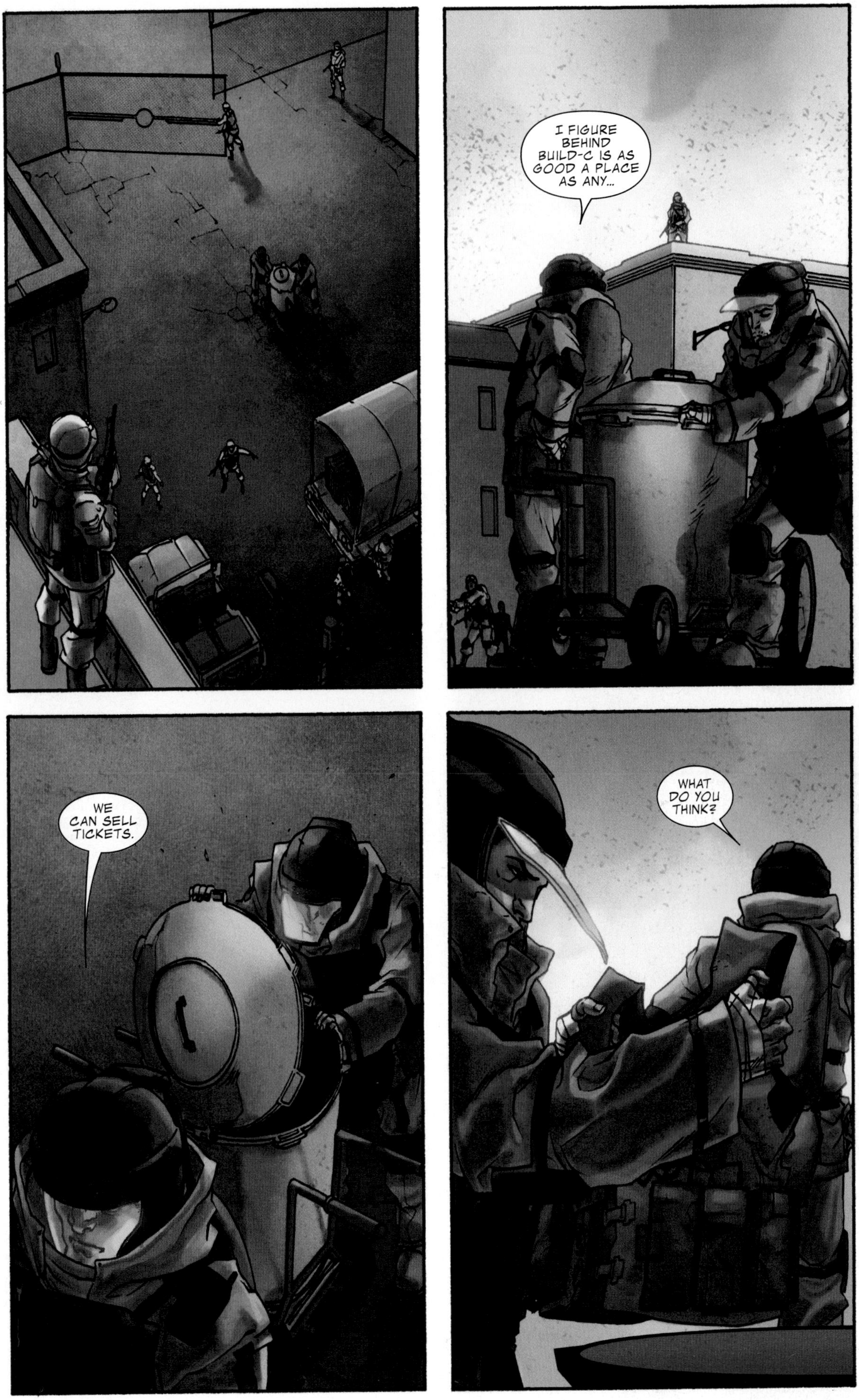
I FIGURE BEHIND BUILD-C IS AS GOOD A PLACE AS ANY...
WE CAN SELL TICKETS.
WHAT DO YOU THINK?

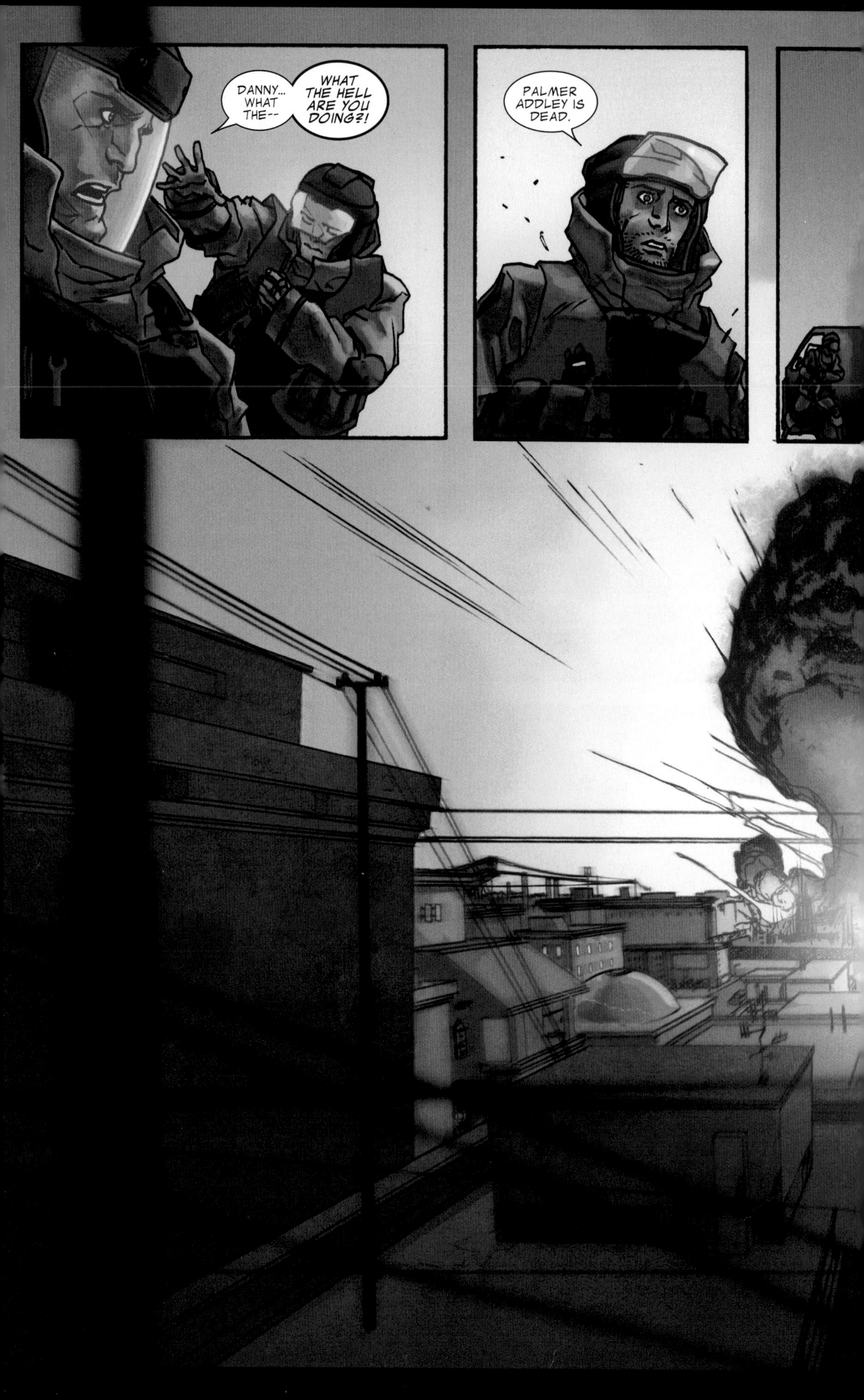
DANNY... WHAT THE--
WHAT THE HELL ARE YOU DOING?!
PALMER ADDLEY IS DEAD.

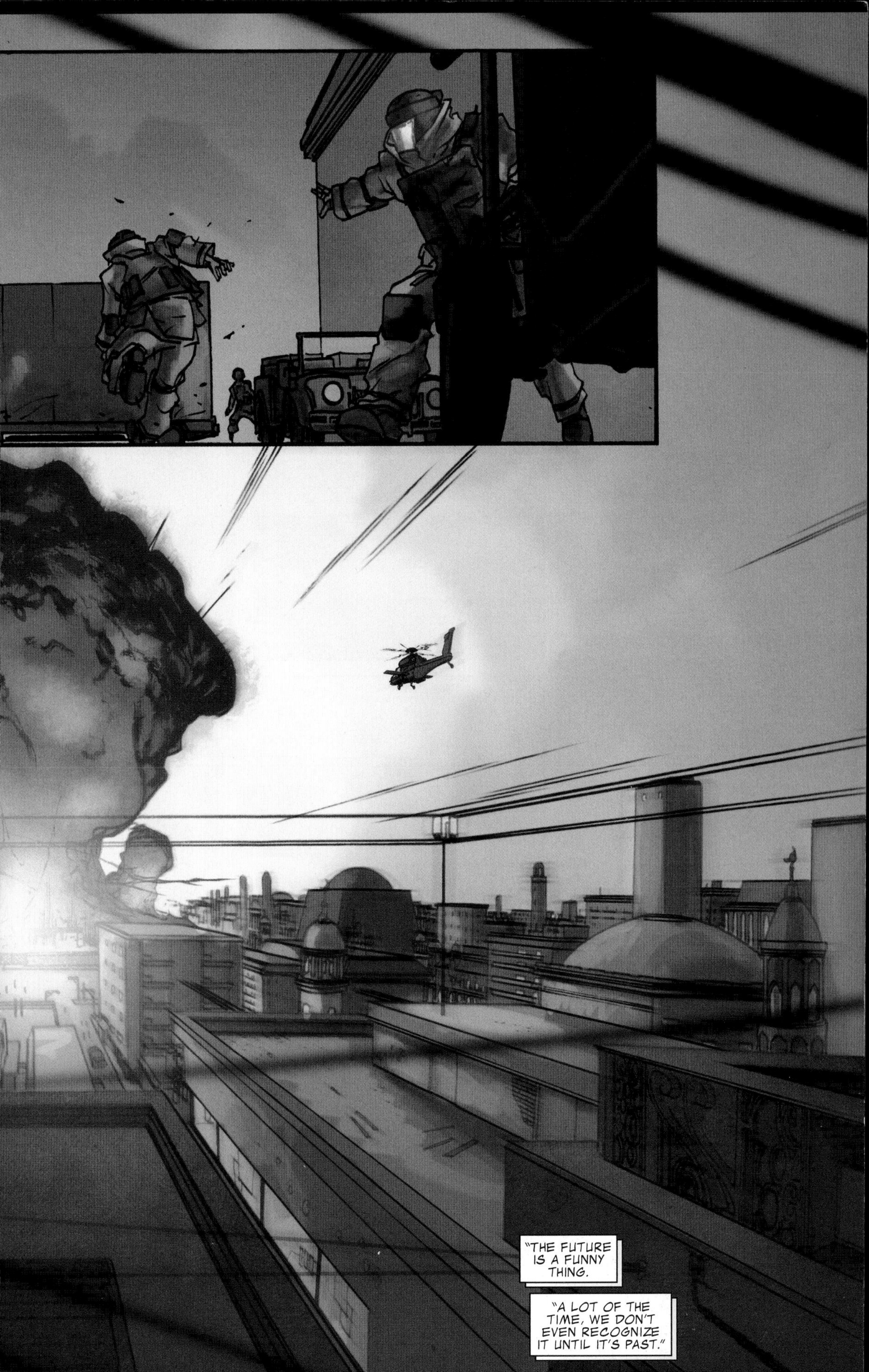
"THE FUTURE IS A FUNNY THING.
"A LOT OF THE TIME, WE DON'T EVEN RECOGNIZE IT UNTIL IT'S PAST."

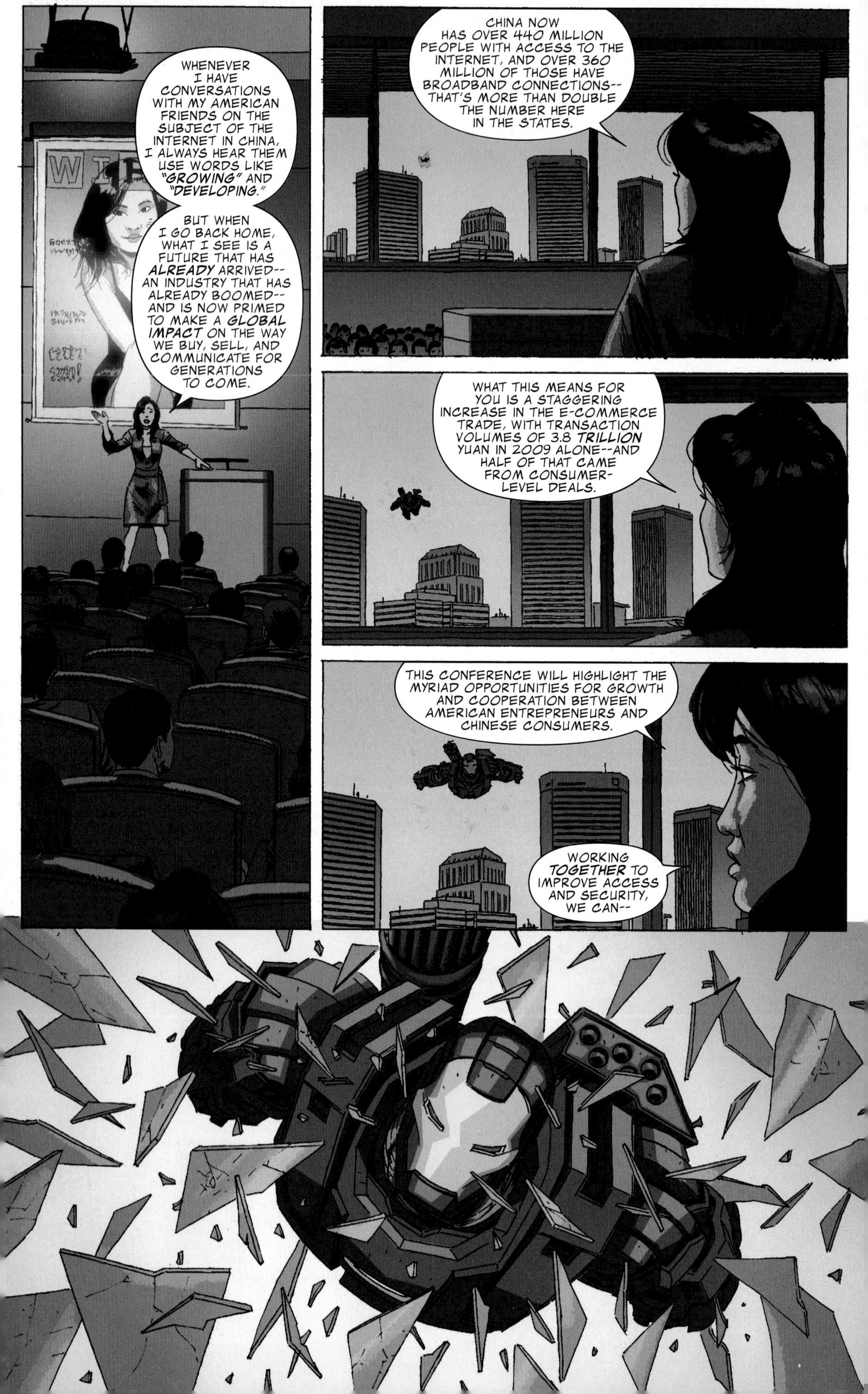

WHENEVER I HAVE CONVERSATIONS WITH MY AMERICAN FRIENDS ON THE SUBJECT OF THE INTERNET IN CHINA, I ALWAYS HEAR THEM USE WORDS LIKE "GROWING" AND "DEVELOPING."
BUT WHEN I GO BACK HOME, WHAT I SEE IS A FUTURE THAT HAS ALREADY ARRIVED--AN INDUSTRY THAT HAS ALREADY BOOMED--AND IS NOW PRIMED TO MAKE A GLOBAL IMPACT ON THE WAY WE BUY, SELL, AND COMMUNICATE FOR GENERATIONS TO COME.
CHINA NOW HAS OVER 440 MILLION PEOPLE WITH ACCESS TO THE INTERNET, AND OVER 360 MILLION OF THOSE HAVE BROADBAND CONNECTIONS--THAT'S MORE THAN DOUBLE THE NUMBER HERE IN THE STATES.
WHAT THIS MEANS FOR YOU IS A STAGGERING INCREASE IN THE E-COMMERCE TRADE, WITH TRANSACTION VOLUMES OF 3.8 TRILLION YUAN IN 2009 ALONE--AND HALF OF THAT CAME FROM CONSUMER-LEVEL DEALS.
THIS CONFERENCE WILL HIGHLIGHT THE MYRIAD OPPORTUNITIES FOR GROWTH AND COOPERATION BETWEEN AMERICAN ENTREPRENEURS AND CHINESE CONSUMERS.
WORKING TOGETHER TO IMPROVE ACCESS AND SECURITY, WE CAN--

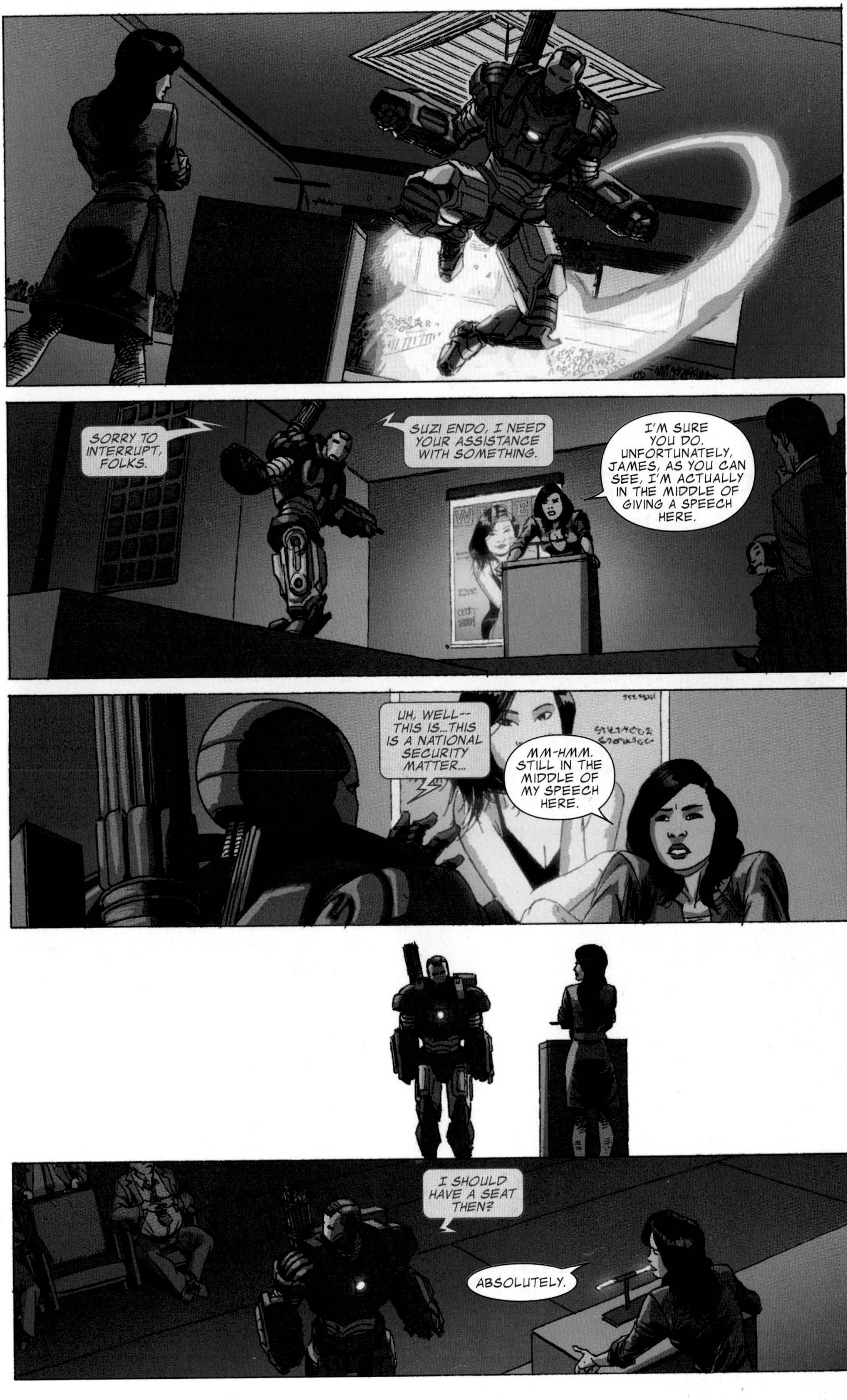
SORRY TO INTERRUPT, FOLKS.
SUZI ENDO, I NEED YOUR ASSISTANCE WITH SOMETHING.
I'M SURE YOU DO. UNFORTUNATELY, JAMES, AS YOU CAN SEE, I'M ACTUALLY IN THE MIDDLE OF GIVING A SPEECH HERE.
UH, WELL-- THIS IS...THIS IS A NATIONAL SECURITY MATTER...
MM-HMM. STILL IN THE MIDDLE OF MY SPEECH HERE.
I SHOULD HAVE A SEAT THEN?
ABSOLUTELY.

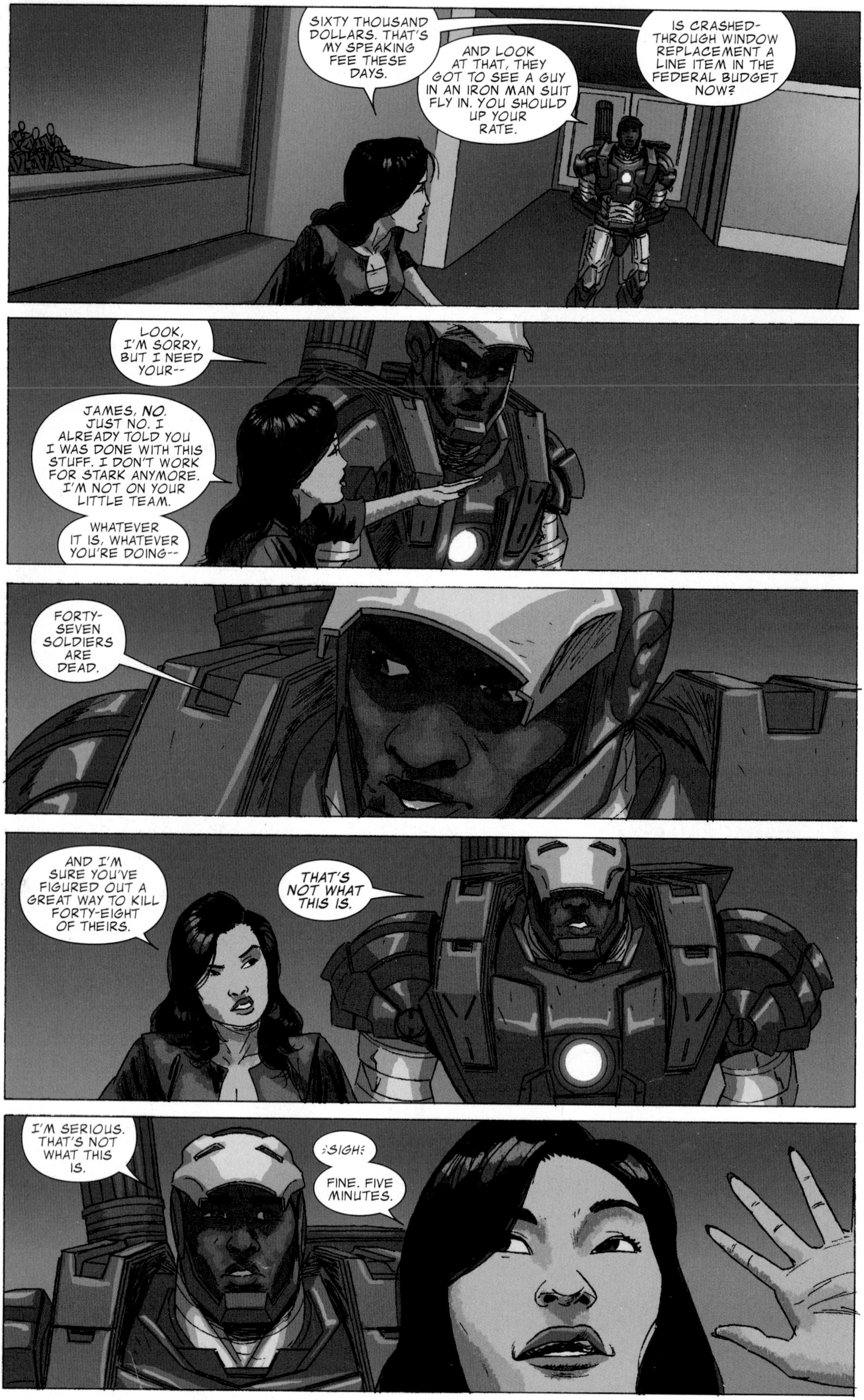
SIXTY THOUSAND DOLLARS. THAT'S MY SPEAKING FEE THESE DAYS.
AND LOOK AT THAT, THEY GOT TO SEE A GUY IN AN IRON MAN SUIT FLY IN. YOU SHOULD UP YOUR RATE.
IS CRASHED-THROUGH WINDOW REPLACEMENT A LINE ITEM IN THE FEDERAL BUDGET NOW?
LOOK, I'M SORRY, BUT I NEED YOUR--
JAMES, NO. JUST NO. I ALREADY TOLD YOU I WAS DONE WITH THIS STUFF. I DON'T WORK FOR STARK ANYMORE. I'M NOT ON YOUR LITTLE TEAM.
WHATEVER IT IS, WHATEVER YOU'RE DOING--
FORTY-SEVEN SOLDIERS ARE DEAD.
AND I'M SURE YOU'VE FIGURED OUT A GREAT WAY TO KILL FORTY-EIGHT OF THEIRS.
THAT'S NOT WHAT THIS IS.
I'M SERIOUS. THAT'S NOT WHAT THIS IS.
SIGH
FINE. FIVE MINUTES.

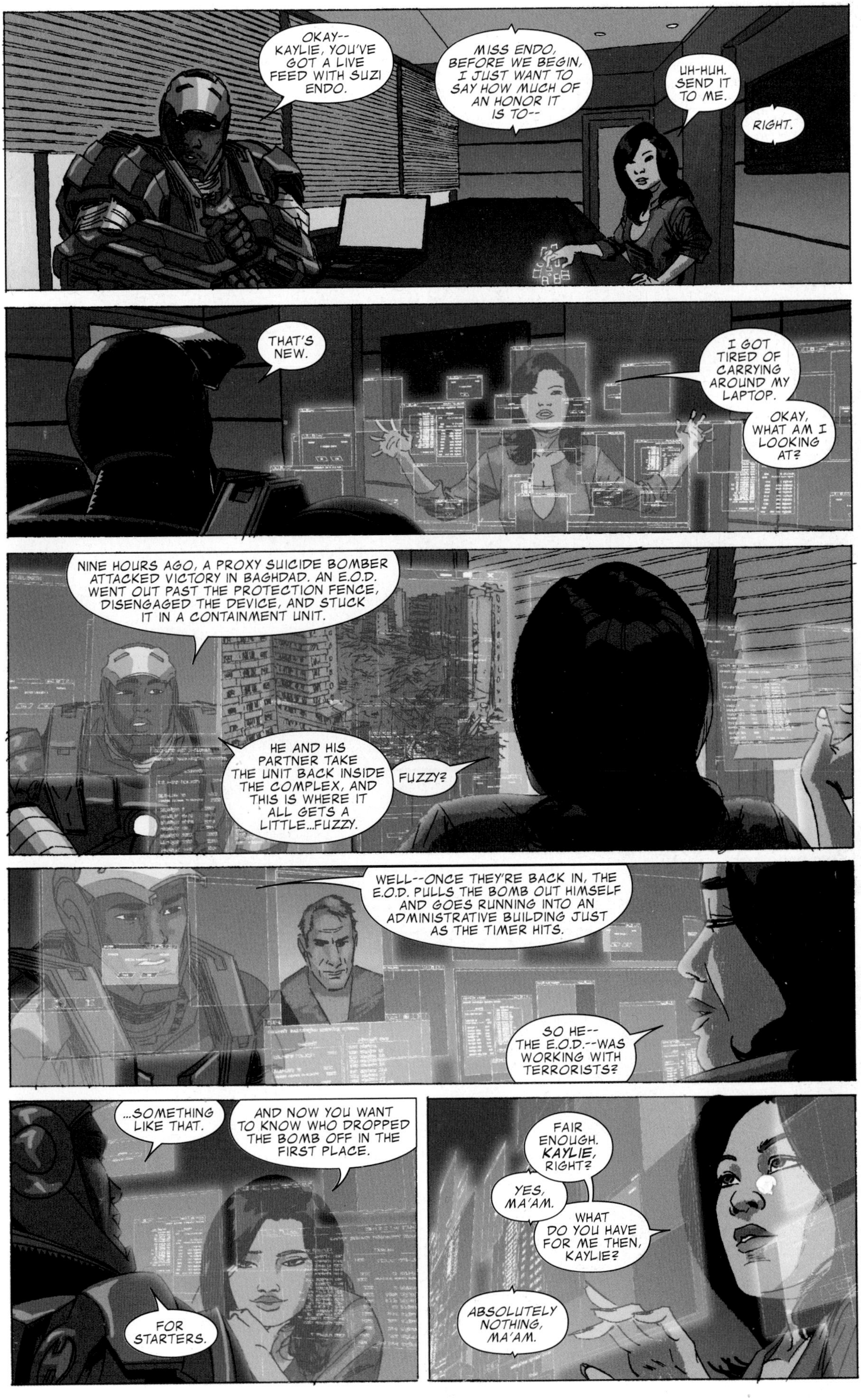
OKAY-- KAYLIE, YOU'VE GOT A LIVE FEED WITH SUZI ENDO.
MISS ENDO, BEFORE WE BEGIN, I JUST WANT TO SAY HOW MUCH OF AN HONOR IT IS TO--
UH-HUH. SEND IT TO ME.
RIGHT.
THAT'S NEW.
I GOT TIRED OF CARRYING AROUND MY LAPTOP.
OKAY, WHAT AM I LOOKING AT?
NINE HOURS AGO, A PROXY SUICIDE BOMBER ATTACKED VICTORY IN BAGHDAD. AN E.O.D. WENT OUT PAST THE PROTECTION FENCE, DISENGAGED THE DEVICE, AND STUCK IT IN A CONTAINMENT UNIT.
HE AND HIS PARTNER TAKE THE UNIT BACK INSIDE THE COMPLEX, AND THIS IS WHERE IT ALL GETS A LITTLE...FUZZY.
FUZZY?
WELL--ONCE THEY'RE BACK IN, THE E.O.D. PULLS THE BOMB OUT HIMSELF AND GOES RUNNING INTO AN ADMINISTRATIVE BUILDING JUST AS THE TIMER HITS.
SO HE-- THE E.O.D.--WAS WORKING WITH TERRORISTS?
...SOMETHING LIKE THAT.
AND NOW YOU WANT TO KNOW WHO DROPPED THE BOMB OFF IN THE FIRST PLACE.
FOR STARTERS.
FAIR ENOUGH. KAYLIE, RIGHT?
YES, MA'AM.
WHAT DO YOU HAVE FOR ME THEN, KAYLIE?
ABSOLUTELY NOTHING, MA'AM.

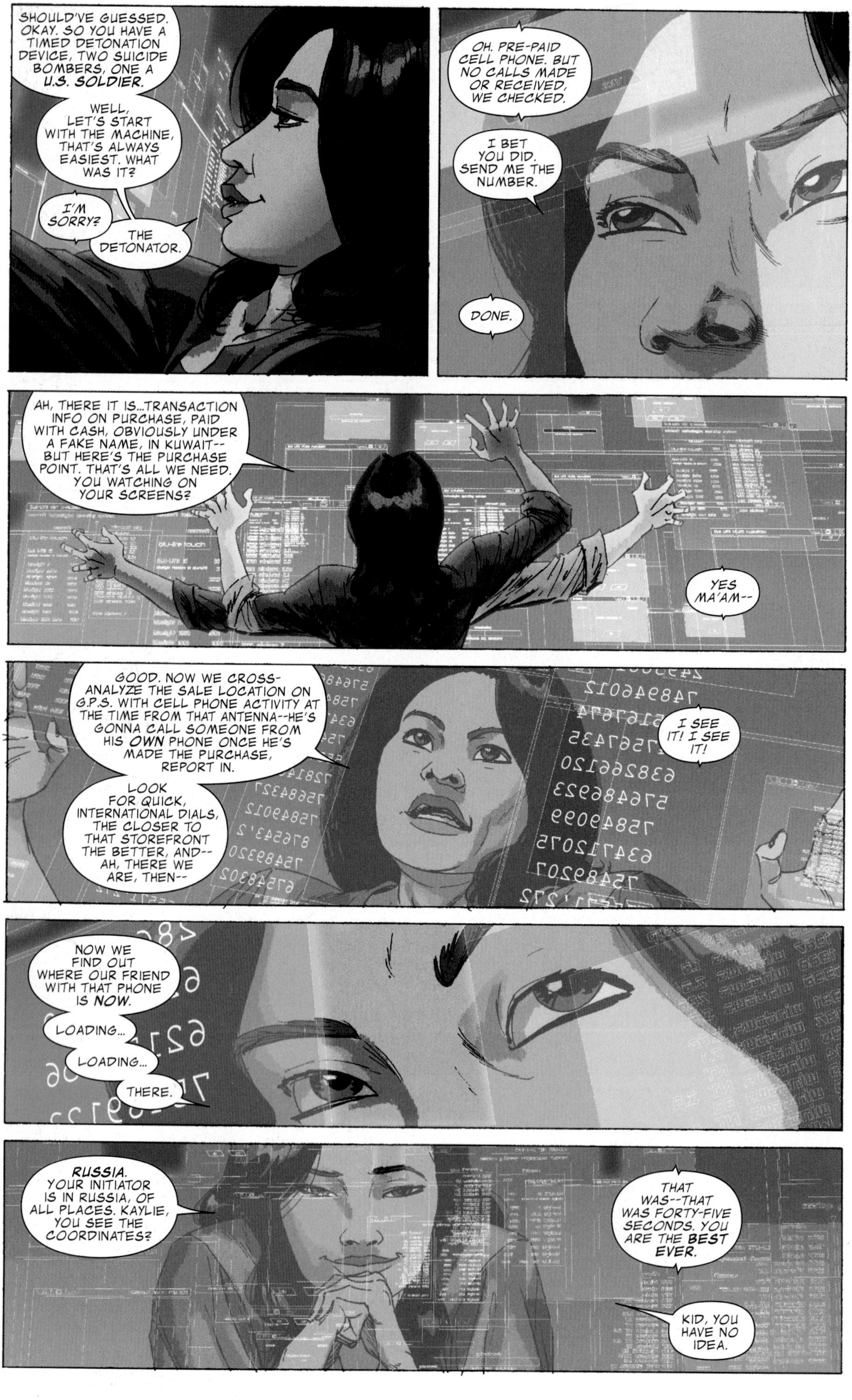

SHOULD'VE GUESSED. OKAY. SO YOU HAVE A TIMED DETONATION DEVICE, TWO SUICIDE BOMBERS, ONE A U.S. SOLDIER.
WELL, LET'S START WITH THE MACHINE, THAT'S ALWAYS EASIEST. WHAT WAS IT?
I'M SORRY?
THE DETONATOR.
OH. PRE-PAID CELL PHONE. BUT NO CALLS MADE OR RECEIVED, WE CHECKED.
I BET YOU DID. SEND ME THE NUMBER.
DONE.
AH, THERE IT IS...TRANSACTION INFO ON PURCHASE, PAID WITH CASH, OBVIOUSLY UNDER A FAKE NAME, IN KUWAIT-- BUT HERE'S THE PURCHASE POINT. THAT'S ALL WE NEED. YOU WATCHING ON YOUR SCREENS?
YES MA'AM--
GOOD. NOW WE CROSS-ANALYZE THE SALE LOCATION ON G.P.S. WITH CELL PHONE ACTIVITY AT THE TIME FROM THAT ANTENNA--HE'S GONNA CALL SOMEONE FROM HIS OWN PHONE ONCE HE'S MADE THE PURCHASE, REPORT IN.
LOOK FOR QUICK, INTERNATIONAL DIALS, THE CLOSER TO THAT STOREFRONT THE BETTER, AND-- AH, THERE WE ARE, THEN--
I SEE IT! I SEE IT!
NOW WE FIND OUT WHERE OUR FRIEND WITH THAT PHONE IS NOW.
LOADING...
LOADING...
THERE.
RUSSIA. YOUR INITIATOR IS IN RUSSIA, OF ALL PLACES. KAYLIE, YOU SEE THE COORDINATES?
THAT WAS--THAT WAS FORTY-FIVE SECONDS. YOU ARE THE BEST EVER.
KID, YOU HAVE NO IDEA.

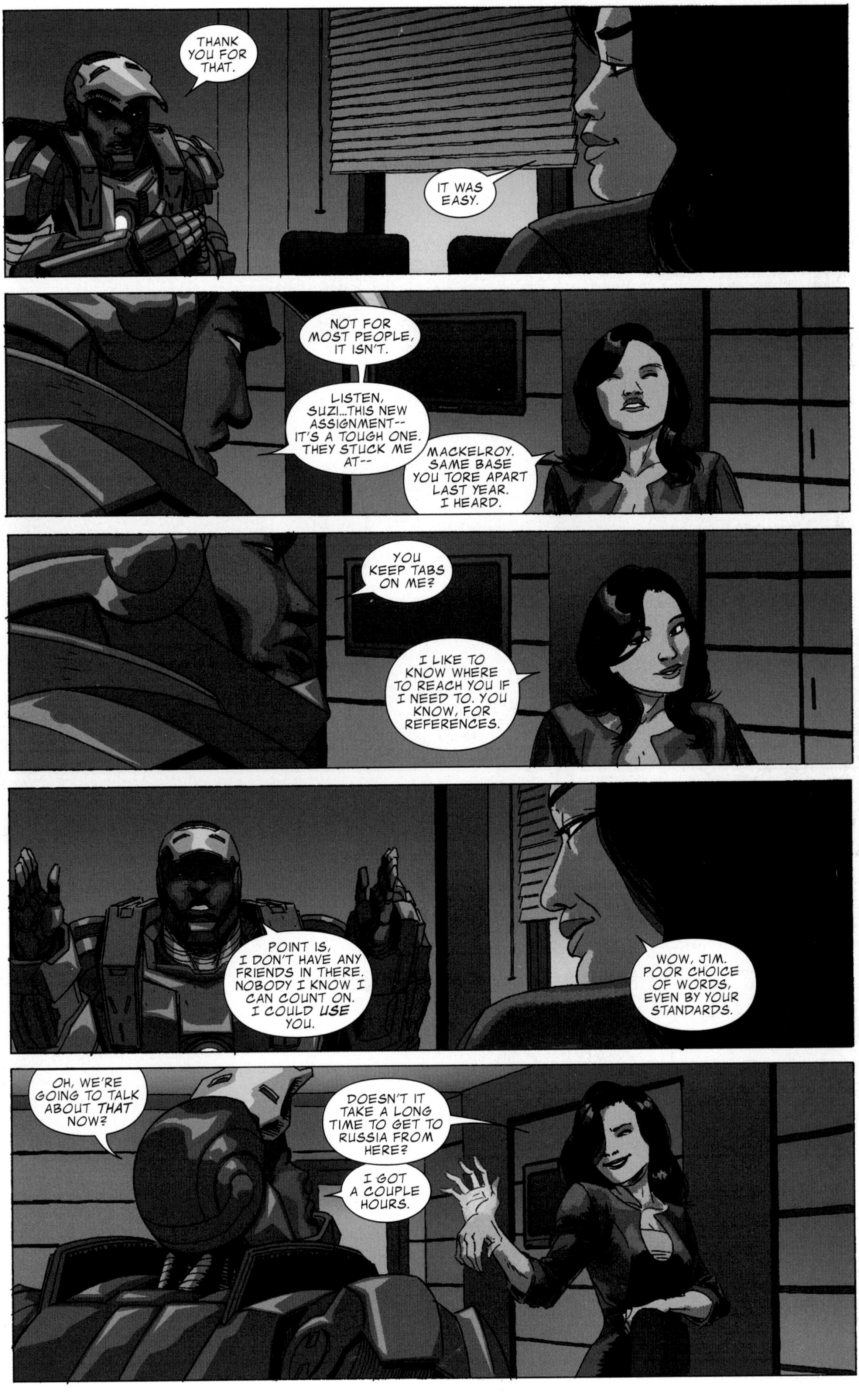
THANK YOU FOR THAT.
IT WAS EASY.
NOT FOR MOST PEOPLE, IT ISN'T.
LISTEN, SUZI...THIS NEW ASSIGNMENT-- IT'S A TOUGH ONE. THEY STUCK ME AT--
MACKELROY. SAME BASE YOU TORE APART LAST YEAR. I HEARD.
YOU KEEP TABS ON ME?
I LIKE TO KNOW WHERE TO REACH YOU IF I NEED TO. YOU KNOW, FOR REFERENCES.
POINT IS, I DON'T HAVE ANY FRIENDS IN THERE. NOBODY I KNOW I CAN COUNT ON. I COULD USE YOU.
WOW, JIM. POOR CHOICE OF WORDS, EVEN BY YOUR STANDARDS.
OH, WE'RE GOING TO TALK ABOUT THAT NOW?
DOESN'T IT TAKE A LONG TIME TO GET TO RUSSIA FROM HERE?
I GOT A COUPLE HOURS.

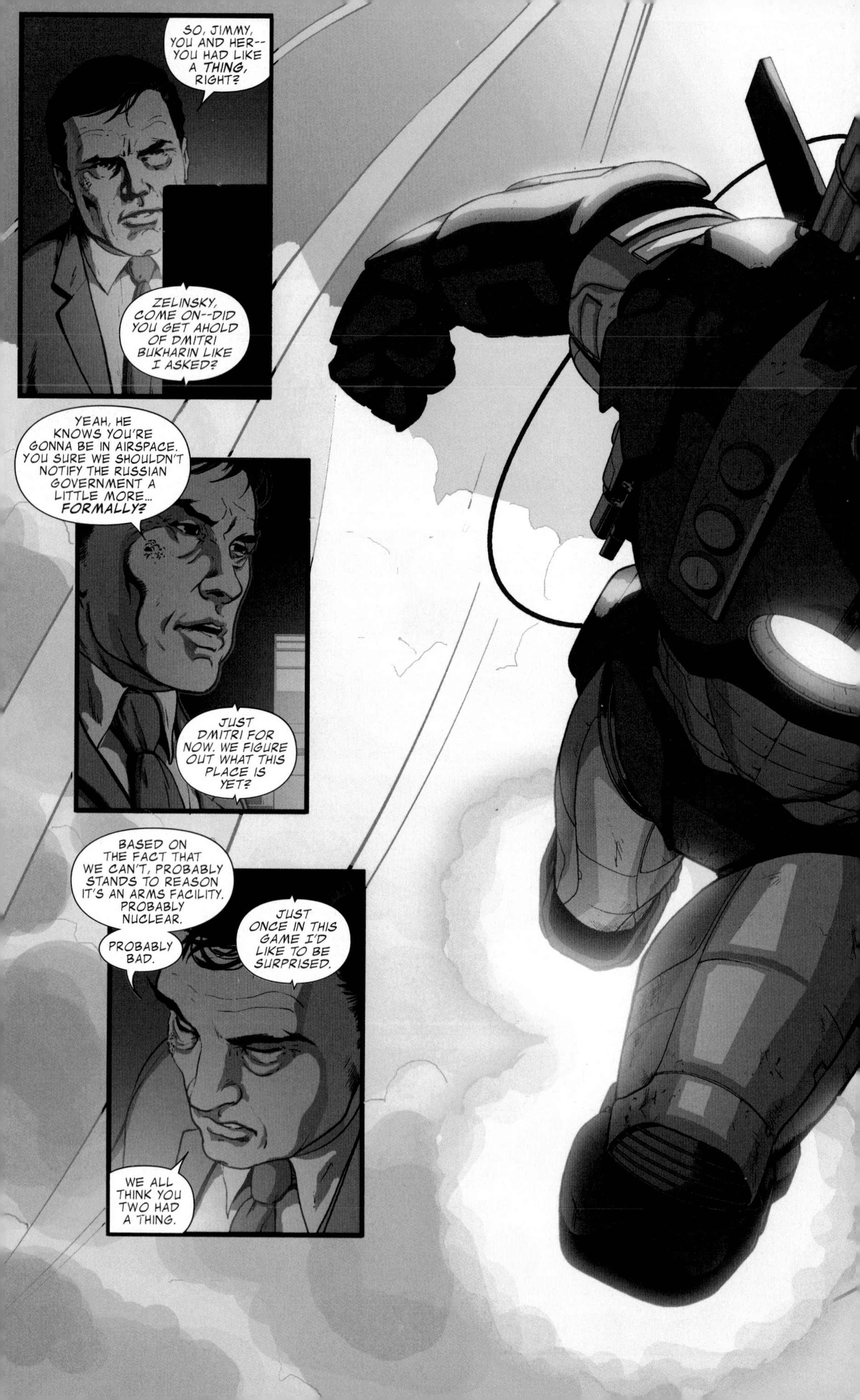
SO, JIMMY, YOU AND HER-- YOU HAD LIKE A THING, RIGHT?
ZELINSKY, COME ON--DID YOU GET AHOLD OF DMITRI BUKHARIN LIKE I ASKED?
YEAH, HE KNOWS YOU'RE GONNA BE IN AIRSPACE. YOU SURE WE SHOULDN'T NOTIFY THE RUSSIAN GOVERNMENT A LITTLE MORE... FORMALLY?
JUST DMITRI FOR NOW. WE FIGURE OUT WHAT THIS PLACE IS YET?
BASED ON THE FACT THAT WE CAN'T, PROBABLY STANDS TO REASON IT'S AN ARMS FACILITY. PROBABLY NUCLEAR.
PROBABLY BAD.
JUST ONCE IN THIS GAME I'D LIKE TO BE SURPRISED.
WE ALL THINK YOU TWO HAD A THING.

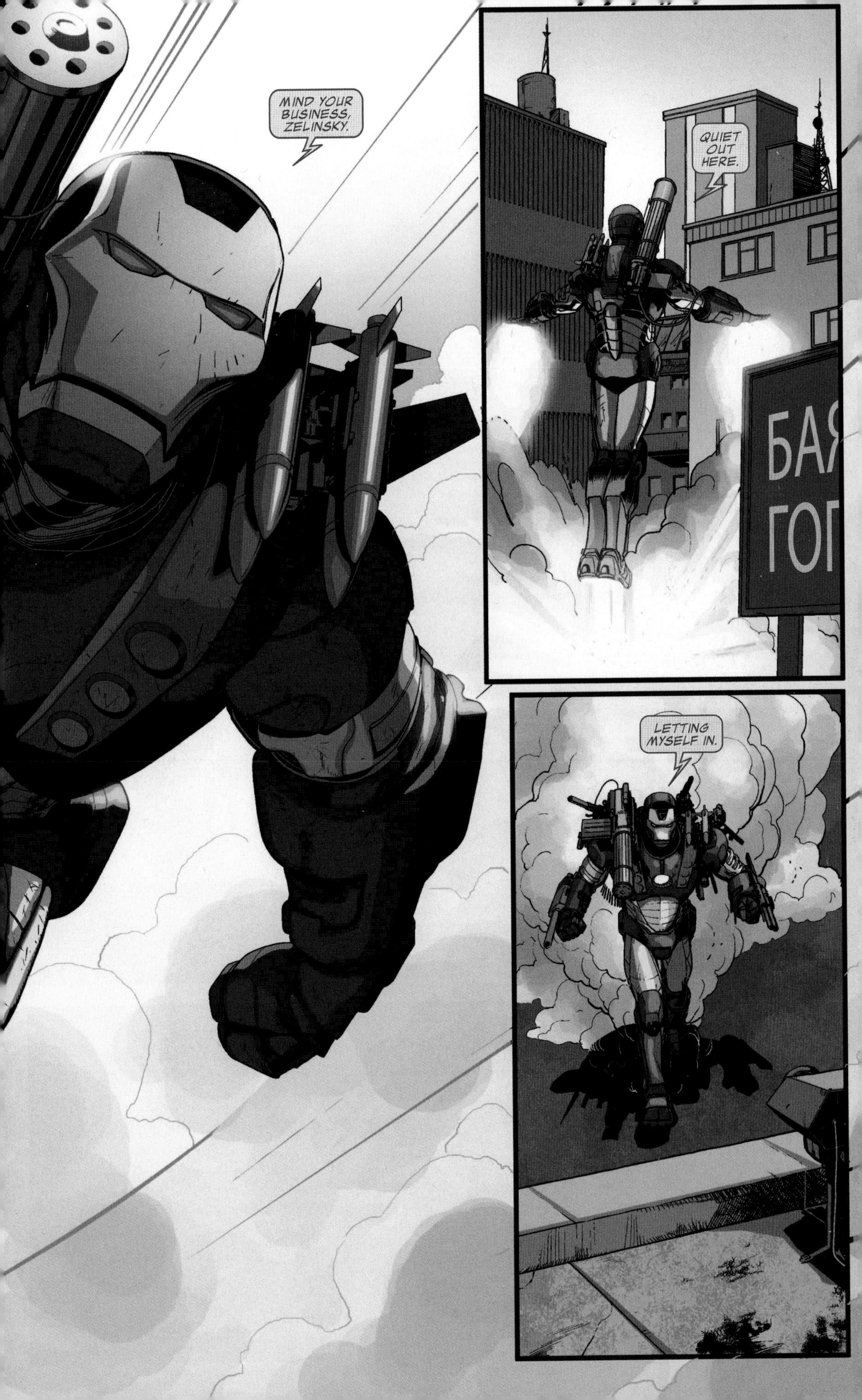
MIND YOUR BUSINESS, ZELINSKY.
QUIET OUT HERE.
LETTING MYSELF IN.

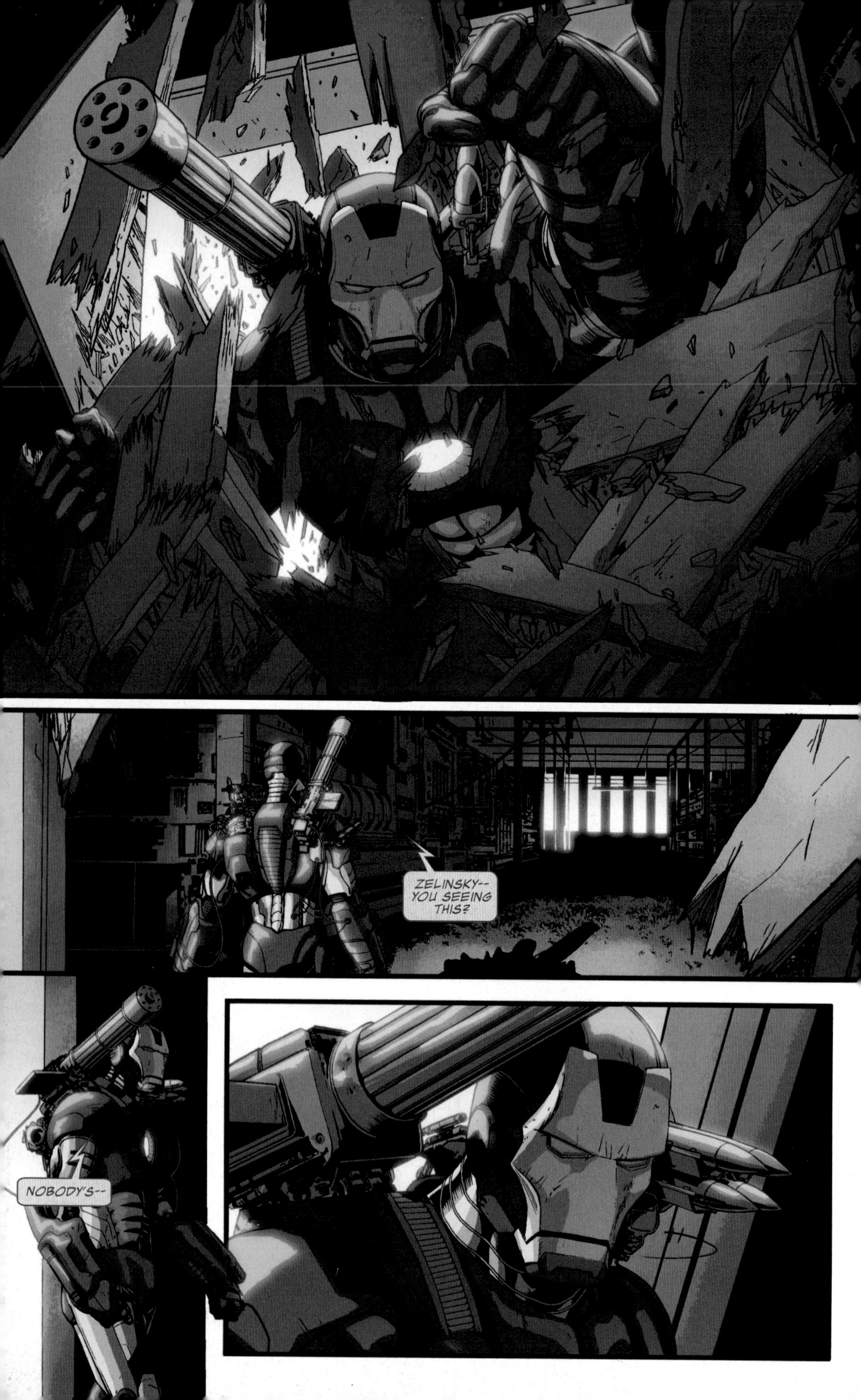
ZELINSKY--
YOU SEEING
THIS?
NOBODY'S--

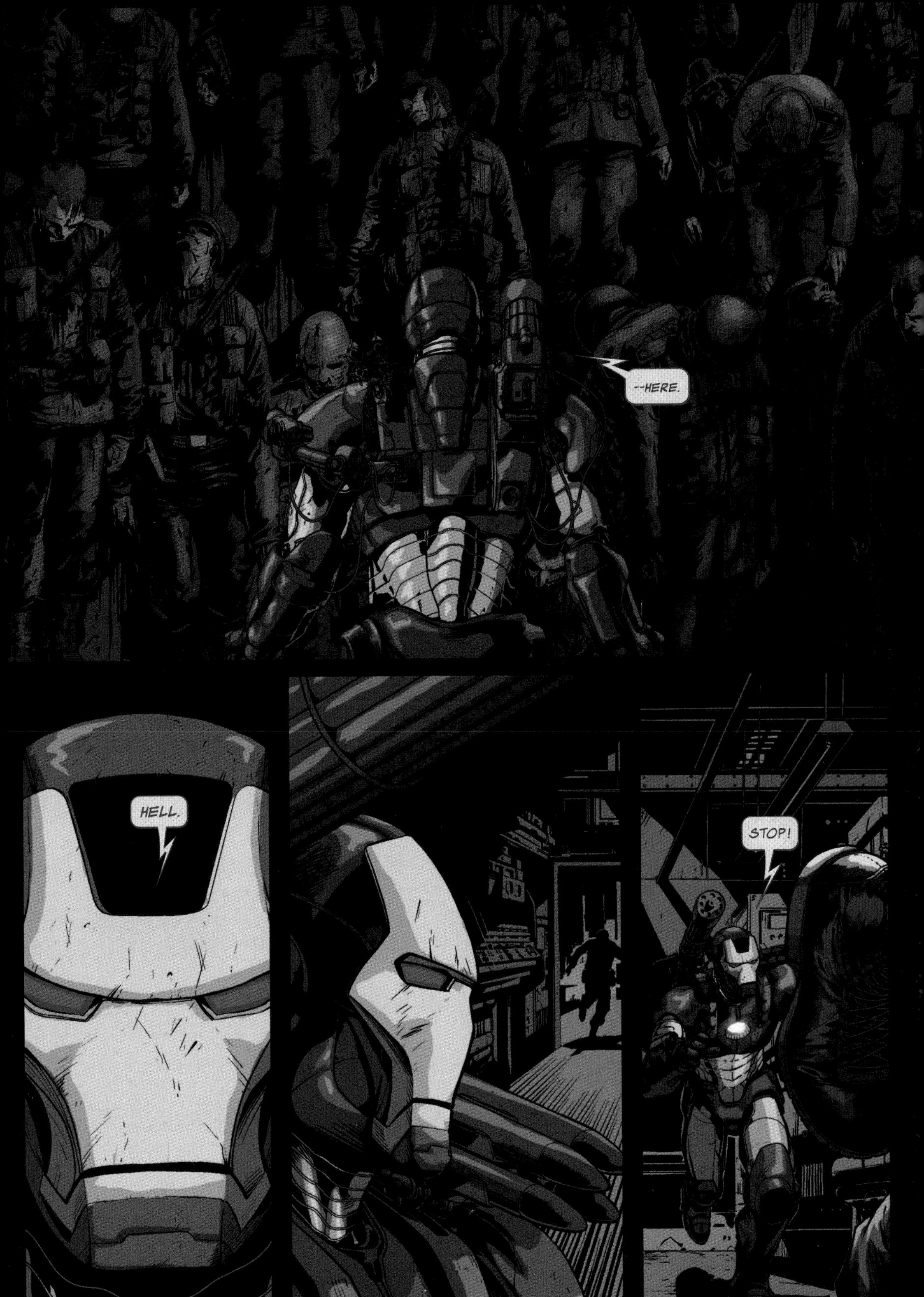
--HERE.
HELL.
STOP!

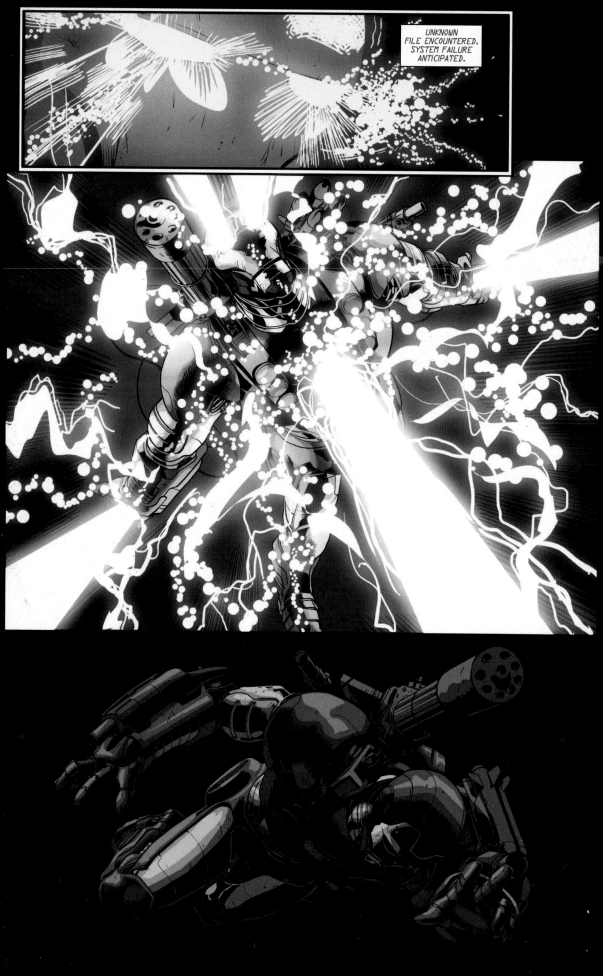

UNKNOWN FILE ENCOUNTERED. SYSTEM FAILURE ANTICIPATED.

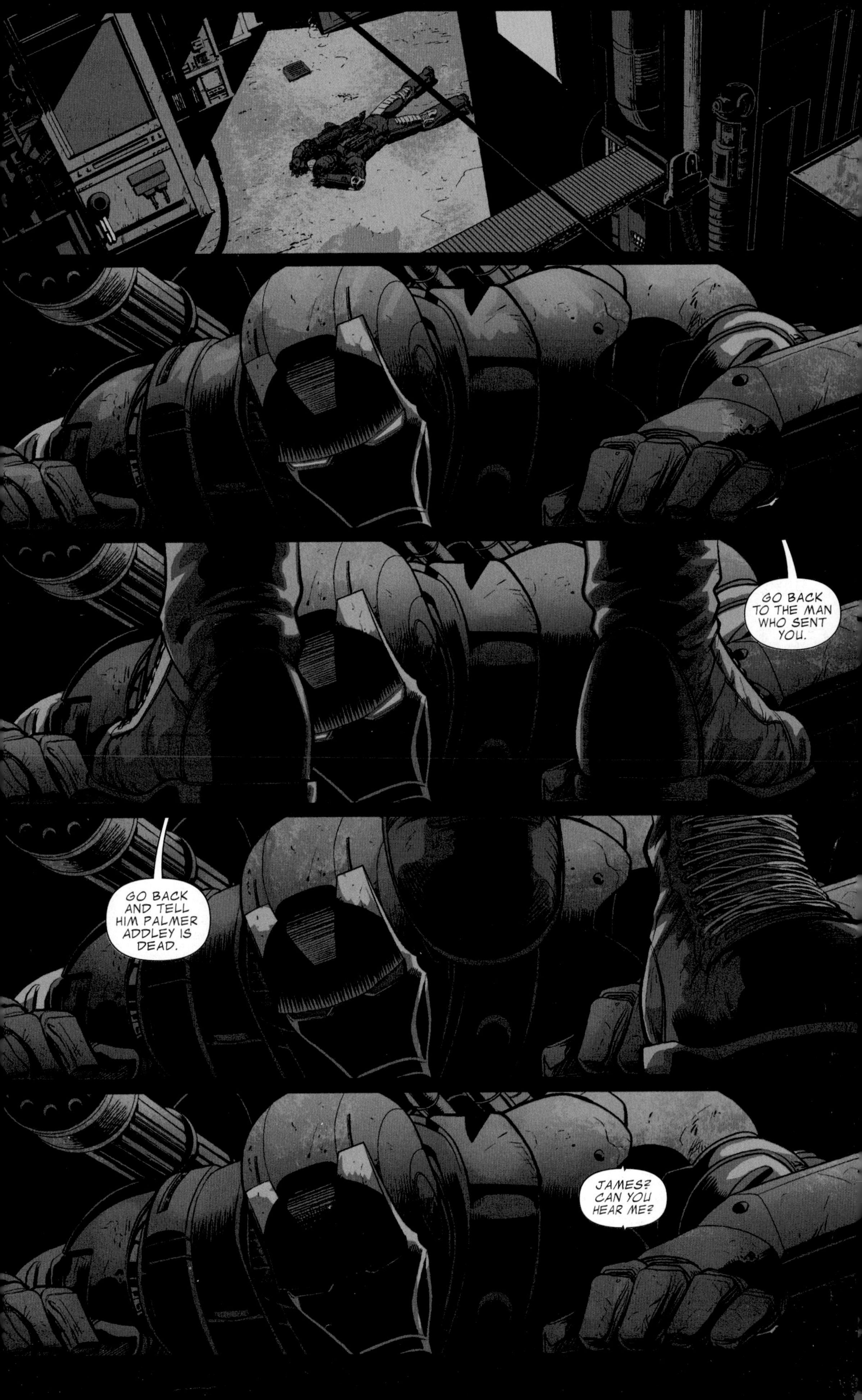
GO BACK TO THE MAN WHO SENT YOU.
GO BACK AND TELL HIM PALMER ADDLEY IS DEAD.
JAMES? CAN YOU HEAR ME?

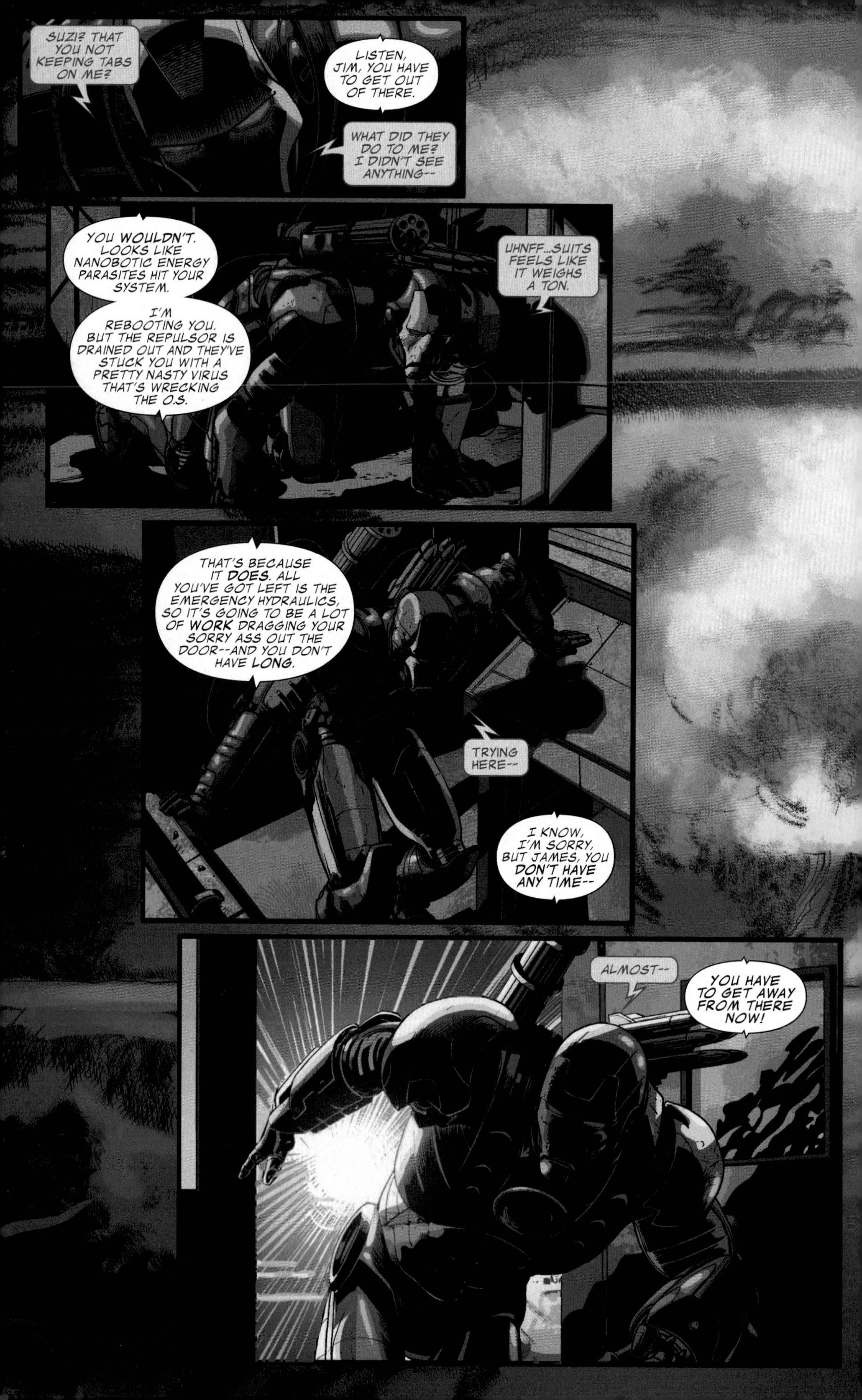
SUZI? THAT YOU NOT KEEPING TABS ON ME?
LISTEN, JIM, YOU HAVE TO GET OUT OF THERE.
WHAT DID THEY DO TO ME? I DIDN'T SEE ANYTHING--
YOU WOULDN'T. LOOKS LIKE NANOBOTIC ENERGY PARASITES HIT YOUR SYSTEM.
I'M REBOOTING YOU. BUT THE REPULSOR IS DRAINED OUT AND THEY'VE STUCK YOU WITH A PRETTY NASTY VIRUS THAT'S WRECKING THE O.S.
UHNFF...SUITS FEELS LIKE IT WEIGHS A TON.
THAT'S BECAUSE IT DOES. ALL YOU'VE GOT LEFT IS THE EMERGENCY HYDRAULICS, SO IT'S GOING TO BE A LOT OF WORK DRAGGING YOUR SORRY ASS OUT THE DOOR--AND YOU DON'T HAVE LONG.
TRYING HERE--
I KNOW, I'M SORRY, BUT JAMES, YOU DON'T HAVE ANY TIME--
ALMOST--
YOU HAVE TO GET AWAY FROM THERE NOW!

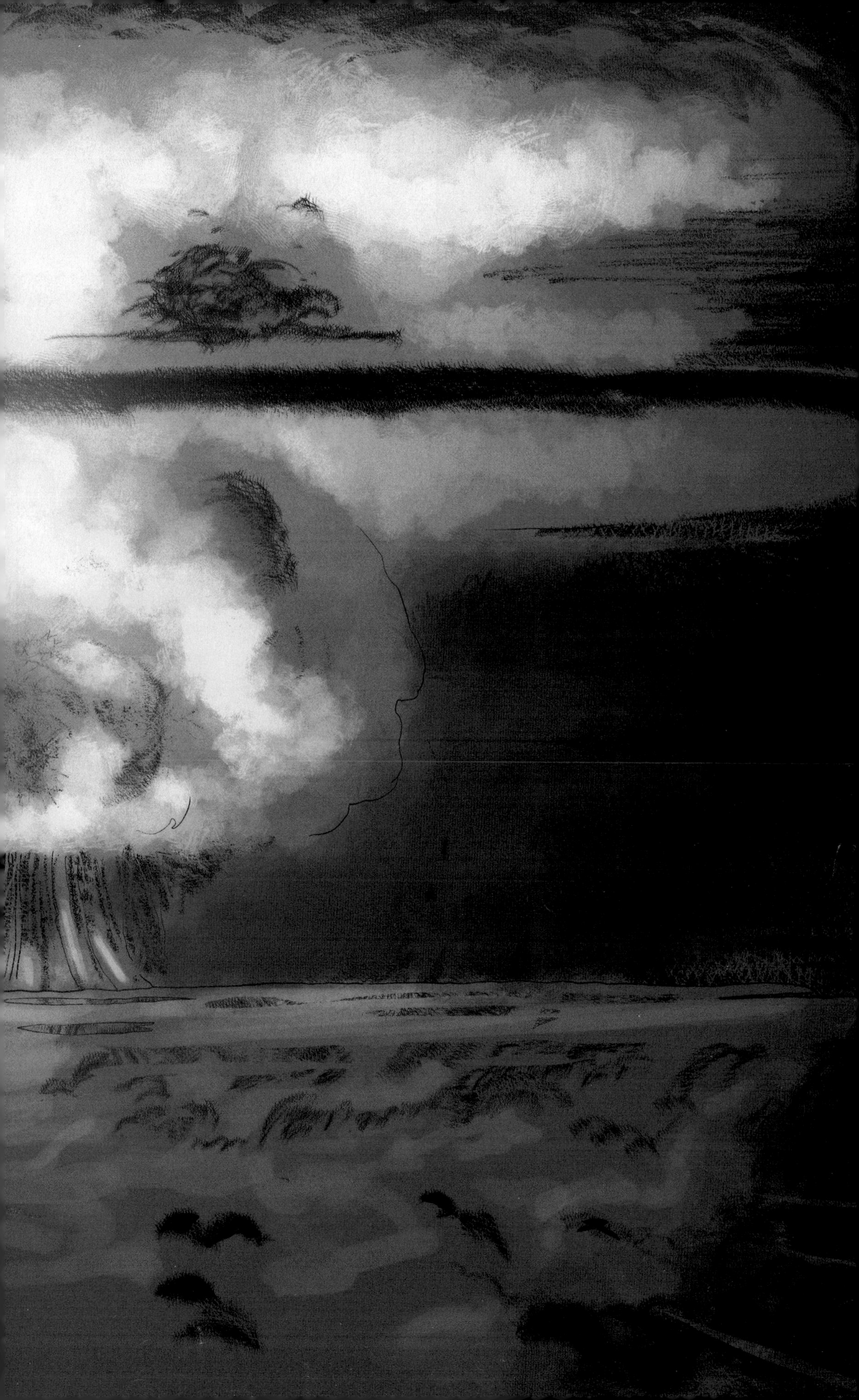

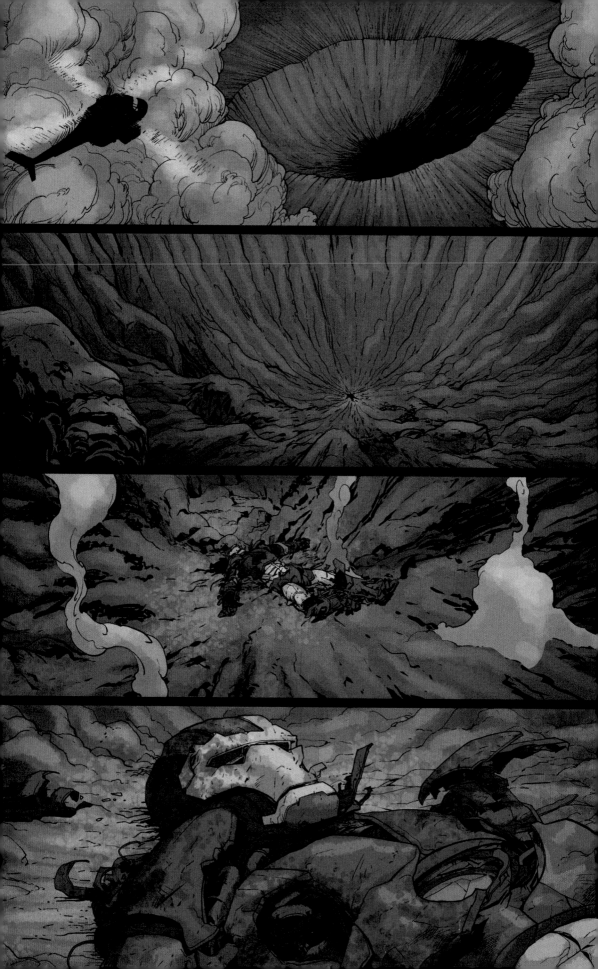

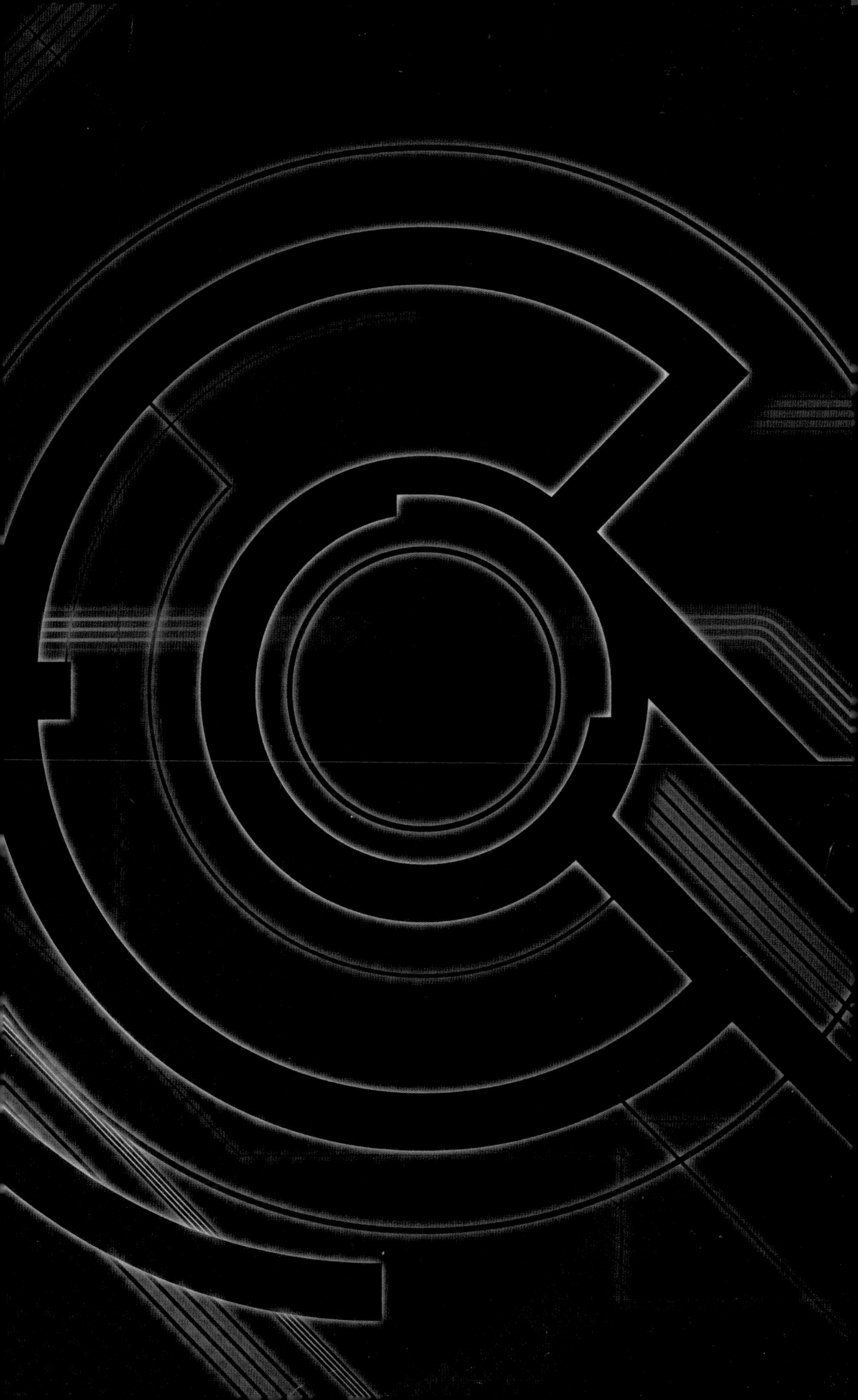

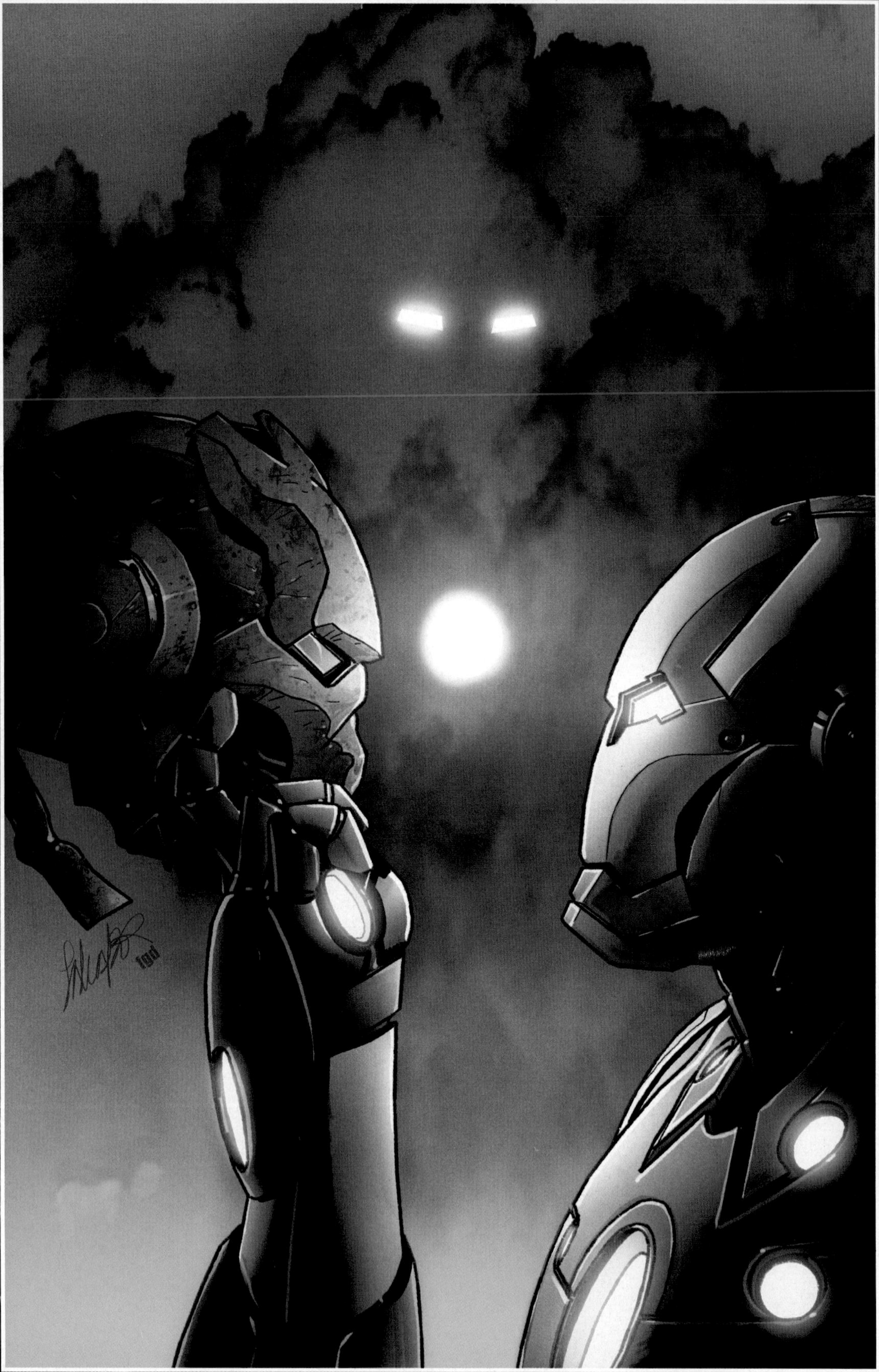

3

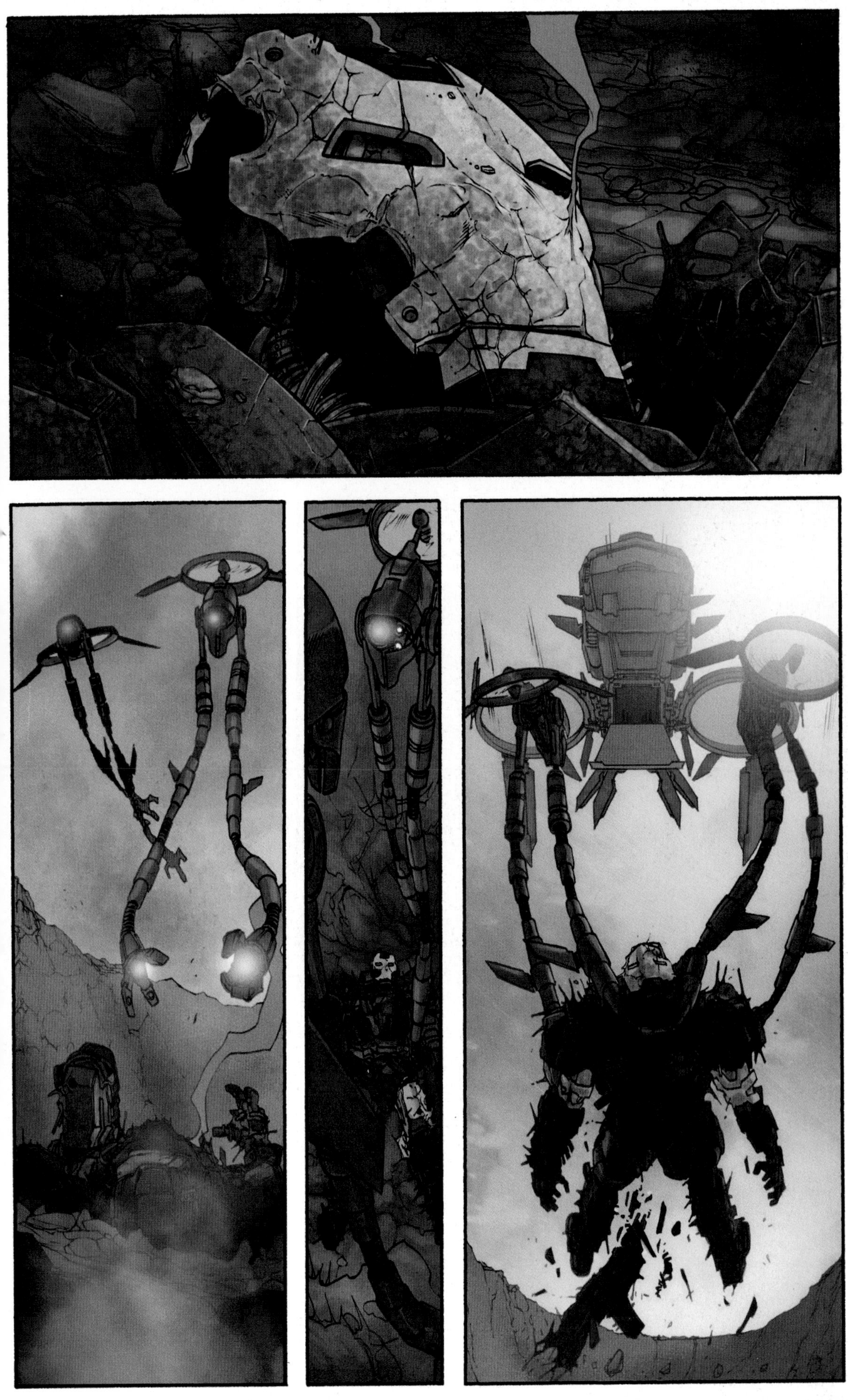

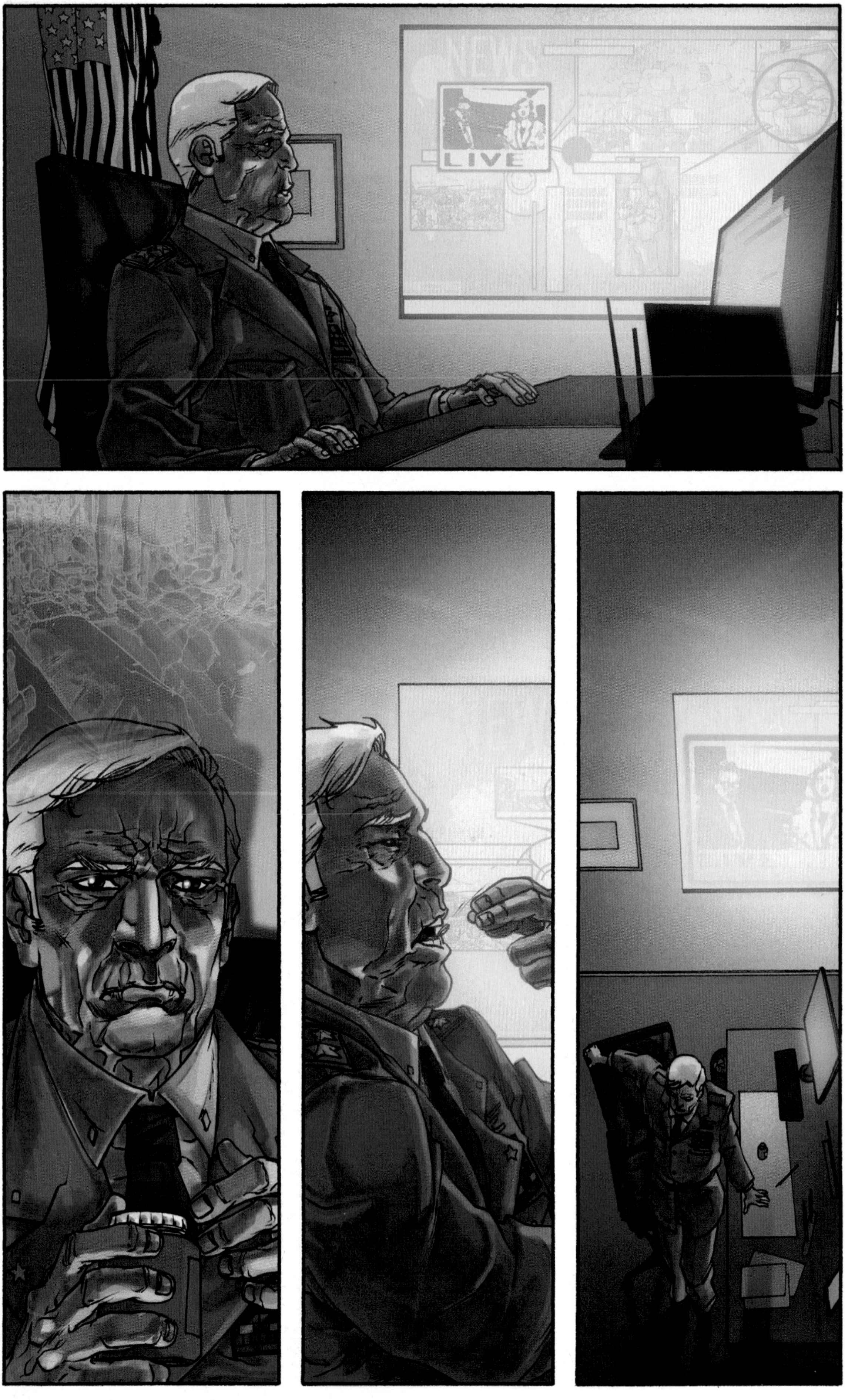
NEWS
LIVE

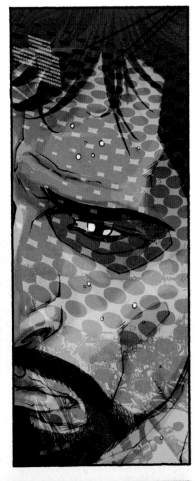
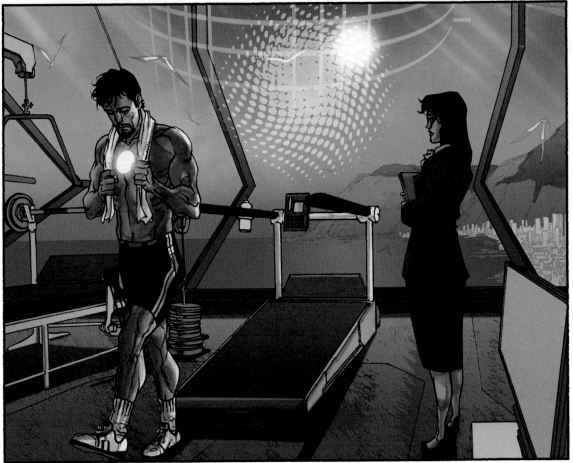

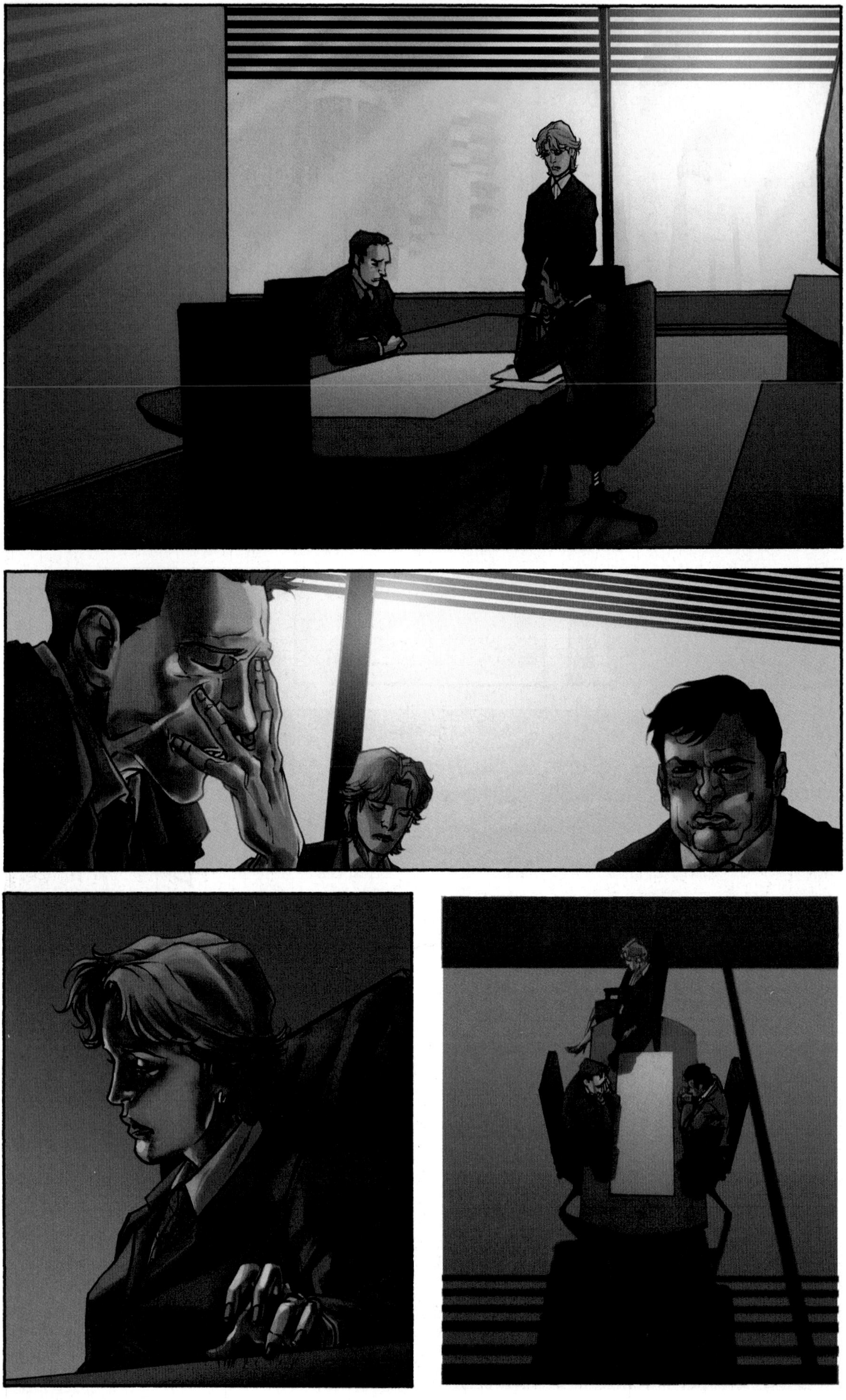

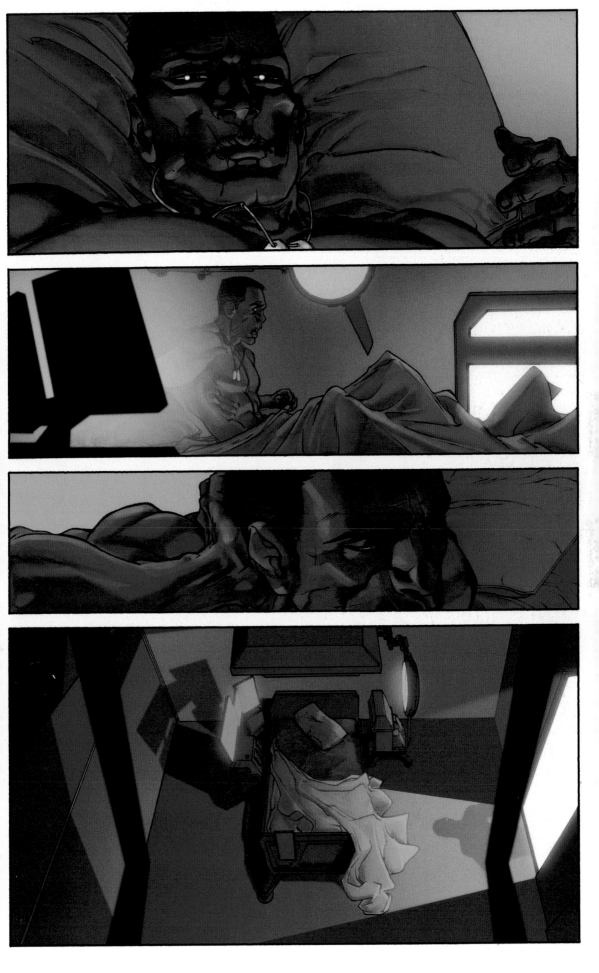

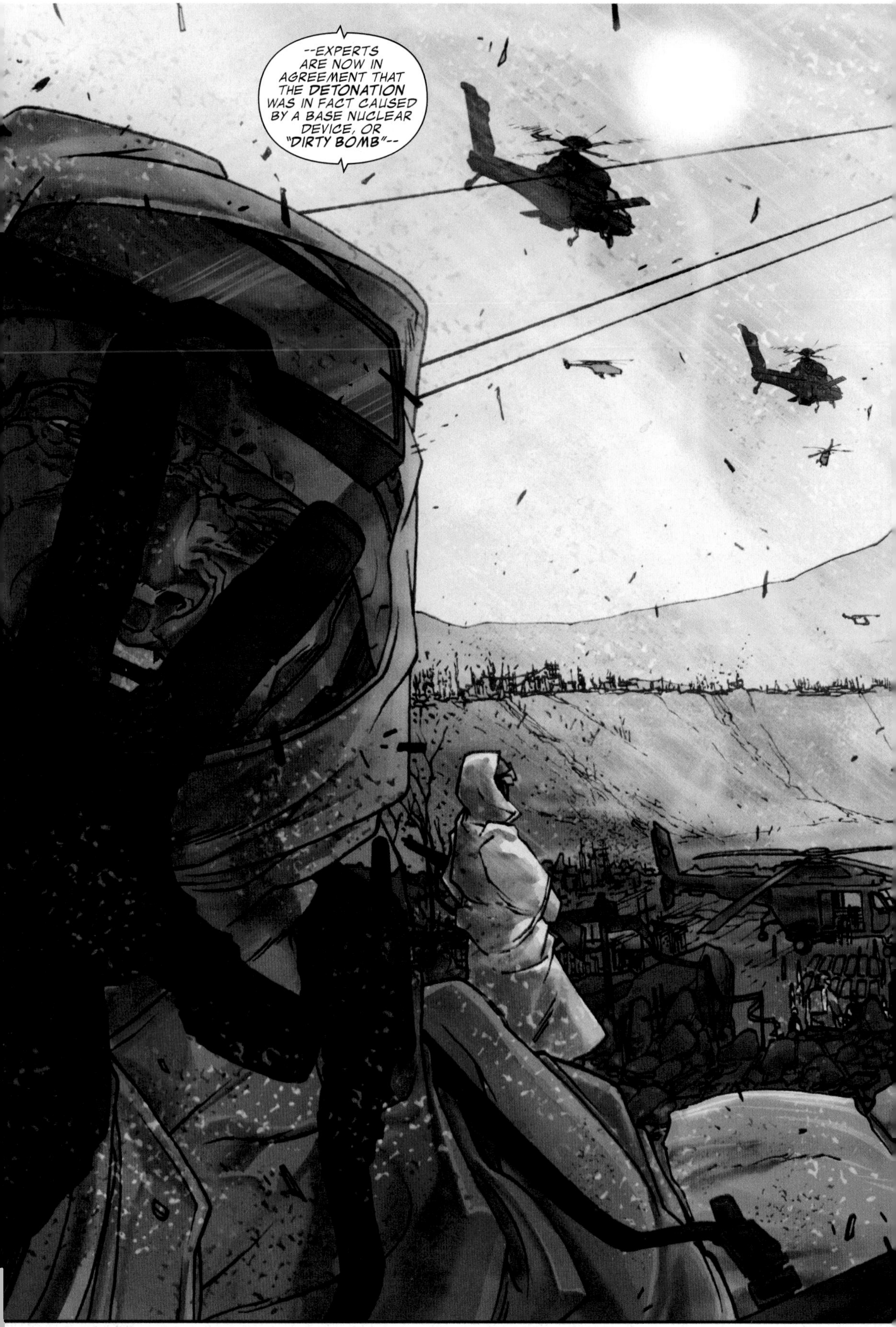
--EXPERTS ARE NOW IN AGREEMENT THAT THE DETONATION WAS IN FACT CAUSED BY A BASE NUCLEAR DEVICE, OR "DIRTY BOMB"--

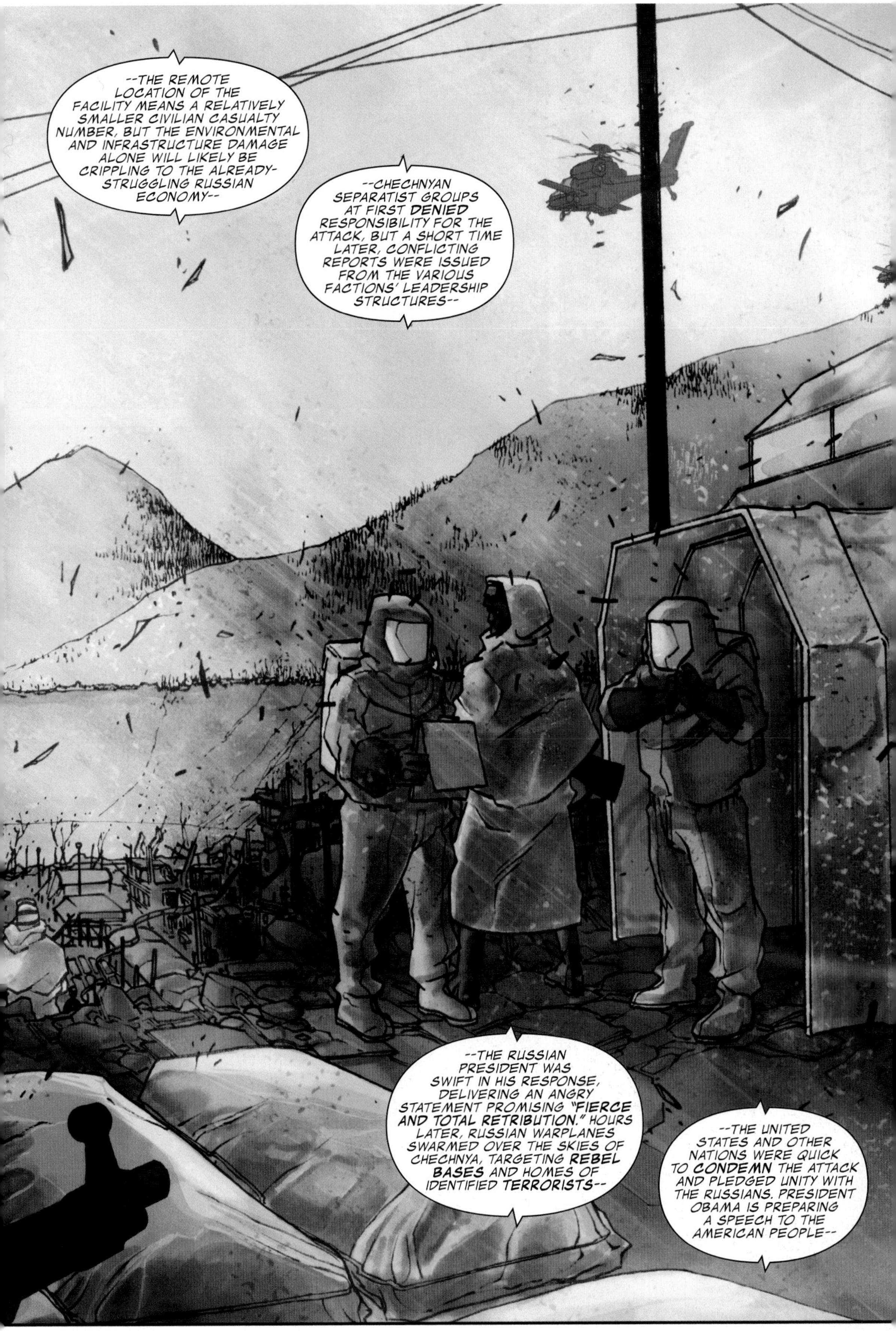
--THE REMOTE LOCATION OF THE FACILITY MEANS A RELATIVELY SMALLER CIVILIAN CASUALTY NUMBER, BUT THE ENVIRONMENTAL AND INFRASTRUCTURE DAMAGE ALONE WILL LIKELY BE CRIPPLING TO THE ALREADY-STRUGGLING RUSSIAN ECONOMY--
--CHECHNYAN SEPARATIST GROUPS AT FIRST DENIED RESPONSIBILITY FOR THE ATTACK, BUT A SHORT TIME LATER, CONFLICTING REPORTS WERE ISSUED FROM THE VARIOUS FACTIONS' LEADERSHIP STRUCTURES--
--THE RUSSIAN PRESIDENT WAS SWIFT IN HIS RESPONSE, DELIVERING AN ANGRY STATEMENT PROMISING "FIERCE AND TOTAL RETRIBUTION." HOURS LATER, RUSSIAN WARPLANES SWARMED OVER THE SKIES OF CHECHNYA, TARGETING REBEL BASES AND HOMES OF IDENTIFIED TERRORISTS--
--THE UNITED STATES AND OTHER NATIONS WERE QUICK TO CONDEMN THE ATTACK AND PLEDGED UNITY WITH THE RUSSIANS. PRESIDENT OBAMA IS PREPARING A SPEECH TO THE AMERICAN PEOPLE--

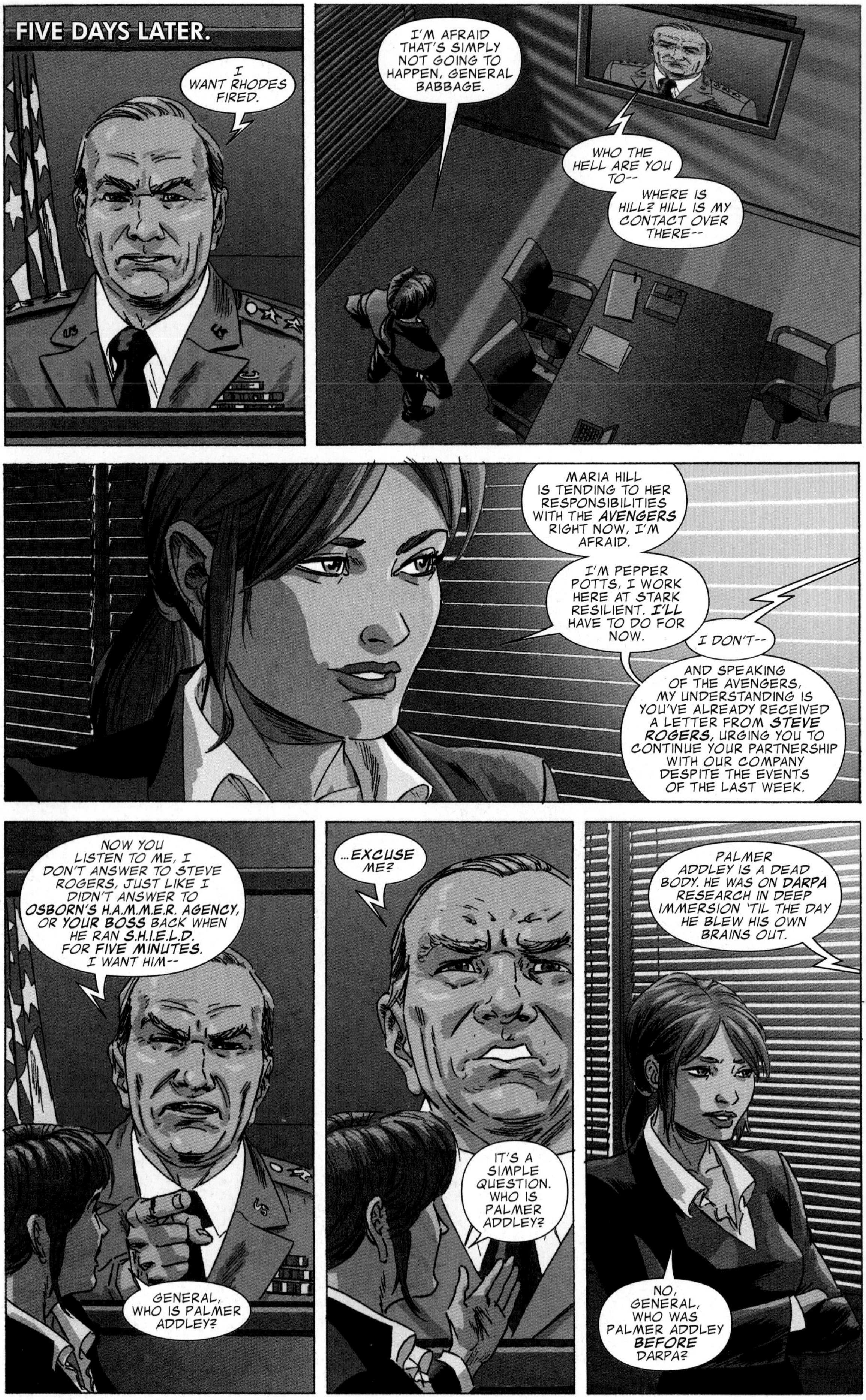
FIVE DAYS LATER.
I WANT RHODES FIRED.
I'M AFRAID THAT'S SIMPLY NOT GOING TO HAPPEN, GENERAL BABBAGE.
WHO THE HELL ARE YOU TO--
WHERE IS HILL? HILL IS MY CONTACT OVER THERE--
MARIA HILL IS TENDING TO HER RESPONSIBILITIES WITH THE AVENGERS RIGHT NOW, I'M AFRAID.
I'M PEPPER POTTS, I WORK HERE AT STARK RESILIENT. I'LL HAVE TO DO FOR NOW.
I DON'T--
AND SPEAKING OF THE AVENGERS, MY UNDERSTANDING IS YOU'VE ALREADY RECEIVED A LETTER FROM STEVE ROGERS, URGING YOU TO CONTINUE YOUR PARTNERSHIP WITH OUR COMPANY DESPITE THE EVENTS OF THE LAST WEEK.
NOW YOU LISTEN TO ME, I DON'T ANSWER TO STEVE ROGERS, JUST LIKE I DIDN'T ANSWER TO OSBORN'S H.A.M.M.E.R. AGENCY, OR YOUR BOSS BACK WHEN HE RAN S.H.I.E.L.D. FOR FIVE MINUTES. I WANT HIM--
GENERAL, WHO IS PALMER ADDLEY?
...EXCUSE ME?
IT'S A SIMPLE QUESTION. WHO IS PALMER ADDLEY?
PALMER ADDLEY IS A DEAD BODY. HE WAS ON DARPA RESEARCH IN DEEP IMMERSION 'TIL THE DAY HE BLEW HIS OWN BRAINS OUT.
NO, GENERAL, WHO WAS PALMER ADDLEY BEFORE DARPA?

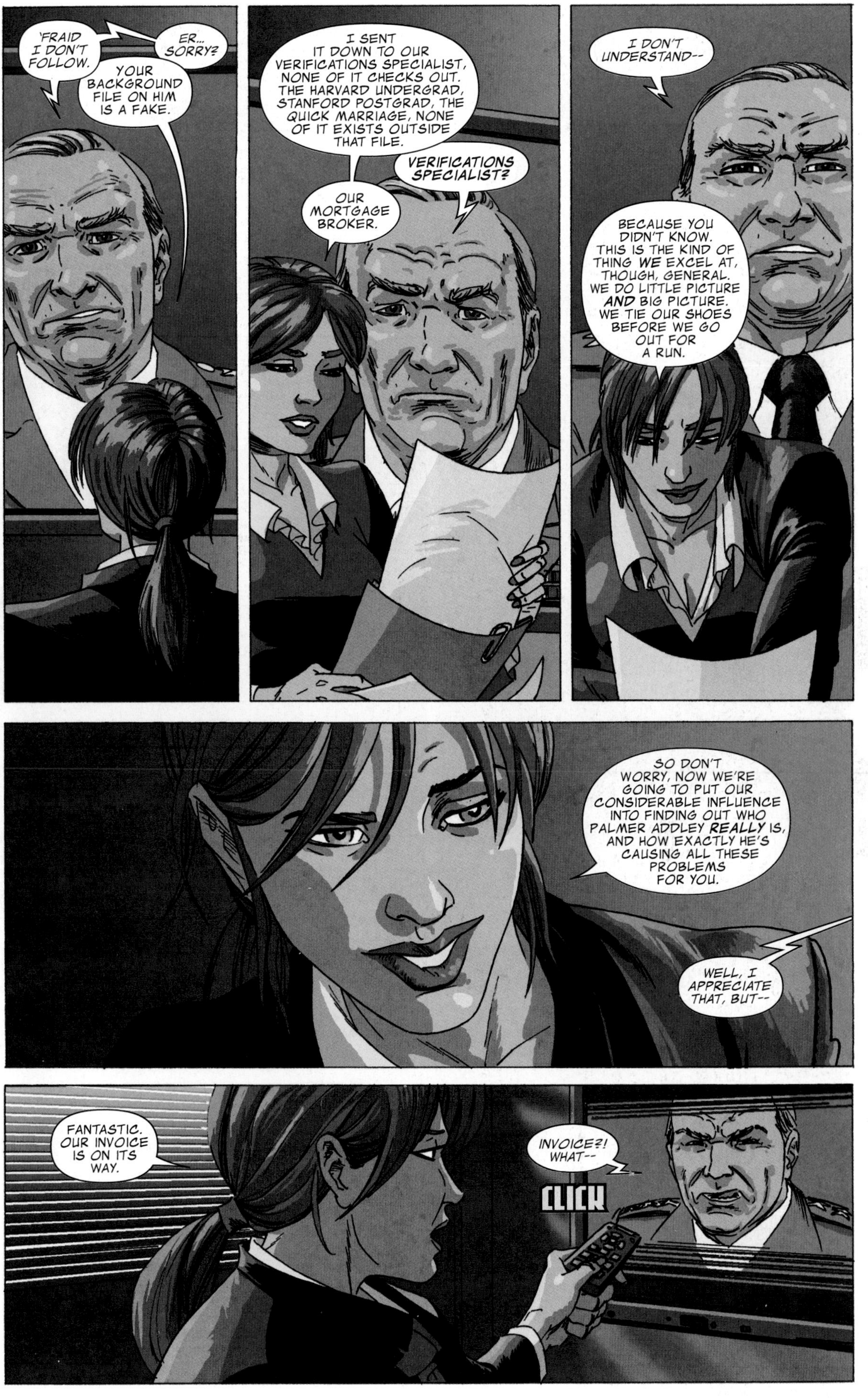
'FRAID I DON'T FOLLOW.
ER... SORRY?
YOUR BACKGROUND FILE ON HIM IS A FAKE.
I SENT IT DOWN TO OUR VERIFICATIONS SPECIALIST, NONE OF IT CHECKS OUT. THE HARVARD UNDERGRAD, STANFORD POSTGRAD, THE QUICK MARRIAGE, NONE OF IT EXISTS OUTSIDE THAT FILE.
VERIFICATIONS SPECIALIST?
OUR MORTGAGE BROKER.
I DON'T UNDERSTAND--
BECAUSE YOU DIDN'T KNOW. THIS IS THE KIND OF THING WE EXCEL AT, THOUGH, GENERAL. WE DO LITTLE PICTURE AND BIG PICTURE. WE TIE OUR SHOES BEFORE WE GO OUT FOR A RUN.
SO DON'T WORRY, NOW WE'RE GOING TO PUT OUR CONSIDERABLE INFLUENCE INTO FINDING OUT WHO PALMER ADDLEY REALLY IS, AND HOW EXACTLY HE'S CAUSING ALL THESE PROBLEMS FOR YOU.
WELL, I APPRECIATE THAT, BUT--
FANTASTIC. OUR INVOICE IS ON ITS WAY.
INVOICE?! WHAT--
CLICK

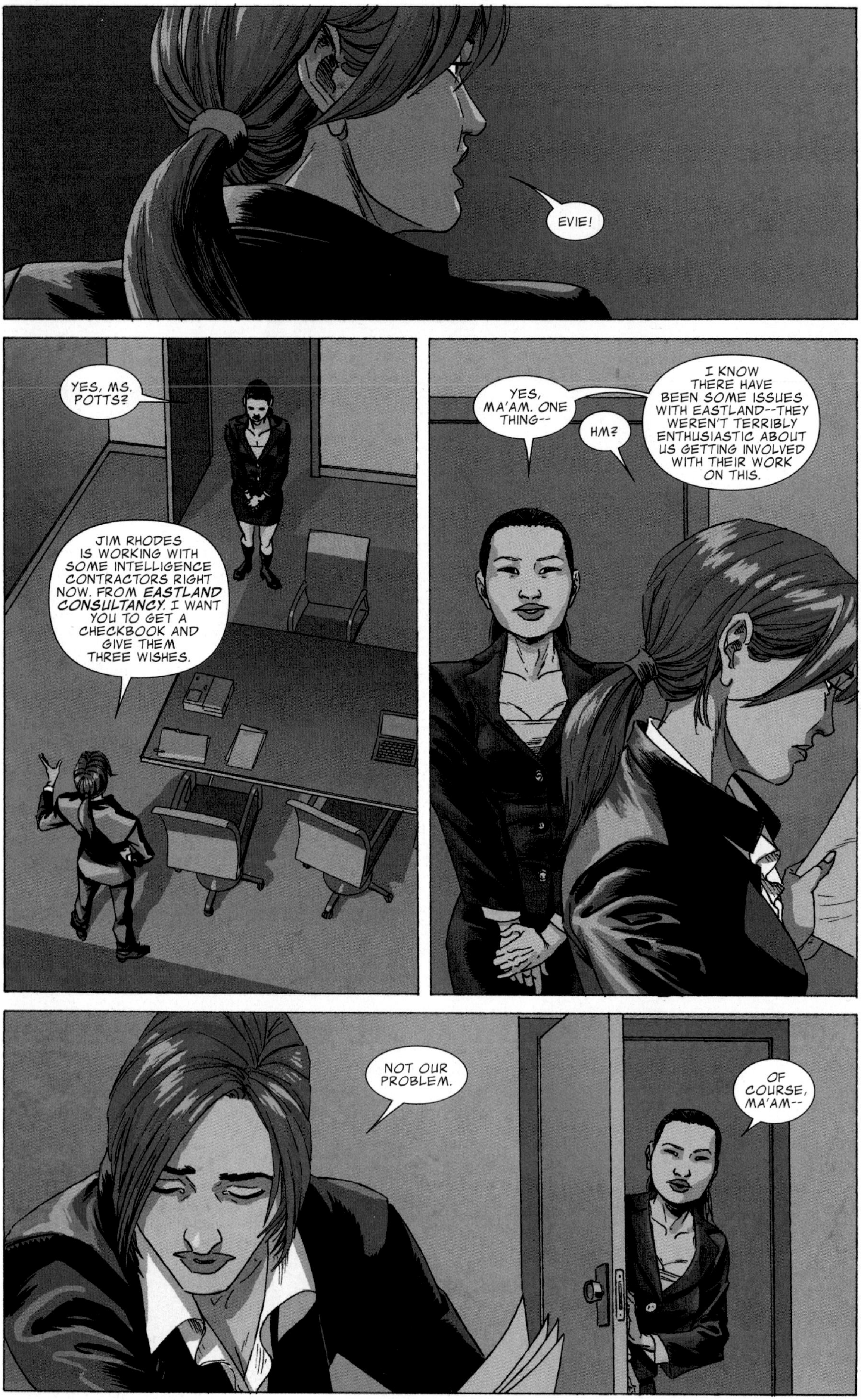
EVIE!
YES, MS. POTTS?
JIM RHODES IS WORKING WITH SOME INTELLIGENCE CONTRACTORS RIGHT NOW. FROM EASTLAND CONSULTANCY. I WANT YOU TO GET A CHECKBOOK AND GIVE THEM THREE WISHES.
YES, MA'AM. ONE THING--
HM?
I KNOW THERE HAVE BEEN SOME ISSUES WITH EASTLAND--THEY WEREN'T TERRIBLY ENTHUSIASTIC ABOUT US GETTING INVOLVED WITH THEIR WORK ON THIS.
NOT OUR PROBLEM.
OF COURSE, MA'AM--

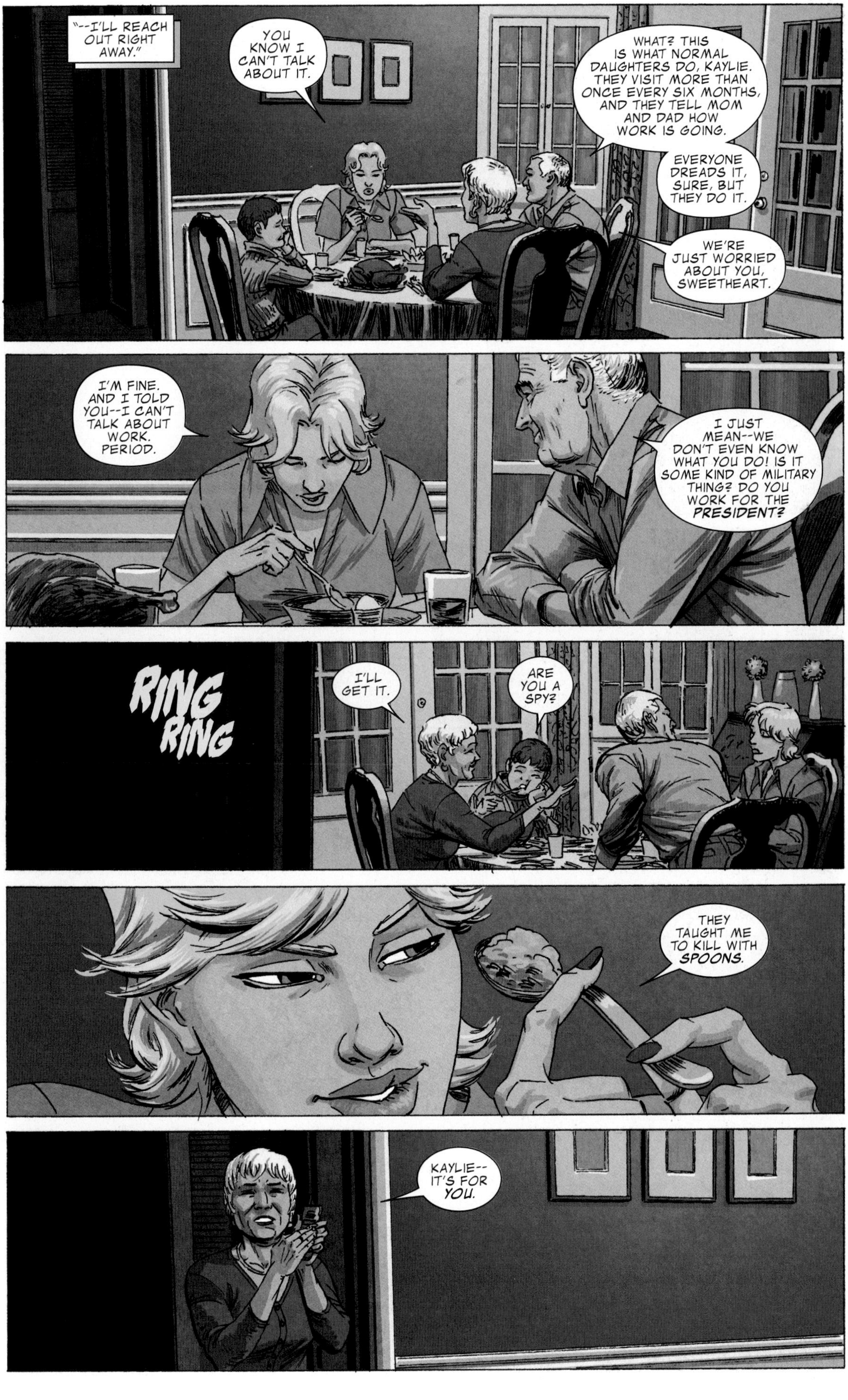
"--I'LL REACH OUT RIGHT AWAY."
YOU KNOW I CAN'T TALK ABOUT IT.
WHAT? THIS IS WHAT NORMAL DAUGHTERS DO, KAYLIE. THEY VISIT MORE THAN ONCE EVERY SIX MONTHS, AND THEY TELL MOM AND DAD HOW WORK IS GOING.
EVERYONE DREADS IT, SURE, BUT THEY DO IT.
WE'RE JUST WORRIED ABOUT YOU, SWEETHEART.
I'M FINE. AND I TOLD YOU--I CAN'T TALK ABOUT WORK. PERIOD.
I JUST MEAN--WE DON'T EVEN KNOW WHAT YOU DO! IS IT SOME KIND OF MILITARY THING? DO YOU WORK FOR THE PRESIDENT?
RING RING
I'LL GET IT.
ARE YOU A SPY?
THEY TAUGHT ME TO KILL WITH SPOONS.
KAYLIE-- IT'S FOR YOU.

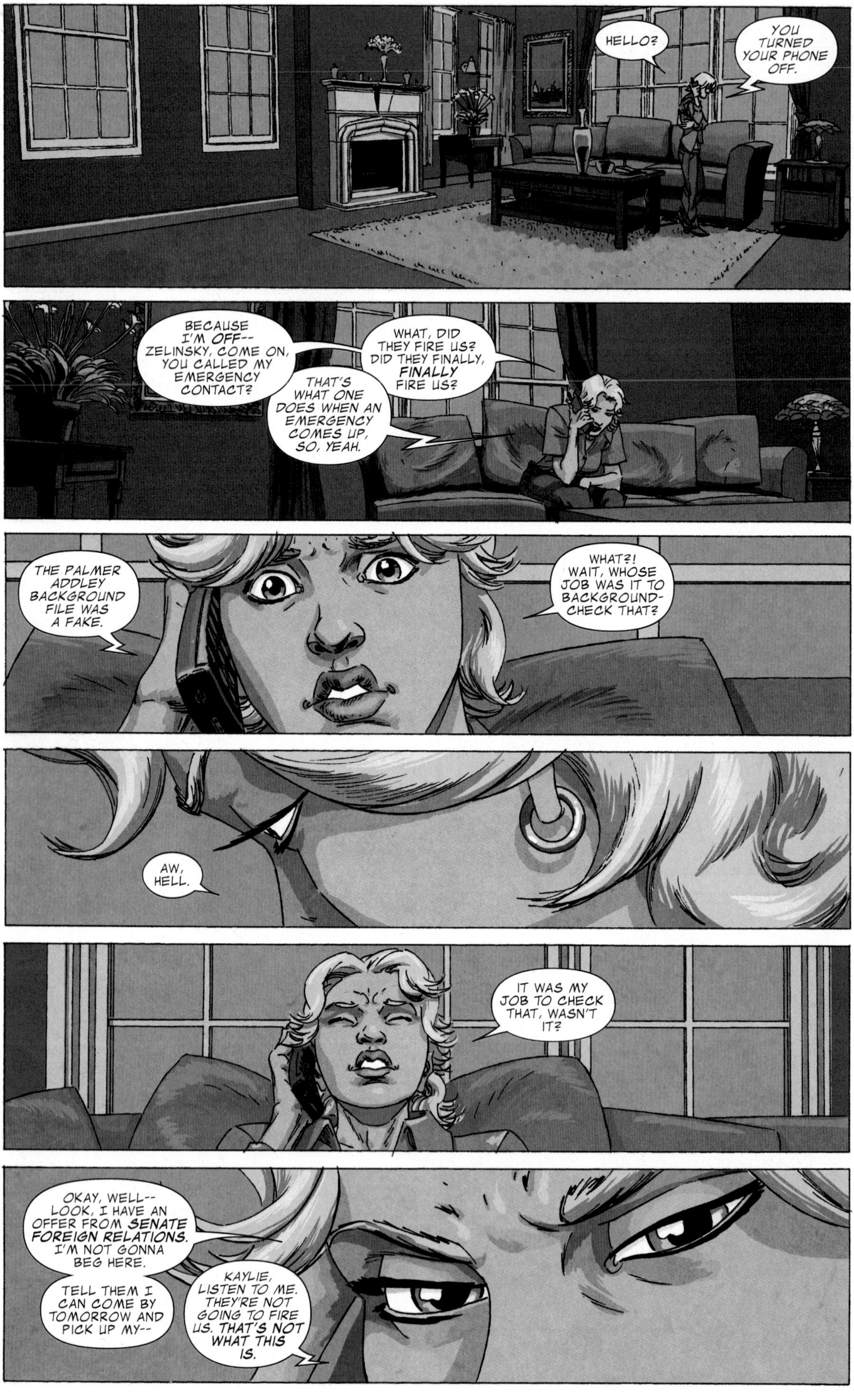
HELLO?
YOU TURNED YOUR PHONE OFF.
BECAUSE I'M OFF-- ZELINSKY, COME ON, YOU CALLED MY EMERGENCY CONTACT?
THAT'S WHAT ONE DOES WHEN AN EMERGENCY COMES UP, SO, YEAH.
WHAT, DID THEY FIRE US? DID THEY FINALLY, FINALLY FIRE US?
THE PALMER ADDLEY BACKGROUND FILE WAS A FAKE.
WHAT?! WAIT, WHOSE JOB WAS IT TO BACKGROUND-CHECK THAT?
AW, HELL.
IT WAS MY JOB TO CHECK THAT, WASN'T IT?
OKAY, WELL-- LOOK, I HAVE AN OFFER FROM SENATE FOREIGN RELATIONS. I'M NOT GONNA BEG HERE.
TELL THEM I CAN COME BY TOMORROW AND PICK UP MY--
KAYLIE, LISTEN TO ME. THEY'RE NOT GOING TO FIRE US. THAT'S NOT WHAT THIS IS.

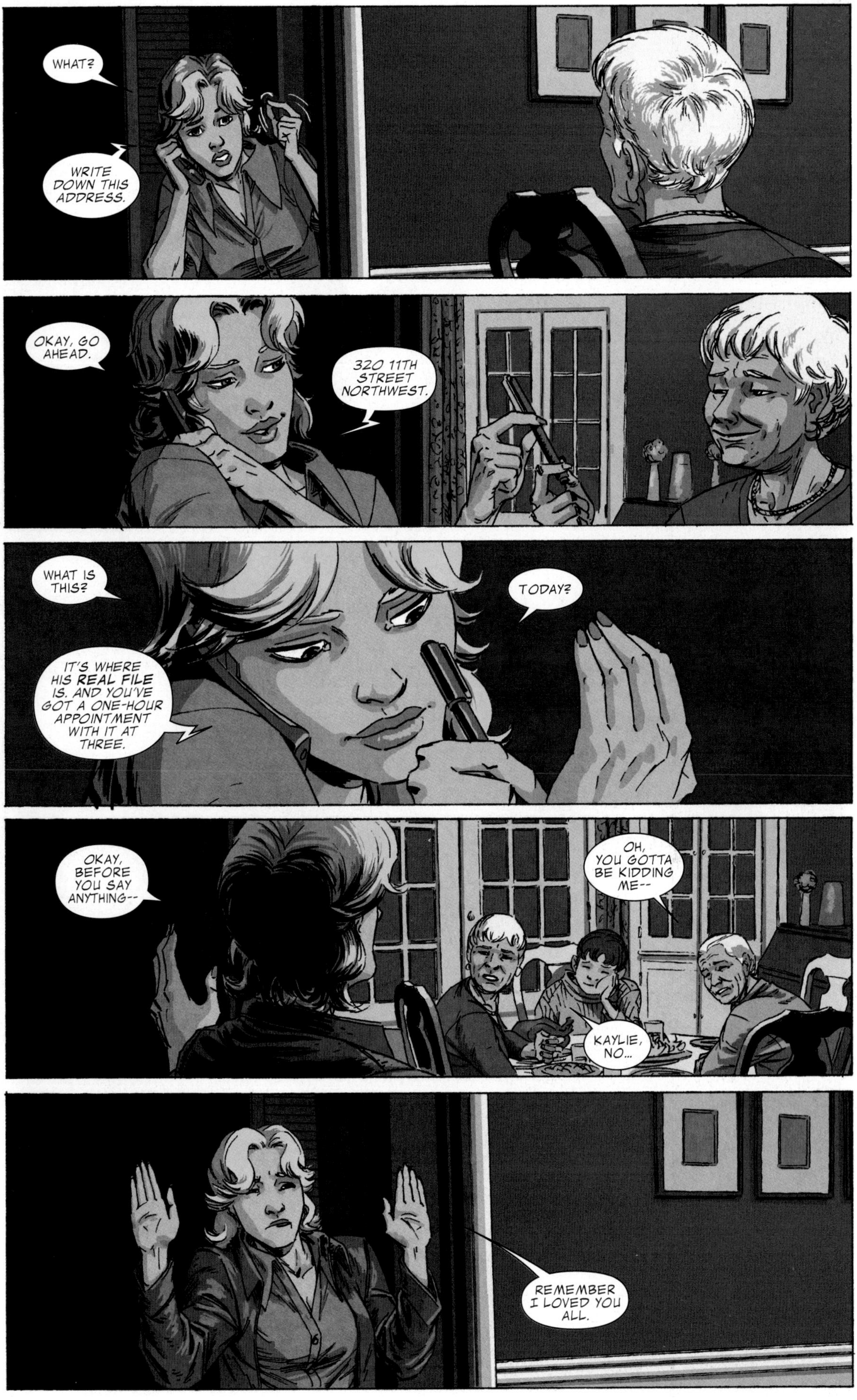
WHAT?
WRITE DOWN THIS ADDRESS.
OKAY, GO AHEAD.
320 11TH STREET NORTHWEST.
WHAT IS THIS?
IT'S WHERE HIS **REAL FILE** IS. AND YOU'VE GOT A ONE-HOUR APPOINTMENT WITH IT AT THREE.
TODAY?
OKAY, BEFORE YOU SAY ANYTHING--
OH, YOU GOTTA BE KIDDING ME--
KAYLIE, NO...
REMEMBER I LOVED YOU ALL.

I GOTTA TELL YOU, JIM--

I FEEL LIKE WE *MIGHT* BE DROPPING THE BALL A LITTLE BIT.

YOU DON'T SAY.

BABBAGE WANTS HIS MONEY BACK, WE GOT NEXT TO *NOTHING* ON THIS PALMER ADDLEY, AND THE STRATEGIC IMPORTANCE MAP HAS A LOT OF THOSE LITTLE RED *THUMBTACKS* IN IT.

WE GOT CLOSER THAN ANYONE'S GOTTEN TO THIS GUY BEFORE--

AND NOW WE'VE GOT NUCLEAR WINTER TO SHOW FOR IT.

DON'T--

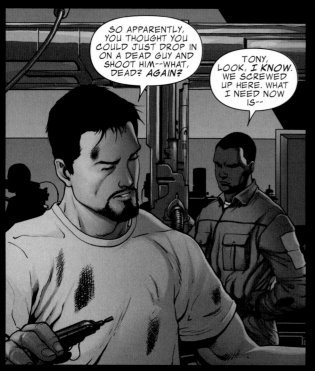

SO APPARENTLY, YOU THOUGHT YOU COULD JUST DROP IN ON A DEAD GUY AND SHOOT HIM--WHAT, DEAD? *AGAIN?*

TONY, LOOK, *I KNOW.* WE SCREWED UP HERE. WHAT I NEED NOW IS--

OKAY, FORGET IT. *FORGET* IT.

BUT I AM GONNA ASK YOU A QUESTION, AND I WANT YOU TO TELL ME THE TRUTH--

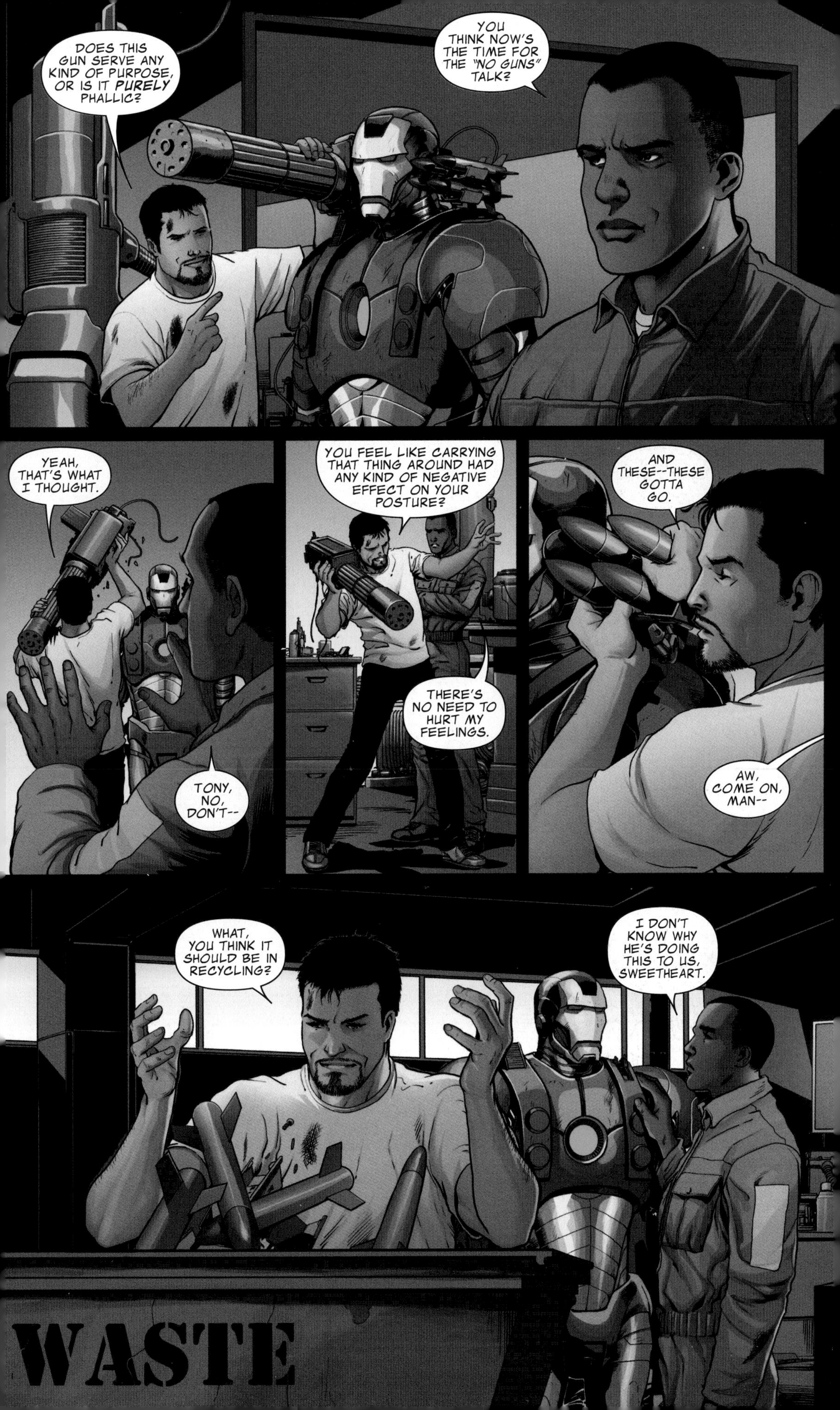
DOES THIS GUN SERVE ANY KIND OF PURPOSE, OR IS IT *PURELY* PHALLIC?
YOU THINK NOW'S THE TIME FOR THE *"NO GUNS"* TALK?
YEAH, THAT'S WHAT I THOUGHT.
TONY, NO, DON'T--
YOU FEEL LIKE CARRYING THAT THING AROUND HAD ANY KIND OF NEGATIVE EFFECT ON YOUR POSTURE?
THERE'S NO NEED TO HURT MY FEELINGS.
AND THESE--THESE GOTTA GO.
AW, COME ON, MAN--
WHAT, YOU THINK IT SHOULD BE IN RECYCLING?
I DON'T KNOW WHY HE'S DOING THIS TO US, SWEETHEART.
WASTE

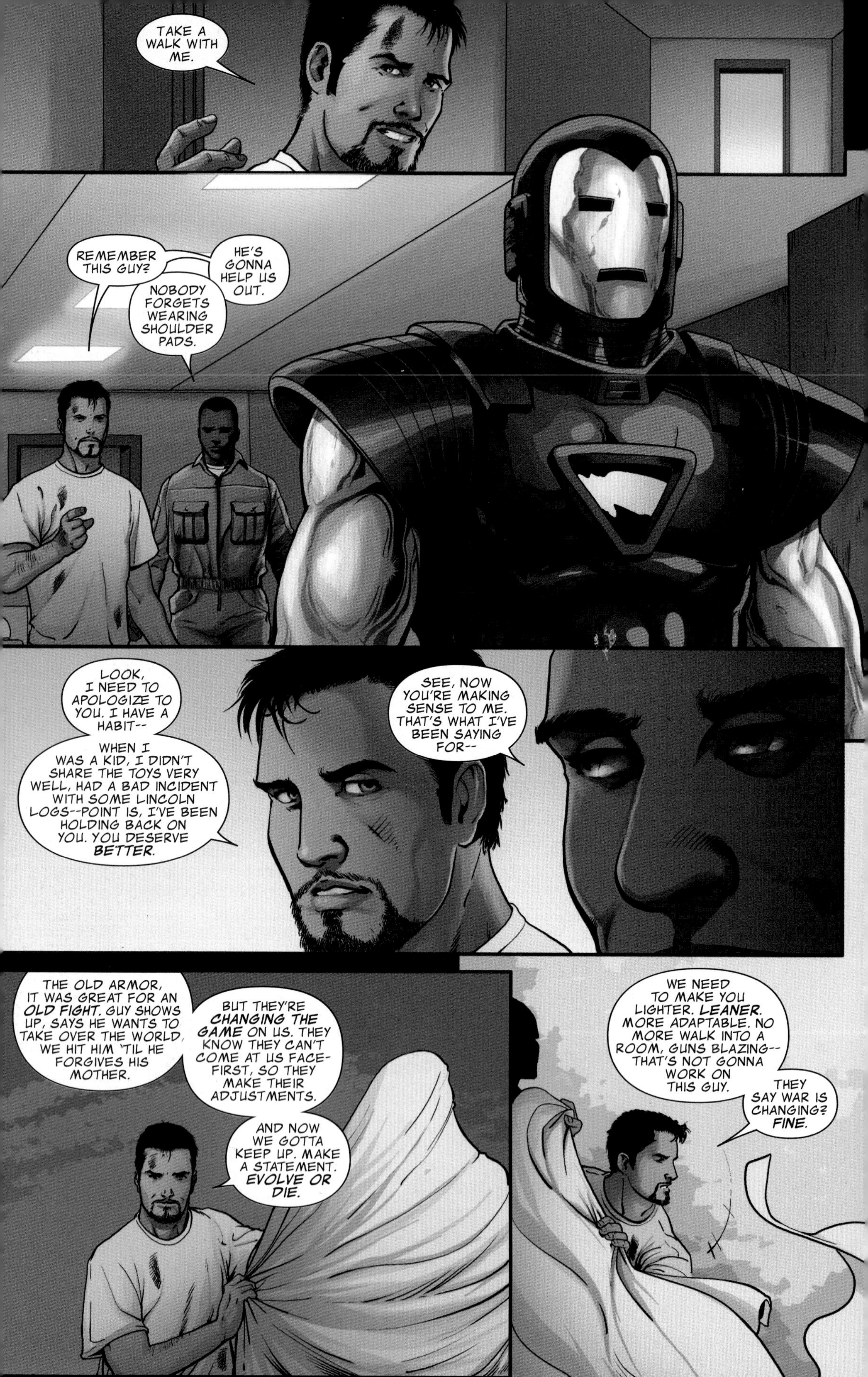
TAKE A WALK WITH ME.
REMEMBER THIS GUY?
HE'S GONNA HELP US OUT.
NOBODY FORGETS WEARING SHOULDER PADS.
LOOK, I NEED TO APOLOGIZE TO YOU. I HAVE A HABIT--
WHEN I WAS A KID, I DIDN'T SHARE THE TOYS VERY WELL, HAD A BAD INCIDENT WITH SOME LINCOLN LOGS--POINT IS, I'VE BEEN HOLDING BACK ON YOU. YOU DESERVE **BETTER**.
SEE, NOW YOU'RE MAKING SENSE TO ME. THAT'S WHAT I'VE BEEN SAYING FOR--
THE OLD ARMOR, IT WAS GREAT FOR AN **OLD FIGHT**. GUY SHOWS UP, SAYS HE WANTS TO TAKE OVER THE WORLD, WE HIT HIM 'TIL HE FORGIVES HIS MOTHER.
BUT THEY'RE **CHANGING THE GAME** ON US. THEY KNOW THEY CAN'T COME AT US FACE-FIRST, SO THEY MAKE THEIR ADJUSTMENTS.
AND NOW WE GOTTA KEEP UP. MAKE A STATEMENT. **EVOLVE OR DIE**.
WE NEED TO MAKE YOU LIGHTER. **LEANER**. MORE ADAPTABLE. NO MORE WALK INTO A ROOM, GUNS BLAZING--THAT'S NOT GONNA WORK ON THIS GUY.
THEY SAY WAR IS CHANGING? **FINE**.

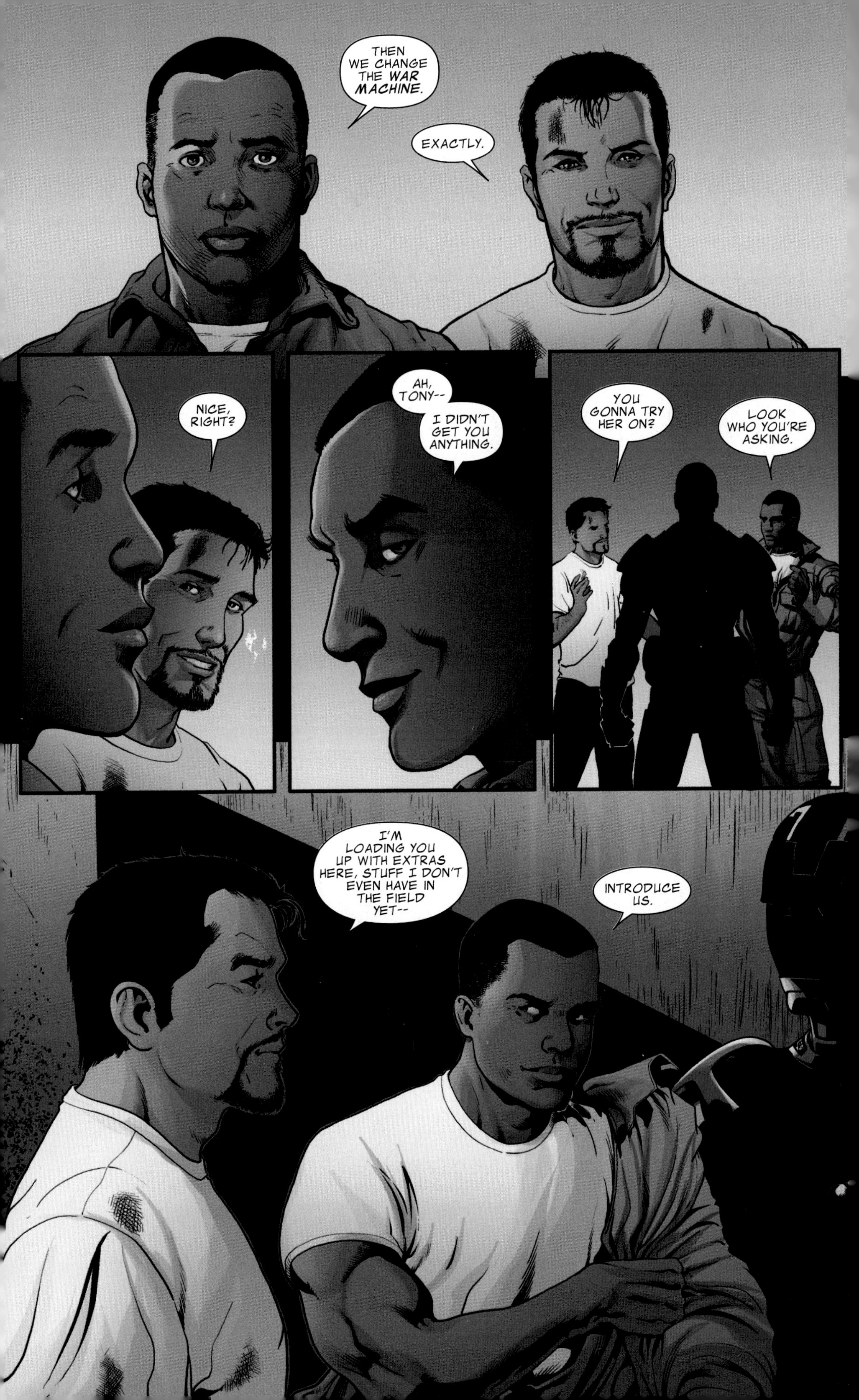
THEN WE CHANGE THE WAR MACHINE.
EXACTLY.
NICE, RIGHT?
AH, TONY--
I DIDN'T GET YOU ANYTHING.
YOU GONNA TRY HER ON?
LOOK WHO YOU'RE ASKING.
I'M LOADING YOU UP WITH EXTRAS HERE, STUFF I DON'T EVEN HAVE IN THE FIELD YET--
INTRODUCE US.

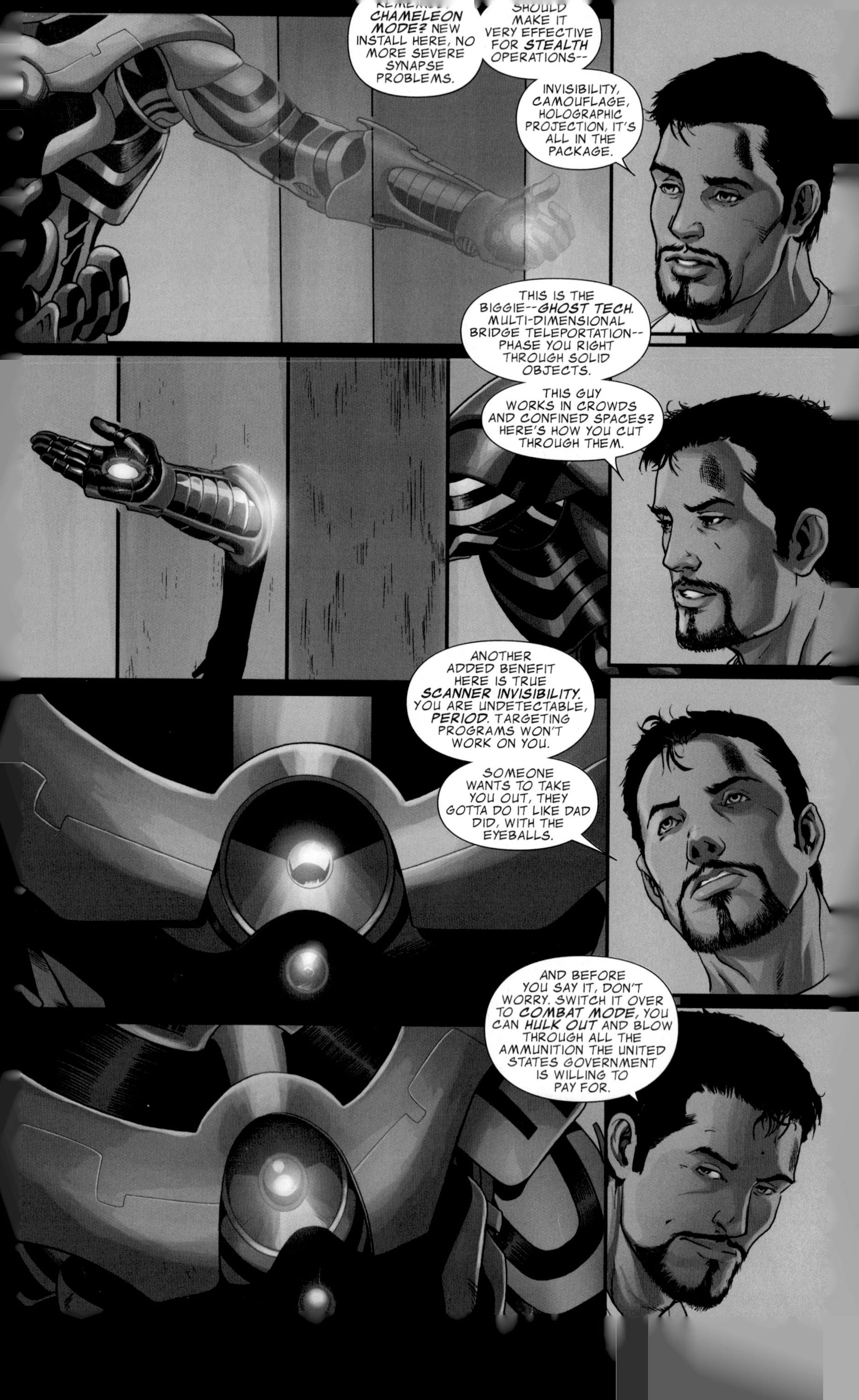
CHAMELEON MODE? NEW INSTALL HERE, NO MORE SEVERE SYNAPSE PROBLEMS.
SHOULD MAKE IT VERY EFFECTIVE FOR STEALTH OPERATIONS--
INVISIBILITY, CAMOUFLAGE, HOLOGRAPHIC PROJECTION, IT'S ALL IN THE PACKAGE.
THIS IS THE BIGGIE--GHOST TECH. MULTI-DIMENSIONAL BRIDGE TELEPORTATION--PHASE YOU RIGHT THROUGH SOLID OBJECTS.
THIS GUY WORKS IN CROWDS AND CONFINED SPACES? HERE'S HOW YOU CUT THROUGH THEM.
ANOTHER ADDED BENEFIT HERE IS TRUE SCANNER INVISIBILITY. YOU ARE UNDETECTABLE, PERIOD. TARGETING PROGRAMS WON'T WORK ON YOU.
SOMEONE WANTS TO TAKE YOU OUT, THEY GOTTA DO IT LIKE DAD DID, WITH THE EYEBALLS.
AND BEFORE YOU SAY IT, DON'T WORRY. SWITCH IT OVER TO COMBAT MODE, YOU CAN HULK OUT AND BLOW THROUGH ALL THE AMMUNITION THE UNITED STATES GOVERNMENT IS WILLING TO PAY FOR.

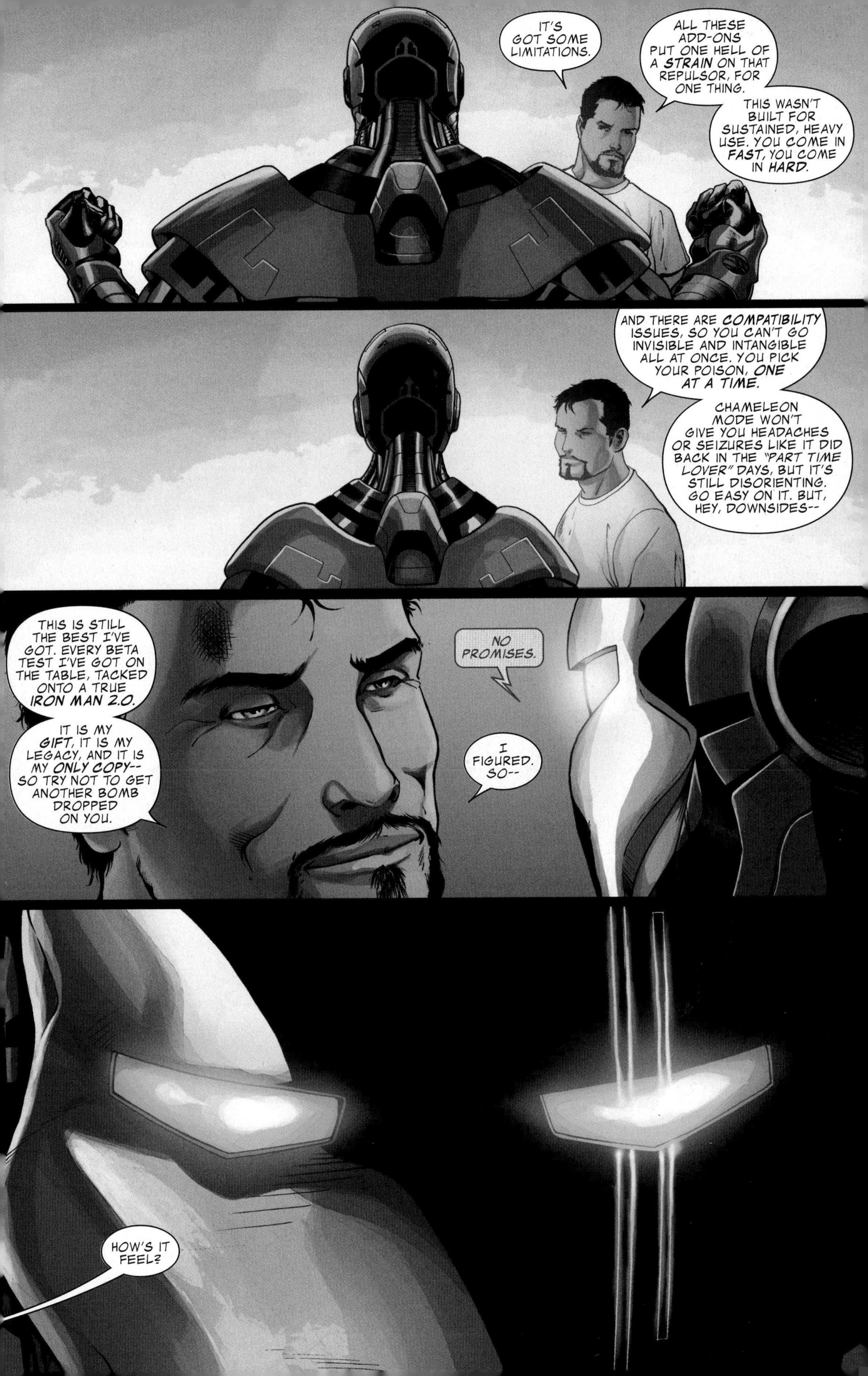
IT'S GOT SOME LIMITATIONS.
ALL THESE ADD-ONS PUT ONE HELL OF A STRAIN ON THAT REPULSOR, FOR ONE THING.
THIS WASN'T BUILT FOR SUSTAINED, HEAVY USE. YOU COME IN FAST, YOU COME IN HARD.
AND THERE ARE COMPATIBILITY ISSUES, SO YOU CAN'T GO INVISIBLE AND INTANGIBLE ALL AT ONCE. YOU PICK YOUR POISON, ONE AT A TIME.
CHAMELEON MODE WON'T GIVE YOU HEADACHES OR SEIZURES LIKE IT DID BACK IN THE "PART TIME LOVER" DAYS, BUT IT'S STILL DISORIENTING. GO EASY ON IT. BUT, HEY, DOWNSIDES--
THIS IS STILL THE BEST I'VE GOT. EVERY BETA TEST I'VE GOT ON THE TABLE, TACKED ONTO A TRUE IRON MAN 2.0.
IT IS MY GIFT, IT IS MY LEGACY, AND IT IS MY ONLY COPY-- SO TRY NOT TO GET ANOTHER BOMB DROPPED ON YOU.
NO PROMISES.
I FIGURED. SO--
HOW'S IT FEEL?

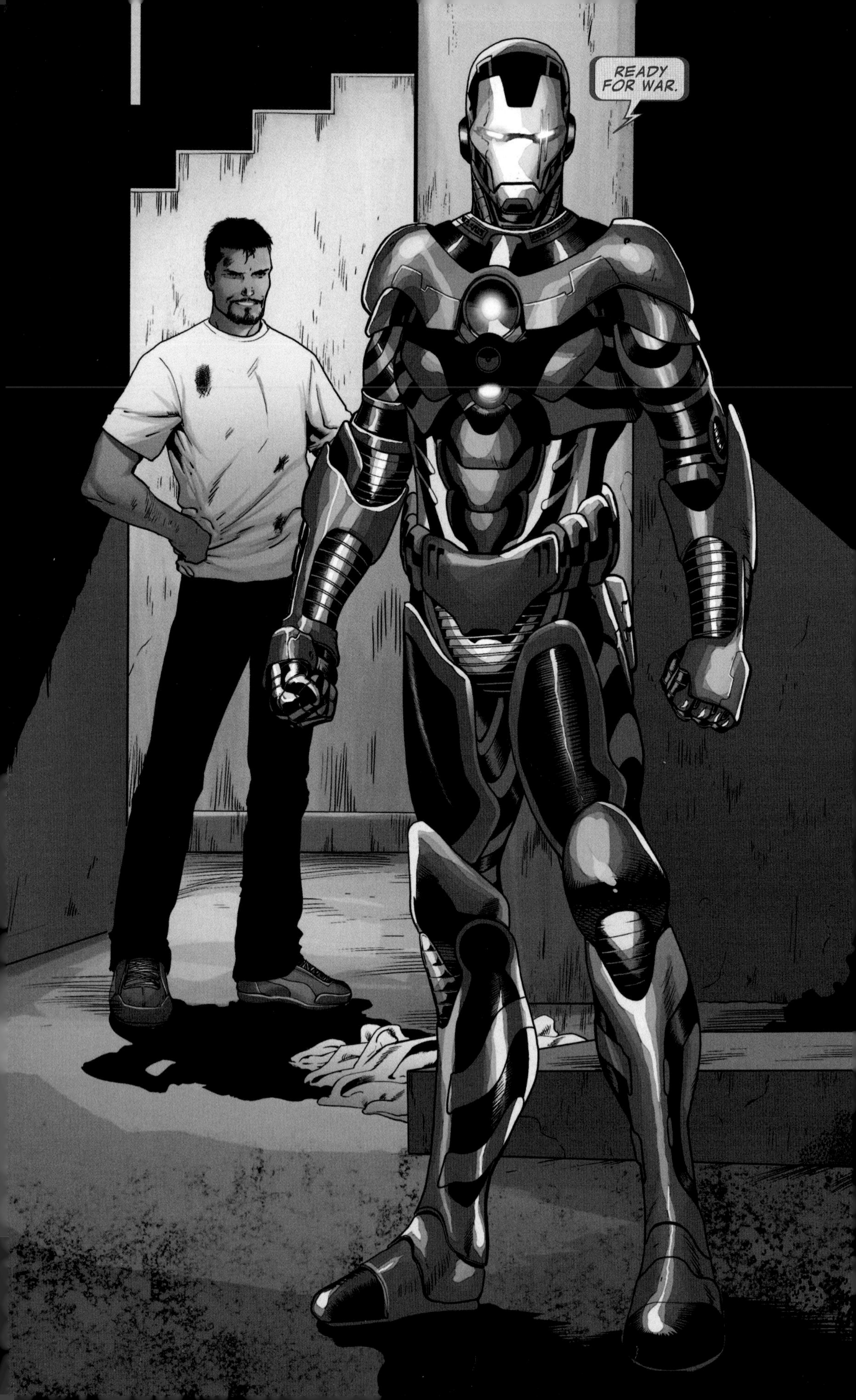
READY FOR WAR.

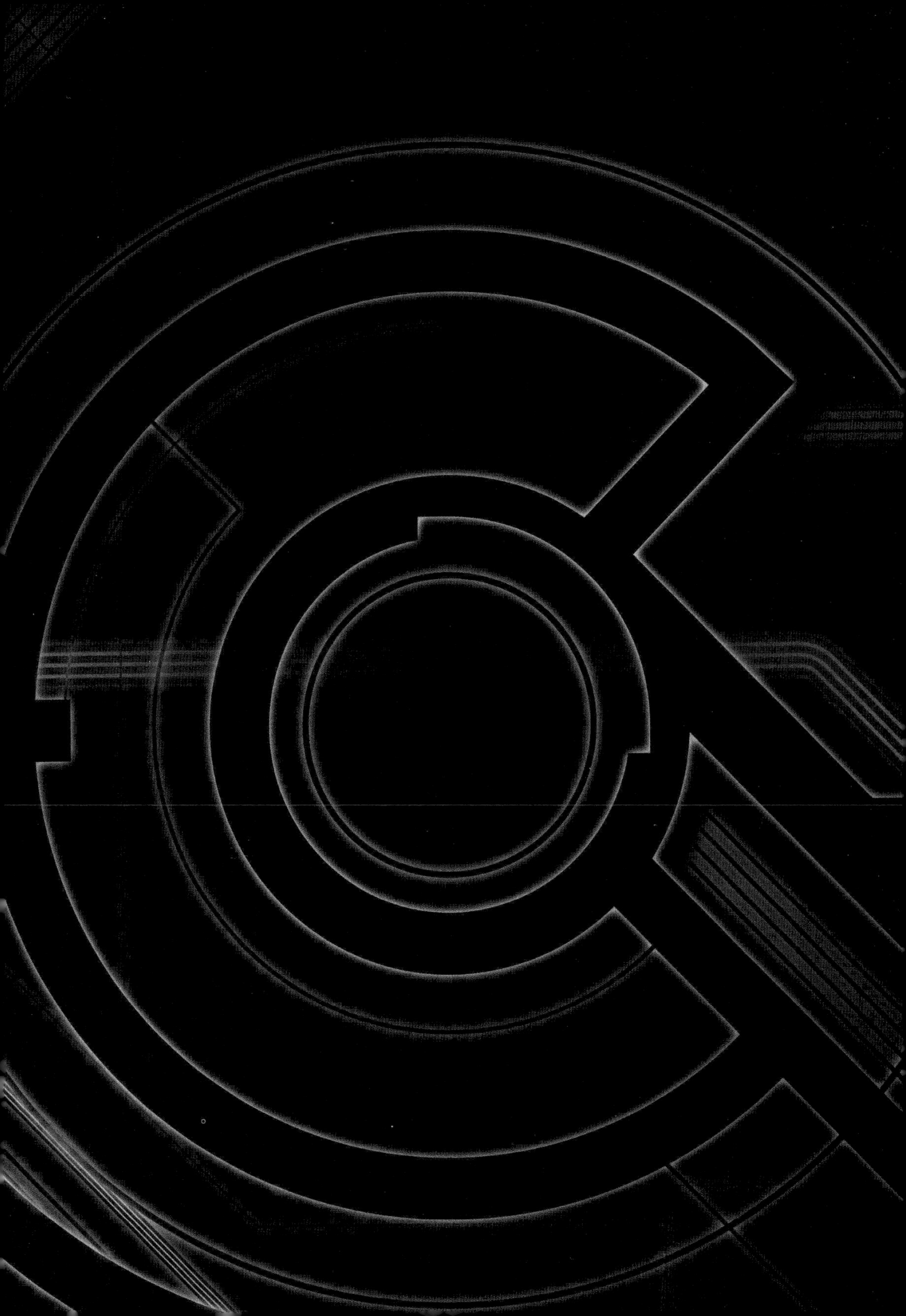

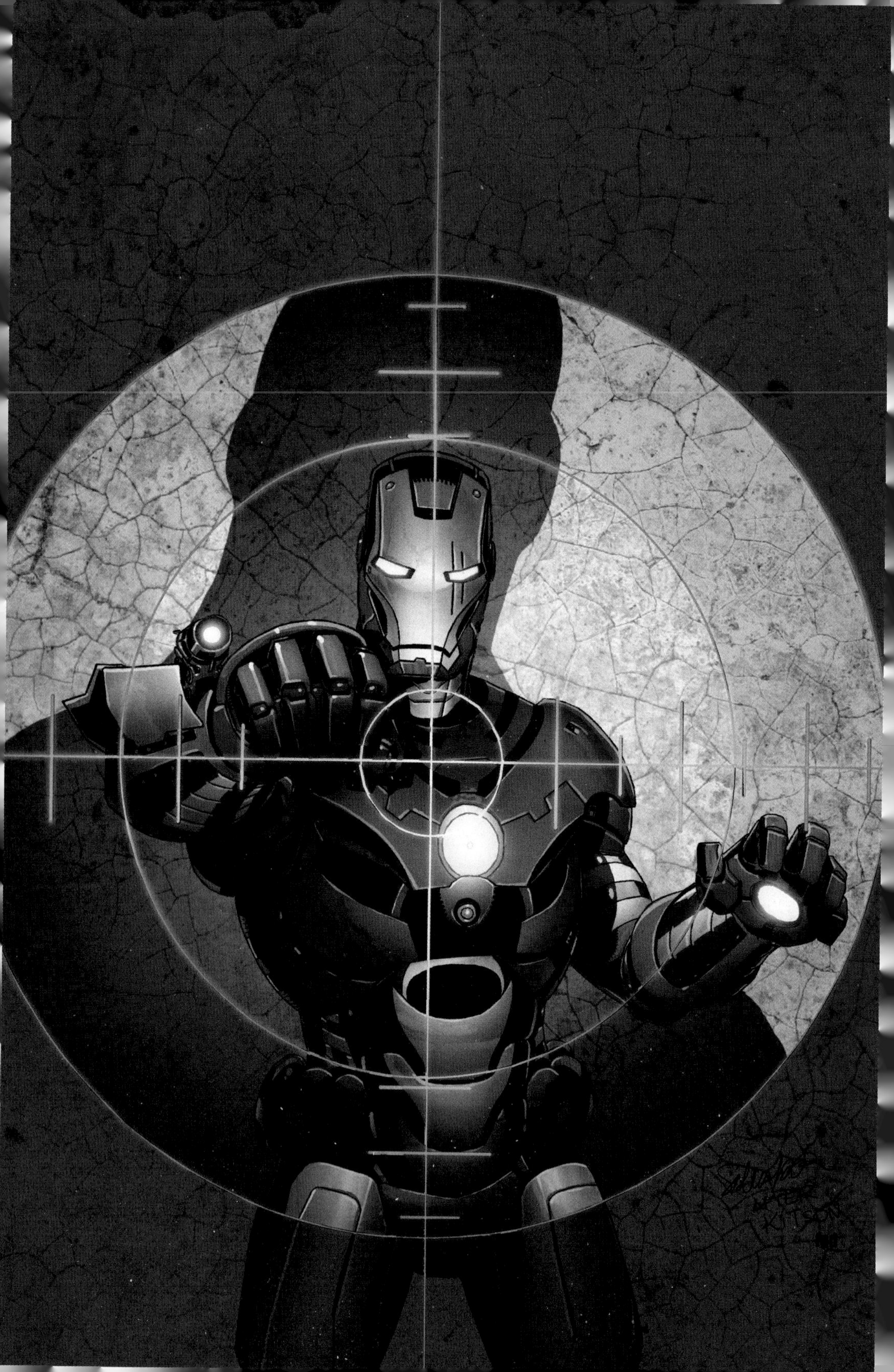

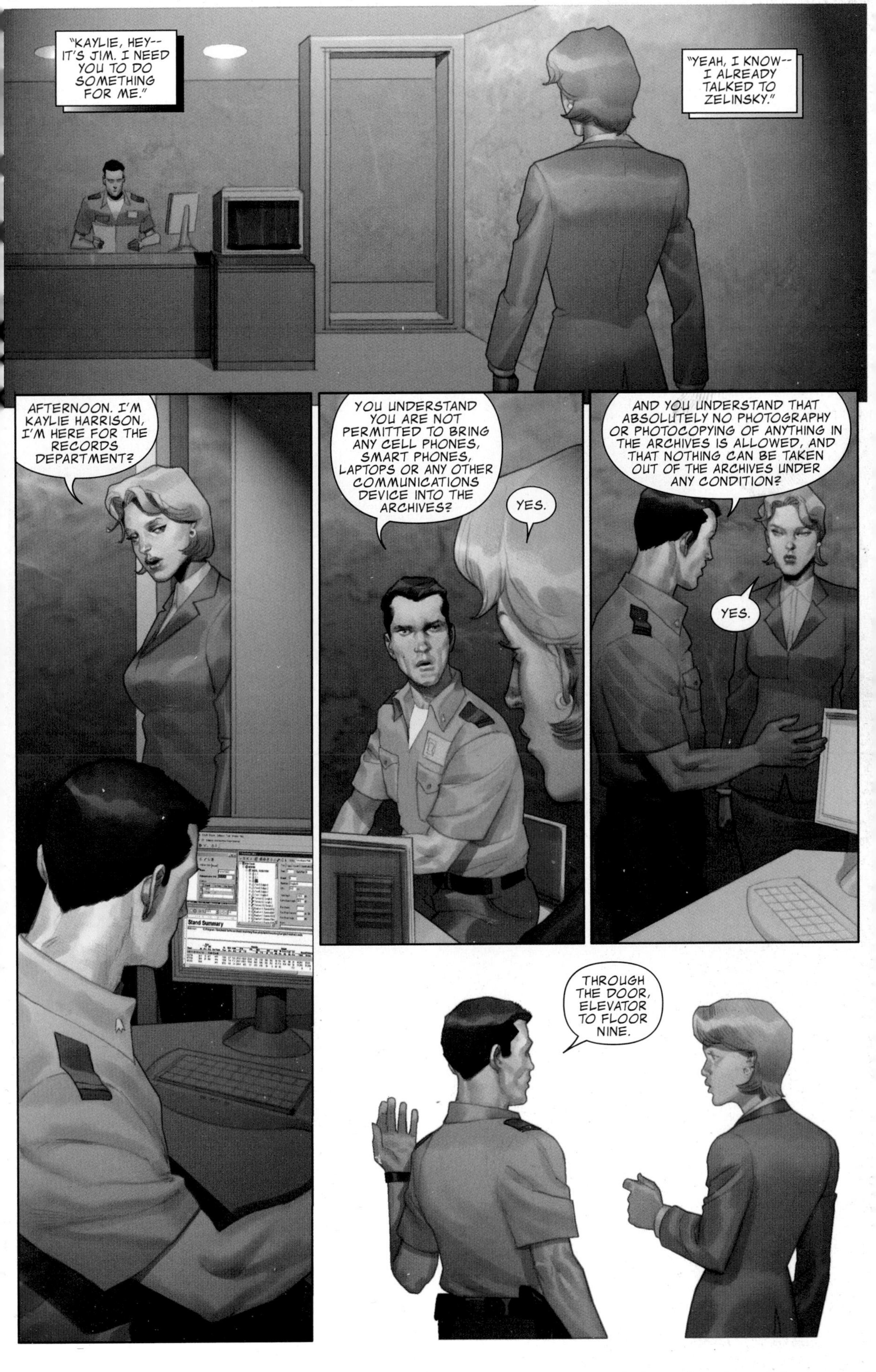
"KAYLIE, HEY-- IT'S JIM. I NEED YOU TO DO SOMETHING FOR ME."
"YEAH, I KNOW-- I ALREADY TALKED TO ZELINSKY."
AFTERNOON. I'M KAYLIE HARRISON, I'M HERE FOR THE RECORDS DEPARTMENT?
YOU UNDERSTAND YOU ARE NOT PERMITTED TO BRING ANY CELL PHONES, SMART PHONES, LAPTOPS OR ANY OTHER COMMUNICATIONS DEVICE INTO THE ARCHIVES?
YES.
AND YOU UNDERSTAND THAT ABSOLUTELY NO PHOTOGRAPHY OR PHOTOCOPYING OF ANYTHING IN THE ARCHIVES IS ALLOWED, AND THAT NOTHING CAN BE TAKEN OUT OF THE ARCHIVES UNDER ANY CONDITION?
YES.
THROUGH THE DOOR, ELEVATOR TO FLOOR NINE.

"THEN YOU KNOW WHAT THIS IS?"

"I UNDERSTAND THE WHAT-IT-IS, I JUST DON'T *UNDERSTAND* WHAT IT IS."

"THIS IS WHERE PALMER ADDLEY'S *REAL* FILE IS."

DING

"RIGHT. MY CONFUSION IS AS TO WHY THERE WAS A FAKE FILE TO BEGIN WITH."

"ADDLEY WAS ONE OF OUR GUYS--

"--BEFORE HE DID THE WHOLE *BLOW-HIS-HEAD-OFF* THING AND WENT THE TERRORIST GHOST ROUTE, I MEAN."

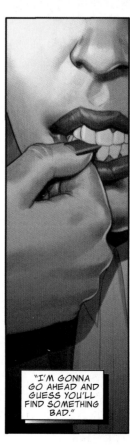

"I'M GONNA GO AHEAD AND GUESS YOU'LL FIND SOMETHING *BAD.*"

DING

"COME WORK IN INTELLIGENCE WITH ME, JIM. YOU WERE *BORN* FOR IT."

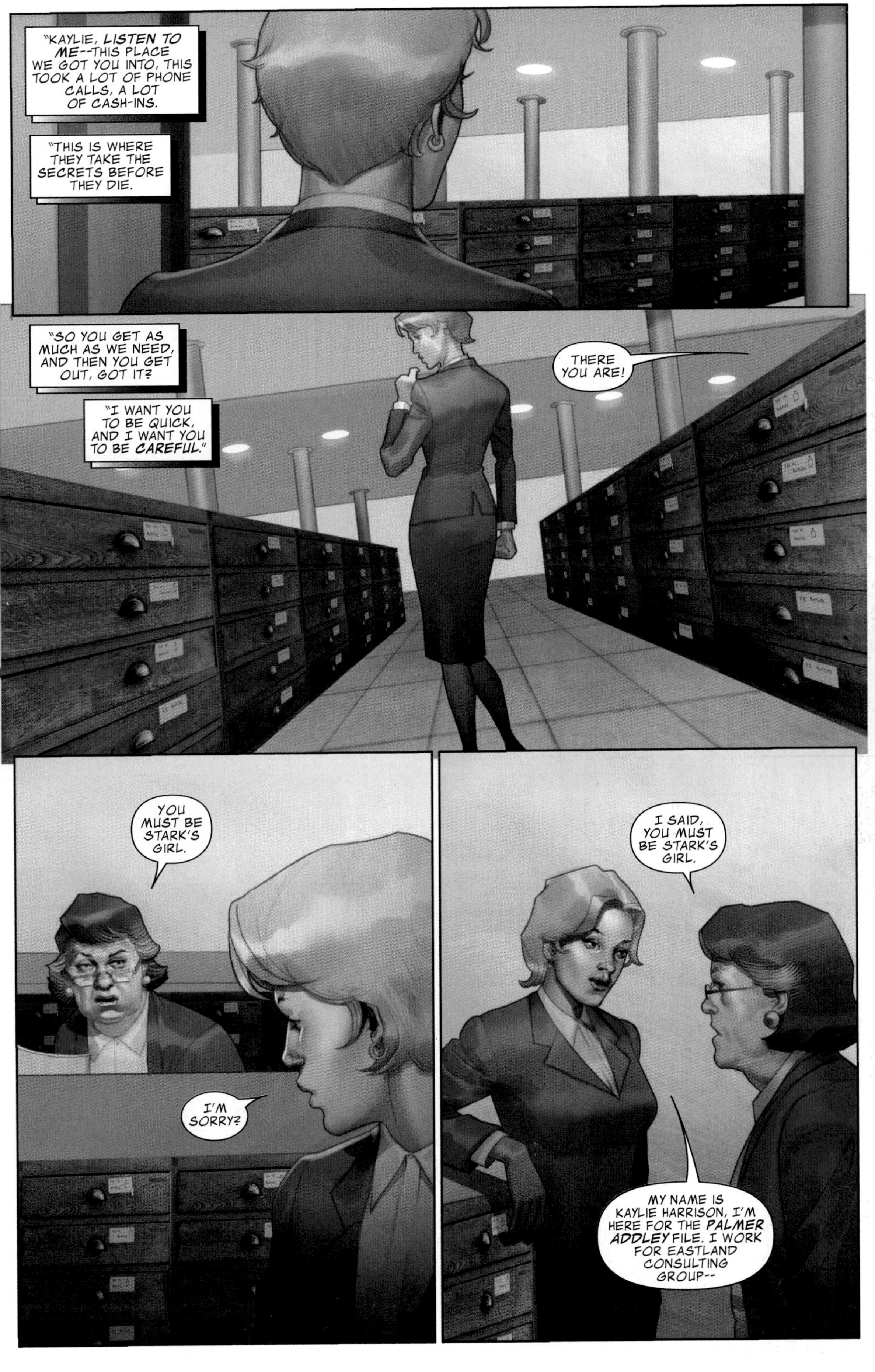
"KAYLIE, LISTEN TO ME--THIS PLACE WE GOT YOU INTO, THIS TOOK A LOT OF PHONE CALLS, A LOT OF CASH-INS.
"THIS IS WHERE THEY TAKE THE SECRETS BEFORE THEY DIE.
"SO YOU GET AS MUCH AS WE NEED, AND THEN YOU GET OUT, GOT IT?
"I WANT YOU TO BE QUICK, AND I WANT YOU TO BE CAREFUL."
THERE YOU ARE!
YOU MUST BE STARK'S GIRL.
I'M SORRY?
I SAID, YOU MUST BE STARK'S GIRL.
MY NAME IS KAYLIE HARRISON, I'M HERE FOR THE PALMER ADDLEY FILE. I WORK FOR EASTLAND CONSULTING GROUP--

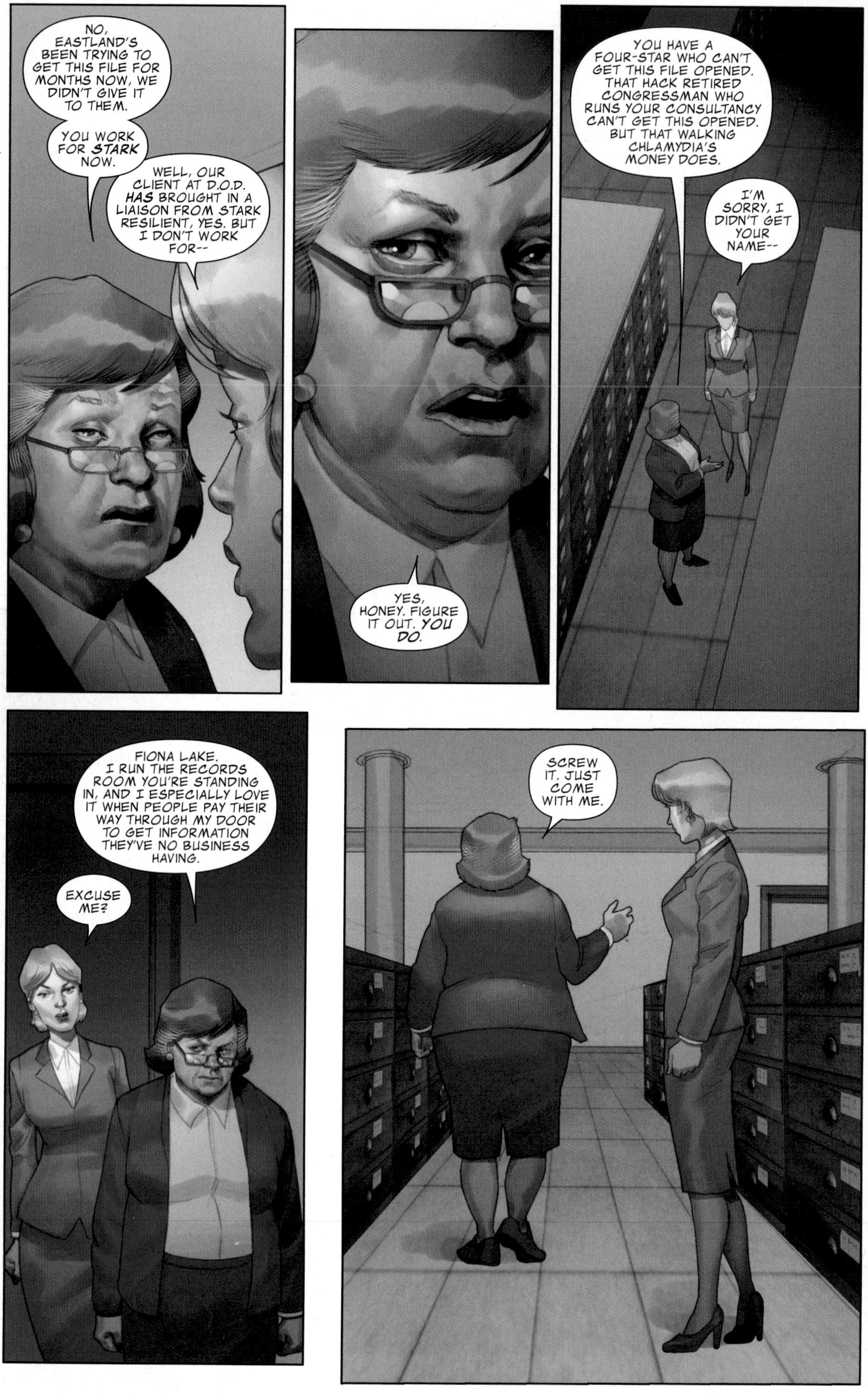
NO, EASTLAND'S BEEN TRYING TO GET THIS FILE FOR MONTHS NOW, WE DIDN'T GIVE IT TO THEM.
YOU WORK FOR **STARK** NOW.
WELL, OUR CLIENT AT D.O.D. **HAS** BROUGHT IN A LIAISON FROM STARK RESILIENT, YES. BUT I DON'T WORK FOR--
YES, HONEY. FIGURE IT OUT. ***YOU DO.***
YOU HAVE A FOUR-STAR WHO CAN'T GET THIS FILE OPENED. THAT HACK RETIRED CONGRESSMAN WHO RUNS YOUR CONSULTANCY CAN'T GET THIS OPENED. BUT THAT WALKING CHLAMYDIA'S MONEY DOES.
I'M SORRY, I DIDN'T GET YOUR NAME--
FIONA LAKE. I RUN THE RECORDS ROOM YOU'RE STANDING IN, AND I ESPECIALLY LOVE IT WHEN PEOPLE PAY THEIR WAY THROUGH MY DOOR TO GET INFORMATION THEY'VE NO BUSINESS HAVING.
EXCUSE ME?
SCREW IT. JUST *COME* WITH ME.

HERE WE GO.

THERE'S A COFFEE MACHINE IN THE BACK, THE BATHROOM IS BROKEN. AND I'M GONNA TELL YOU THIS *ONCE*--

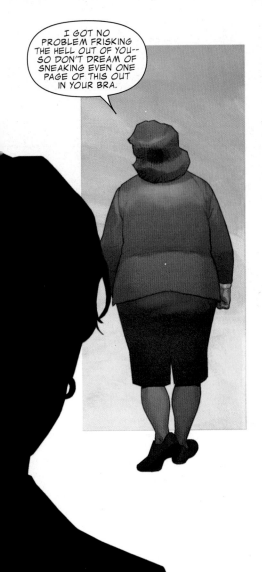

I GOT NO PROBLEM FRISKING THE HELL OUT OF YOU-- SO DON'T DREAM OF SNEAKING EVEN ONE PAGE OF THIS OUT IN YOUR BRA.

OKAY. TRANSCRIPTS.

WHOLE *LOTTA* TRANSCRIPTS.

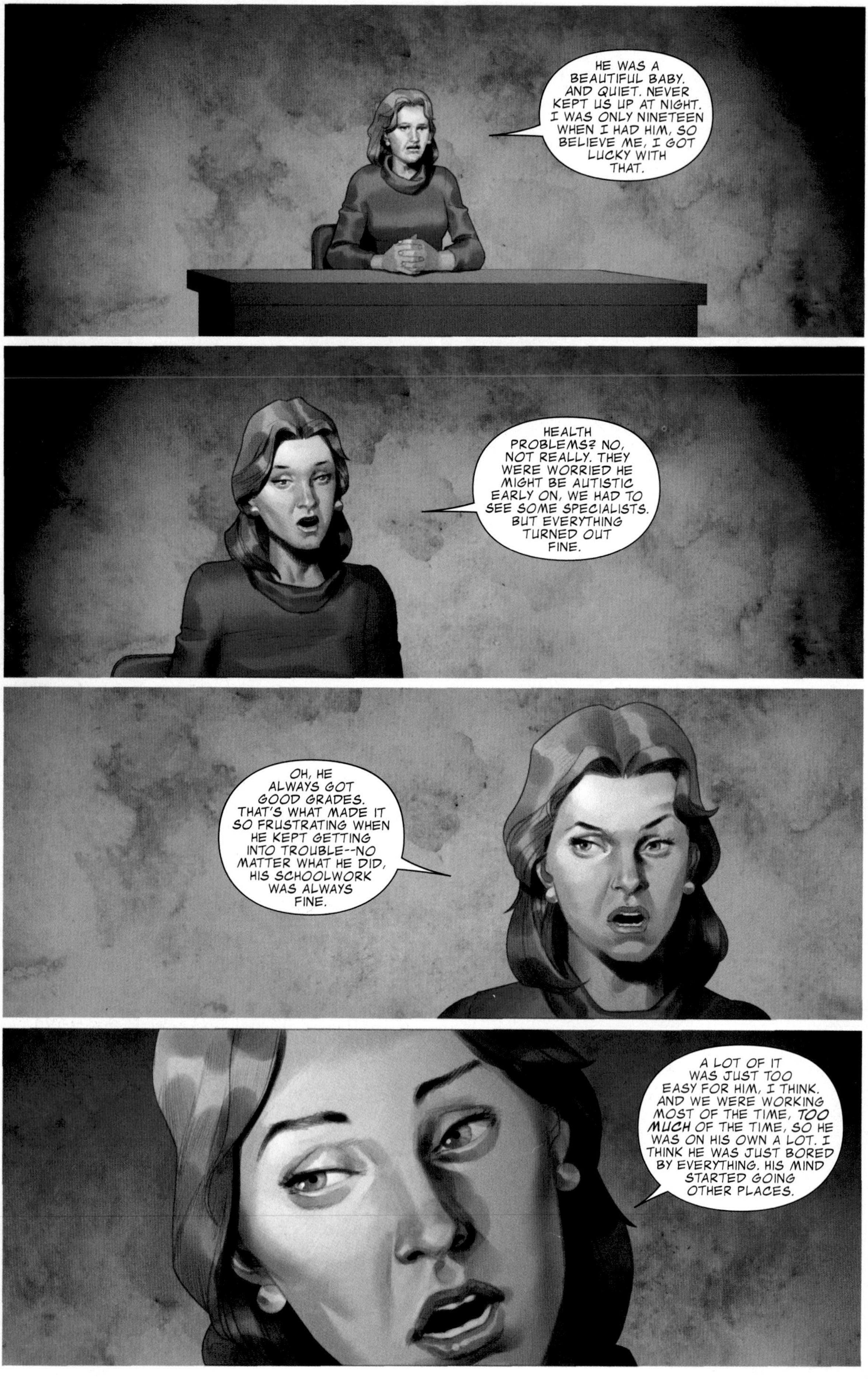
HE WAS A BEAUTIFUL BABY. AND QUIET. NEVER KEPT US UP AT NIGHT. I WAS ONLY NINETEEN WHEN I HAD HIM, SO BELIEVE ME, I GOT LUCKY WITH THAT.
HEALTH PROBLEMS? NO, NOT REALLY. THEY WERE WORRIED HE MIGHT BE AUTISTIC EARLY ON, WE HAD TO SEE SOME SPECIALISTS. BUT EVERYTHING TURNED OUT FINE.
OH, HE ALWAYS GOT GOOD GRADES. THAT'S WHAT MADE IT SO FRUSTRATING WHEN HE KEPT GETTING INTO TROUBLE--NO MATTER WHAT HE DID, HIS SCHOOLWORK WAS ALWAYS FINE.
A LOT OF IT WAS JUST TOO EASY FOR HIM, I THINK. AND WE WERE WORKING MOST OF THE TIME, *TOO MUCH* OF THE TIME, SO HE WAS ON HIS OWN A LOT. I THINK HE WAS JUST BORED BY EVERYTHING. HIS MIND STARTED GOING OTHER PLACES.

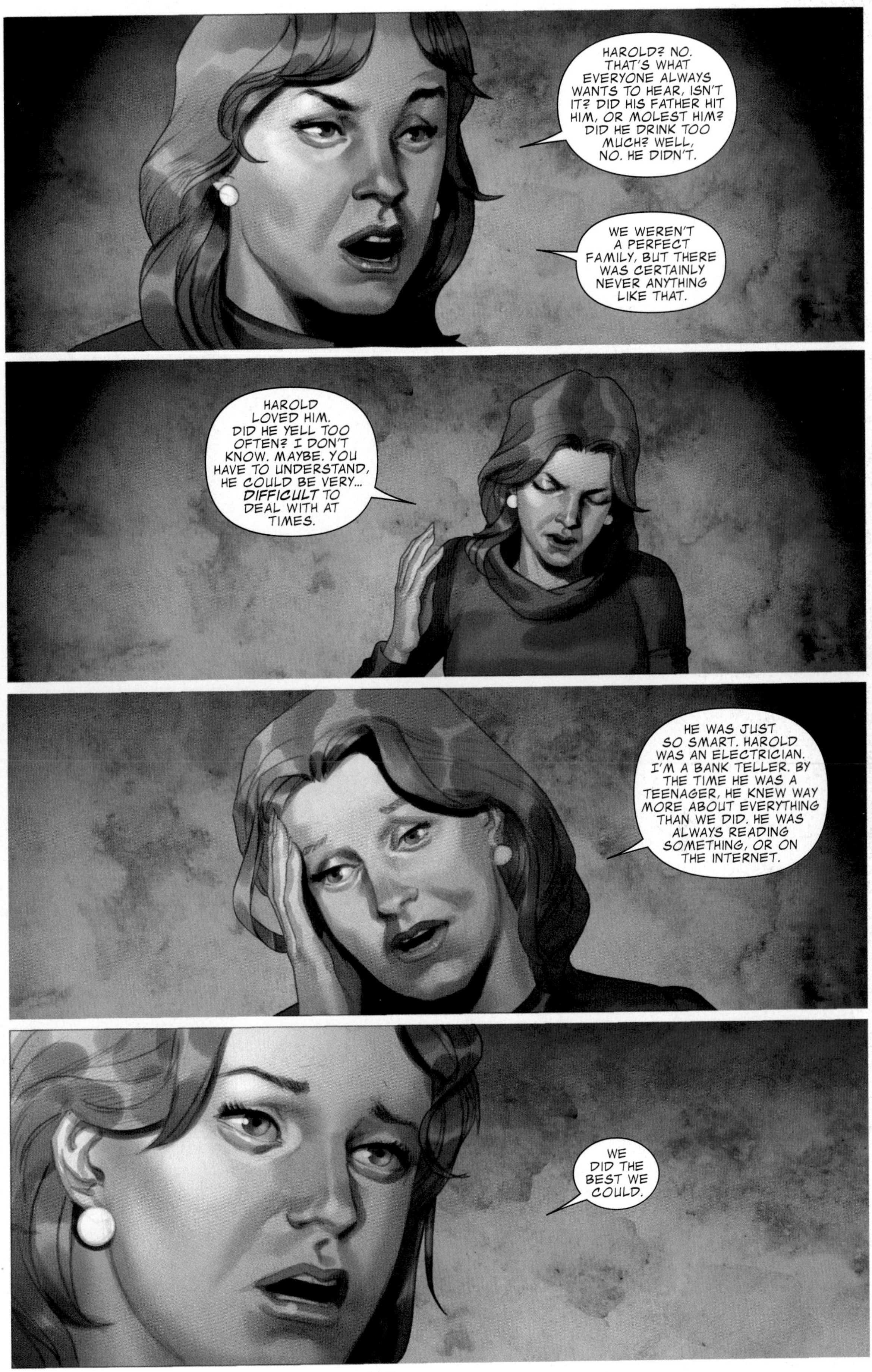
HAROLD? NO. THAT'S WHAT EVERYONE ALWAYS WANTS TO HEAR, ISN'T IT? DID HIS FATHER HIT HIM, OR MOLEST HIM? DID HE DRINK TOO MUCH? WELL, NO. HE DIDN'T.
WE WEREN'T A PERFECT FAMILY, BUT THERE WAS CERTAINLY NEVER ANYTHING LIKE THAT.
HAROLD LOVED HIM. DID HE YELL TOO OFTEN? I DON'T KNOW. MAYBE. YOU HAVE TO UNDERSTAND, HE COULD BE VERY... DIFFICULT TO DEAL WITH AT TIMES.
HE WAS JUST SO SMART. HAROLD WAS AN ELECTRICIAN. I'M A BANK TELLER. BY THE TIME HE WAS A TEENAGER, HE KNEW WAY MORE ABOUT EVERYTHING THAN WE DID. HE WAS ALWAYS READING SOMETHING, OR ON THE INTERNET.
WE DID THE BEST WE COULD.

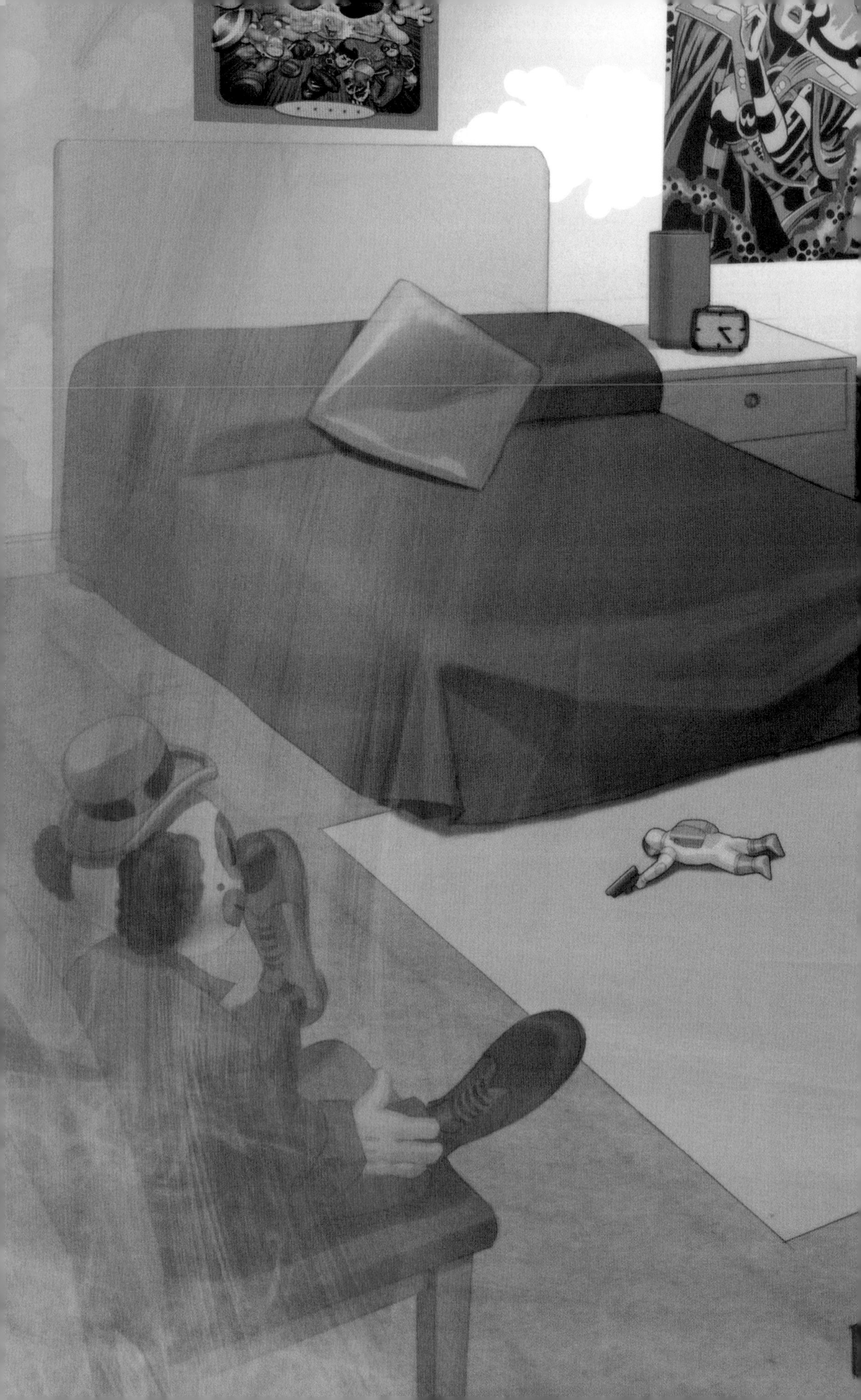

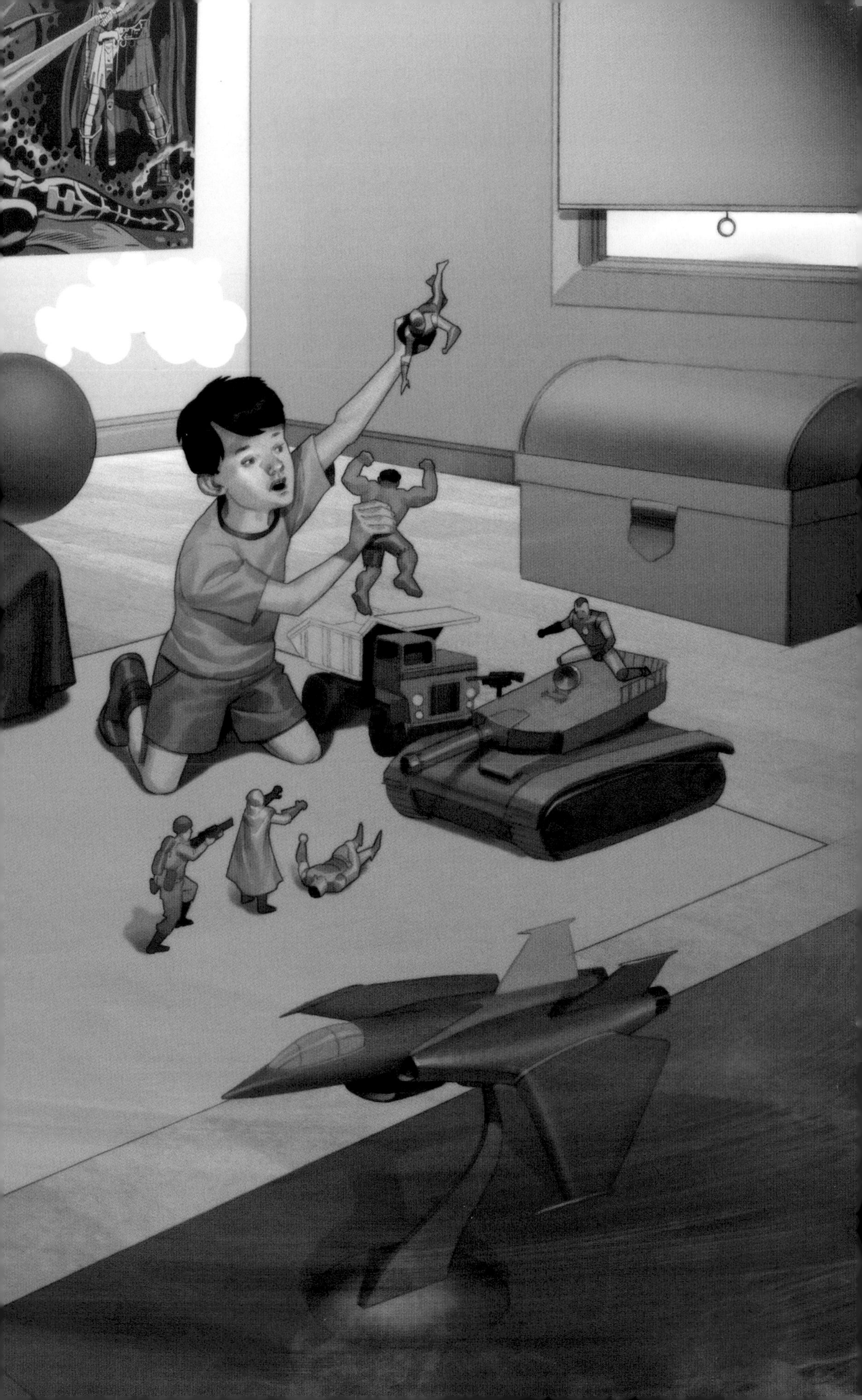

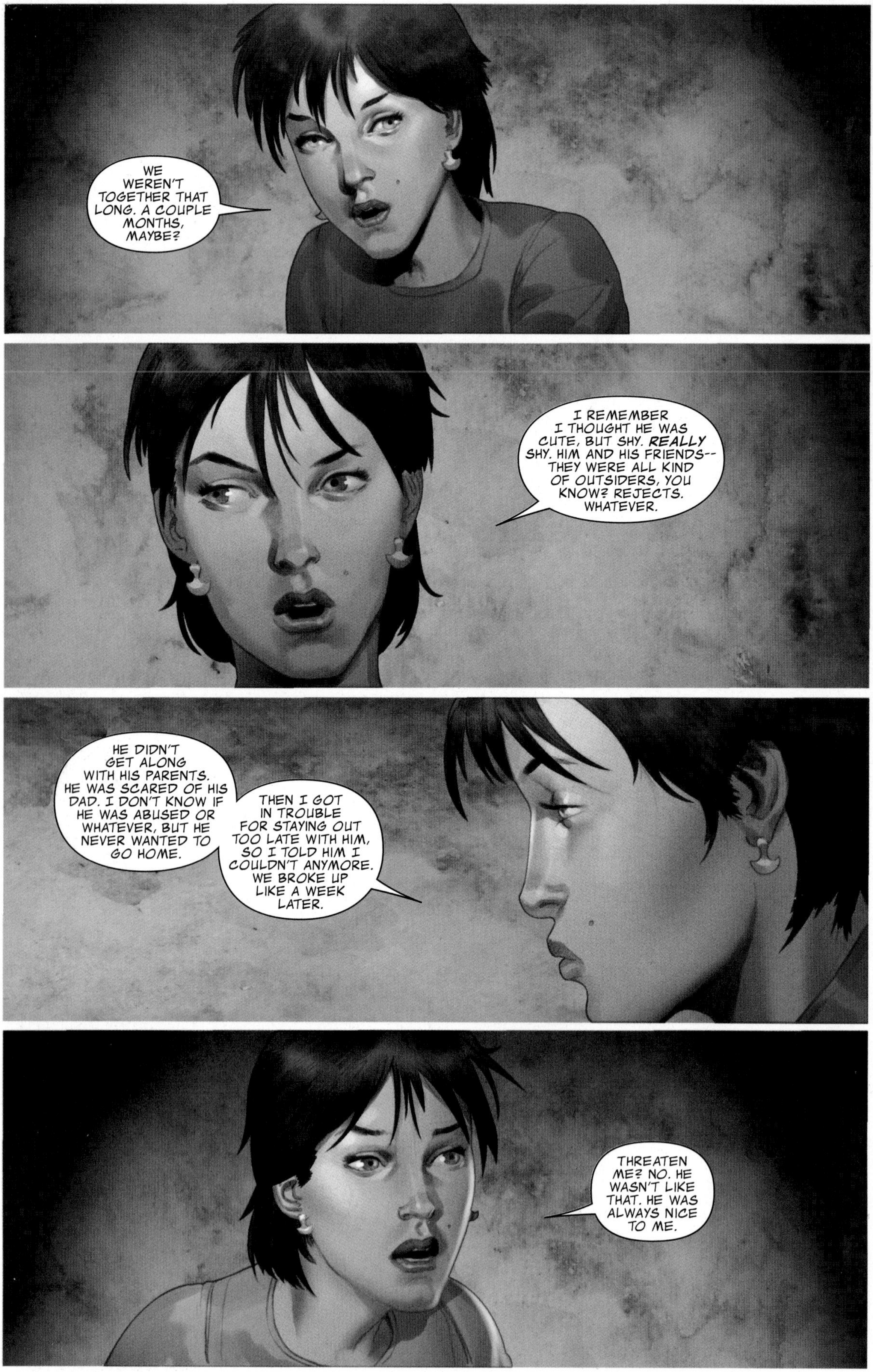
WE WEREN'T TOGETHER THAT LONG. A COUPLE MONTHS, MAYBE?
I REMEMBER I THOUGHT HE WAS CUTE, BUT SHY. *REALLY* SHY. HIM AND HIS FRIENDS-- THEY WERE ALL KIND OF OUTSIDERS, YOU KNOW? REJECTS. WHATEVER.
HE DIDN'T GET ALONG WITH HIS PARENTS. HE WAS SCARED OF HIS DAD. I DON'T KNOW IF HE WAS ABUSED OR WHATEVER, BUT HE NEVER WANTED TO GO HOME.
THEN I GOT IN TROUBLE FOR STAYING OUT TOO LATE WITH HIM, SO I TOLD HIM I COULDN'T ANYMORE. WE BROKE UP LIKE A WEEK LATER.
THREATEN ME? NO. HE WASN'T LIKE THAT. HE WAS ALWAYS NICE TO ME.

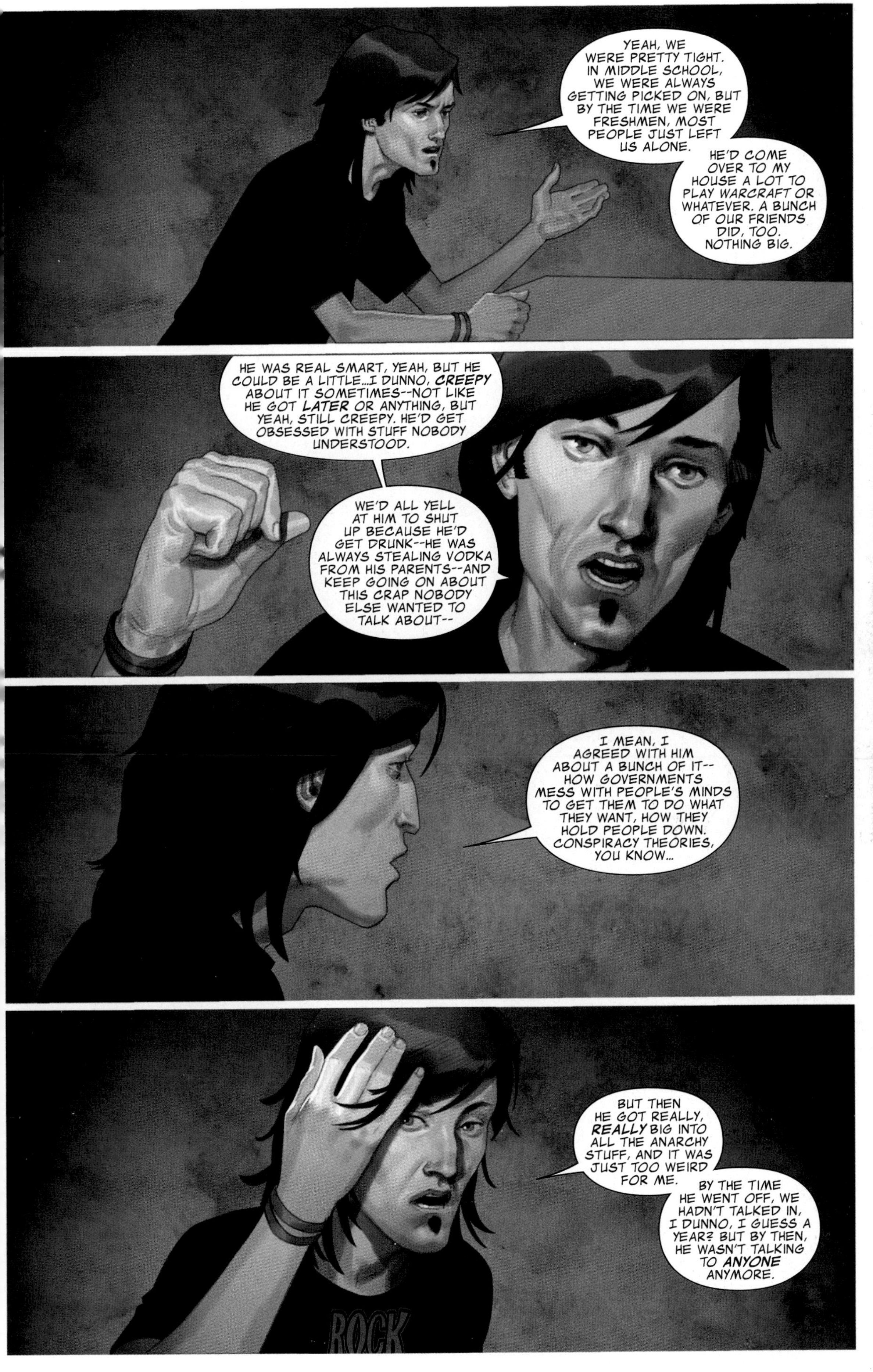
YEAH, WE WERE PRETTY TIGHT. IN MIDDLE SCHOOL, WE WERE ALWAYS GETTING PICKED ON, BUT BY THE TIME WE WERE FRESHMEN, MOST PEOPLE JUST LEFT US ALONE.
HE'D COME OVER TO MY HOUSE A LOT TO PLAY WARCRAFT OR WHATEVER. A BUNCH OF OUR FRIENDS DID, TOO. NOTHING BIG.
HE WAS REAL SMART, YEAH, BUT HE COULD BE A LITTLE...I DUNNO, CREEPY ABOUT IT SOMETIMES--NOT LIKE HE GOT LATER OR ANYTHING, BUT YEAH, STILL CREEPY. HE'D GET OBSESSED WITH STUFF NOBODY UNDERSTOOD.
WE'D ALL YELL AT HIM TO SHUT UP BECAUSE HE'D GET DRUNK--HE WAS ALWAYS STEALING VODKA FROM HIS PARENTS--AND KEEP GOING ON ABOUT THIS CRAP NOBODY ELSE WANTED TO TALK ABOUT--
I MEAN, I AGREED WITH HIM ABOUT A BUNCH OF IT--HOW GOVERNMENTS MESS WITH PEOPLE'S MINDS TO GET THEM TO DO WHAT THEY WANT, HOW THEY HOLD PEOPLE DOWN. CONSPIRACY THEORIES, YOU KNOW...
BUT THEN HE GOT REALLY, REALLY BIG INTO ALL THE ANARCHY STUFF, AND IT WAS JUST TOO WEIRD FOR ME.
BY THE TIME HE WENT OFF, WE HADN'T TALKED IN, I DUNNO, I GUESS A YEAR? BUT BY THEN, HE WASN'T TALKING TO ANYONE ANYMORE.
ROCK

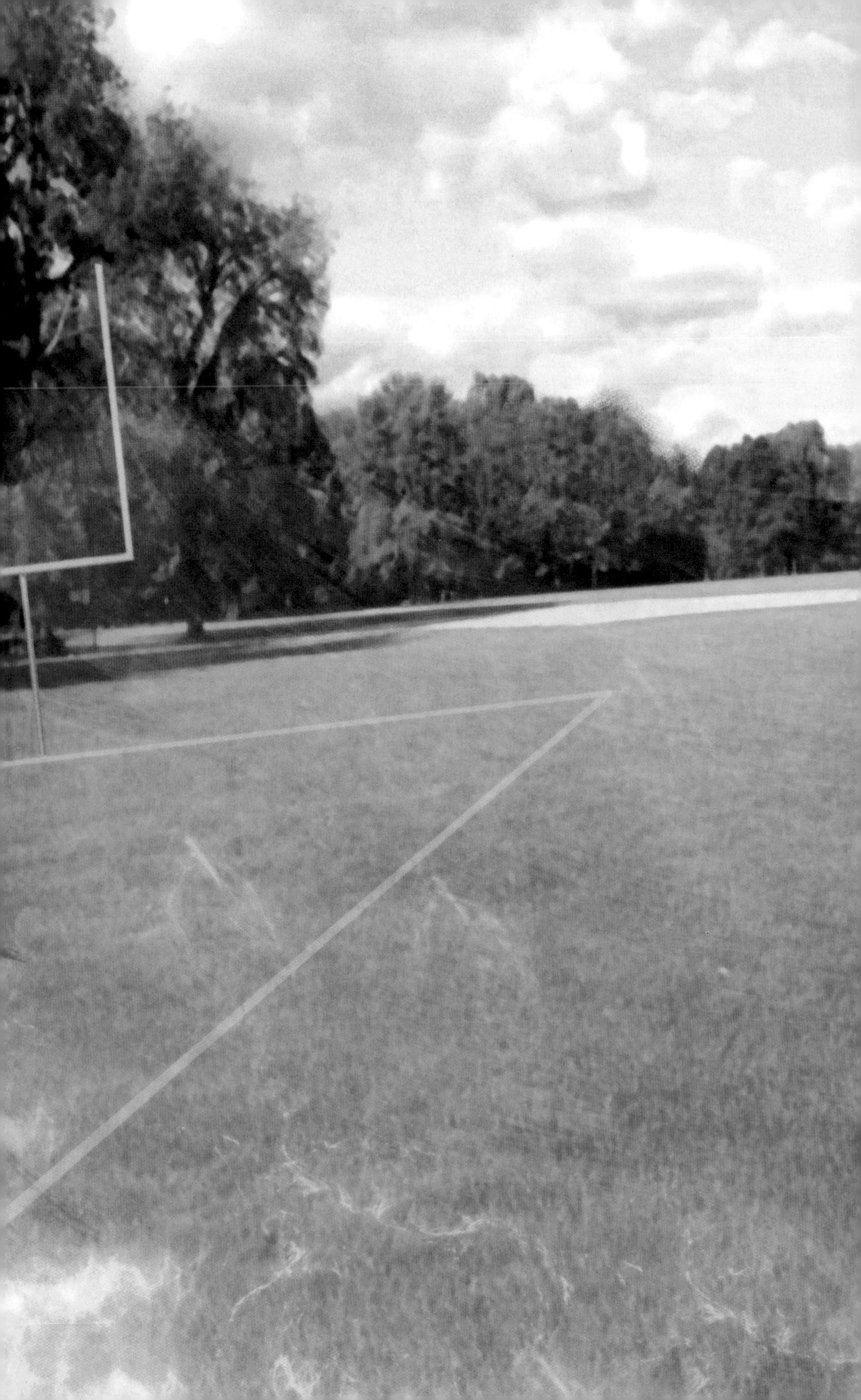

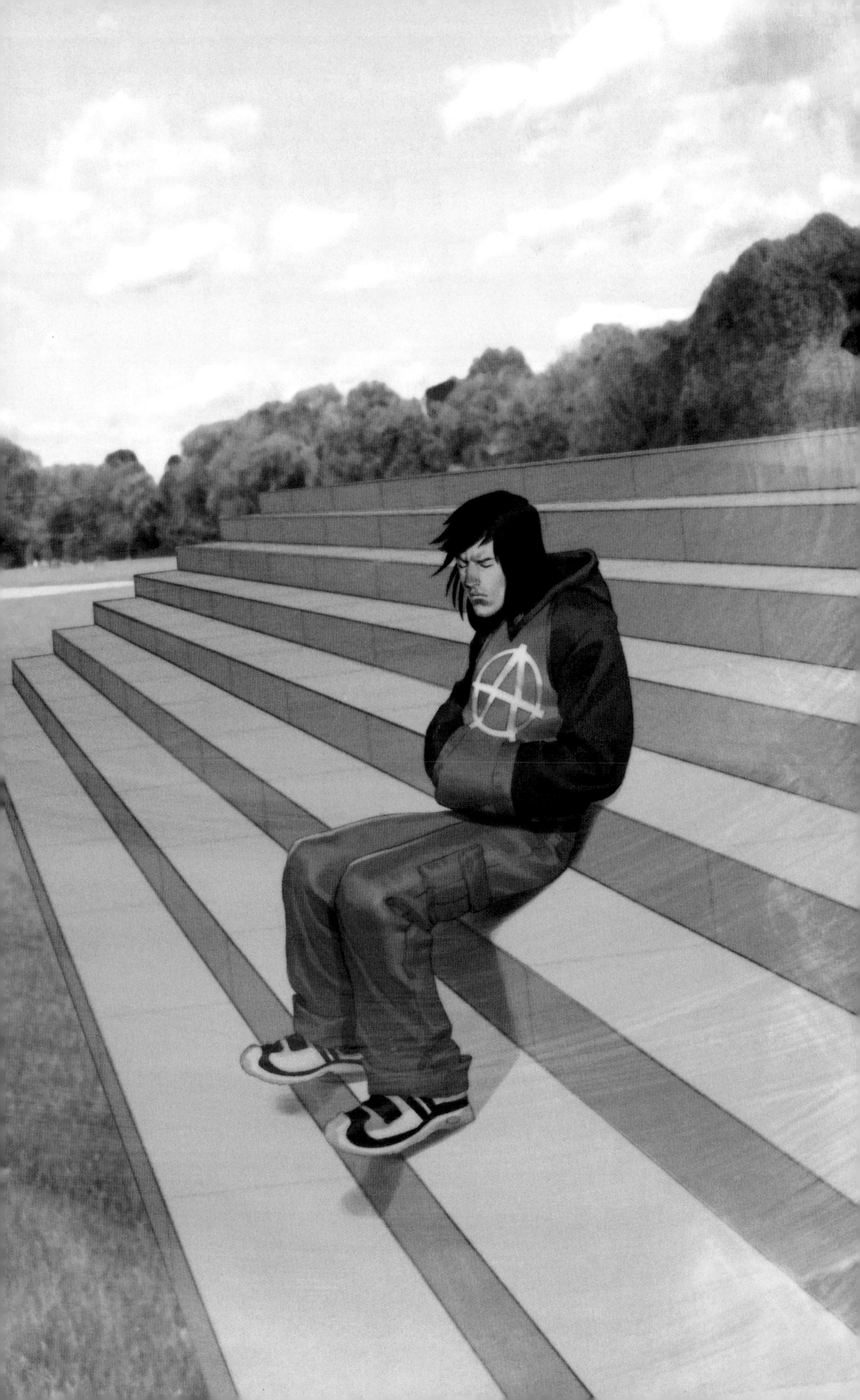

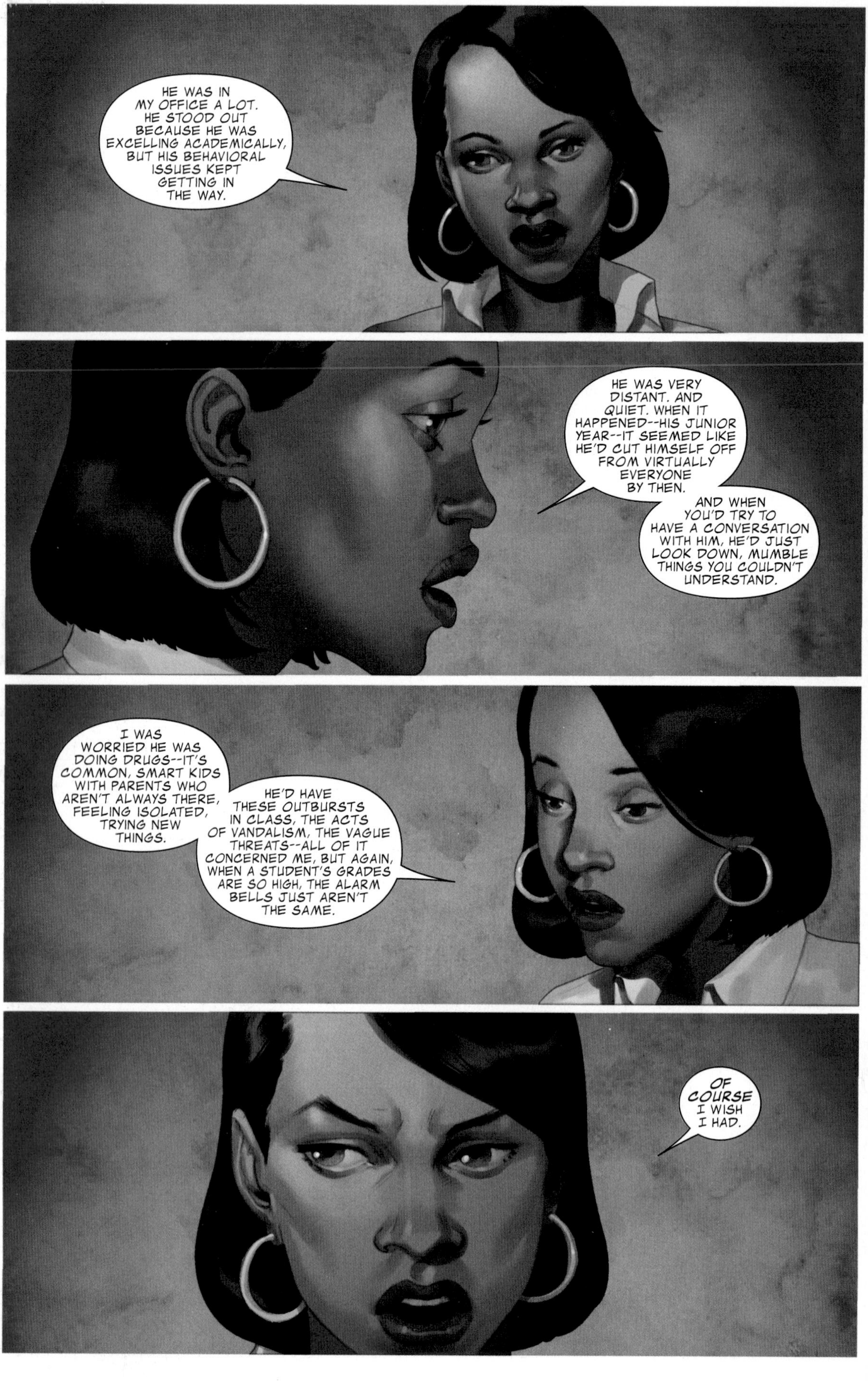
HE WAS IN MY OFFICE A LOT. HE STOOD OUT BECAUSE HE WAS EXCELLING ACADEMICALLY, BUT HIS BEHAVIORAL ISSUES KEPT GETTING IN THE WAY.
HE WAS VERY DISTANT. AND QUIET. WHEN IT HAPPENED--HIS JUNIOR YEAR--IT SEEMED LIKE HE'D CUT HIMSELF OFF FROM VIRTUALLY EVERYONE BY THEN.
AND WHEN YOU'D TRY TO HAVE A CONVERSATION WITH HIM, HE'D JUST LOOK DOWN, MUMBLE THINGS YOU COULDN'T UNDERSTAND.
I WAS WORRIED HE WAS DOING DRUGS--IT'S COMMON, SMART KIDS WITH PARENTS WHO AREN'T ALWAYS THERE, FEELING ISOLATED, TRYING NEW THINGS.
HE'D HAVE THESE OUTBURSTS IN CLASS, THE ACTS OF VANDALISM, THE VAGUE THREATS--ALL OF IT CONCERNED ME, BUT AGAIN, WHEN A STUDENT'S GRADES ARE SO HIGH, THE ALARM BELLS JUST AREN'T THE SAME.
OF COURSE I WISH I HAD.

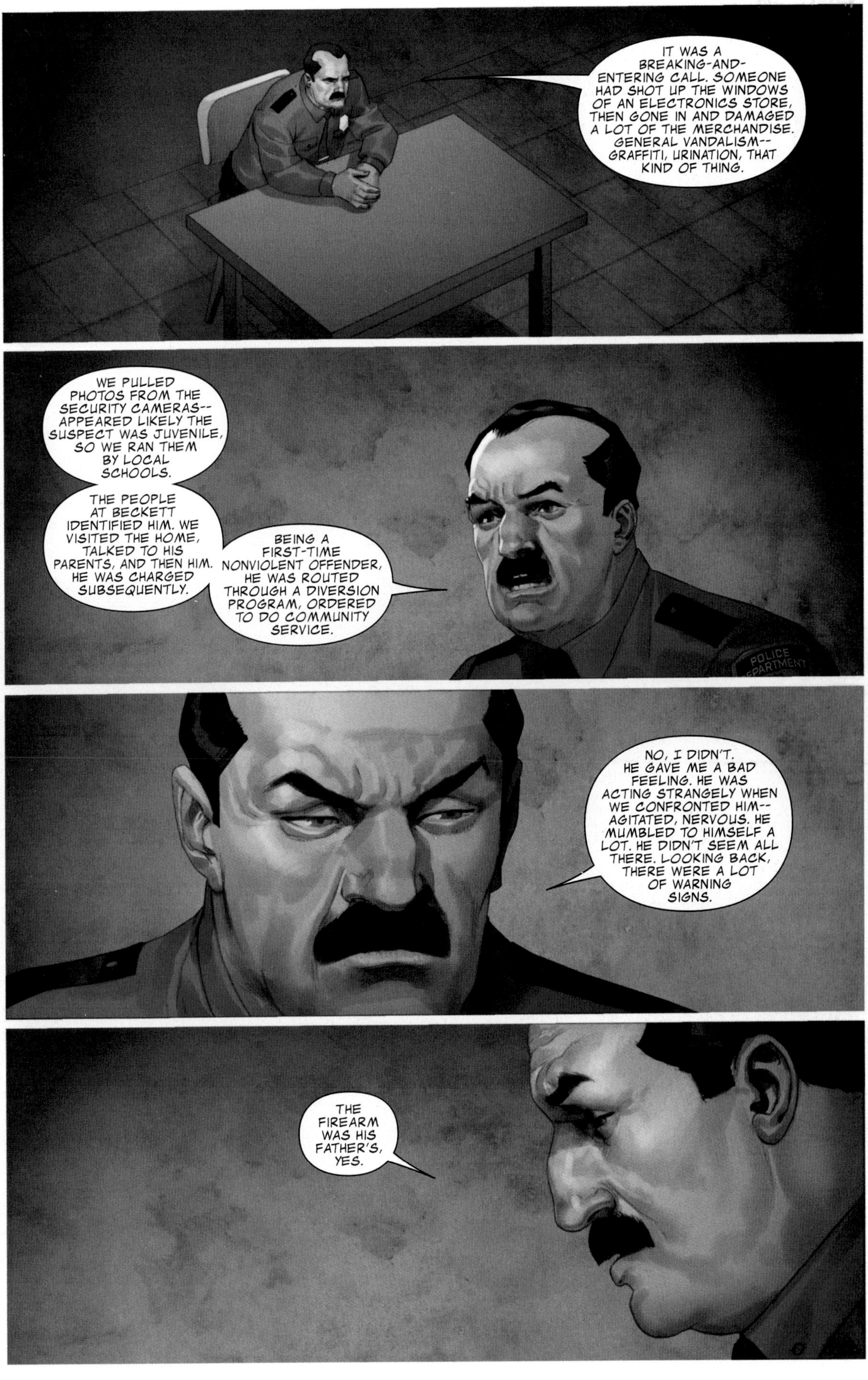
IT WAS A BREAKING-AND-ENTERING CALL. SOMEONE HAD SHOT UP THE WINDOWS OF AN ELECTRONICS STORE, THEN GONE IN AND DAMAGED A LOT OF THE MERCHANDISE. GENERAL VANDALISM--GRAFFITI, URINATION, THAT KIND OF THING.
WE PULLED PHOTOS FROM THE SECURITY CAMERAS--APPEARED LIKELY THE SUSPECT WAS JUVENILE, SO WE RAN THEM BY LOCAL SCHOOLS.
THE PEOPLE AT BECKETT IDENTIFIED HIM. WE VISITED THE HOME, TALKED TO HIS PARENTS, AND THEN HIM. HE WAS CHARGED SUBSEQUENTLY.
BEING A FIRST-TIME NONVIOLENT OFFENDER, HE WAS ROUTED THROUGH A DIVERSION PROGRAM, ORDERED TO DO COMMUNITY SERVICE.
POLICE DEPARTMENT
NO, I DIDN'T. HE GAVE ME A BAD FEELING. HE WAS ACTING STRANGELY WHEN WE CONFRONTED HIM--AGITATED, NERVOUS. HE MUMBLED TO HIMSELF A LOT. HE DIDN'T SEEM ALL THERE. LOOKING BACK, THERE WERE A LOT OF WARNING SIGNS.
THE FIREARM WAS HIS FATHER'S, YES.

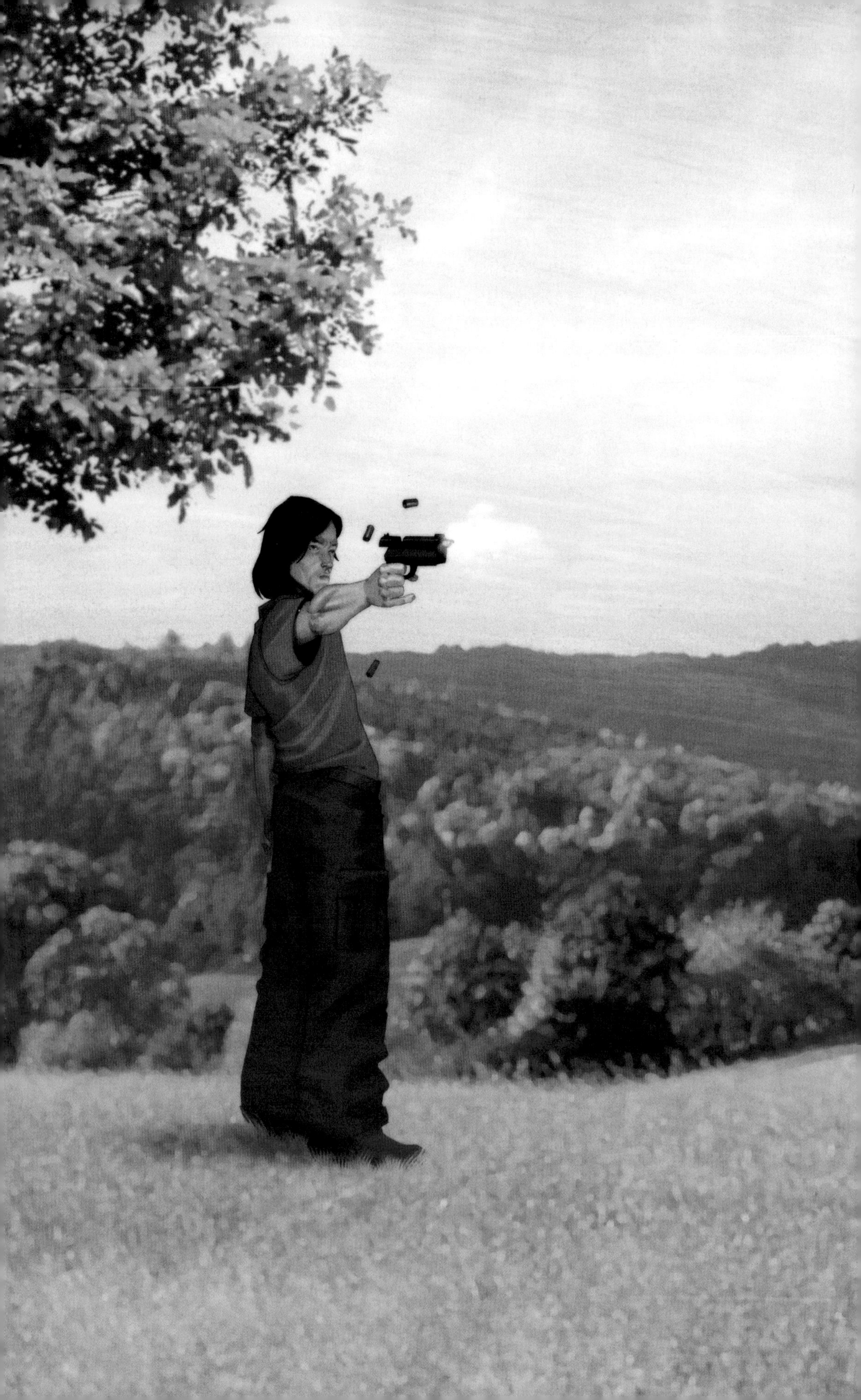

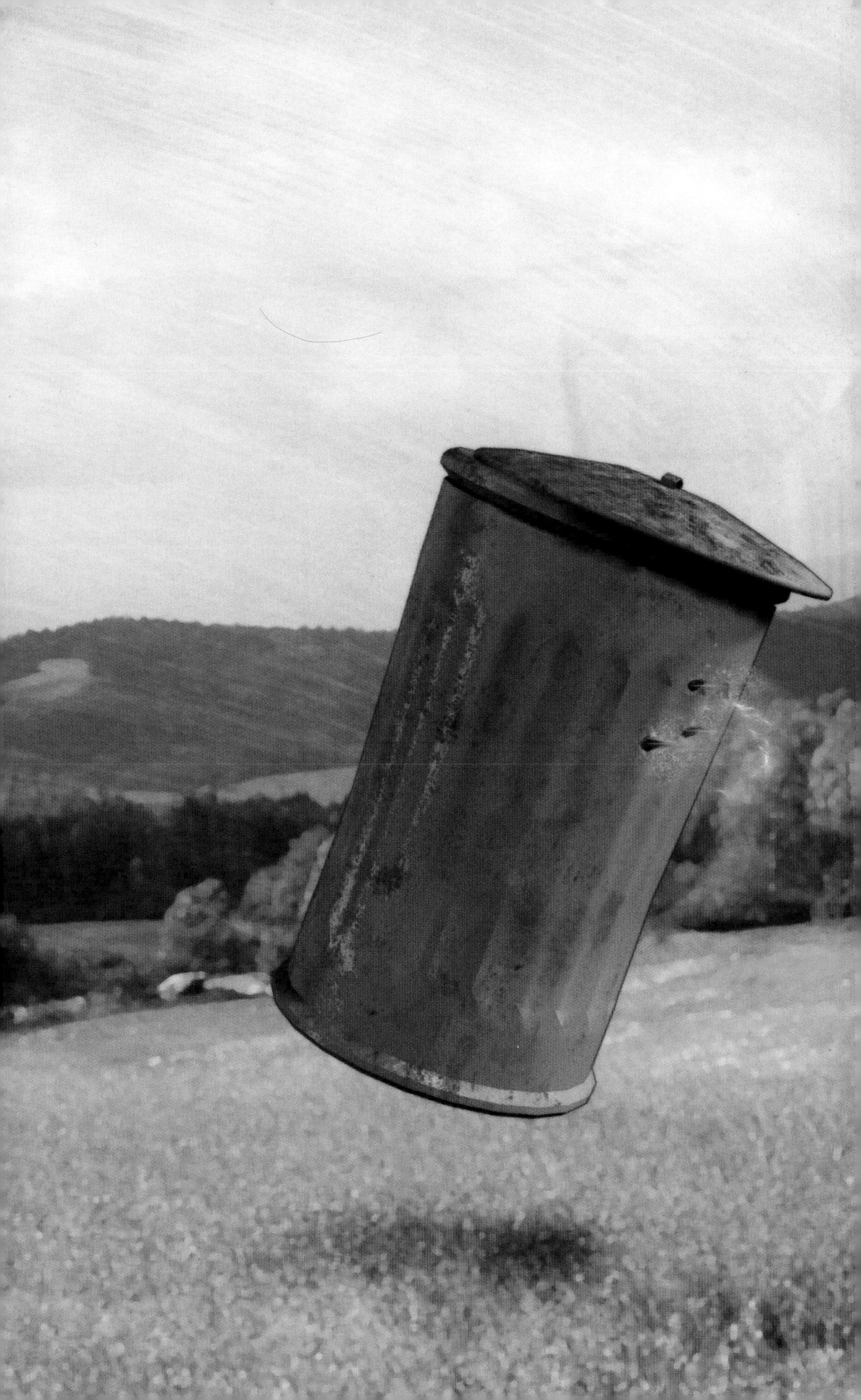

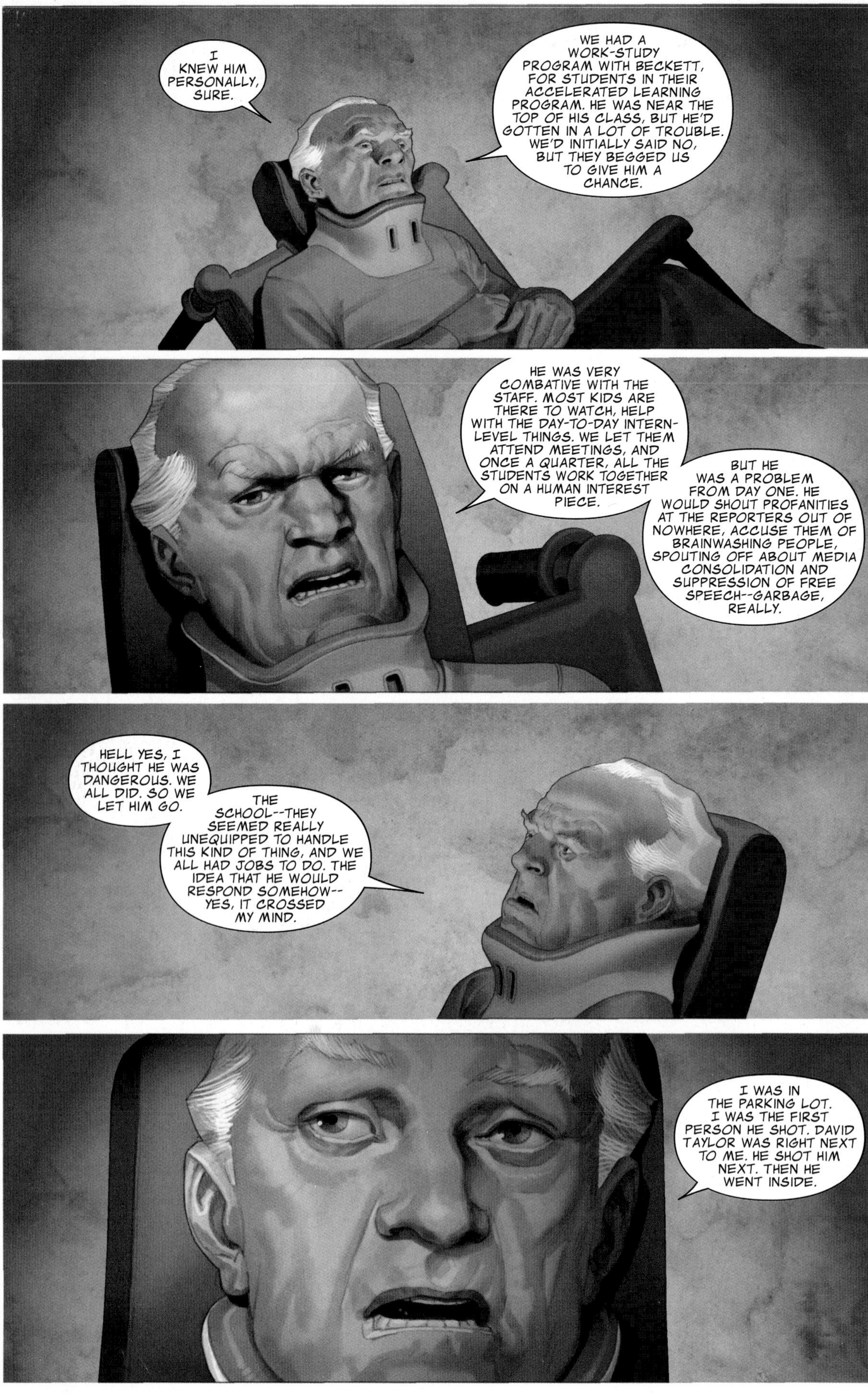
I KNEW HIM PERSONALLY, SURE.
WE HAD A WORK-STUDY PROGRAM WITH BECKETT, FOR STUDENTS IN THEIR ACCELERATED LEARNING PROGRAM. HE WAS NEAR THE TOP OF HIS CLASS, BUT HE'D GOTTEN IN A LOT OF TROUBLE. WE'D INITIALLY SAID NO, BUT THEY BEGGED US TO GIVE HIM A CHANCE.
HE WAS VERY COMBATIVE WITH THE STAFF. MOST KIDS ARE THERE TO WATCH, HELP WITH THE DAY-TO-DAY INTERN-LEVEL THINGS. WE LET THEM ATTEND MEETINGS, AND ONCE A QUARTER, ALL THE STUDENTS WORK TOGETHER ON A HUMAN INTEREST PIECE.
BUT HE WAS A PROBLEM FROM DAY ONE. HE WOULD SHOUT PROFANITIES AT THE REPORTERS OUT OF NOWHERE, ACCUSE THEM OF BRAINWASHING PEOPLE, SPOUTING OFF ABOUT MEDIA CONSOLIDATION AND SUPPRESSION OF FREE SPEECH--GARBAGE, REALLY.
HELL YES, I THOUGHT HE WAS DANGEROUS. WE ALL DID. SO WE LET HIM GO.
THE SCHOOL--THEY SEEMED REALLY UNEQUIPPED TO HANDLE THIS KIND OF THING, AND WE ALL HAD JOBS TO DO. THE IDEA THAT HE WOULD RESPOND SOMEHOW--YES, IT CROSSED MY MIND.
I WAS IN THE PARKING LOT. I WAS THE FIRST PERSON HE SHOT. DAVID TAYLOR WAS RIGHT NEXT TO ME. HE SHOT HIM NEXT. THEN HE WENT INSIDE.

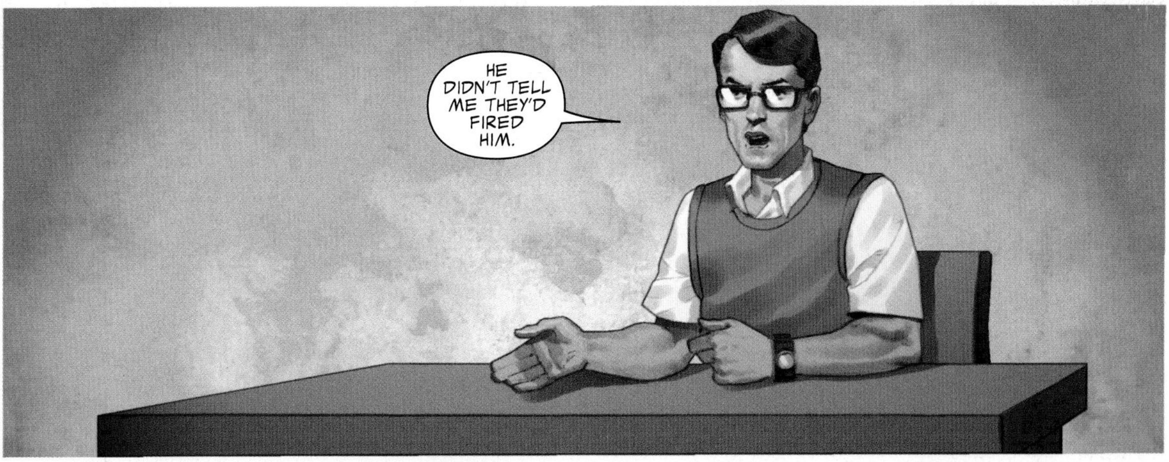
HE DIDN'T TELL ME THEY'D FIRED HIM.

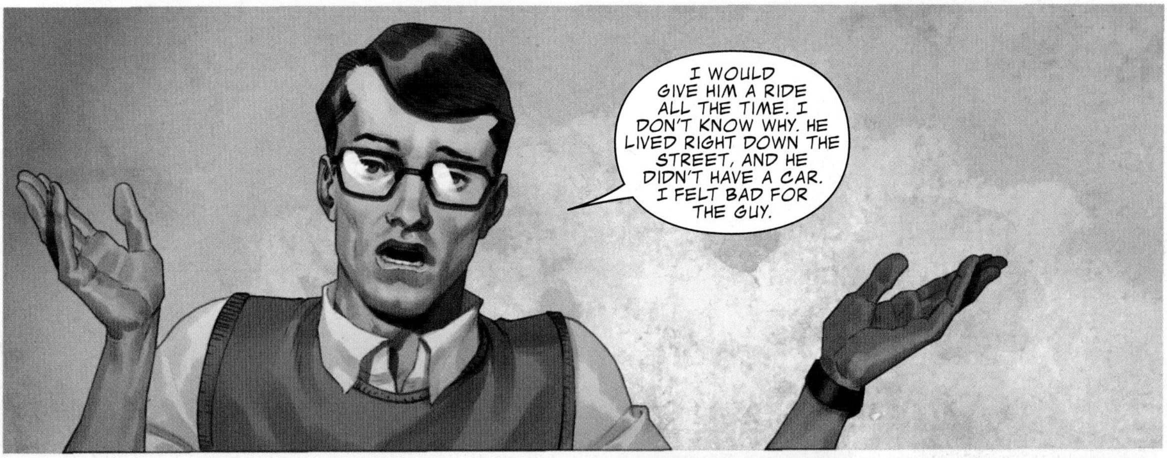
I WOULD GIVE HIM A RIDE ALL THE TIME. I DON'T KNOW WHY. HE LIVED RIGHT DOWN THE STREET, AND HE DIDN'T HAVE A CAR. I FELT BAD FOR THE GUY.

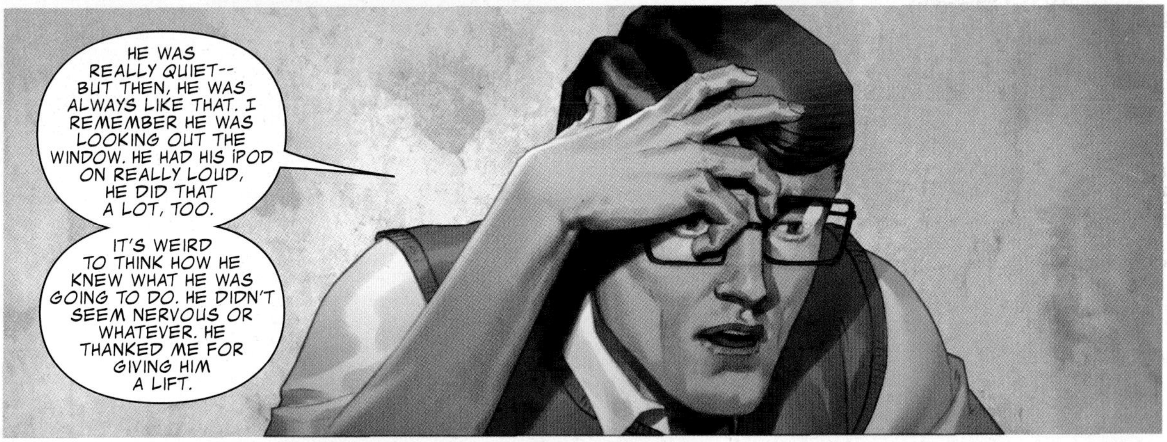
HE WAS REALLY QUIET-- BUT THEN, HE WAS ALWAYS LIKE THAT. I REMEMBER HE WAS LOOKING OUT THE WINDOW. HE HAD HIS iPOD ON REALLY LOUD, HE DID THAT A LOT, TOO.
IT'S WEIRD TO THINK HOW HE KNEW WHAT HE WAS GOING TO DO. HE DIDN'T SEEM NERVOUS OR WHATEVER. HE THANKED ME FOR GIVING HIM A LIFT.

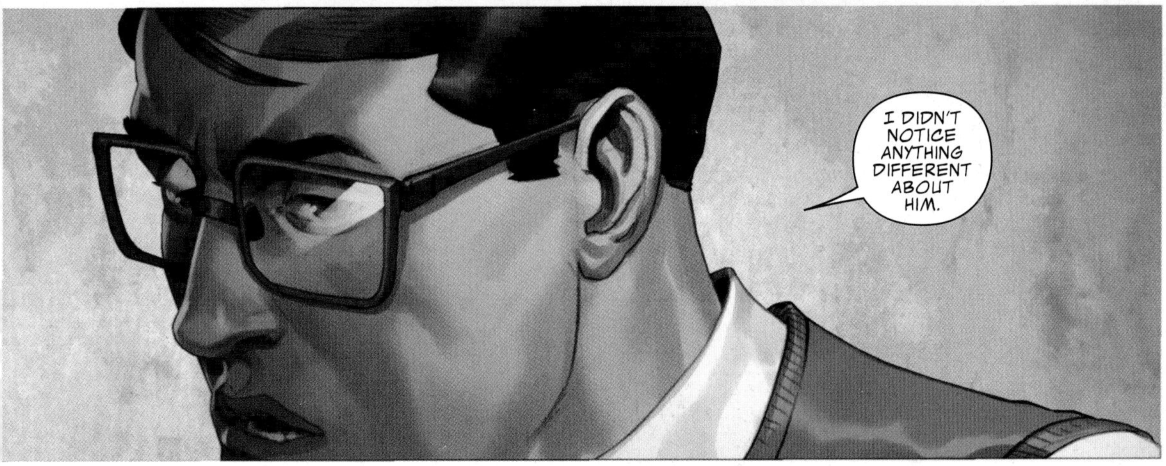
I DIDN'T NOTICE ANYTHING DIFFERENT ABOUT HIM.

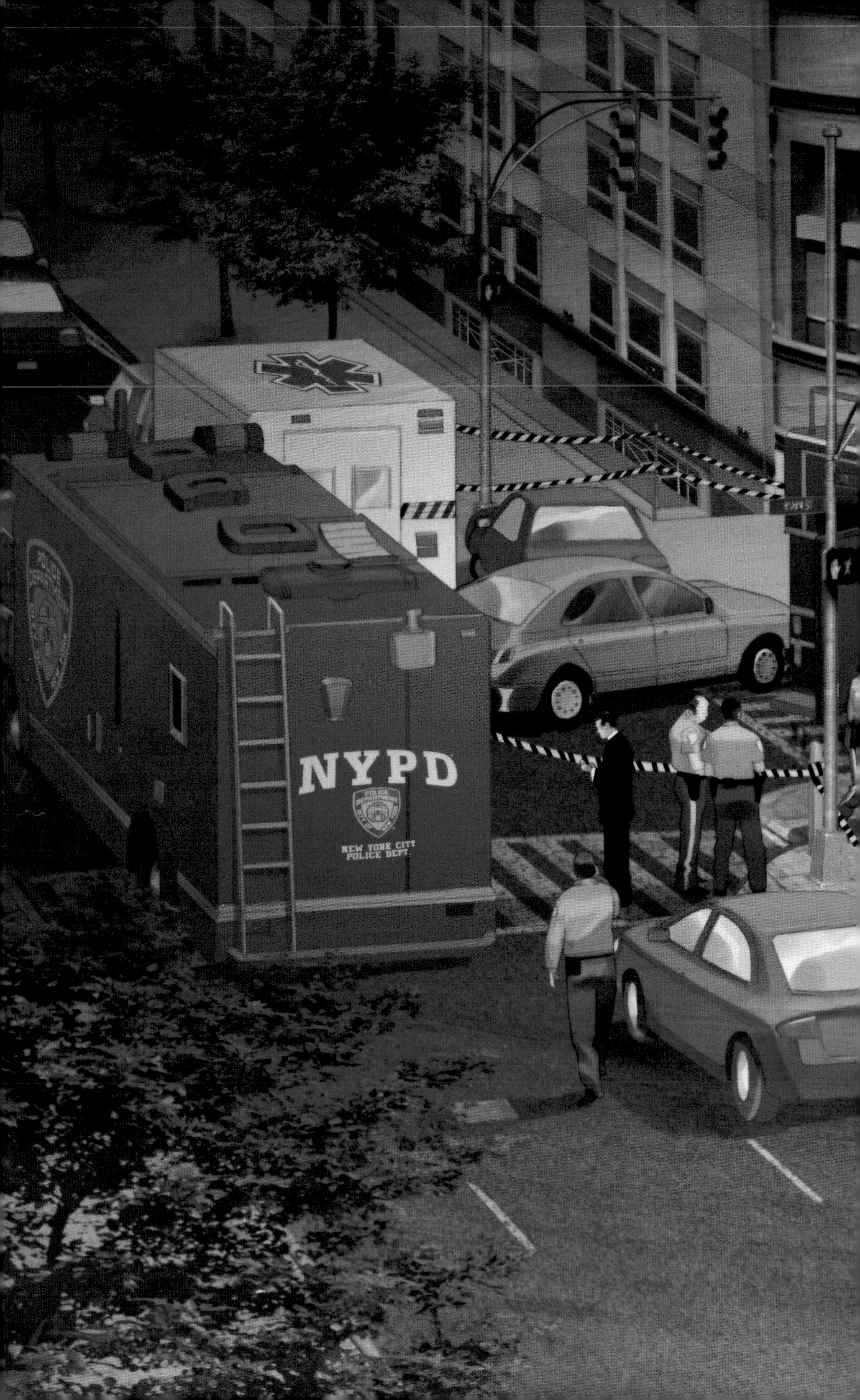
NYPD
NEW YORK CITY
POLICE DEPT.

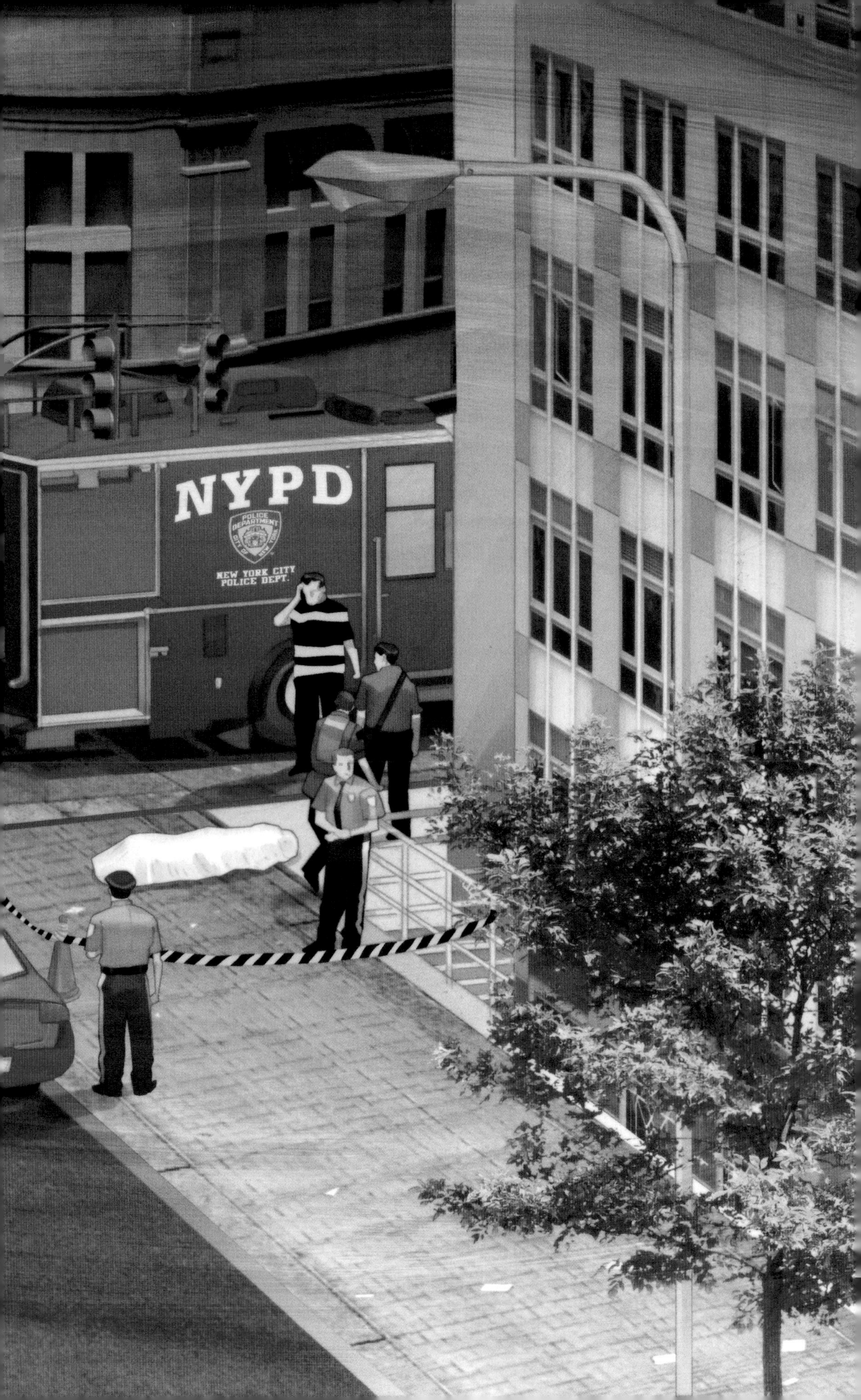
NYPD
POLICE DEPARTMENT CITY OF NEW YORK
NEW YORK CITY
POLICE DEPT.

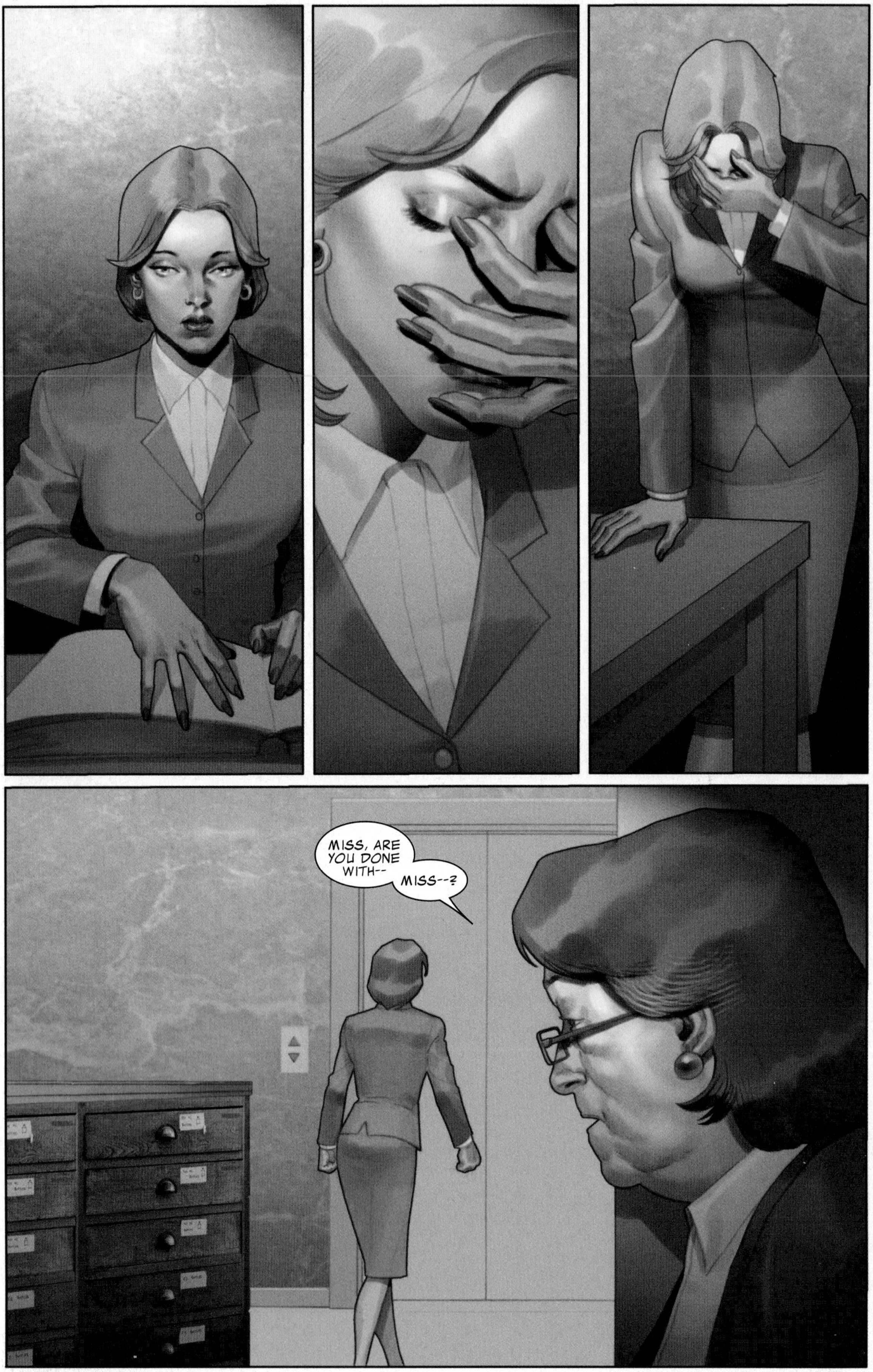
MISS, ARE YOU DONE WITH--
MISS--?

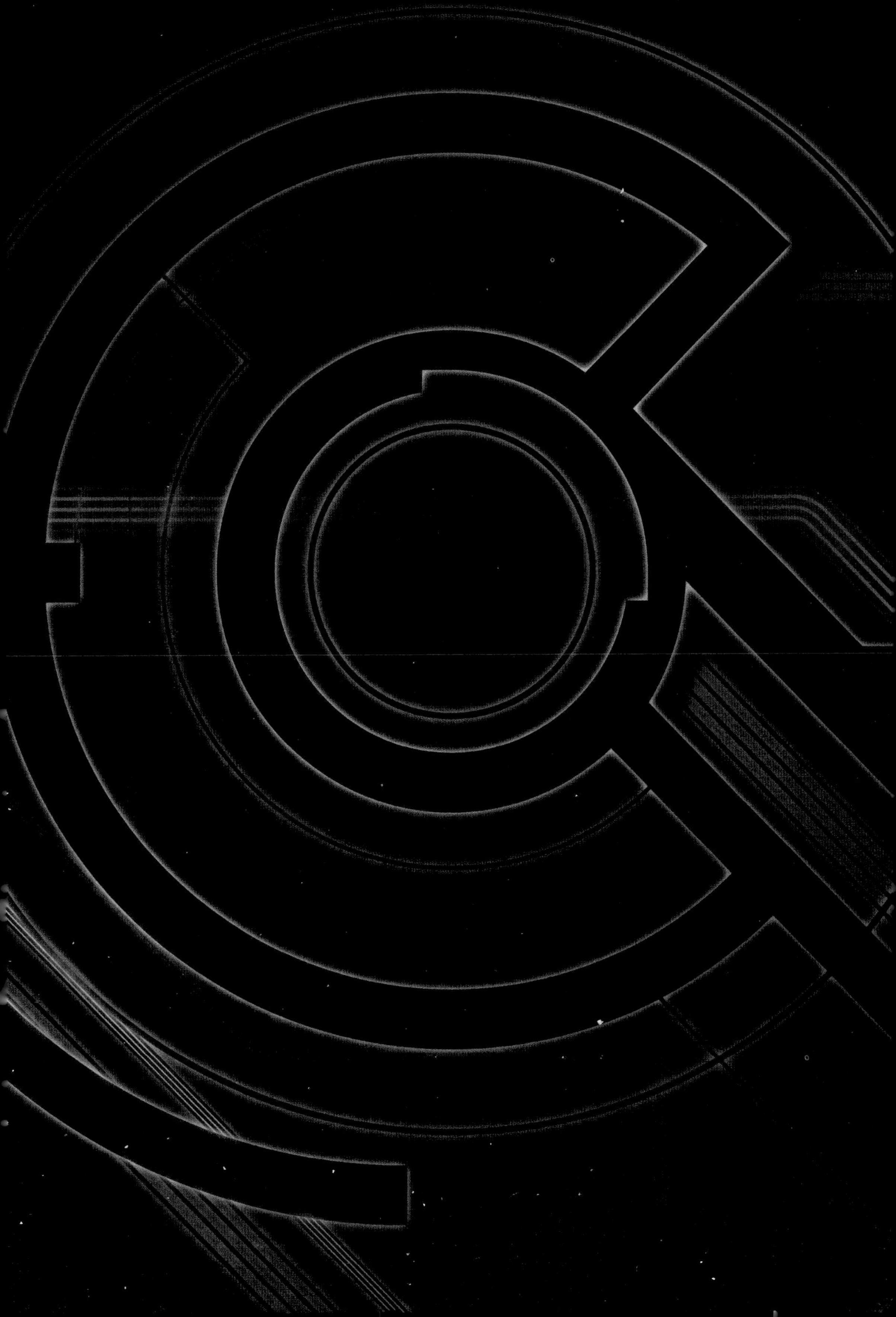

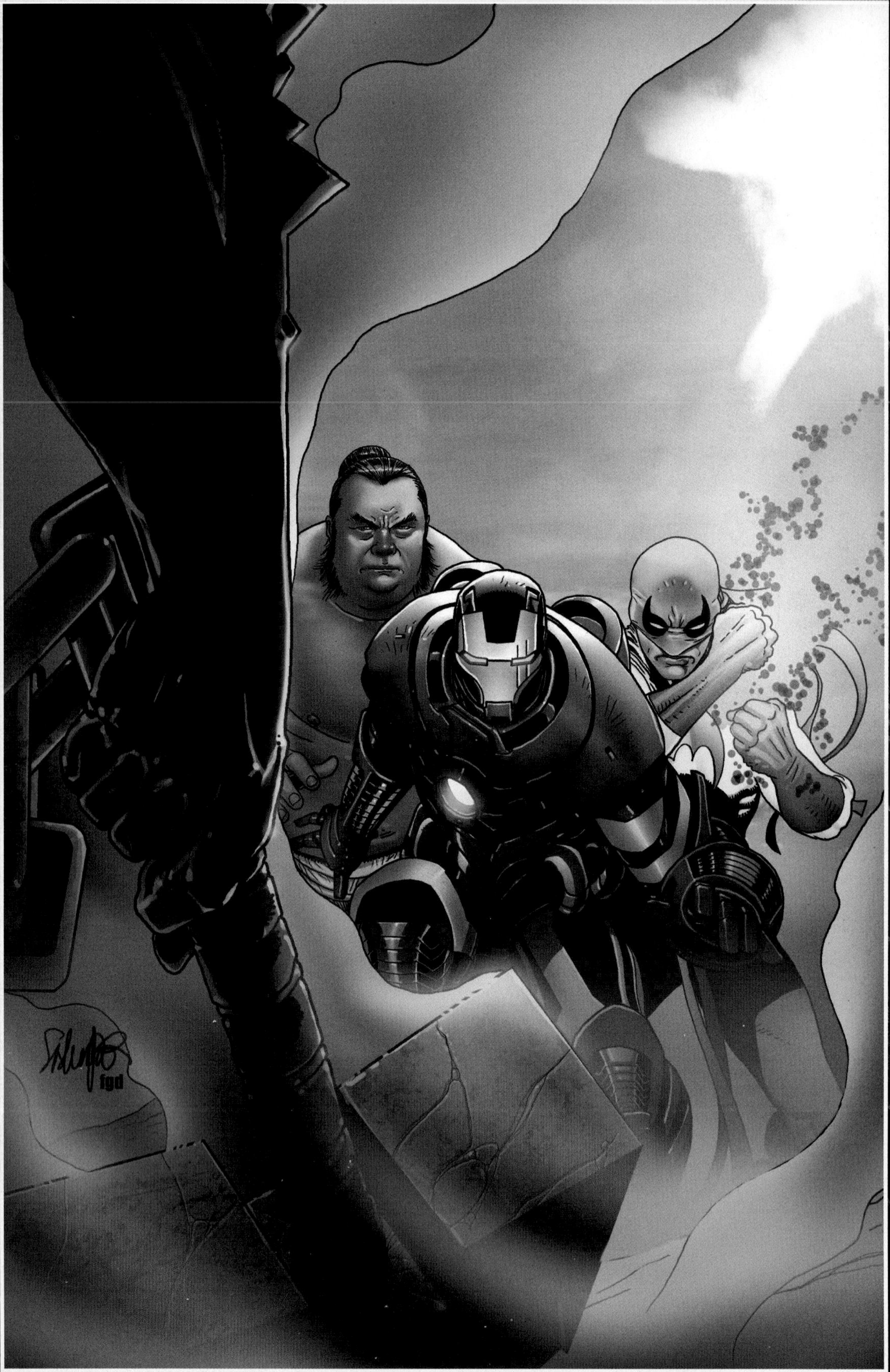

5

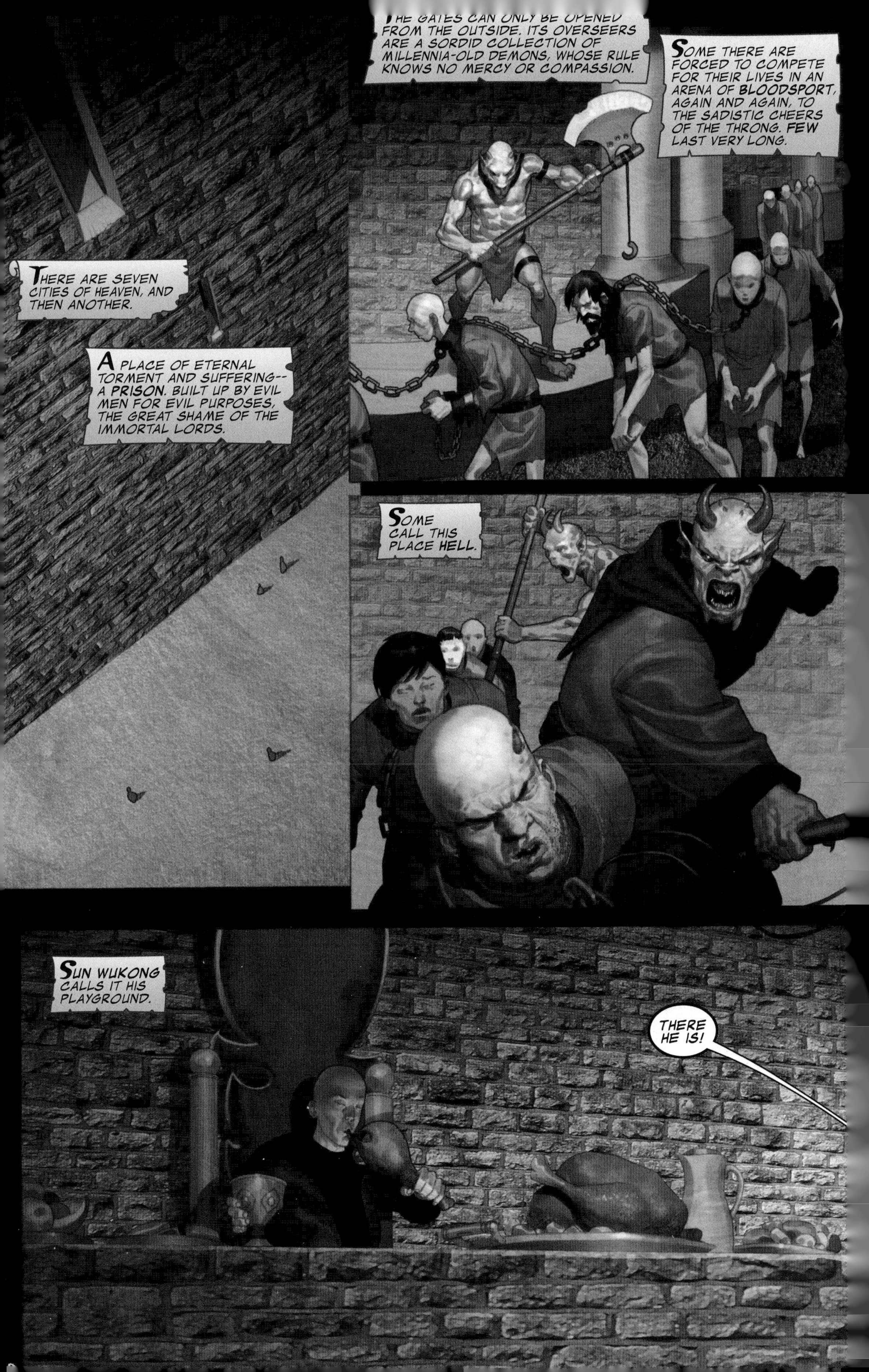
THE GATES CAN ONLY BE OPENED FROM THE OUTSIDE. ITS OVERSEERS ARE A SORDID COLLECTION OF MILLENNIA-OLD DEMONS, WHOSE RULE KNOWS NO MERCY OR COMPASSION.
SOME THERE ARE FORCED TO COMPETE FOR THEIR LIVES IN AN ARENA OF BLOODSPORT, AGAIN AND AGAIN, TO THE SADISTIC CHEERS OF THE THRONG. FEW LAST VERY LONG.
THERE ARE SEVEN CITIES OF HEAVEN, AND THEN ANOTHER.
A PLACE OF ETERNAL TORMENT AND SUFFERING-- A PRISON. BUILT UP BY EVIL MEN FOR EVIL PURPOSES, THE GREAT SHAME OF THE IMMORTAL LORDS.
SOME CALL THIS PLACE HELL.
SUN WUKONG CALLS IT HIS PLAYGROUND.
THERE HE IS!

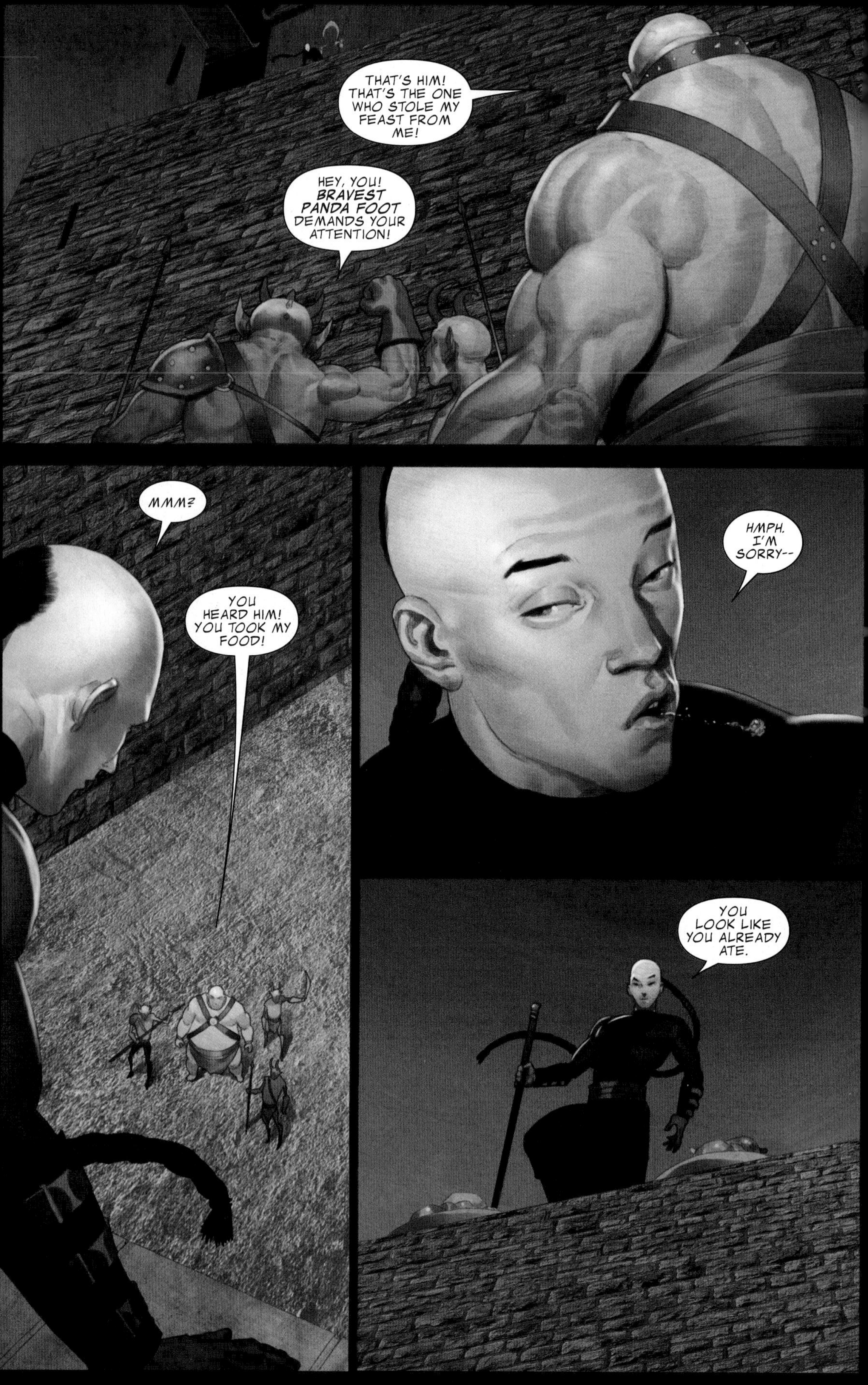
THAT'S HIM! THAT'S THE ONE WHO STOLE MY FEAST FROM ME!
HEY, YOU! BRAVEST PANDA FOOT DEMANDS YOUR ATTENTION!
MMM?
YOU HEARD HIM! YOU TOOK MY FOOD!
HMPH. I'M SORRY--
YOU LOOK LIKE YOU ALREADY ATE.

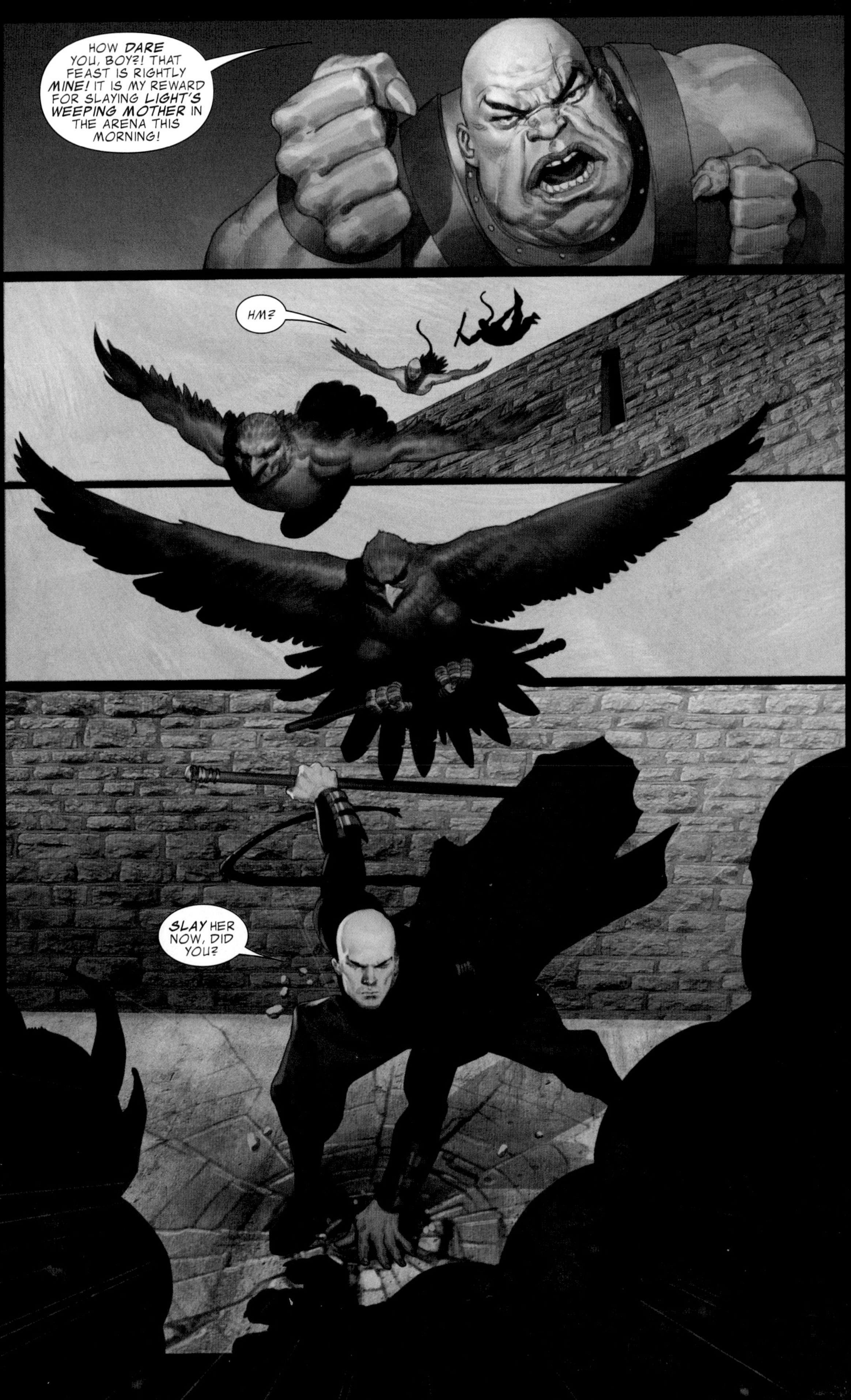

HOW DARE YOU, BOY?! THAT FEAST IS RIGHTLY MINE! IT IS MY REWARD FOR SLAYING LIGHT'S WEEPING MOTHER IN THE ARENA THIS MORNING!
HM?
SLAY HER NOW, DID YOU?

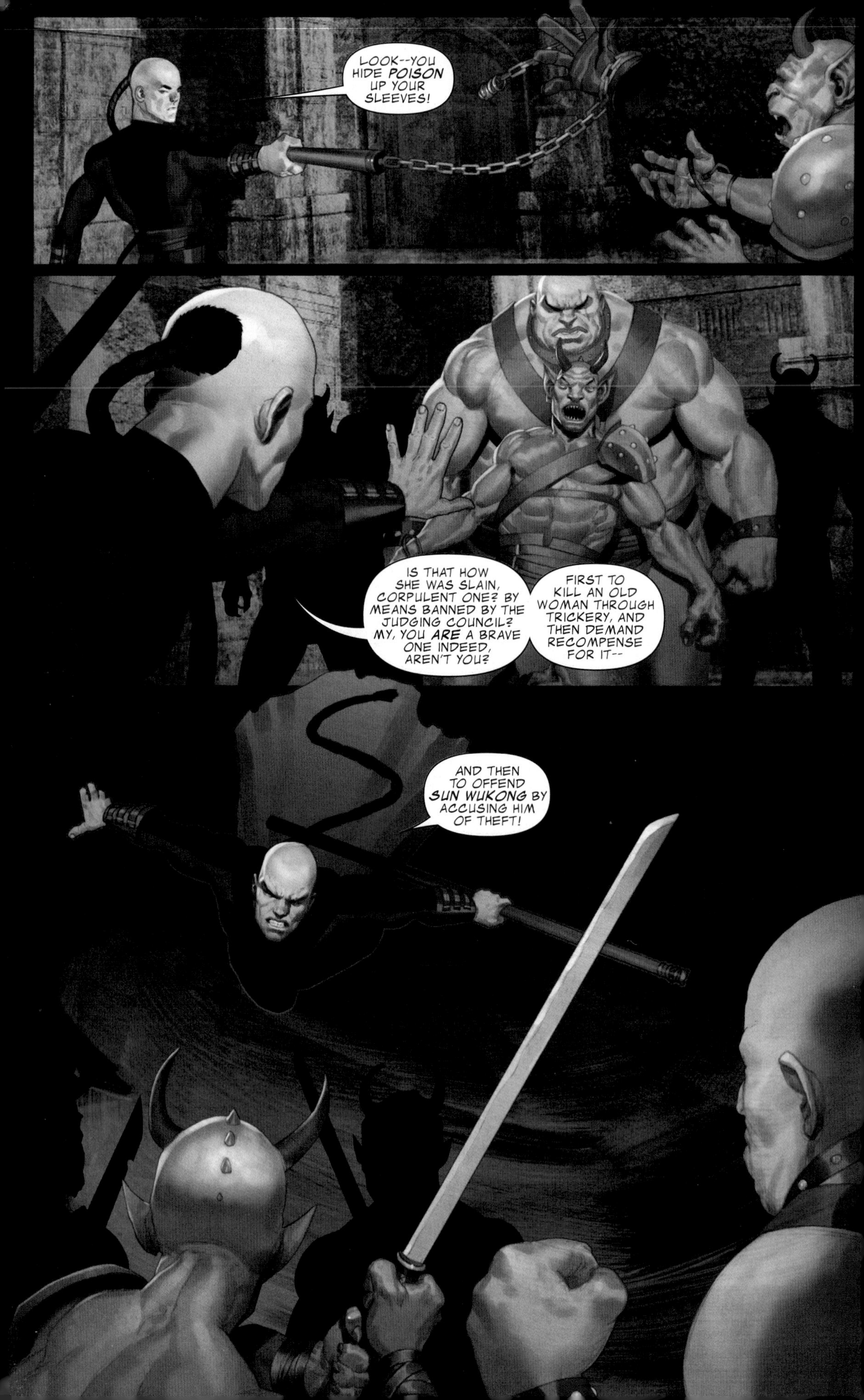
LOOK--YOU HIDE POISON UP YOUR SLEEVES!
IS THAT HOW SHE WAS SLAIN, CORPULENT ONE? BY MEANS BANNED BY THE JUDGING COUNCIL? MY, YOU ARE A BRAVE ONE INDEED, AREN'T YOU?
FIRST TO KILL AN OLD WOMAN THROUGH TRICKERY, AND THEN DEMAND RECOMPENSE FOR IT--
AND THEN TO OFFEND SUN WUKONG BY ACCUSING HIM OF THEFT!

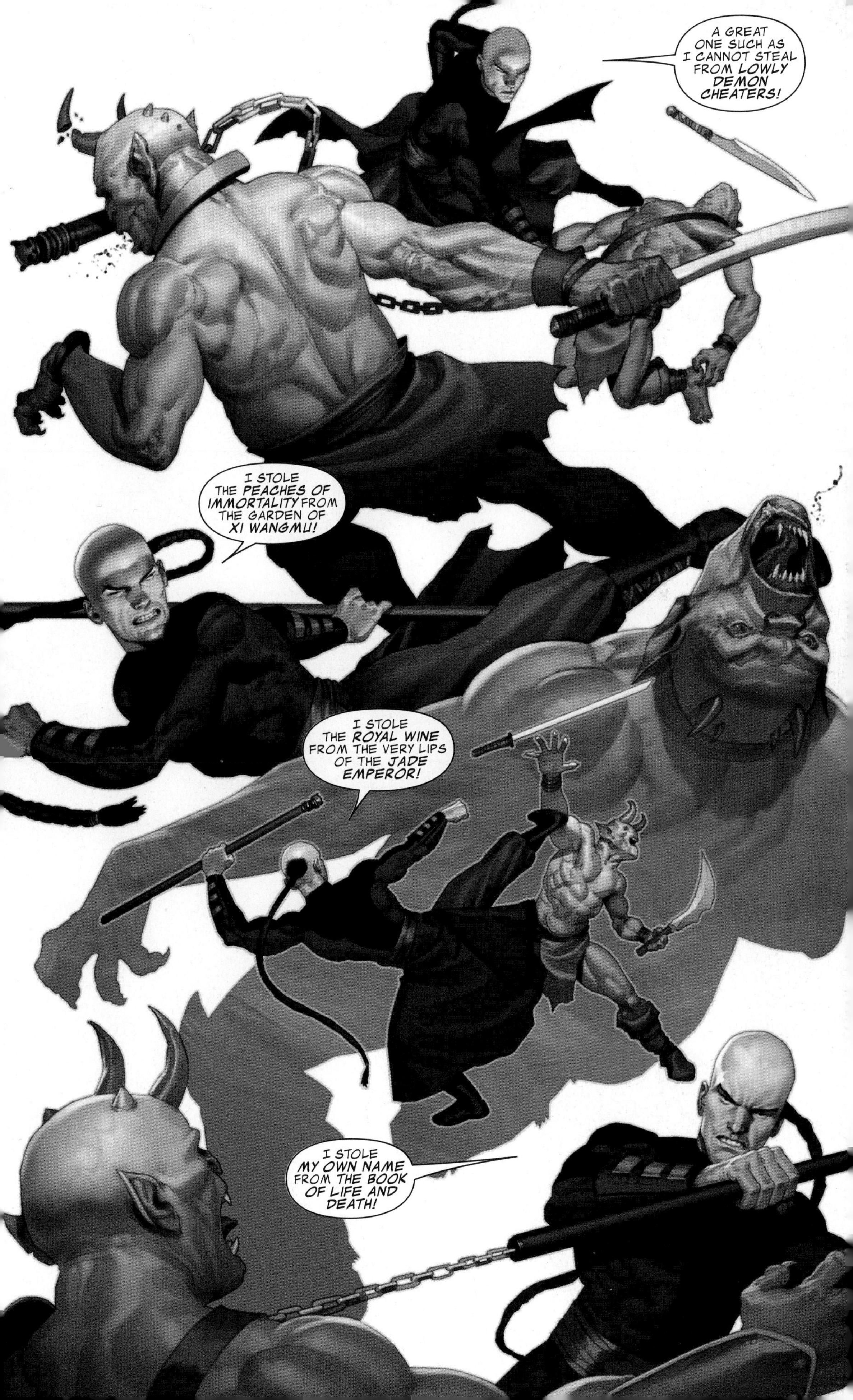
A GREAT ONE SUCH AS I CANNOT STEAL FROM LOWLY DEMON CHEATERS!
I STOLE THE PEACHES OF IMMORTALITY FROM THE GARDEN OF XI WANGMU!
I STOLE THE ROYAL WINE FROM THE VERY LIPS OF THE JADE EMPEROR!
I STOLE MY OWN NAME FROM THE BOOK OF LIFE AND DEATH!

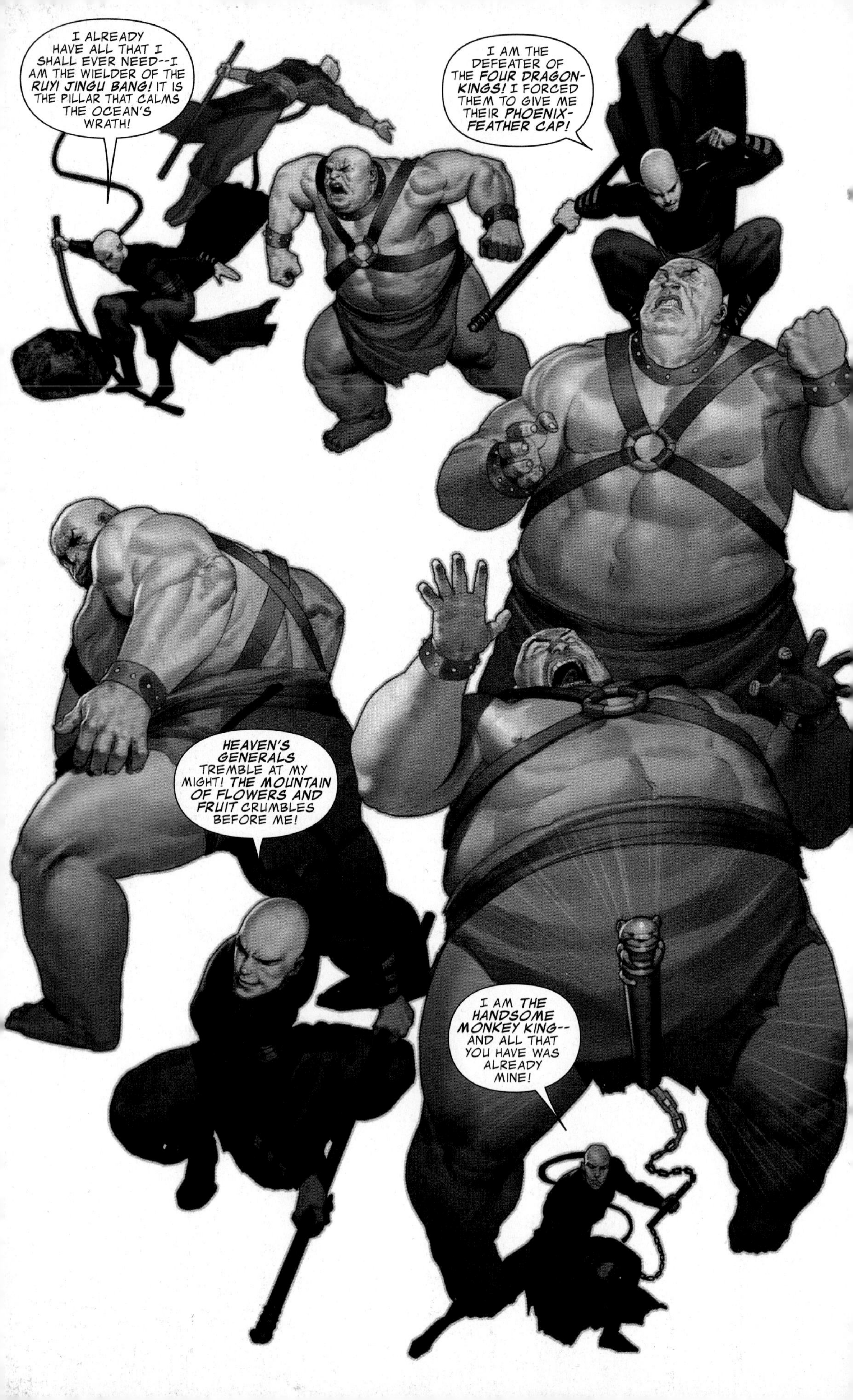
I ALREADY HAVE ALL THAT I SHALL EVER NEED--I AM THE WIELDER OF THE RUYI JINGU BANG! IT IS THE PILLAR THAT CALMS THE OCEAN'S WRATH!
I AM THE DEFEATER OF THE FOUR DRAGON-KINGS! I FORCED THEM TO GIVE ME THEIR PHOENIX-FEATHER CAP!
HEAVEN'S GENERALS TREMBLE AT MY MIGHT! THE MOUNTAIN OF FLOWERS AND FRUIT CRUMBLES BEFORE ME!
I AM THE HANDSOME MONKEY KING--AND ALL THAT YOU HAVE WAS ALREADY MINE!

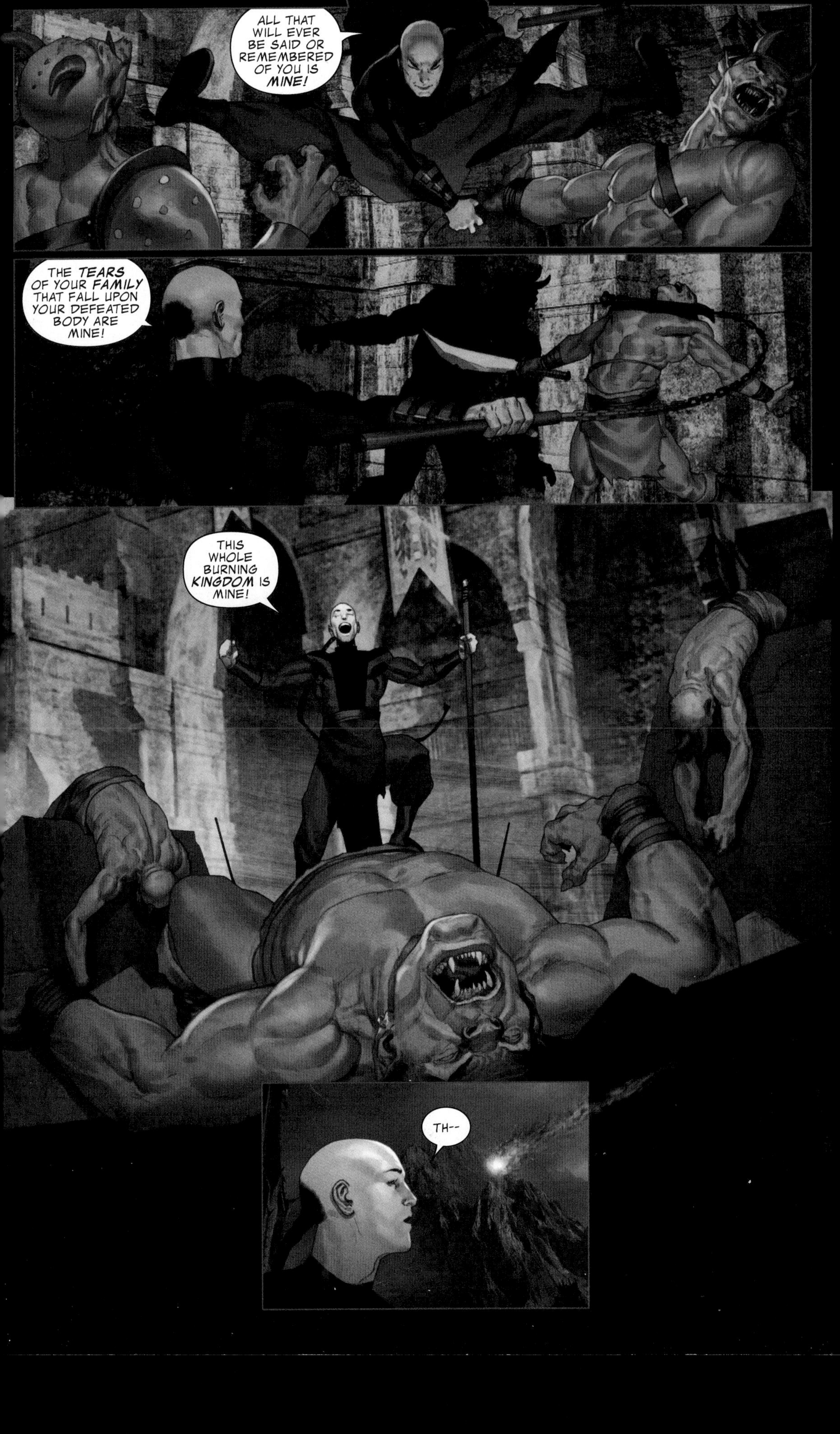
ALL THAT WILL EVER BE SAID OR REMEMBERED OF YOU IS MINE!
THE TEARS OF YOUR FAMILY THAT FALL UPON YOUR DEFEATED BODY ARE MINE!
THIS WHOLE BURNING KINGDOM IS MINE!
TH--

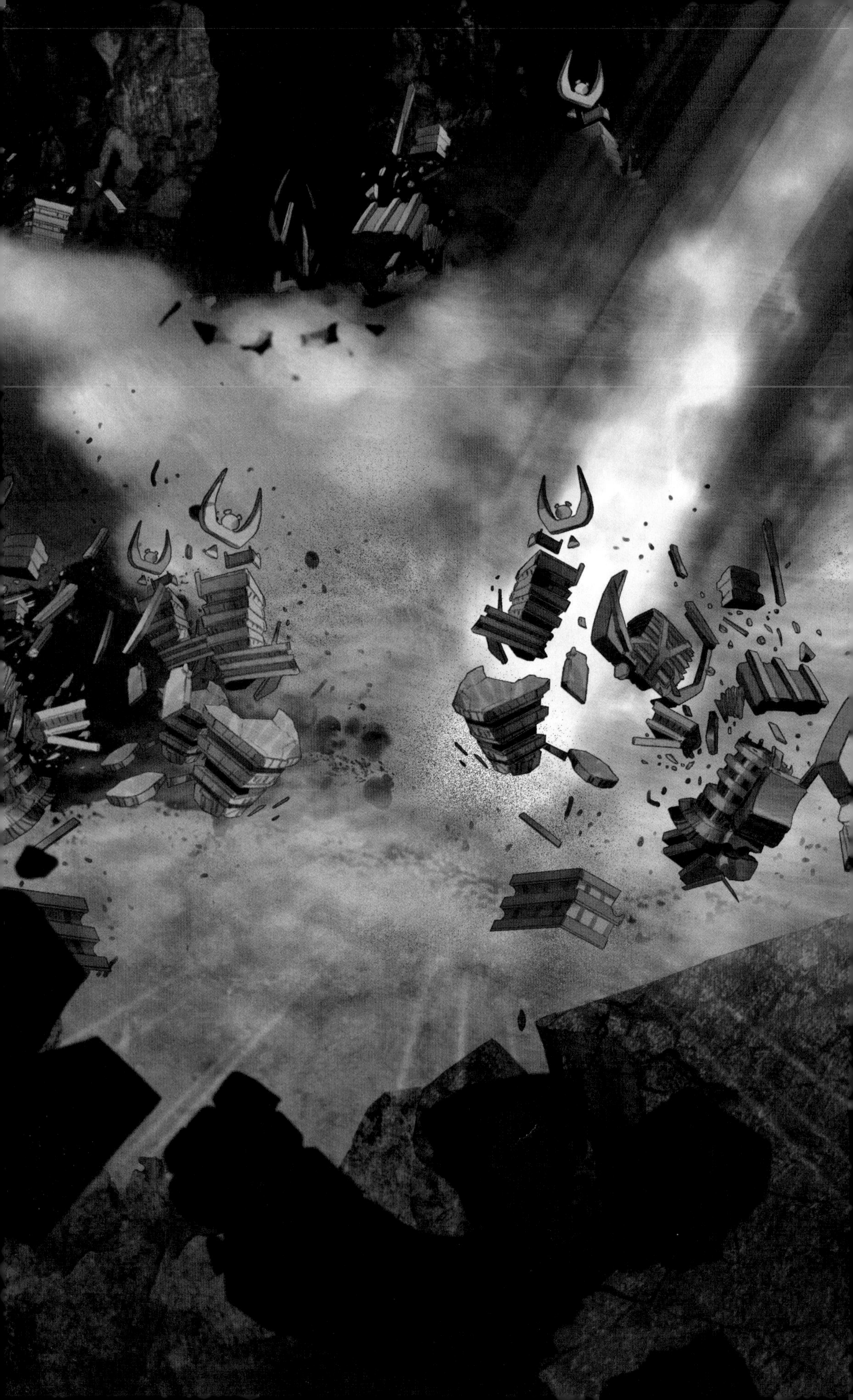

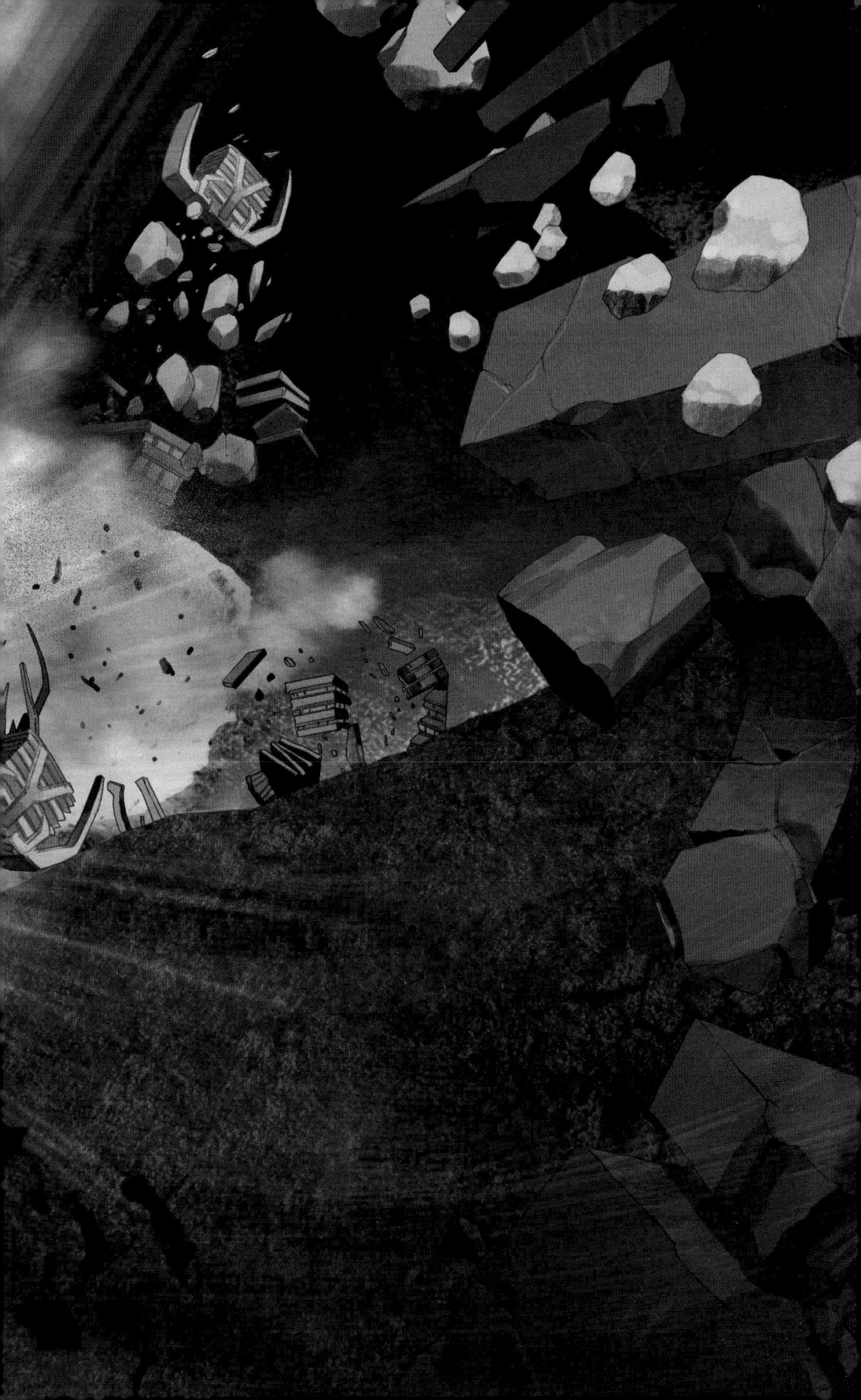

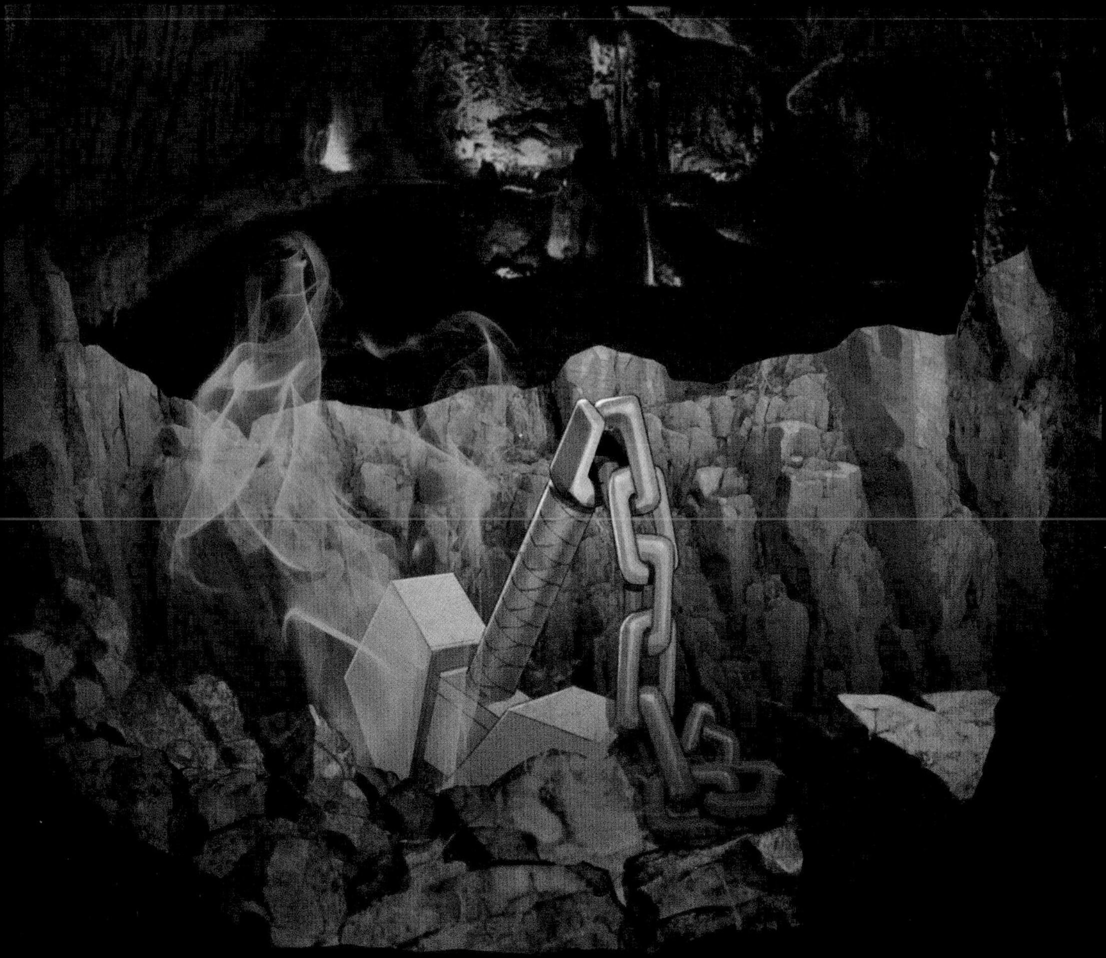

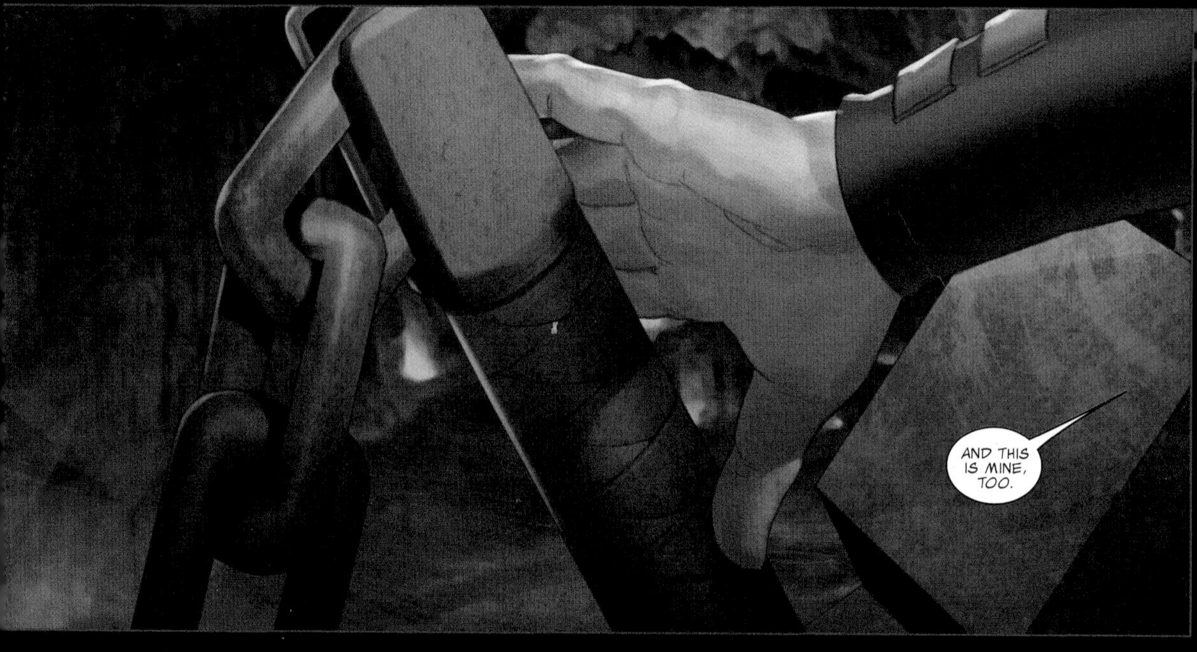
AND THIS IS MINE, TOO.

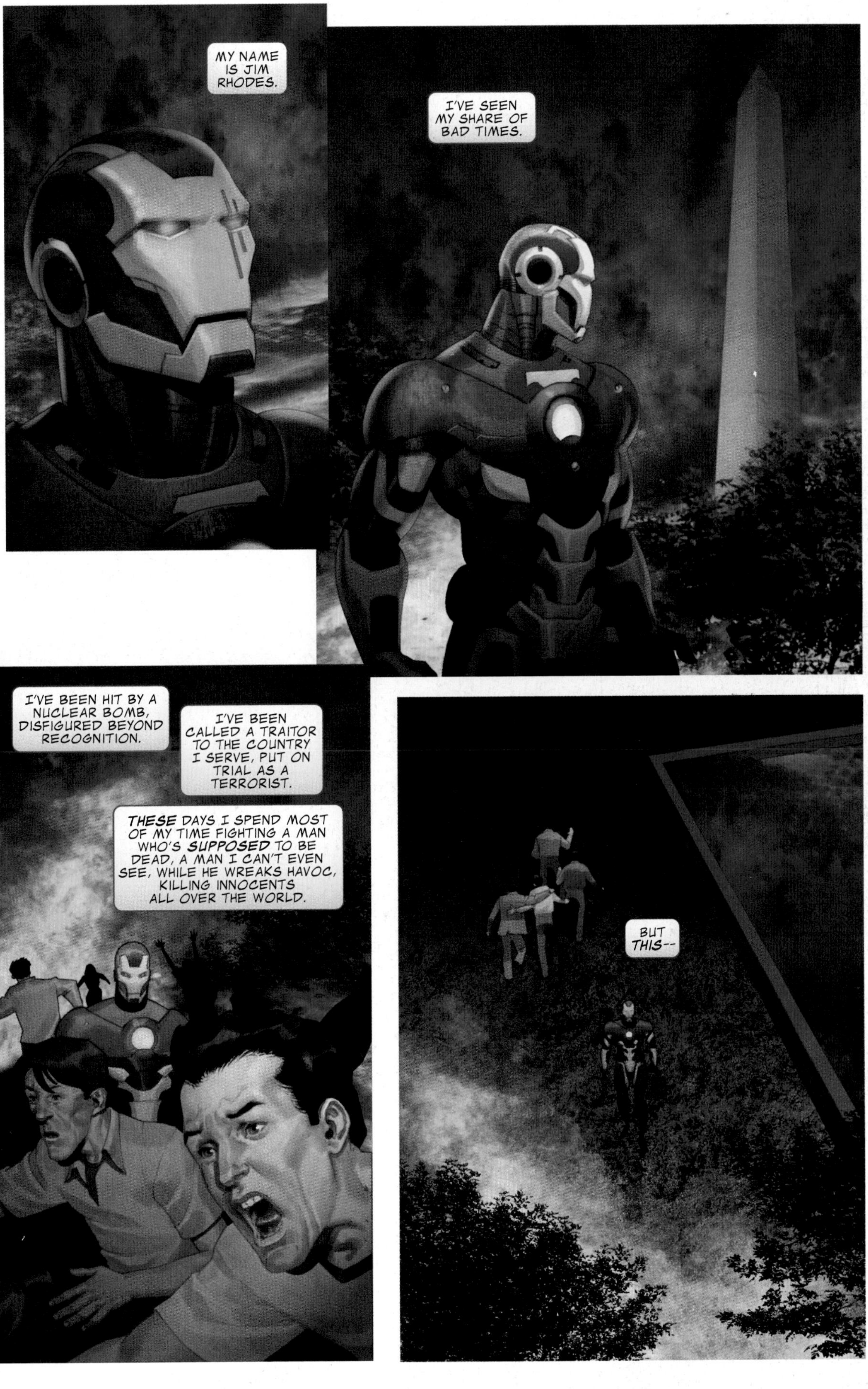
MY NAME IS JIM RHODES.
I'VE SEEN MY SHARE OF BAD TIMES.
I'VE BEEN HIT BY A NUCLEAR BOMB, DISFIGURED BEYOND RECOGNITION.
I'VE BEEN CALLED A TRAITOR TO THE COUNTRY I SERVE, PUT ON TRIAL AS A TERRORIST.
THESE DAYS I SPEND MOST OF MY TIME FIGHTING A MAN WHO'S SUPPOSED TO BE DEAD, A MAN I CAN'T EVEN SEE, WHILE HE WREAKS HAVOC, KILLING INNOCENTS ALL OVER THE WORLD.
BUT THIS--

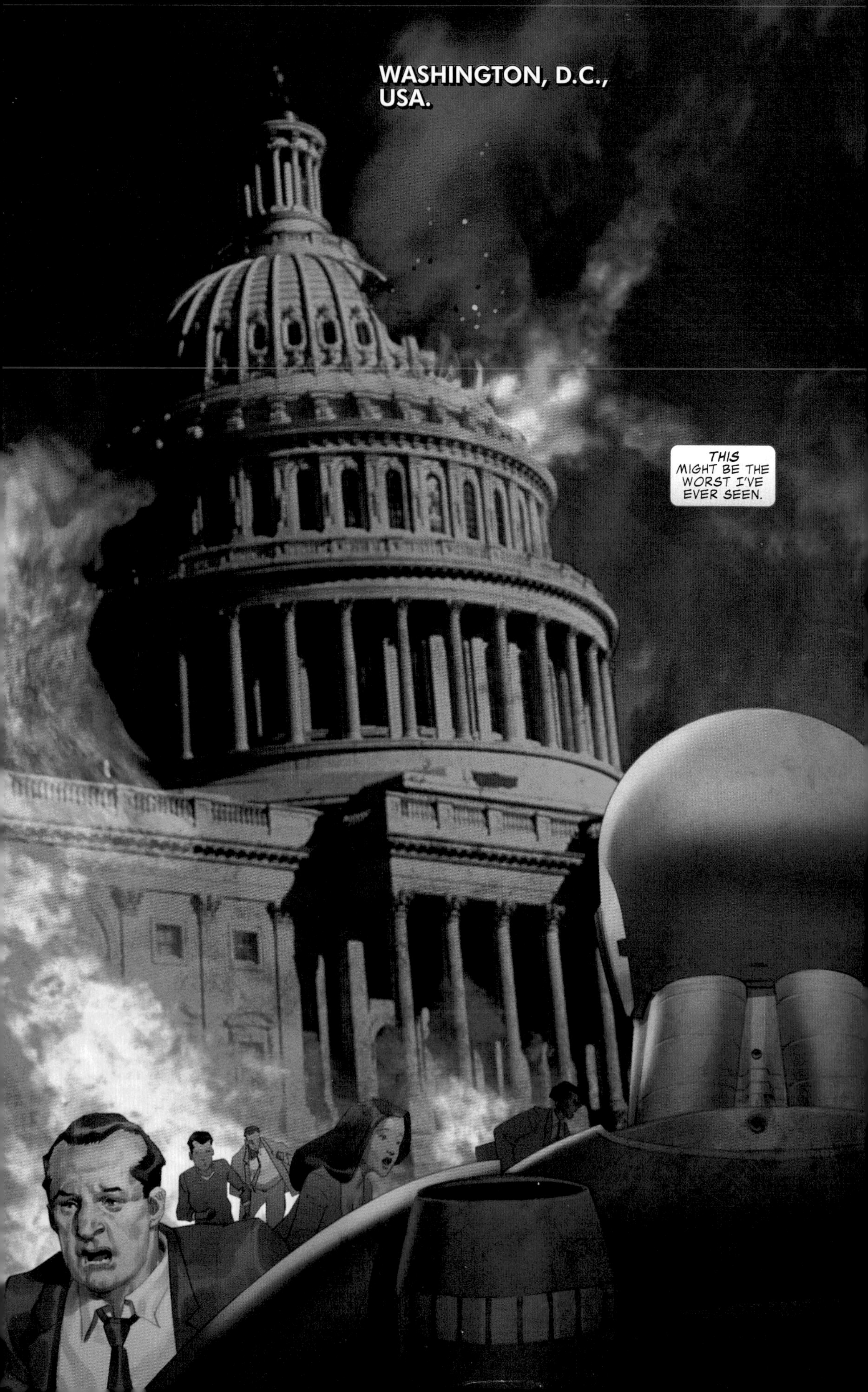

WASHINGTON, D.C., USA.
THIS MIGHT BE THE WORST I'VE EVER SEEN.

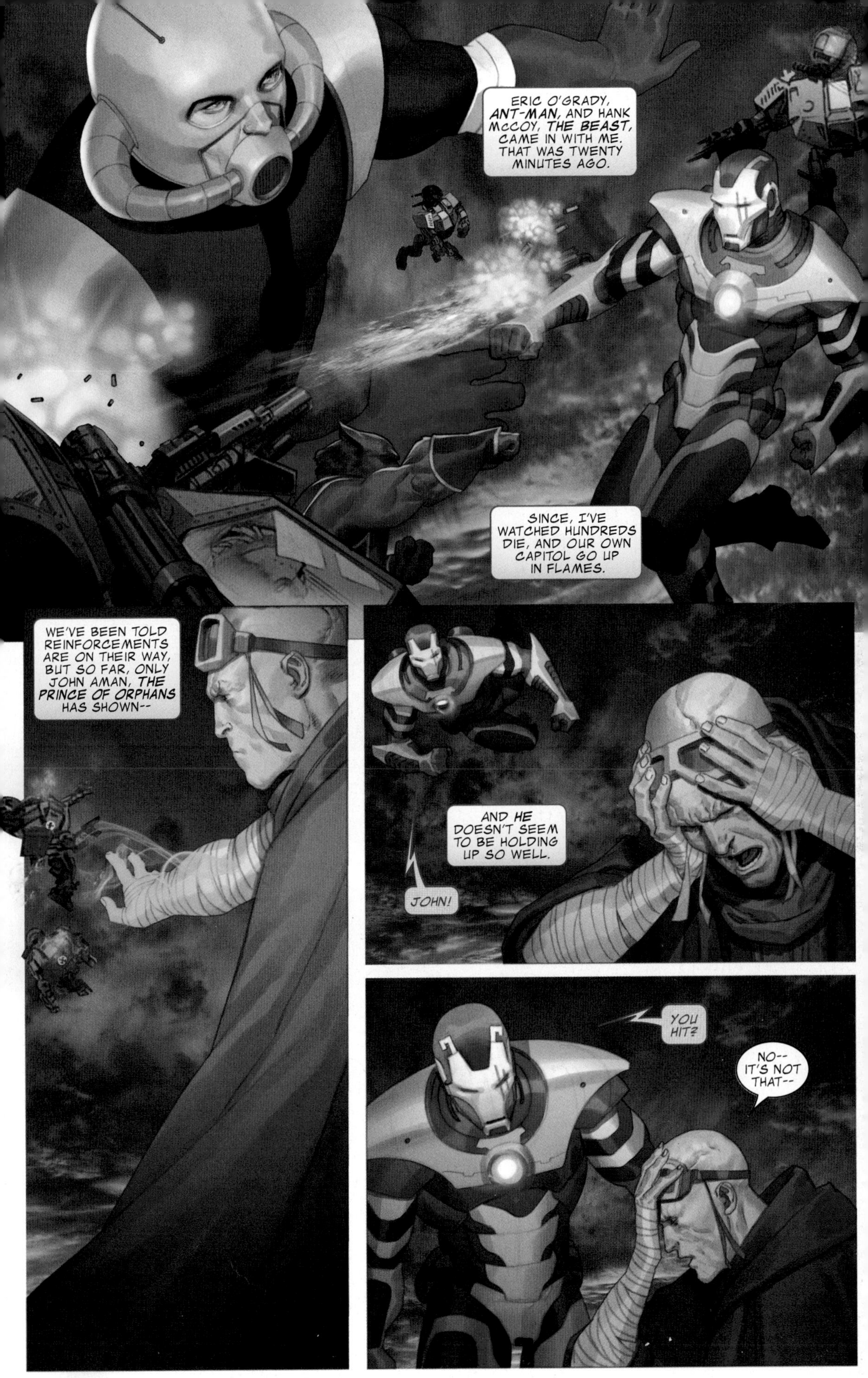
ERIC O'GRADY, ANT-MAN, AND HANK McCOY, THE BEAST, CAME IN WITH ME. THAT WAS TWENTY MINUTES AGO.
SINCE, I'VE WATCHED HUNDREDS DIE, AND OUR OWN CAPITOL GO UP IN FLAMES.
WE'VE BEEN TOLD REINFORCEMENTS ARE ON THEIR WAY, BUT SO FAR, ONLY JOHN AMAN, THE PRINCE OF ORPHANS HAS SHOWN--
AND HE DOESN'T SEEM TO BE HOLDING UP SO WELL.
JOHN!
YOU HIT?
NO-- IT'S NOT THAT--

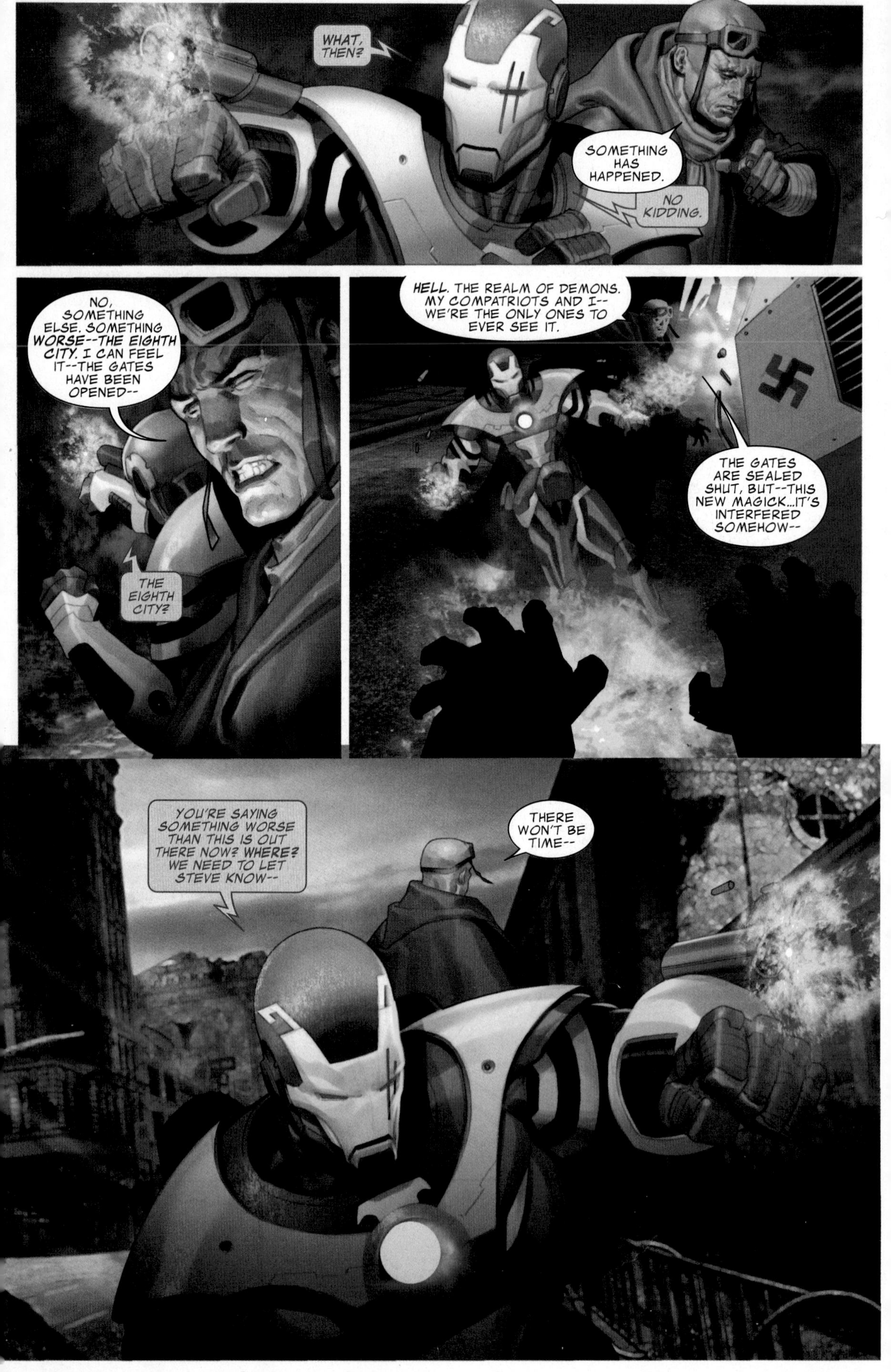

WHAT, THEN?
SOMETHING HAS HAPPENED.
NO KIDDING.
NO, SOMETHING ELSE. SOMETHING WORSE--THE EIGHTH CITY. I CAN FEEL IT--THE GATES HAVE BEEN OPENED--
THE EIGHTH CITY?
HELL. THE REALM OF DEMONS. MY COMPATRIOTS AND I--WE'RE THE ONLY ONES TO EVER SEE IT.
THE GATES ARE SEALED SHUT, BUT--THIS NEW MAGICK...IT'S INTERFERED SOMEHOW--
YOU'RE SAYING SOMETHING WORSE THAN THIS IS OUT THERE NOW? WHERE? WE NEED TO LET STEVE KNOW--
THERE WON'T BE TIME--

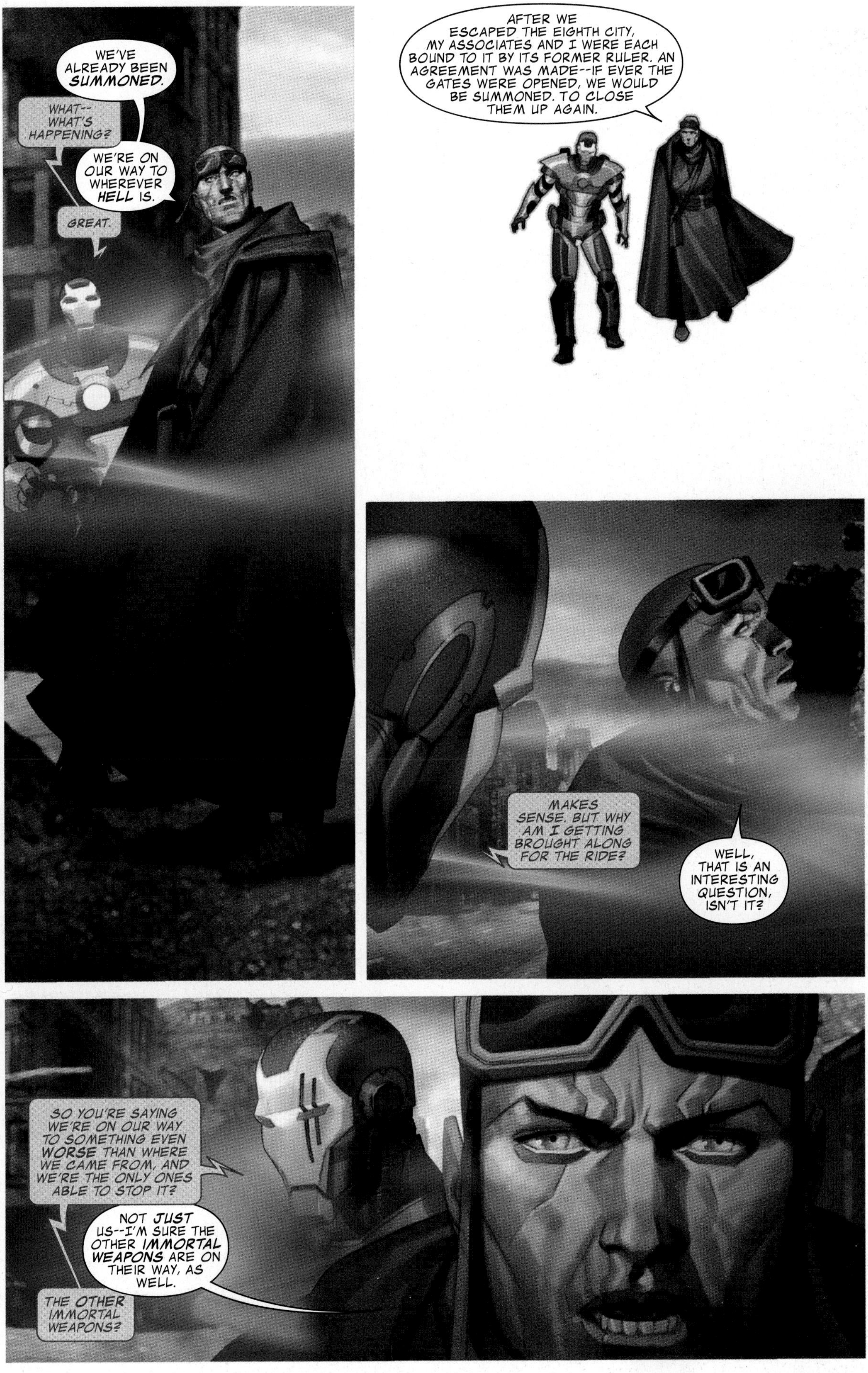
WE'VE ALREADY BEEN SUMMONED.
WHAT-- WHAT'S HAPPENING?
WE'RE ON OUR WAY TO WHEREVER HELL IS.
GREAT.
AFTER WE ESCAPED THE EIGHTH CITY, MY ASSOCIATES AND I WERE EACH BOUND TO IT BY ITS FORMER RULER. AN AGREEMENT WAS MADE--IF EVER THE GATES WERE OPENED, WE WOULD BE SUMMONED. TO CLOSE THEM UP AGAIN.
MAKES SENSE. BUT WHY AM I GETTING BROUGHT ALONG FOR THE RIDE?
WELL, THAT IS AN INTERESTING QUESTION, ISN'T IT?
SO YOU'RE SAYING WE'RE ON OUR WAY TO SOMETHING EVEN WORSE THAN WHERE WE CAME FROM, AND WE'RE THE ONLY ONES ABLE TO STOP IT?
NOT JUST US--I'M SURE THE OTHER IMMORTAL WEAPONS ARE ON THEIR WAY, AS WELL.
THE OTHER IMMORTAL WEAPONS?

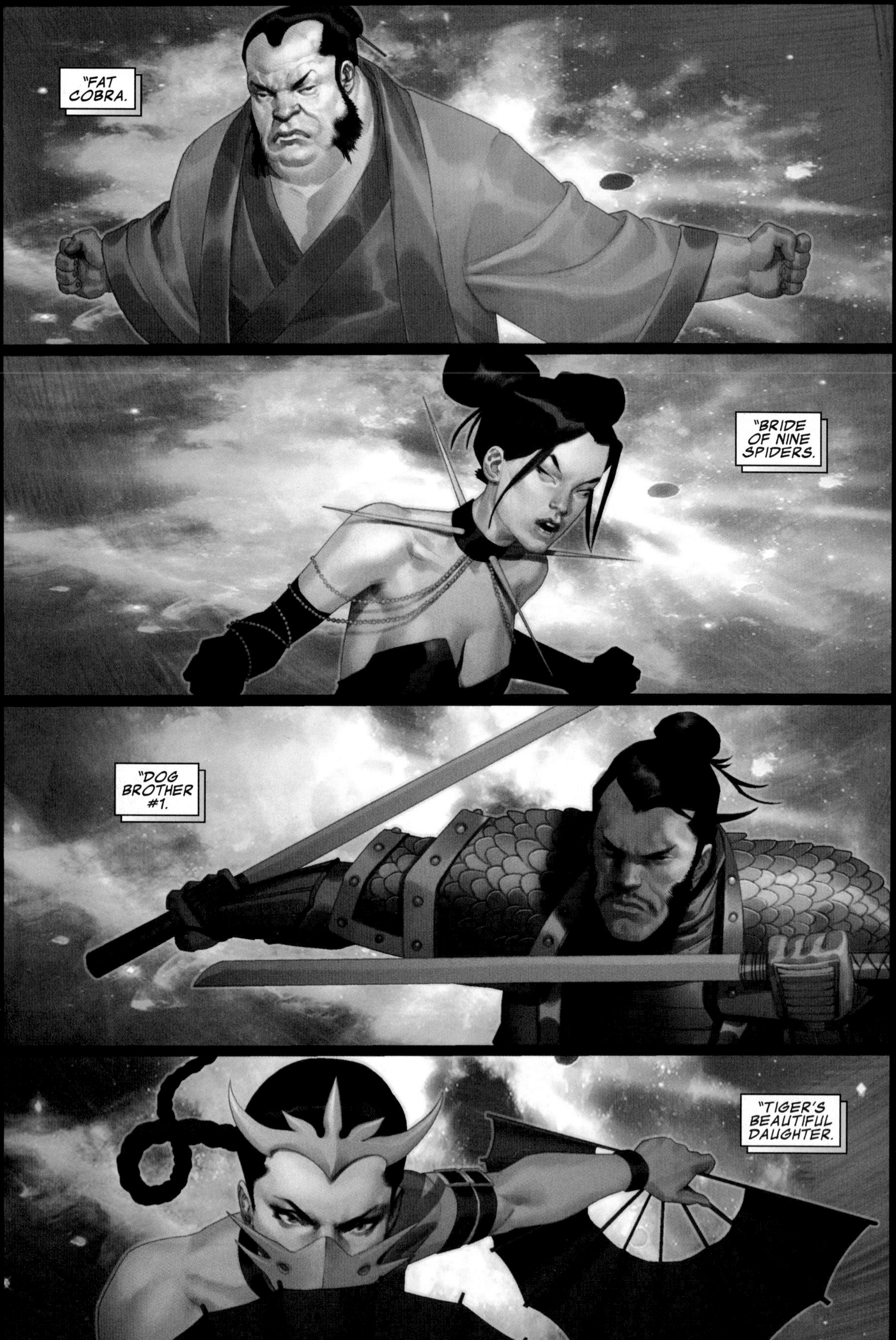
"FAT COBRA.
"BRIDE OF NINE SPIDERS.
"DOG BROTHER #1.
"TIGER'S BEAUTIFUL DAUGHTER.

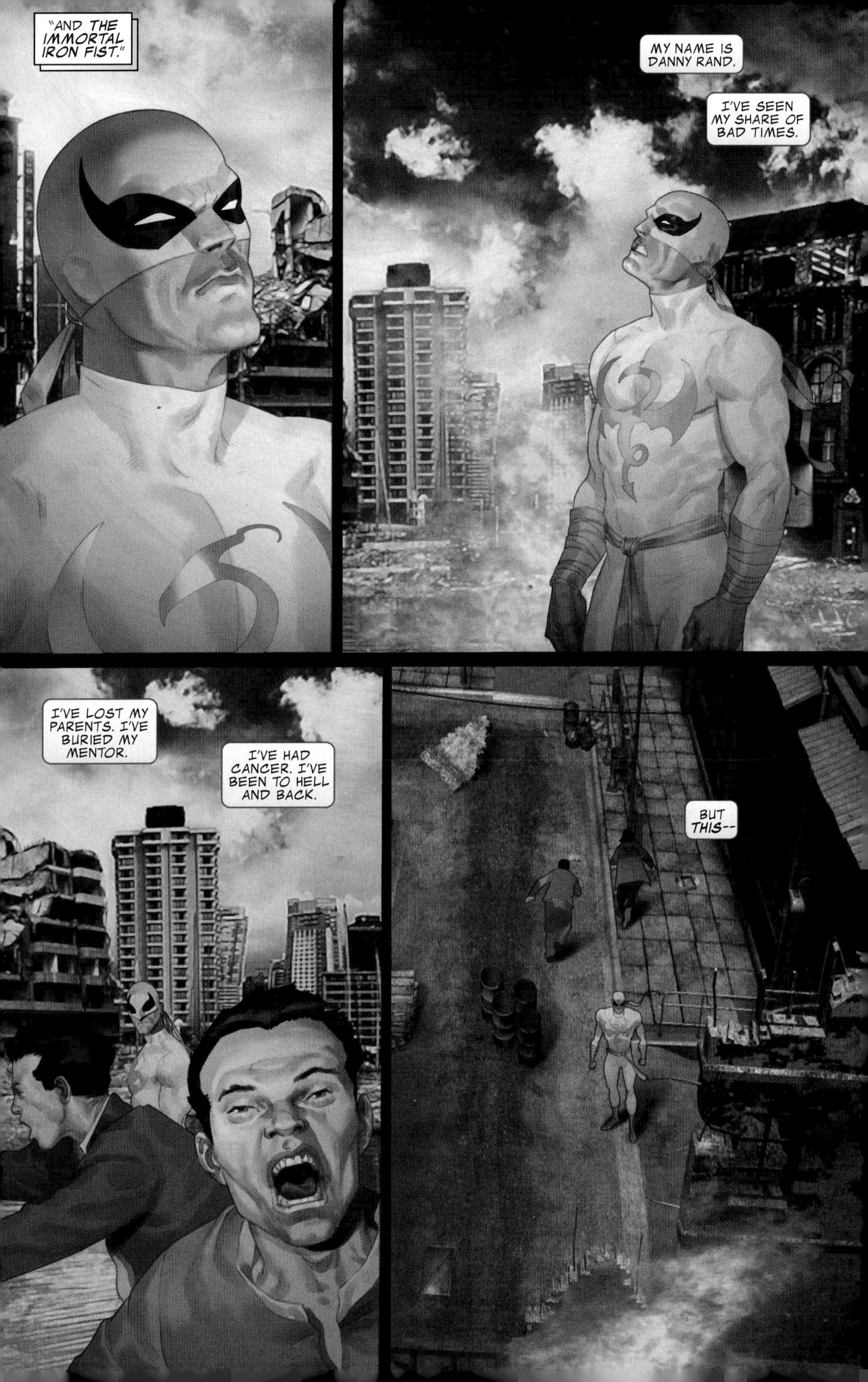
"AND THE IMMORTAL IRON FIST."
MY NAME IS DANNY RAND.
I'VE SEEN MY SHARE OF BAD TIMES.
I'VE LOST MY PARENTS. I'VE BURIED MY MENTOR.
I'VE HAD CANCER. I'VE BEEN TO HELL AND BACK.
BUT THIS--

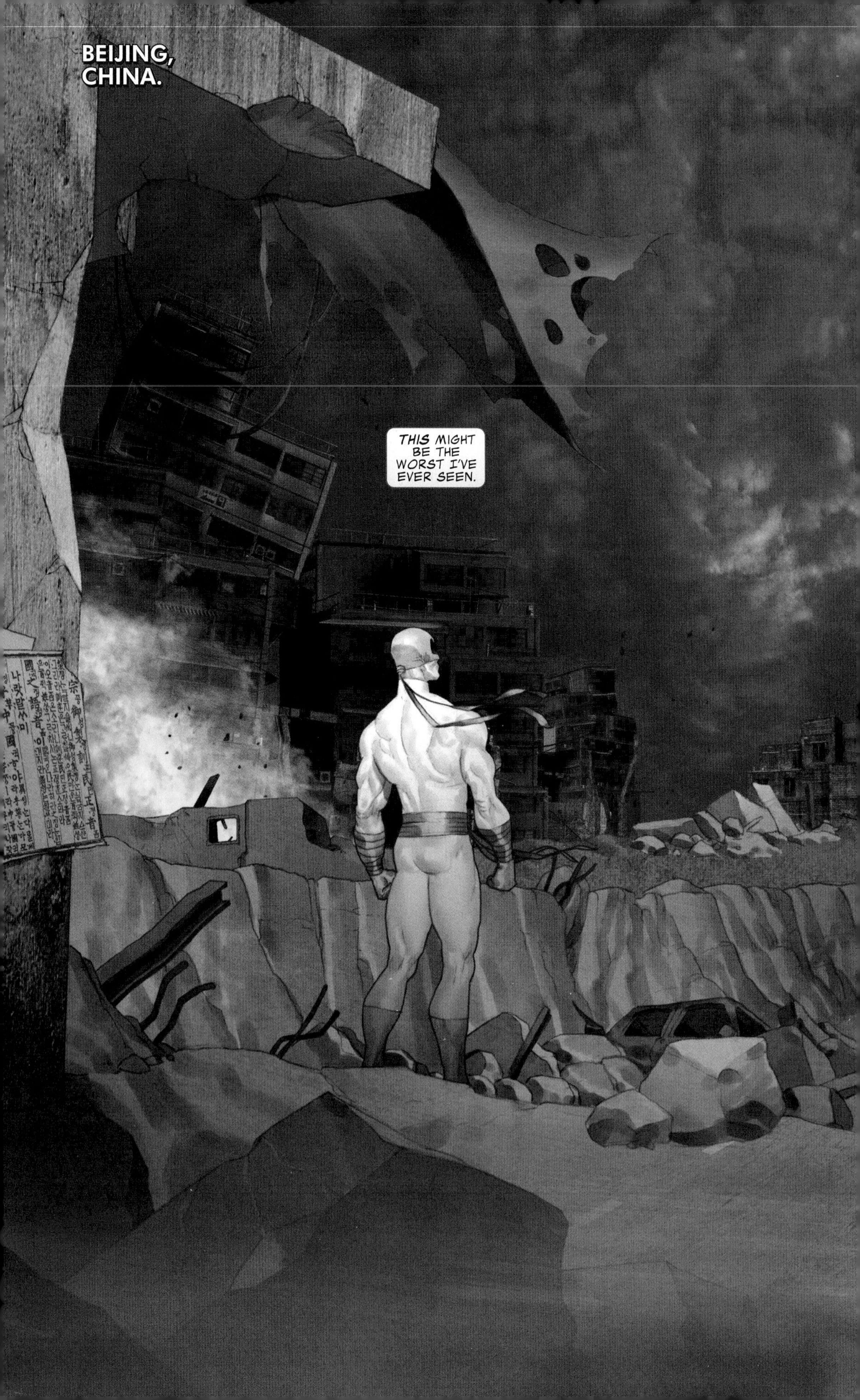
BEIJING, CHINA.
THIS MIGHT BE THE WORST I'VE EVER SEEN.

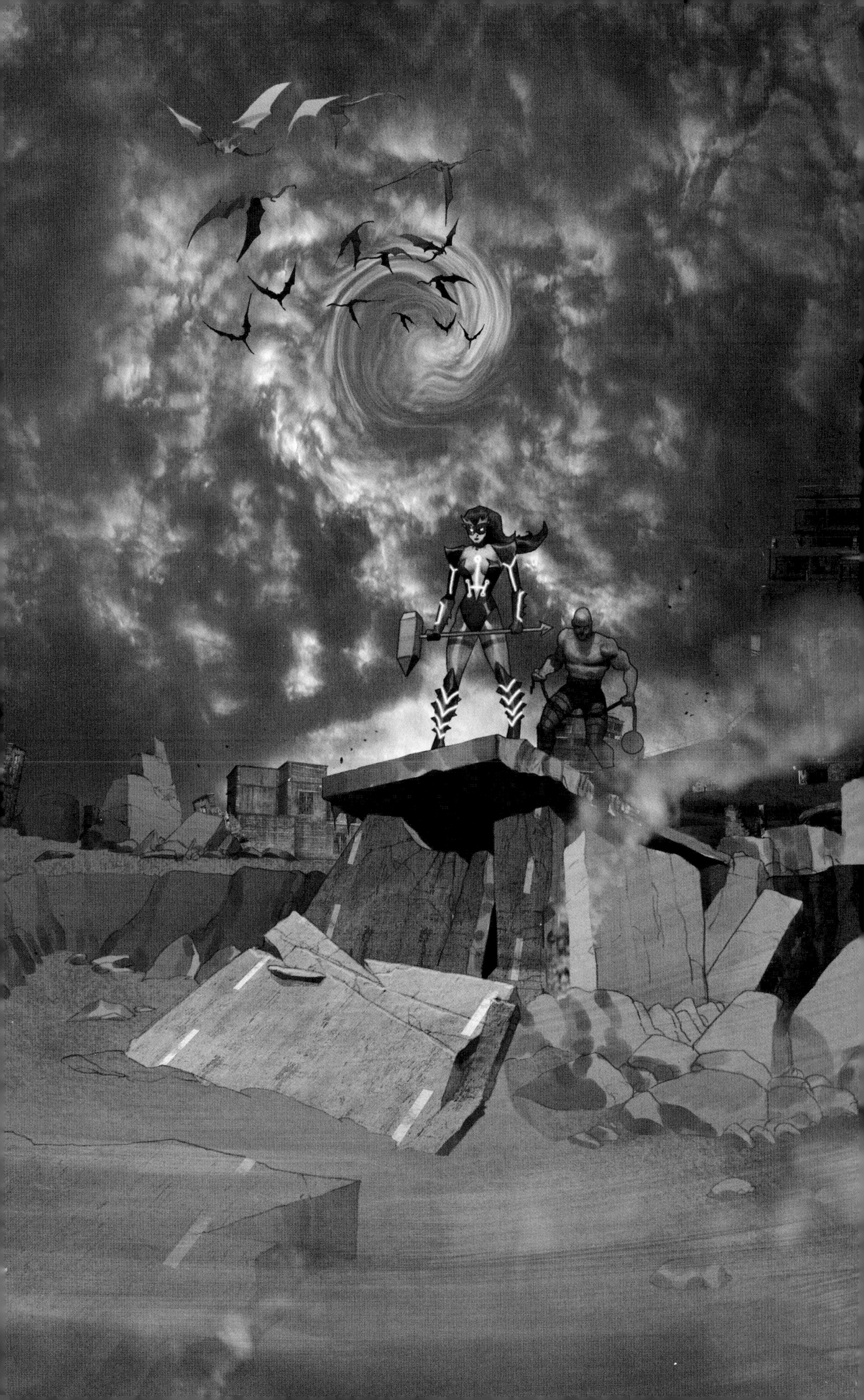

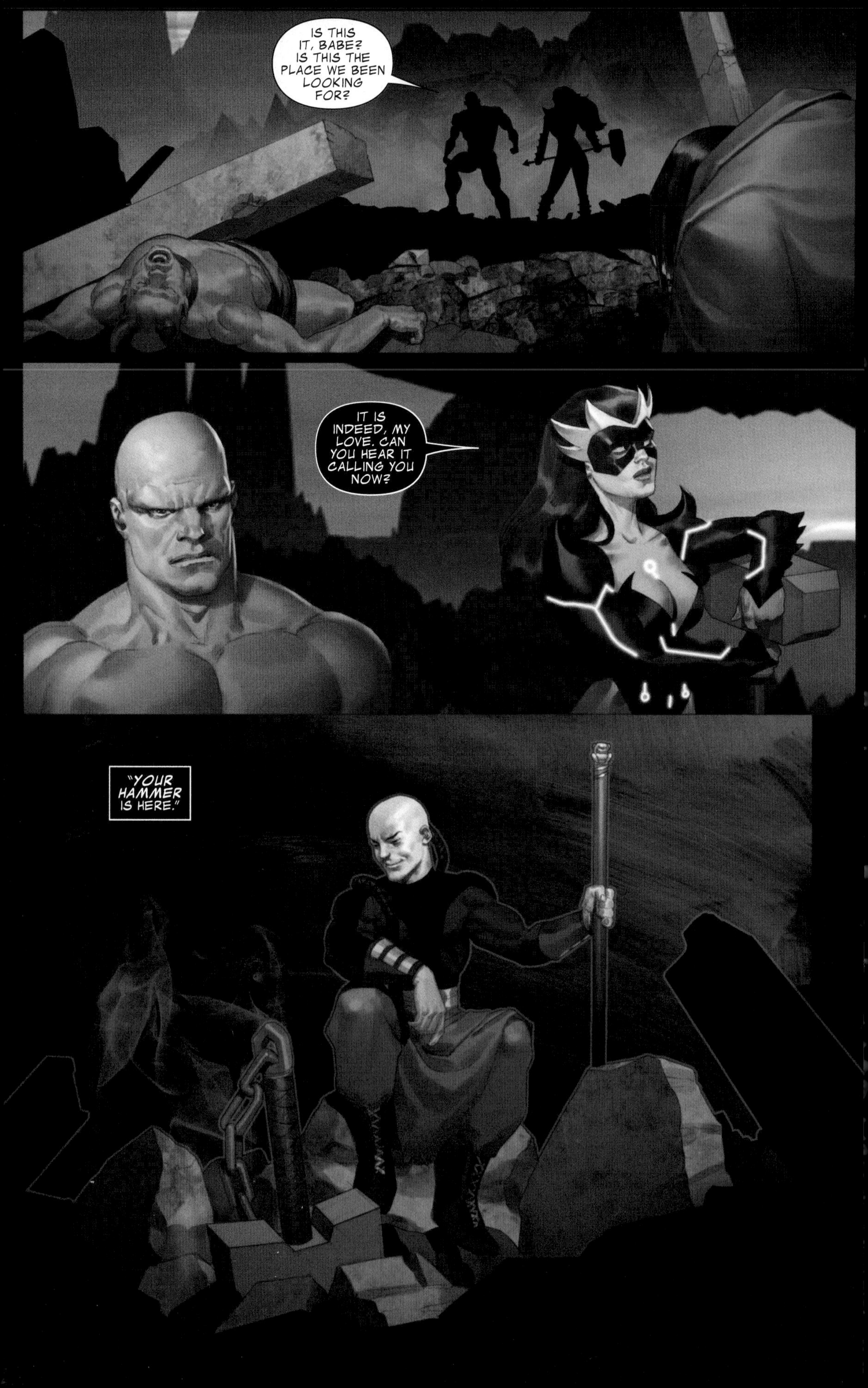
IS THIS IT, BABE? IS THIS THE PLACE WE BEEN LOOKING FOR?
IT IS INDEED, MY LOVE. CAN YOU HEAR IT CALLING YOU NOW?
"YOUR HAMMER IS HERE."

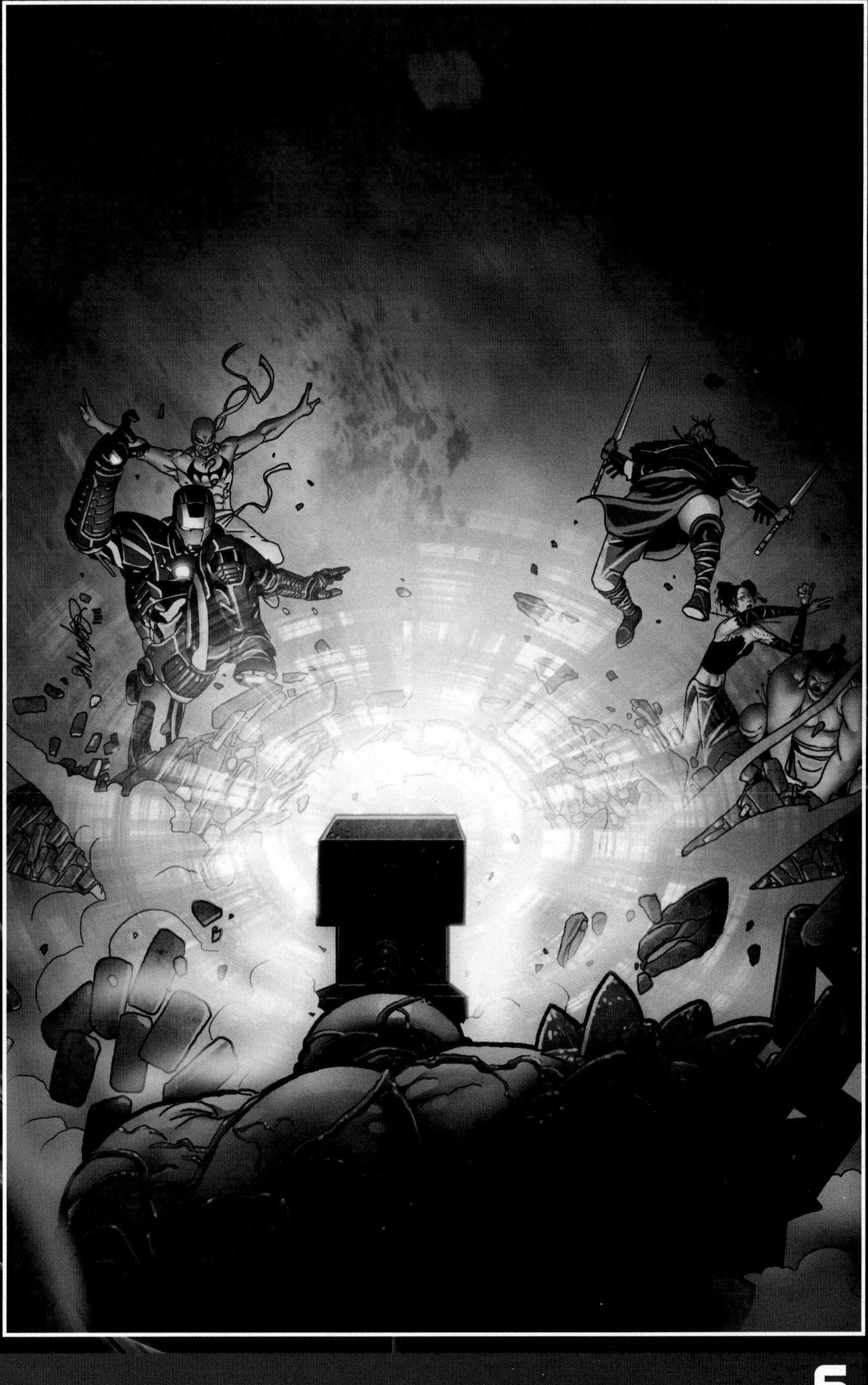

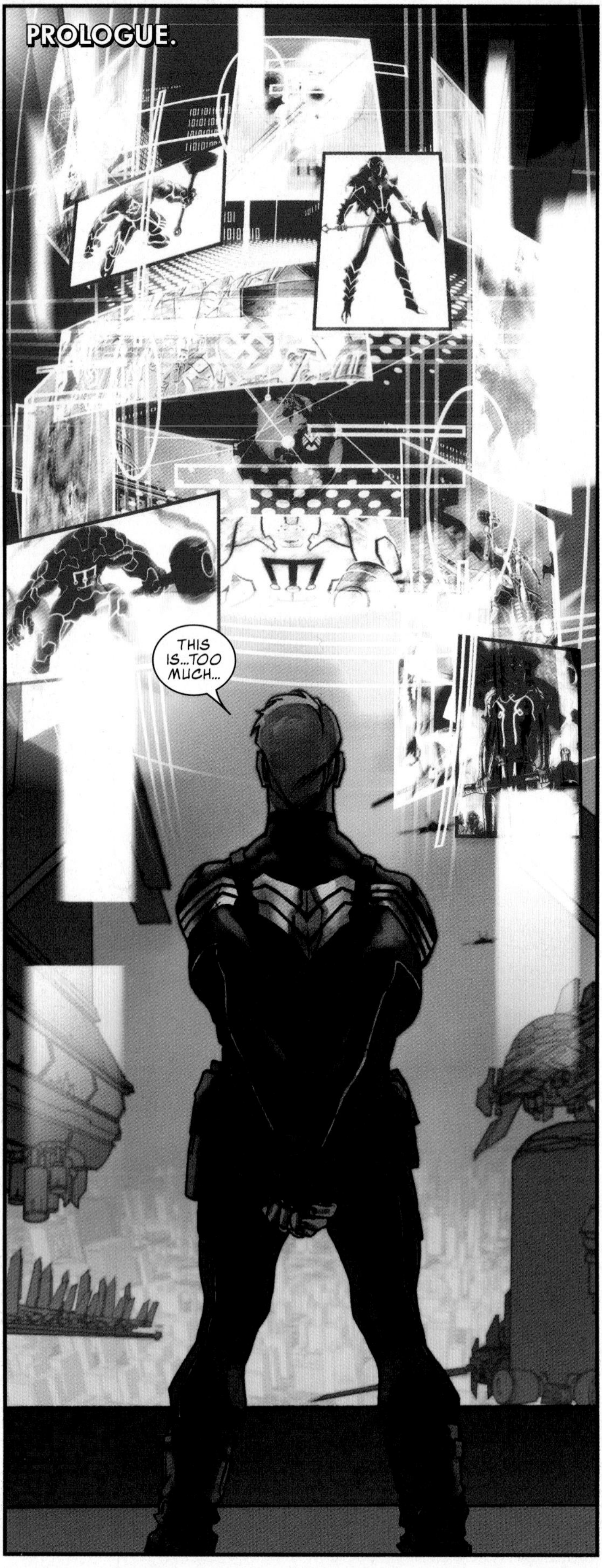
PROLOGUE.
THIS IS...TOO MUCH...

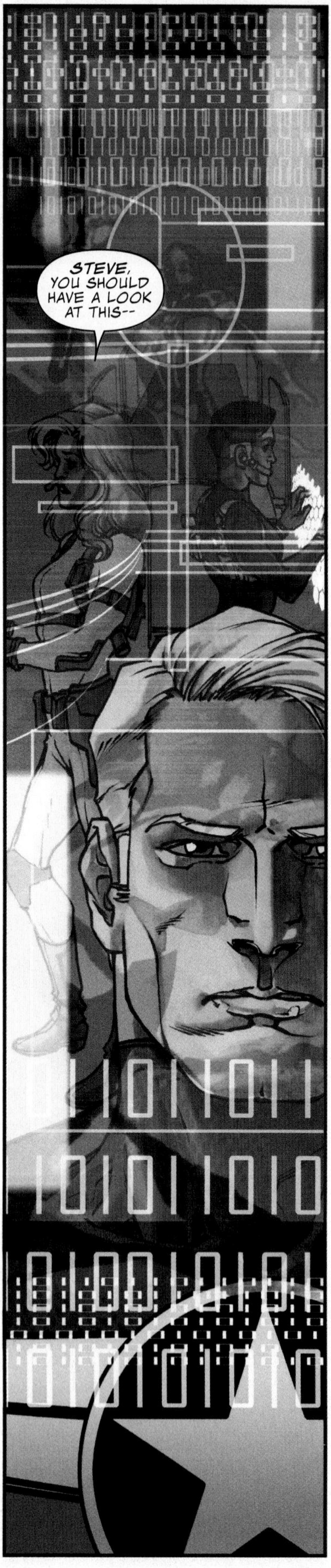
STEVE, YOU SHOULD HAVE A LOOK AT THIS--

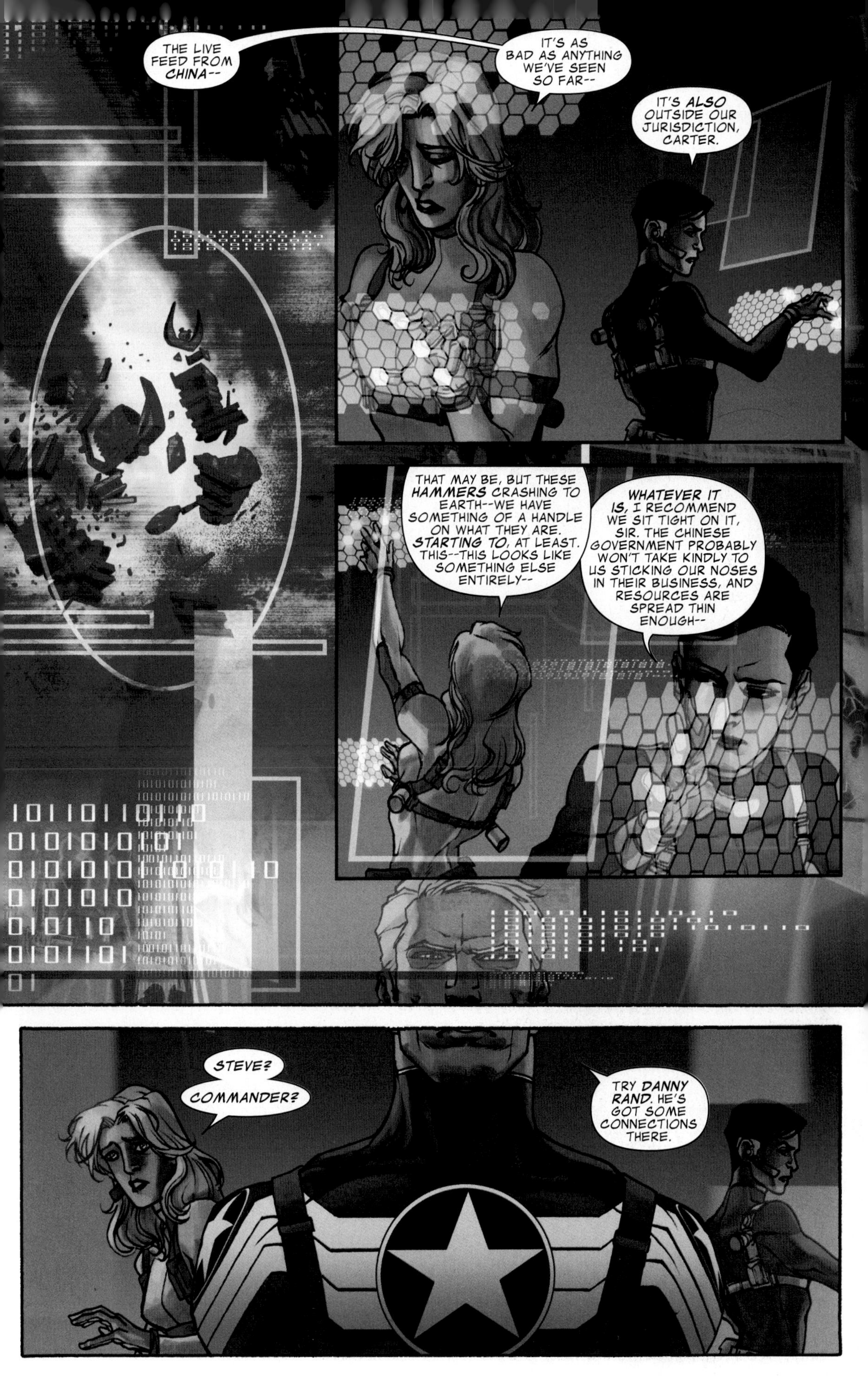

THE LIVE FEED FROM CHINA--
IT'S AS BAD AS ANYTHING WE'VE SEEN SO FAR--
IT'S ALSO OUTSIDE OUR JURISDICTION, CARTER.
THAT MAY BE, BUT THESE HAMMERS CRASHING TO EARTH--WE HAVE SOMETHING OF A HANDLE ON WHAT THEY ARE. STARTING TO, AT LEAST. THIS--THIS LOOKS LIKE SOMETHING ELSE ENTIRELY--
WHATEVER IT IS, I RECOMMEND WE SIT TIGHT ON IT, SIR. THE CHINESE GOVERNMENT PROBABLY WON'T TAKE KINDLY TO US STICKING OUR NOSES IN THEIR BUSINESS, AND RESOURCES ARE SPREAD THIN ENOUGH--
STEVE?
COMMANDER?
TRY DANNY RAND. HE'S GOT SOME CONNECTIONS THERE.

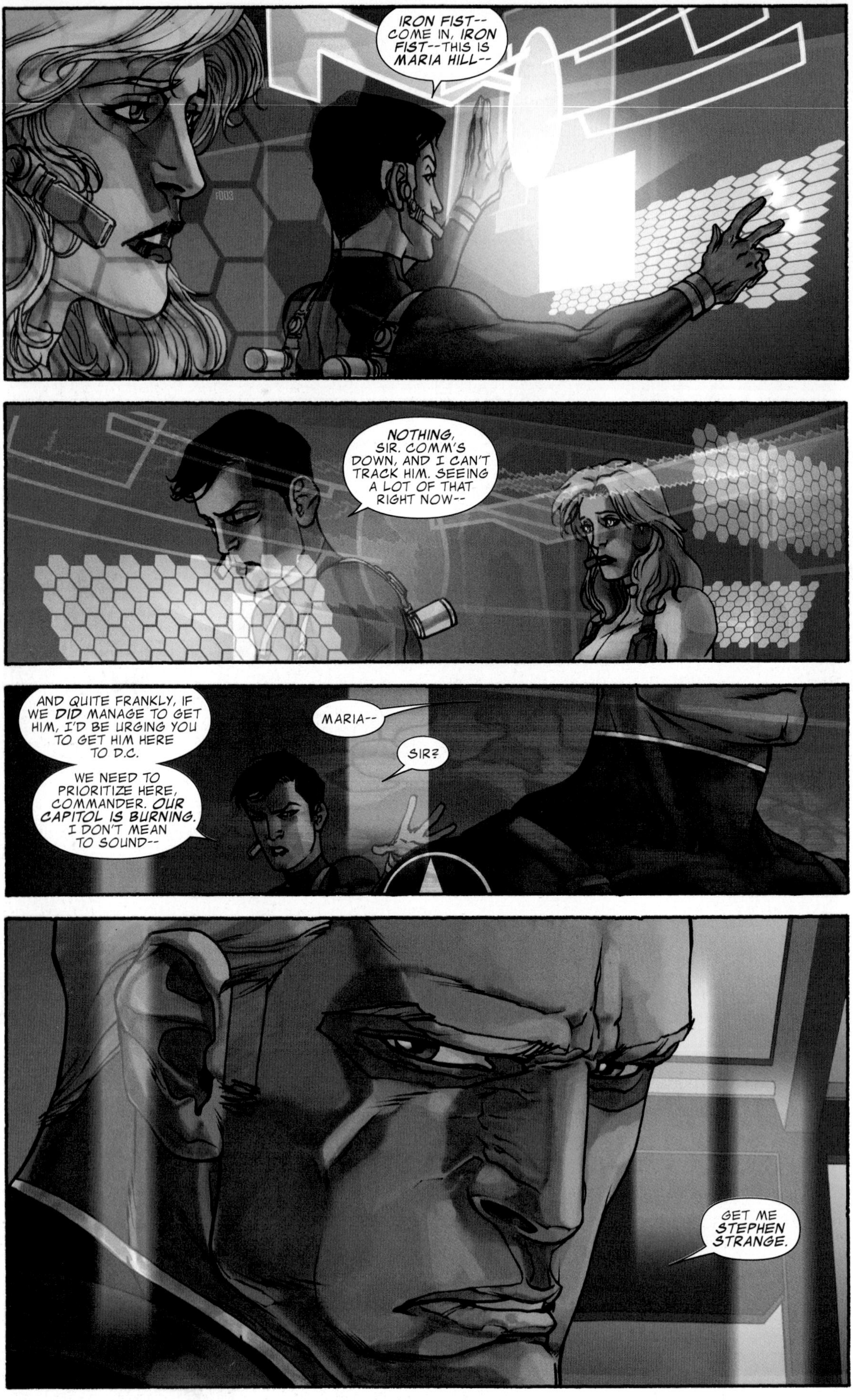
IRON FIST--COME IN, IRON FIST--THIS IS MARIA HILL--
NOTHING, SIR. COMM'S DOWN, AND I CAN'T TRACK HIM. SEEING A LOT OF THAT RIGHT NOW--
AND QUITE FRANKLY, IF WE DID MANAGE TO GET HIM, I'D BE URGING YOU TO GET HIM HERE TO D.C.
WE NEED TO PRIORITIZE HERE, COMMANDER. OUR CAPITOL IS BURNING. I DON'T MEAN TO SOUND--
MARIA--
SIR?
GET ME STEPHEN STRANGE.

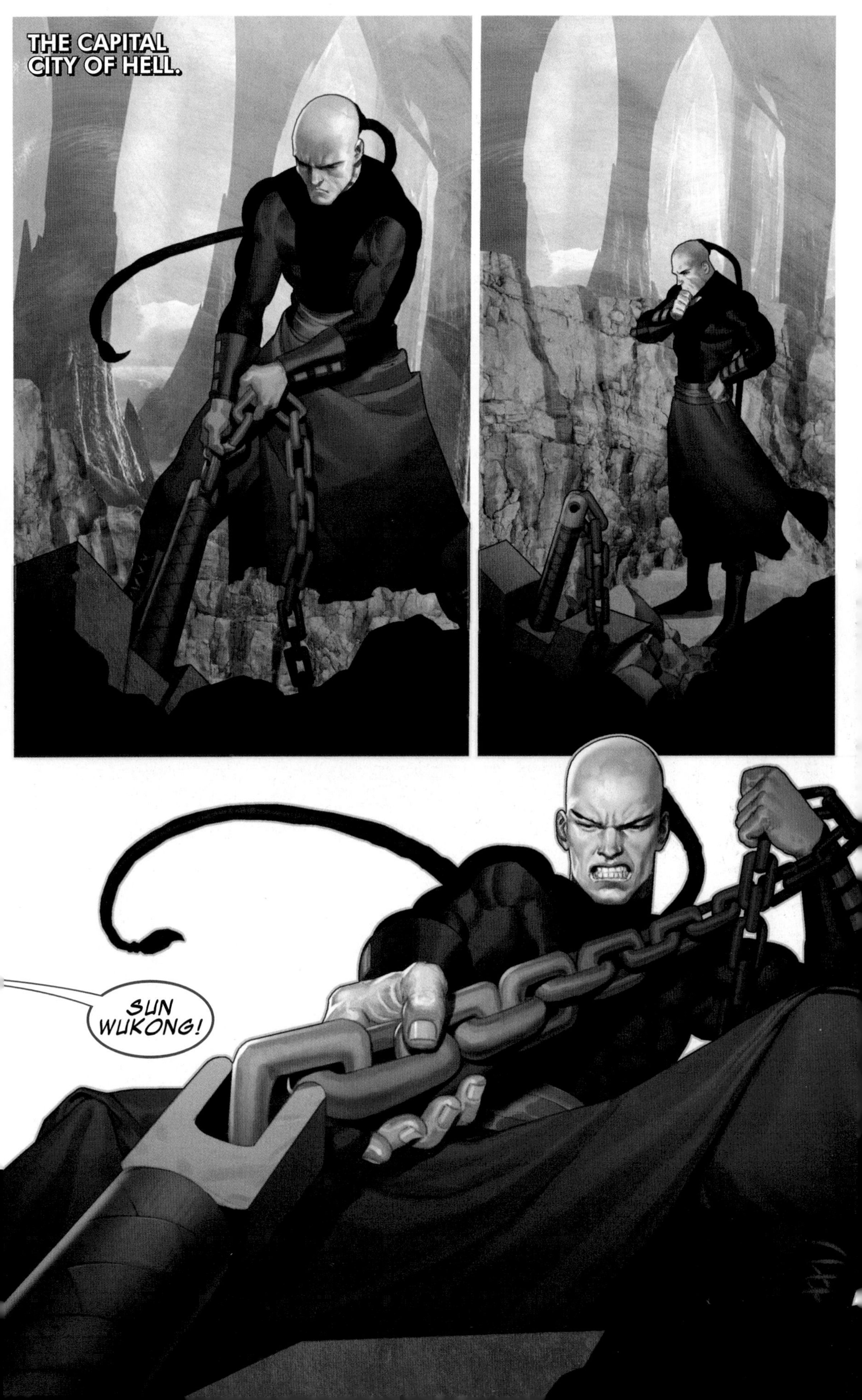
THE CAPITAL CITY OF HELL.
SUN WUKONG!

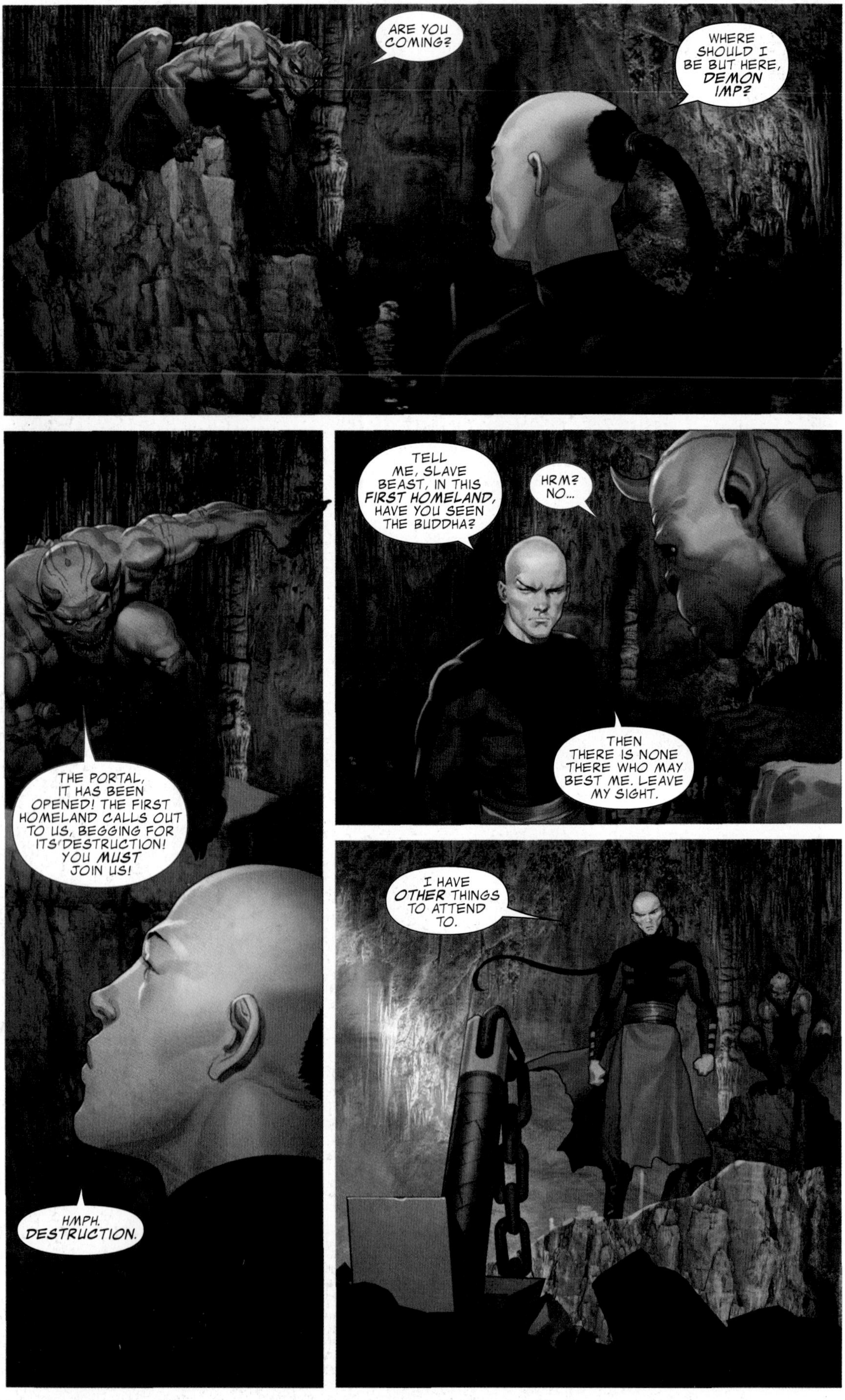
ARE YOU COMING?
WHERE SHOULD I BE BUT HERE, DEMON IMP?
THE PORTAL, IT HAS BEEN OPENED! THE FIRST HOMELAND CALLS OUT TO US, BEGGING FOR ITS DESTRUCTION! YOU MUST JOIN US!
HMPH. DESTRUCTION.
TELL ME, SLAVE BEAST, IN THIS FIRST HOMELAND, HAVE YOU SEEN THE BUDDHA?
HRM? NO...
THEN THERE IS NONE THERE WHO MAY BEST ME. LEAVE MY SIGHT.
I HAVE OTHER THINGS TO ATTEND TO.

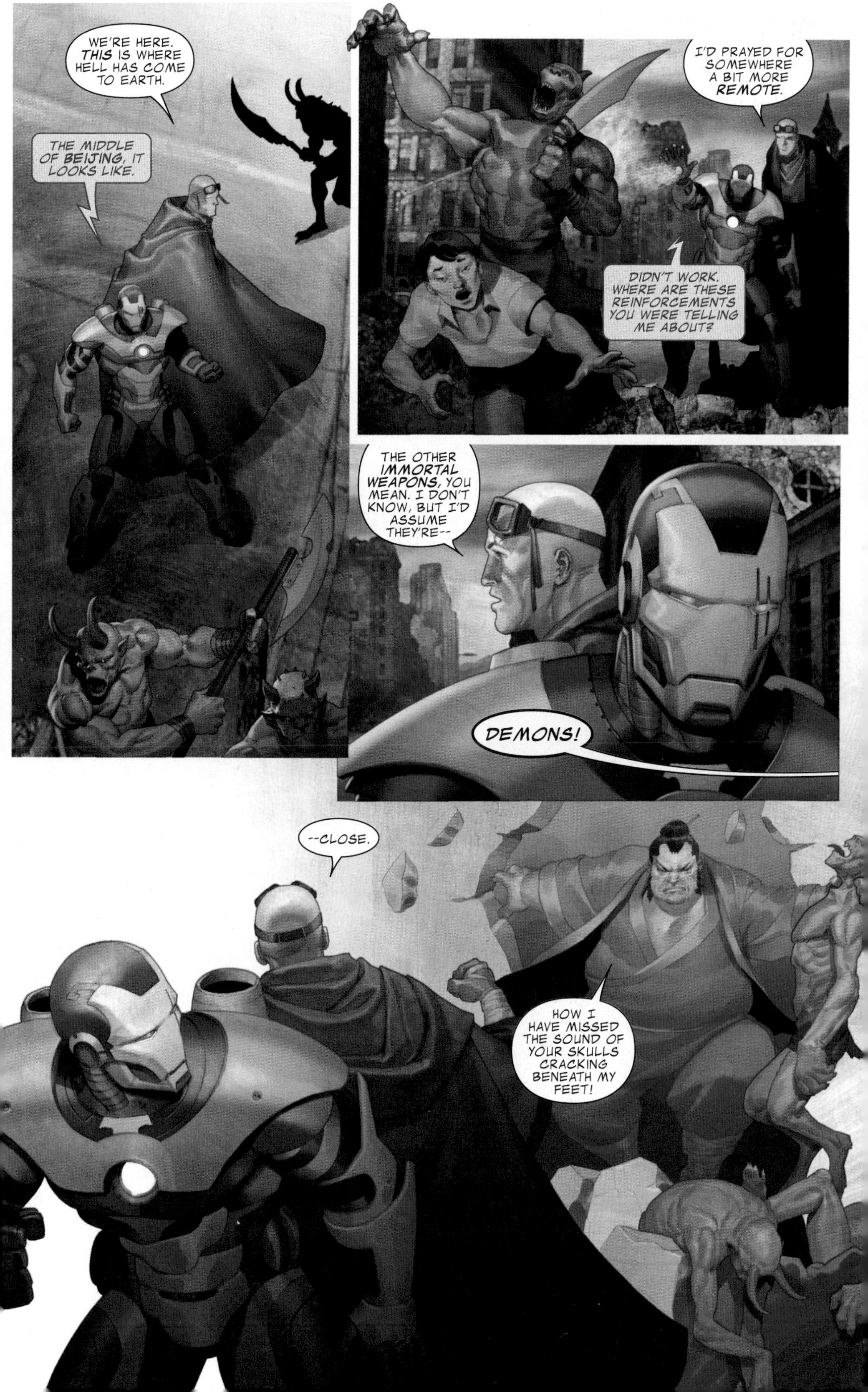
WE'RE HERE. THIS IS WHERE HELL HAS COME TO EARTH.
THE MIDDLE OF BEIJING, IT LOOKS LIKE.
I'D PRAYED FOR SOMEWHERE A BIT MORE REMOTE.
DIDN'T WORK. WHERE ARE THESE REINFORCEMENTS YOU WERE TELLING ME ABOUT?
THE OTHER IMMORTAL WEAPONS, YOU MEAN. I DON'T KNOW, BUT I'D ASSUME THEY'RE--
DEMONS!
--CLOSE.
HOW I HAVE MISSED THE SOUND OF YOUR SKULLS CRACKING BENEATH MY FEET!

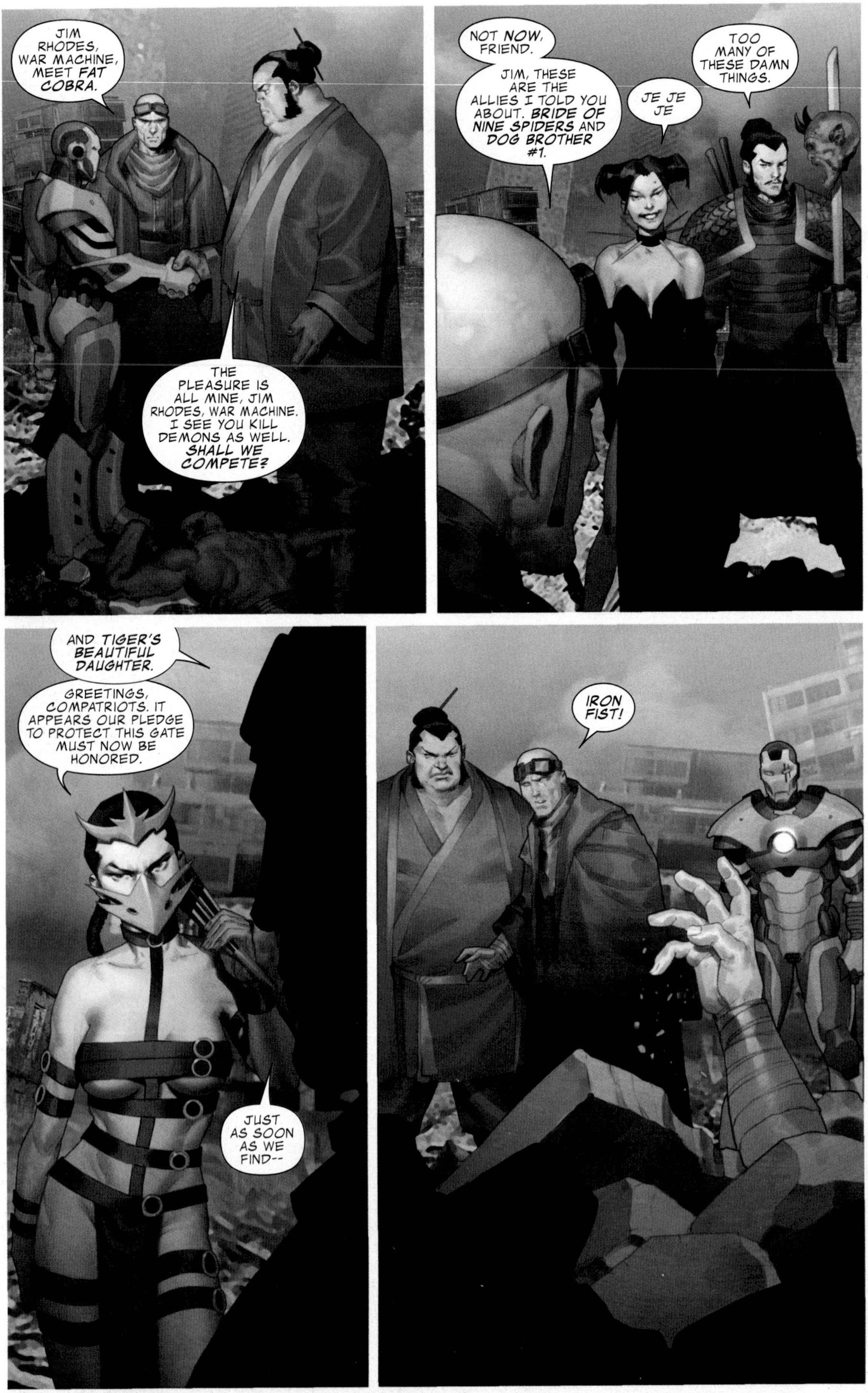
JIM RHODES, WAR MACHINE, MEET FAT COBRA.
THE PLEASURE IS ALL MINE, JIM RHODES, WAR MACHINE. I SEE YOU KILL DEMONS AS WELL. SHALL WE COMPETE?
NOT NOW, FRIEND.
JIM, THESE ARE THE ALLIES I TOLD YOU ABOUT. BRIDE OF NINE SPIDERS AND DOG BROTHER #1.
JE JE JE
TOO MANY OF THESE DAMN THINGS.
AND TIGER'S BEAUTIFUL DAUGHTER.
GREETINGS, COMPATRIOTS. IT APPEARS OUR PLEDGE TO PROTECT THIS GATE MUST NOW BE HONORED.
JUST AS SOON AS WE FIND--
IRON FIST!

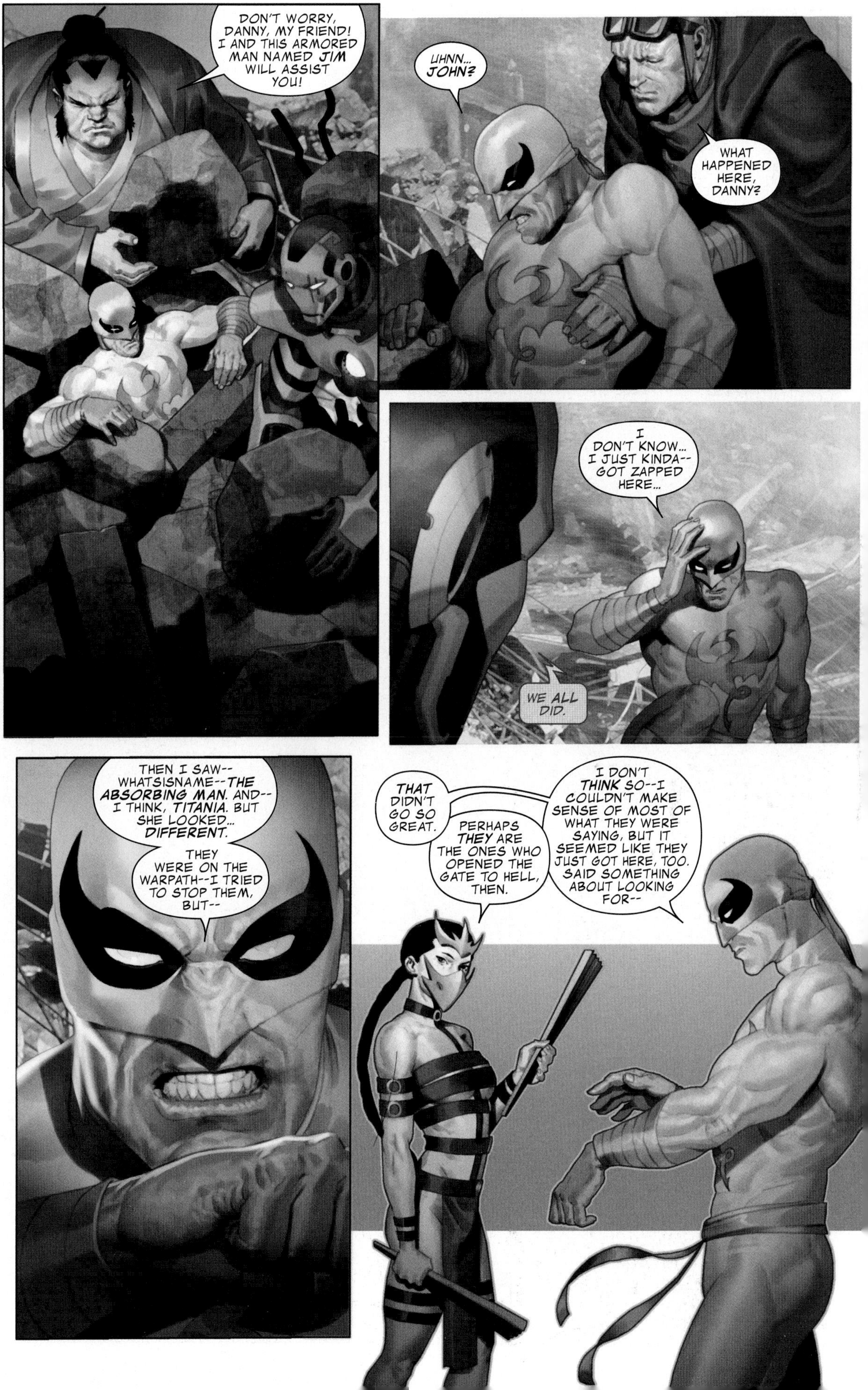
DON'T WORRY, DANNY, MY FRIEND! I AND THIS ARMORED MAN NAMED JIM WILL ASSIST YOU!
UHNN... JOHN?
WHAT HAPPENED HERE, DANNY?
I DON'T KNOW... I JUST KINDA-- GOT ZAPPED HERE...
WE ALL DID.
THEN I SAW-- WHATSISNAME--THE ABSORBING MAN. AND-- I THINK, TITANIA. BUT SHE LOOKED... DIFFERENT.
THEY WERE ON THE WARPATH--I TRIED TO STOP THEM, BUT--
THAT DIDN'T GO SO GREAT.
PERHAPS THEY ARE THE ONES WHO OPENED THE GATE TO HELL, THEN.
I DON'T THINK SO--I COULDN'T MAKE SENSE OF MOST OF WHAT THEY WERE SAYING, BUT IT SEEMED LIKE THEY JUST GOT HERE, TOO. SAID SOMETHING ABOUT LOOKING FOR--

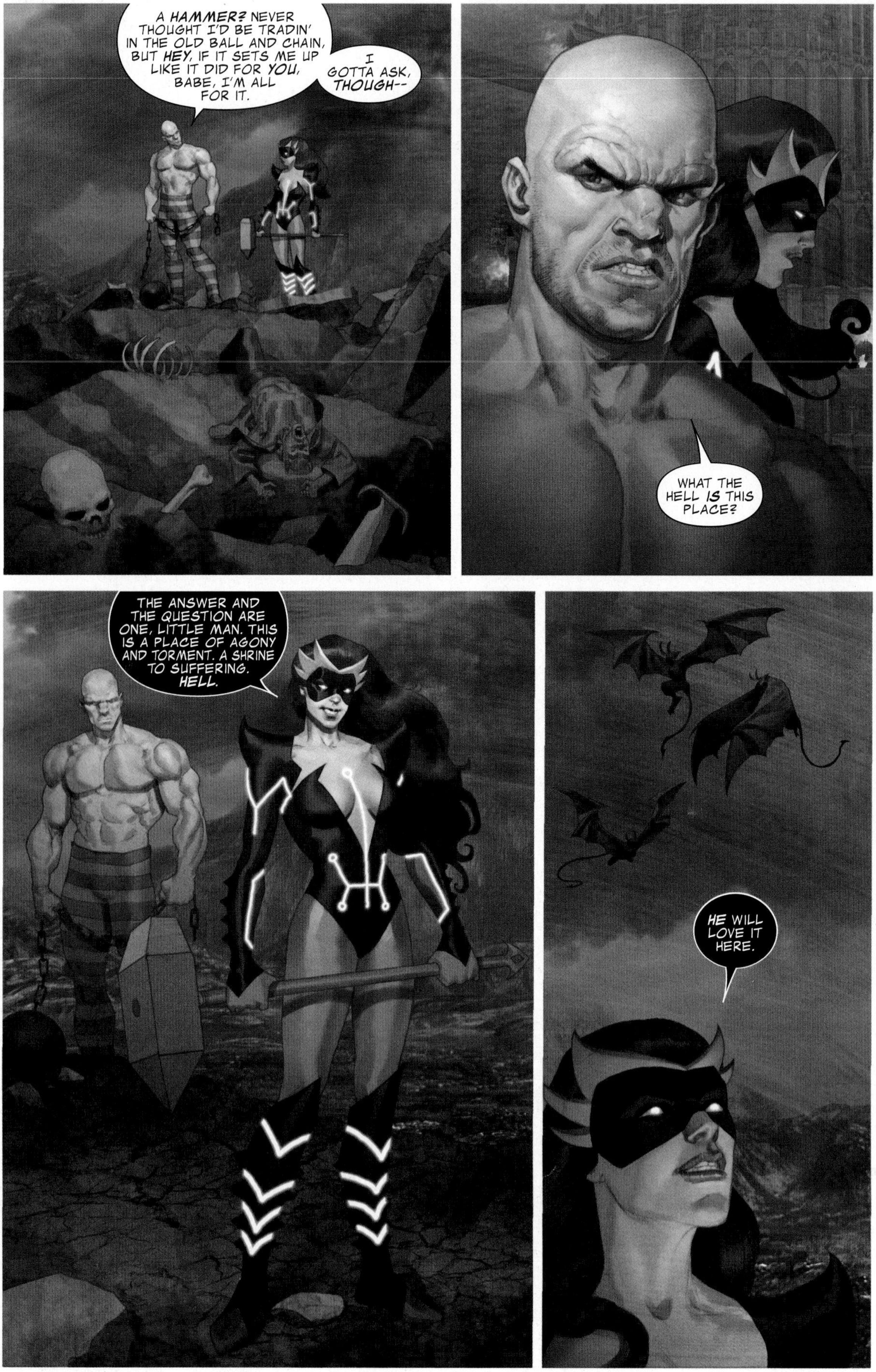

A HAMMER? NEVER THOUGHT I'D BE TRADIN' IN THE OLD BALL AND CHAIN, BUT HEY, IF IT SETS ME UP LIKE IT DID FOR YOU, BABE, I'M ALL FOR IT.
I GOTTA ASK, THOUGH--
WHAT THE HELL IS THIS PLACE?
THE ANSWER AND THE QUESTION ARE ONE, LITTLE MAN. THIS IS A PLACE OF AGONY AND TORMENT. A SHRINE TO SUFFERING. HELL.
HE WILL LOVE IT HERE.

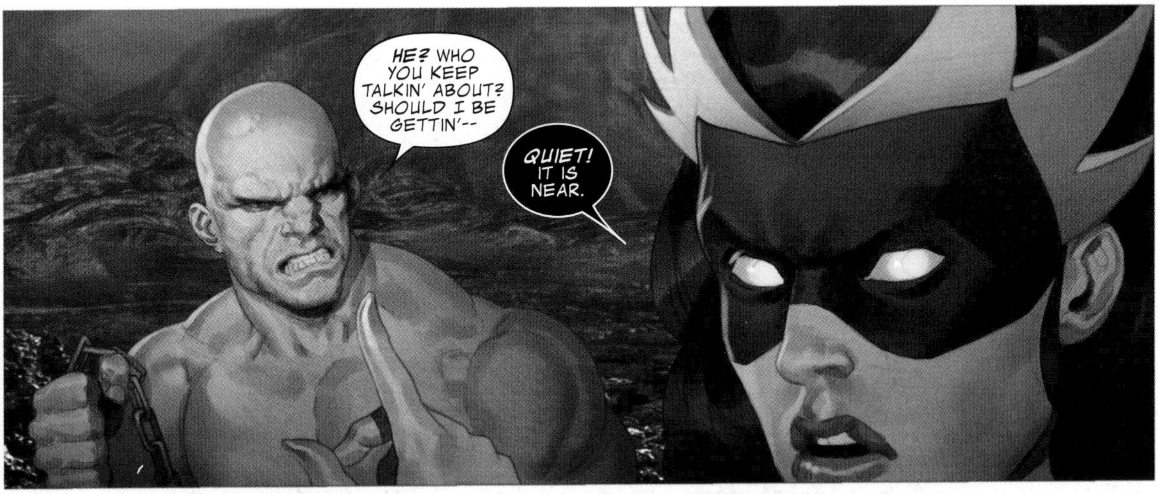
HE? WHO YOU KEEP TALKIN' ABOUT? SHOULD I BE GETTIN'--
QUIET! IT IS NEAR.

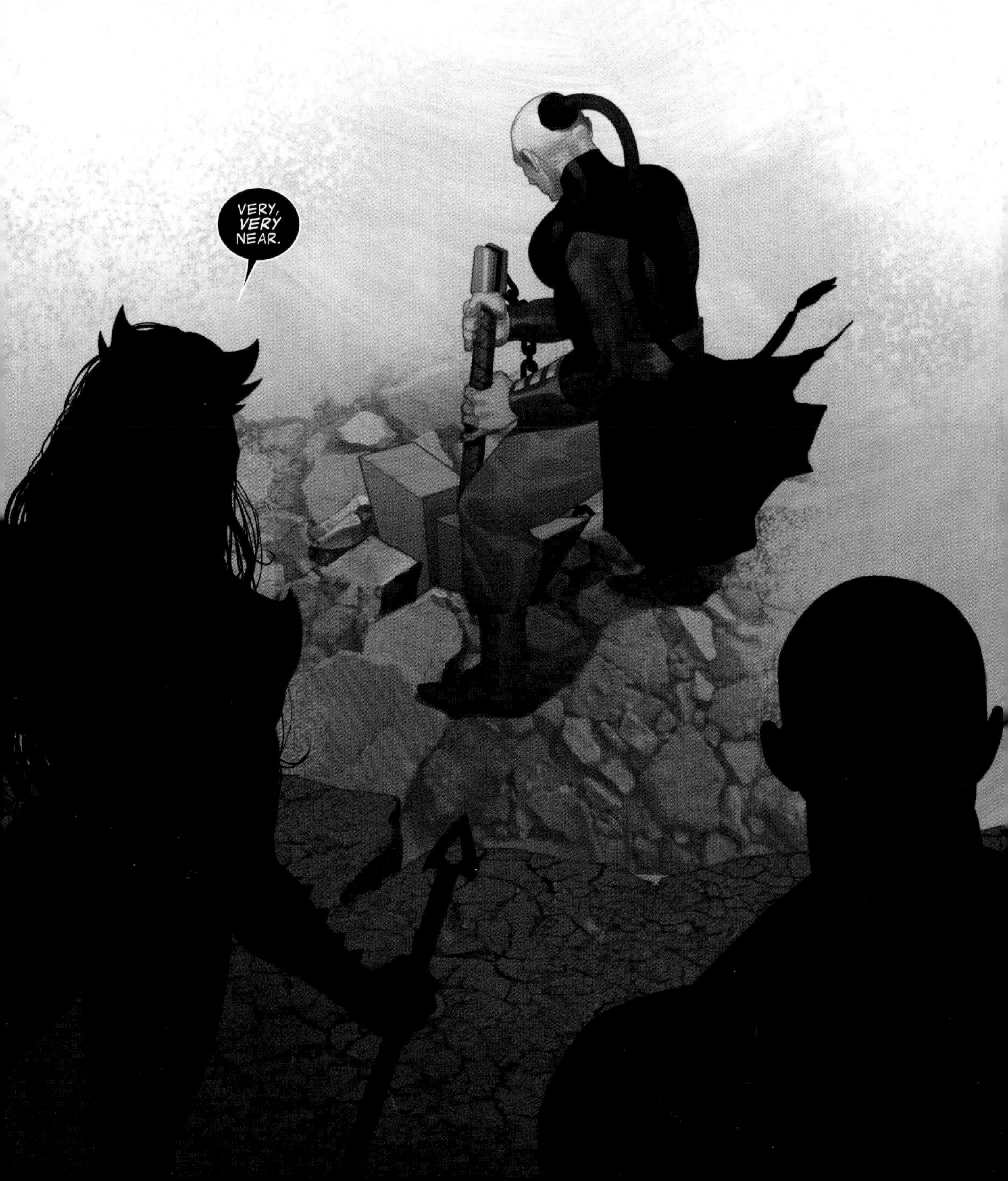
VERY, VERY NEAR.

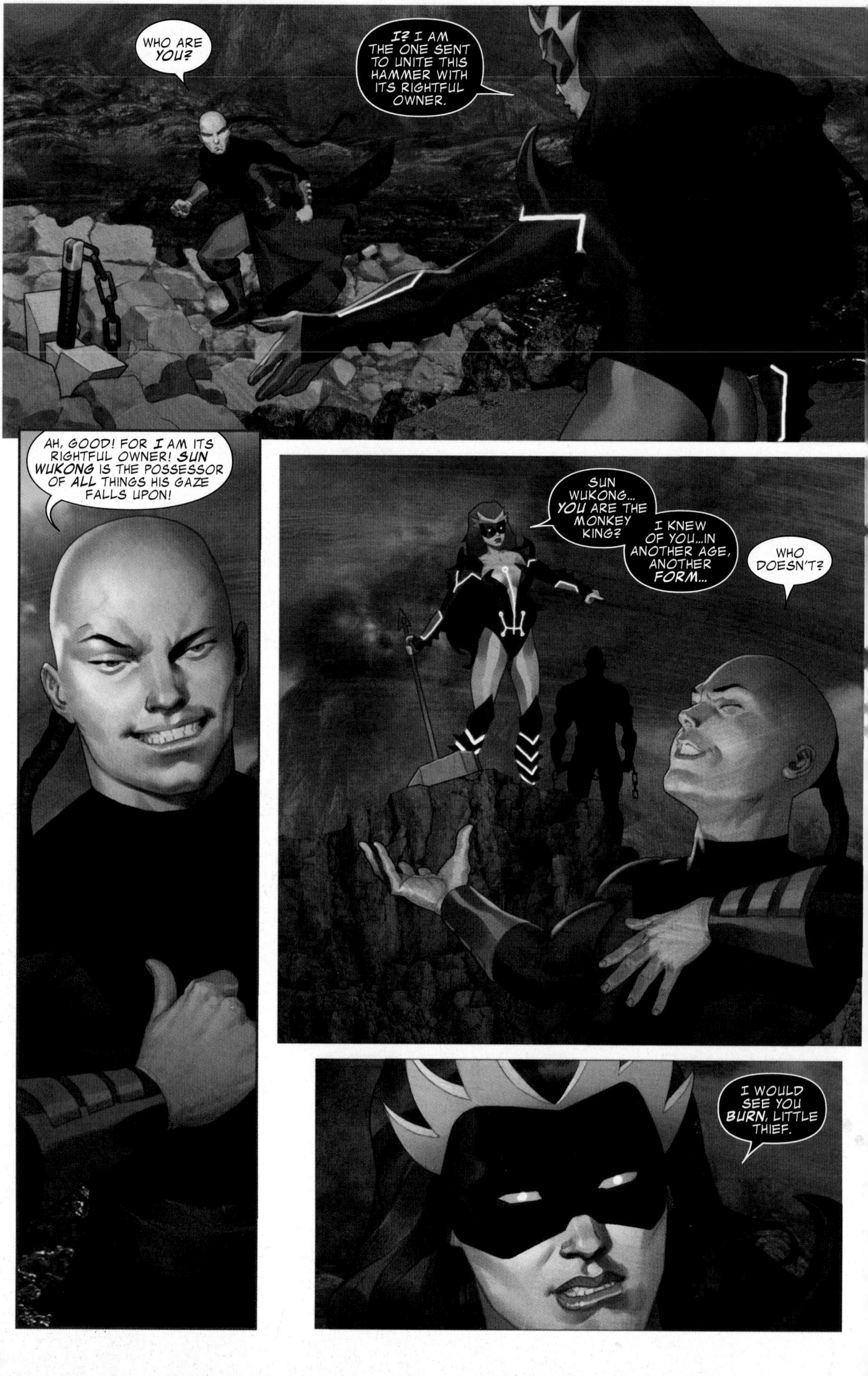
WHO ARE YOU?
I? I AM THE ONE SENT TO UNITE THIS HAMMER WITH ITS RIGHTFUL OWNER.
AH, GOOD! FOR I AM ITS RIGHTFUL OWNER! SUN WUKONG IS THE POSSESSOR OF ALL THINGS HIS GAZE FALLS UPON!
SUN WUKONG... YOU ARE THE MONKEY KING?
I KNEW OF YOU...IN ANOTHER AGE, ANOTHER FORM...
WHO DOESN'T?
I WOULD SEE YOU BURN, LITTLE THIEF.

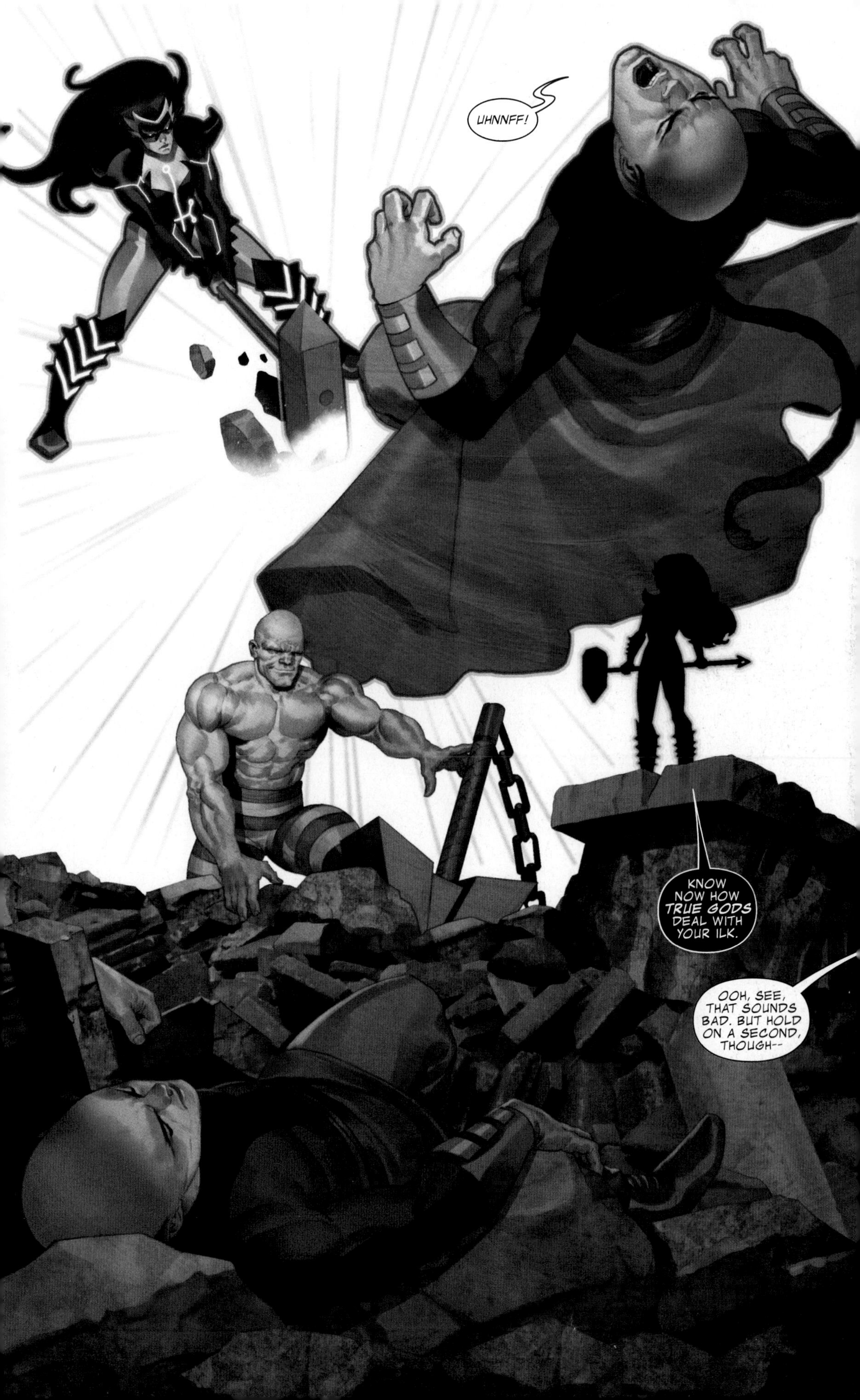
UHNNFF!
KNOW NOW HOW TRUE GODS DEAL WITH YOUR ILK.
OOH, SEE, THAT SOUNDS BAD. BUT HOLD ON A SECOND, THOUGH--

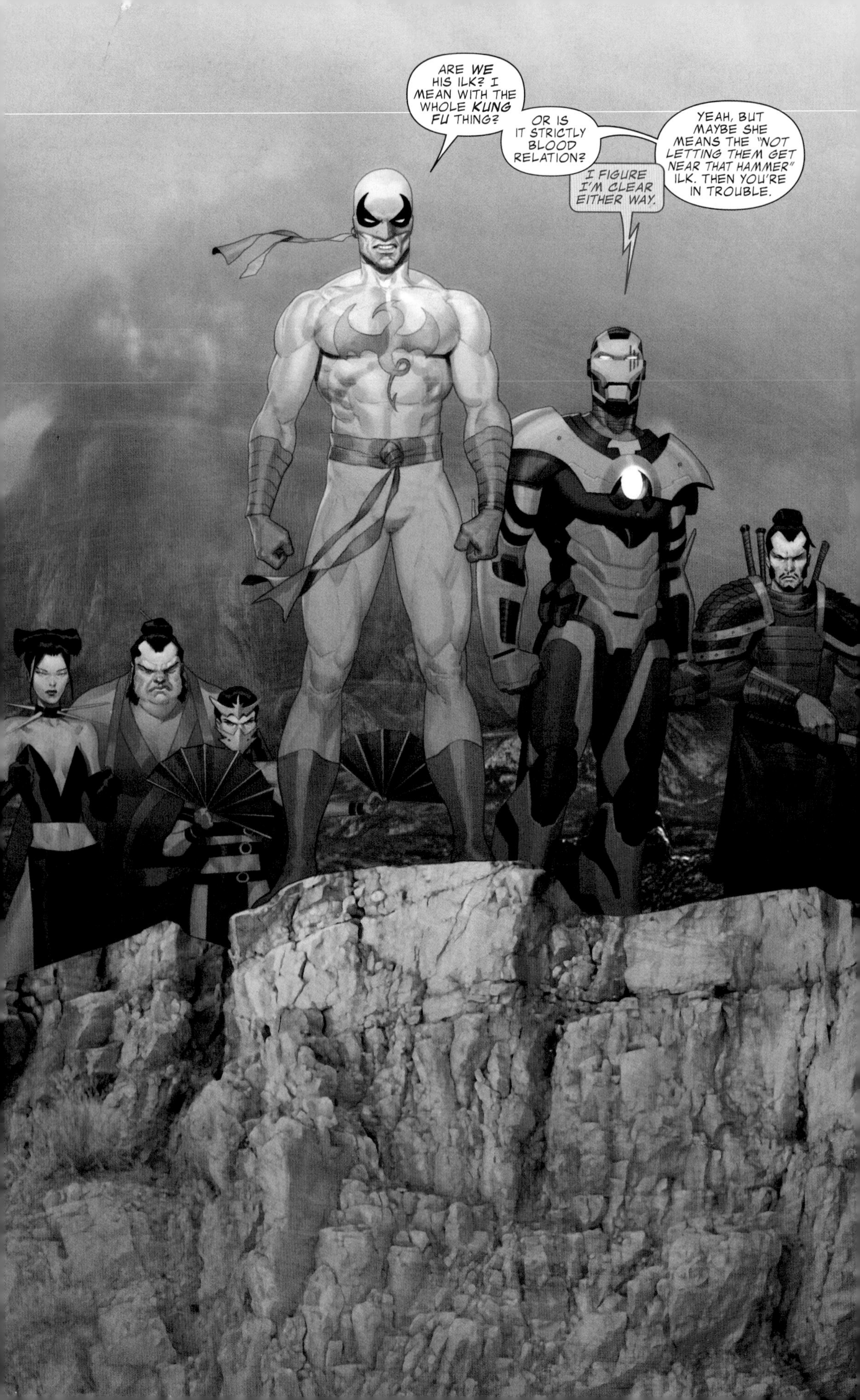
ARE WE HIS ILK? I MEAN WITH THE WHOLE KUNG FU THING?
OR IS IT STRICTLY BLOOD RELATION?
YEAH, BUT MAYBE SHE MEANS THE "NOT LETTING THEM GET NEAR THAT HAMMER" ILK. THEN YOU'RE IN TROUBLE.
I FIGURE I'M CLEAR EITHER WAY.

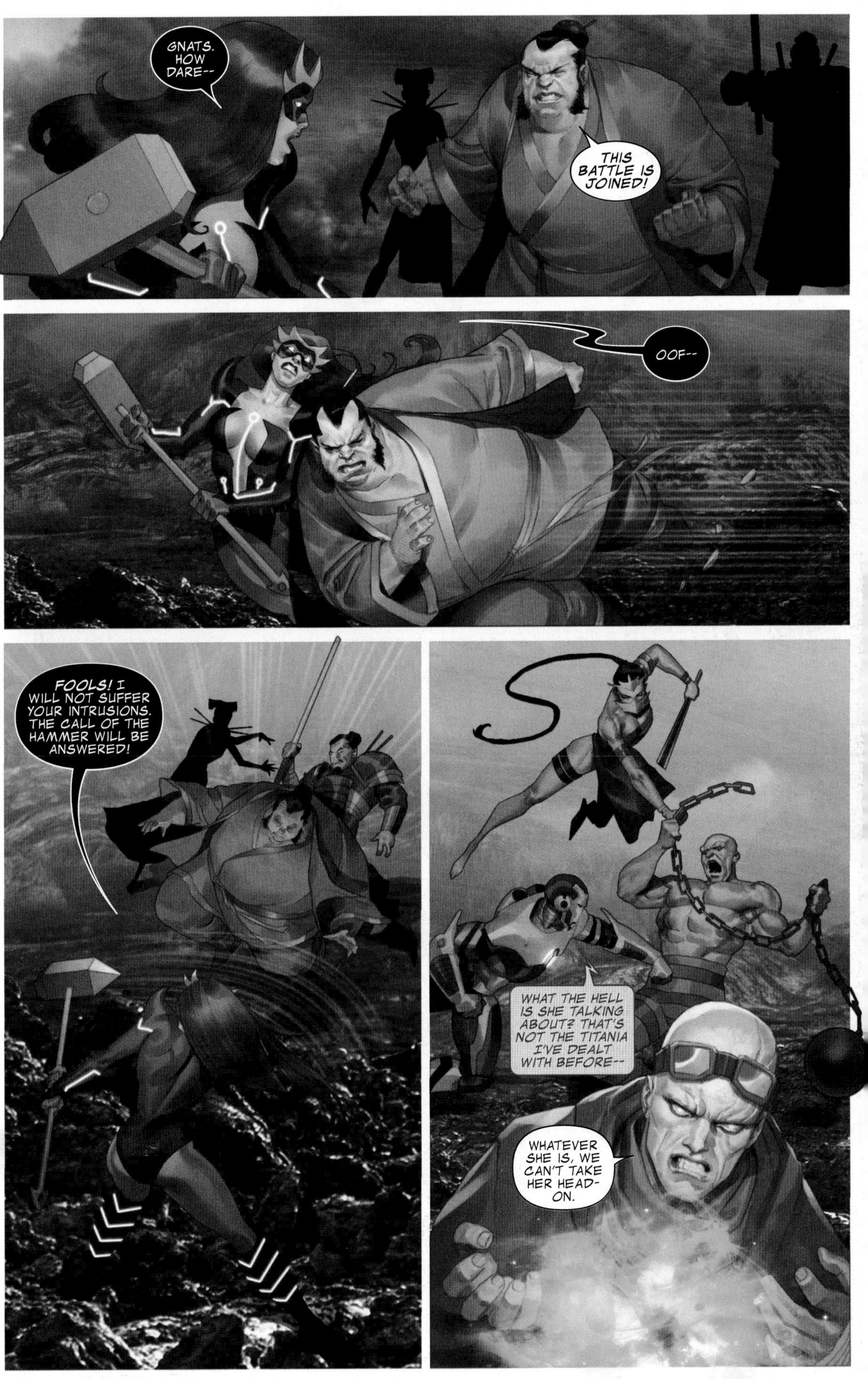
GNATS. HOW DARE--
THIS BATTLE IS JOINED!
OOF--
FOOLS! I WILL NOT SUFFER YOUR INTRUSIONS. THE CALL OF THE HAMMER WILL BE ANSWERED!
WHAT THE HELL IS SHE TALKING ABOUT? THAT'S NOT THE TITANIA I'VE DEALT WITH BEFORE--
WHATEVER SHE IS, WE CAN'T TAKE HER HEAD-ON.

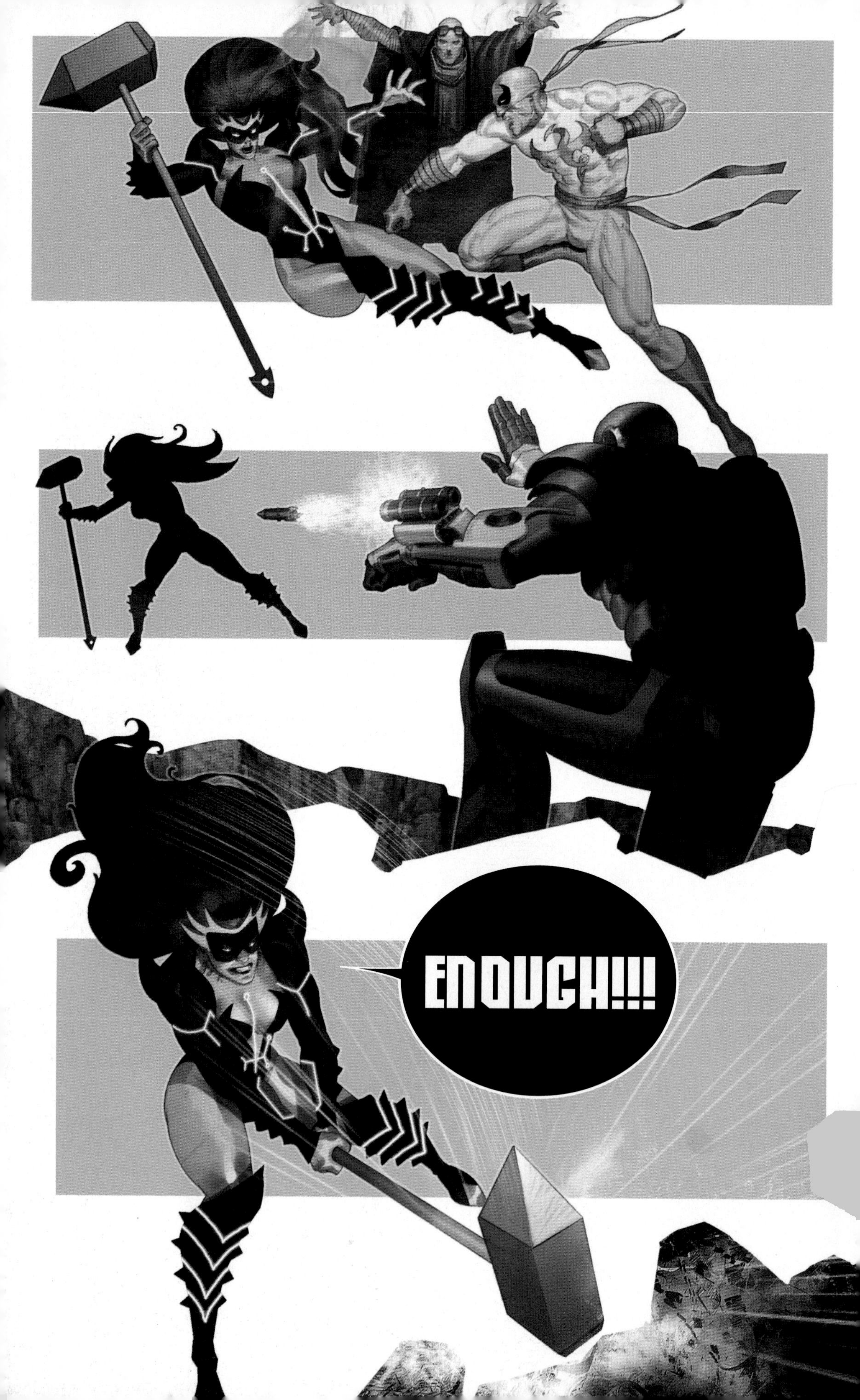
ENOUGH!!!

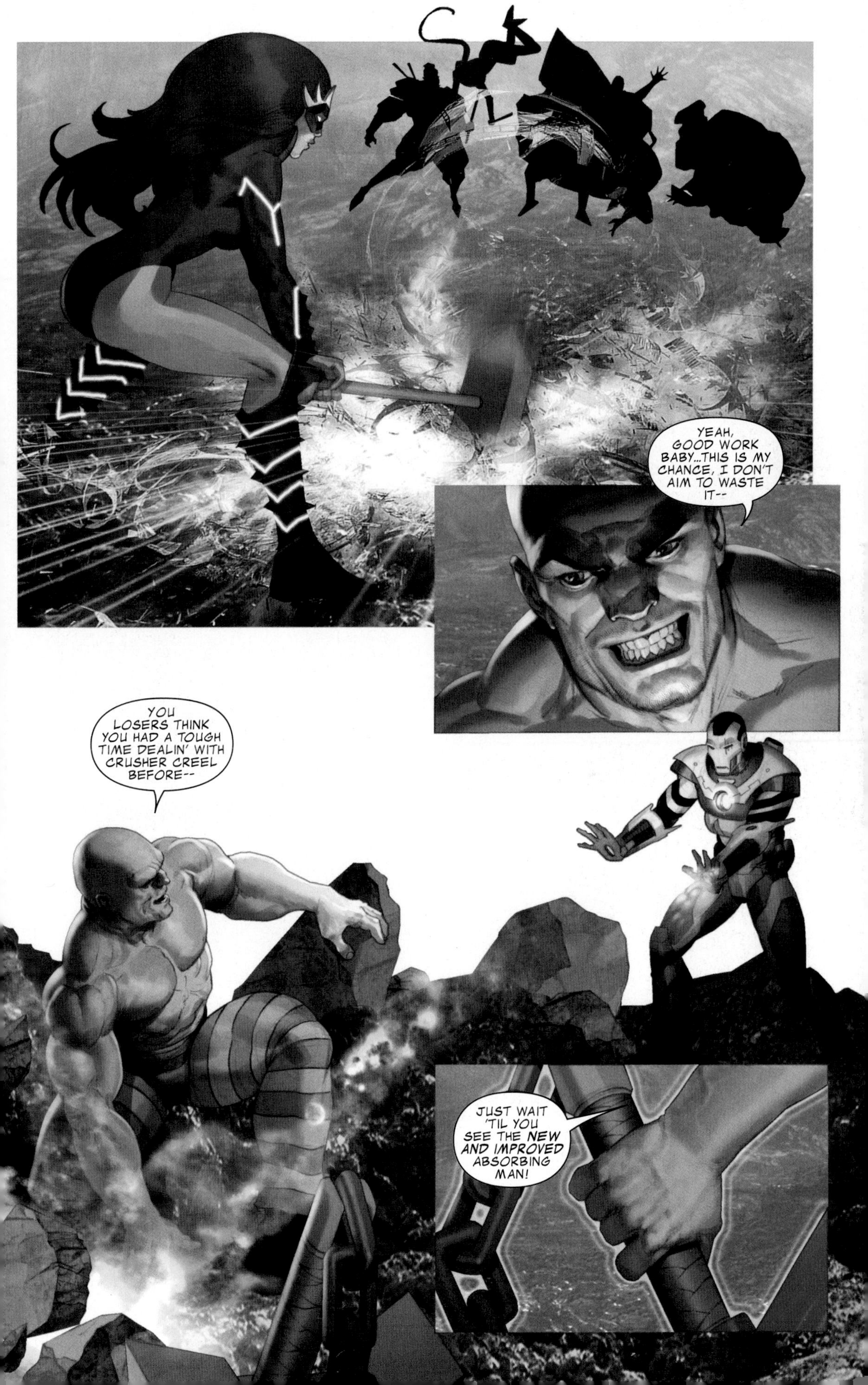
YEAH, GOOD WORK BABY...THIS IS MY CHANCE, I DON'T AIM TO WASTE IT--
YOU LOSERS THINK YOU HAD A TOUGH TIME DEALIN' WITH CRUSHER CREEL BEFORE--
JUST WAIT 'TIL YOU SEE THE NEW AND IMPROVED ABSORBING MAN!

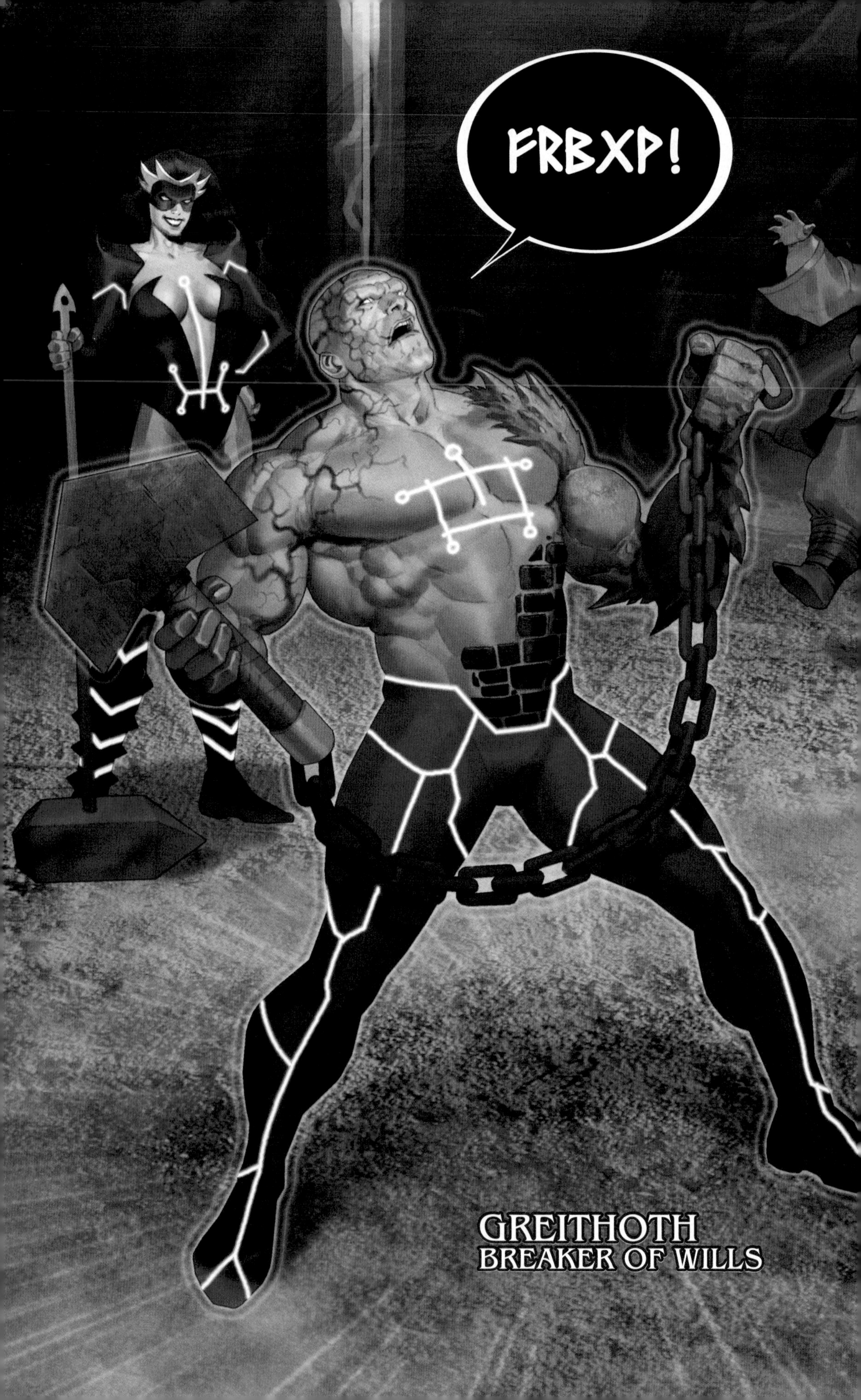
FRBXP!
GREITHOTH
BREAKER OF WILLS

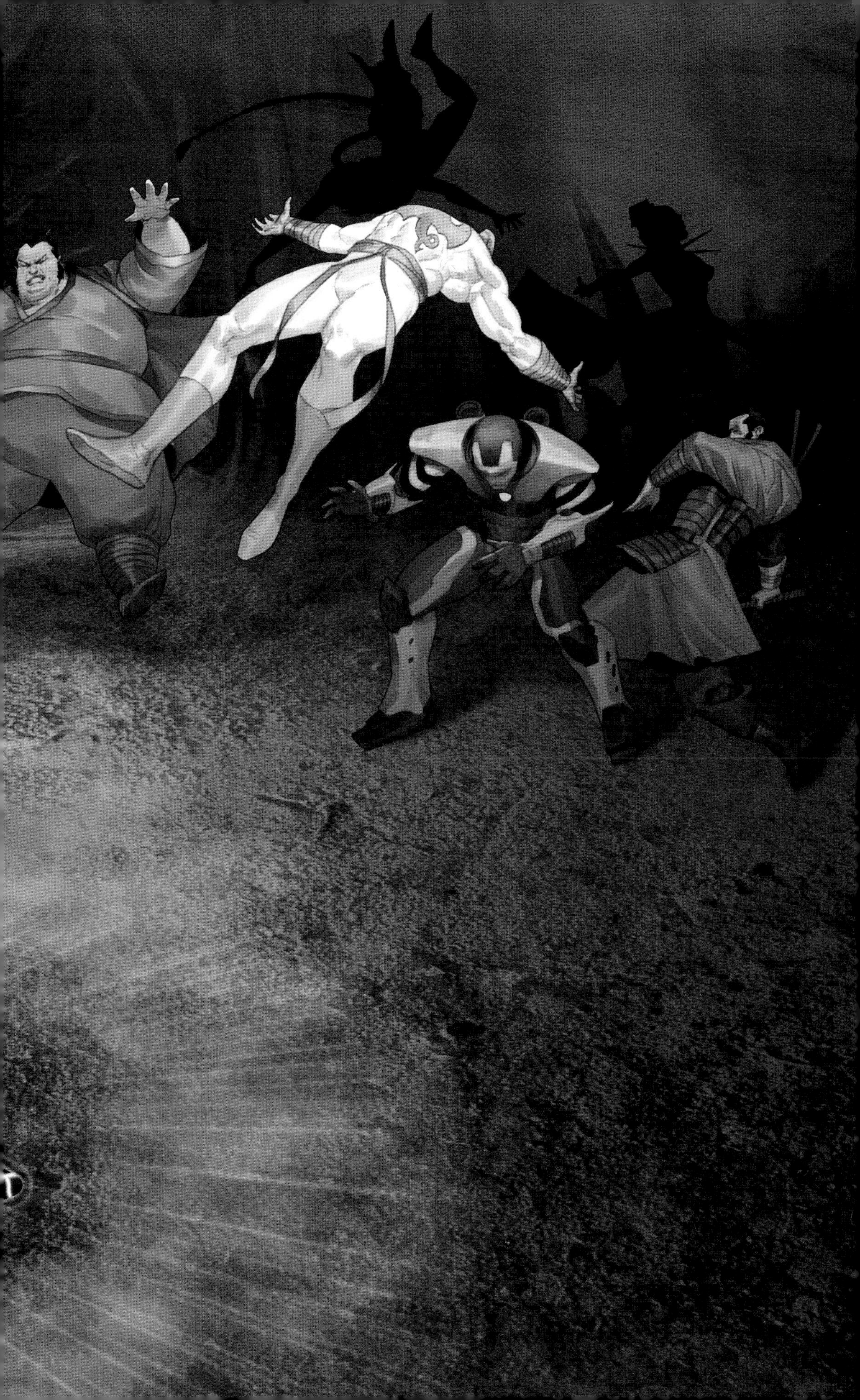

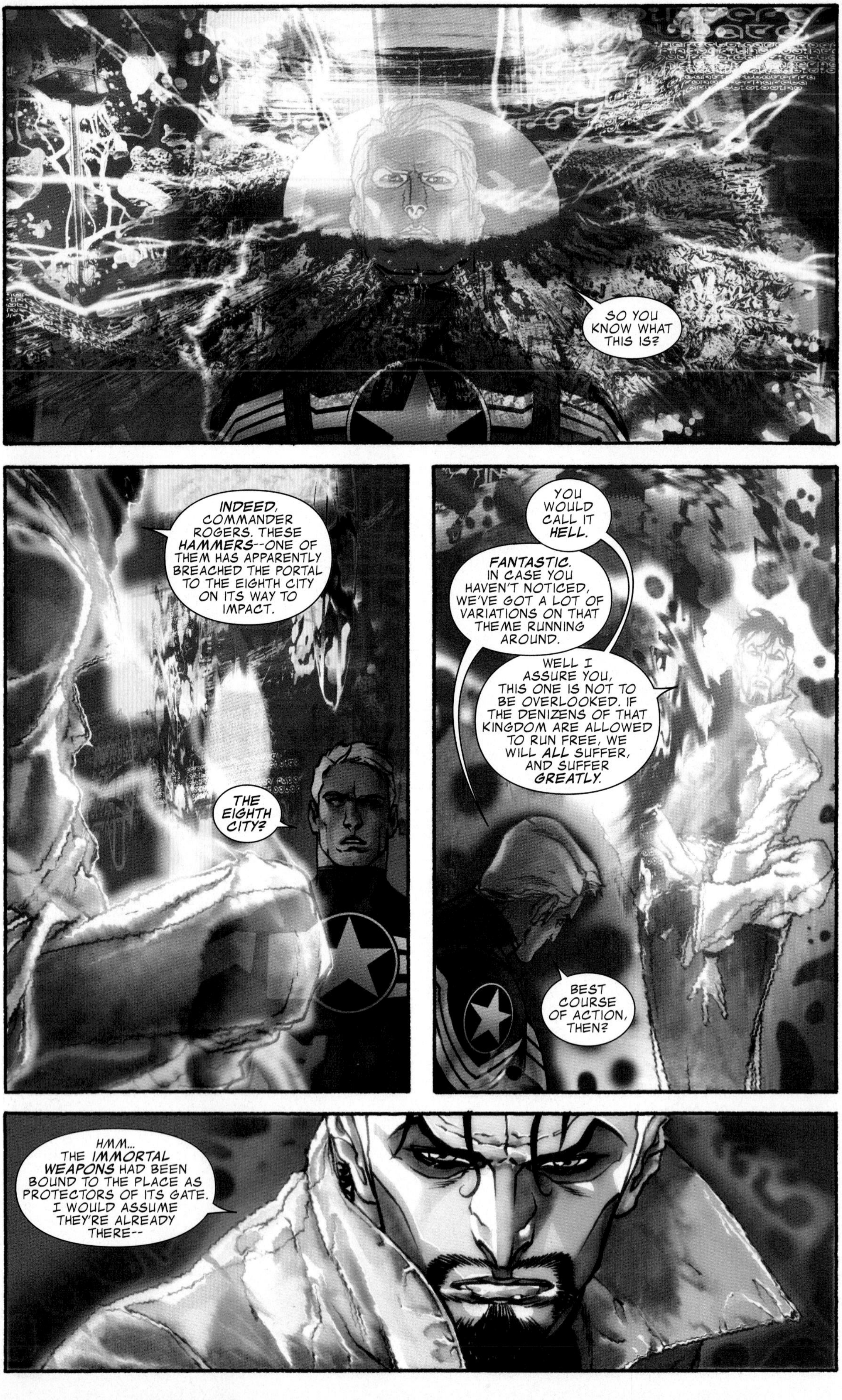
SO YOU KNOW WHAT THIS IS?
INDEED, COMMANDER ROGERS. THESE HAMMERS--ONE OF THEM HAS APPARENTLY BREACHED THE PORTAL TO THE EIGHTH CITY ON ITS WAY TO IMPACT.
THE EIGHTH CITY?
YOU WOULD CALL IT HELL.
FANTASTIC. IN CASE YOU HAVEN'T NOTICED, WE'VE GOT A LOT OF VARIATIONS ON THAT THEME RUNNING AROUND.
WELL I ASSURE YOU, THIS ONE IS NOT TO BE OVERLOOKED. IF THE DENIZENS OF THAT KINGDOM ARE ALLOWED TO RUN FREE, WE WILL ALL SUFFER, AND SUFFER GREATLY.
BEST COURSE OF ACTION, THEN?
HMM... THE IMMORTAL WEAPONS HAD BEEN BOUND TO THE PLACE AS PROTECTORS OF ITS GATE. I WOULD ASSUME THEY'RE ALREADY THERE--

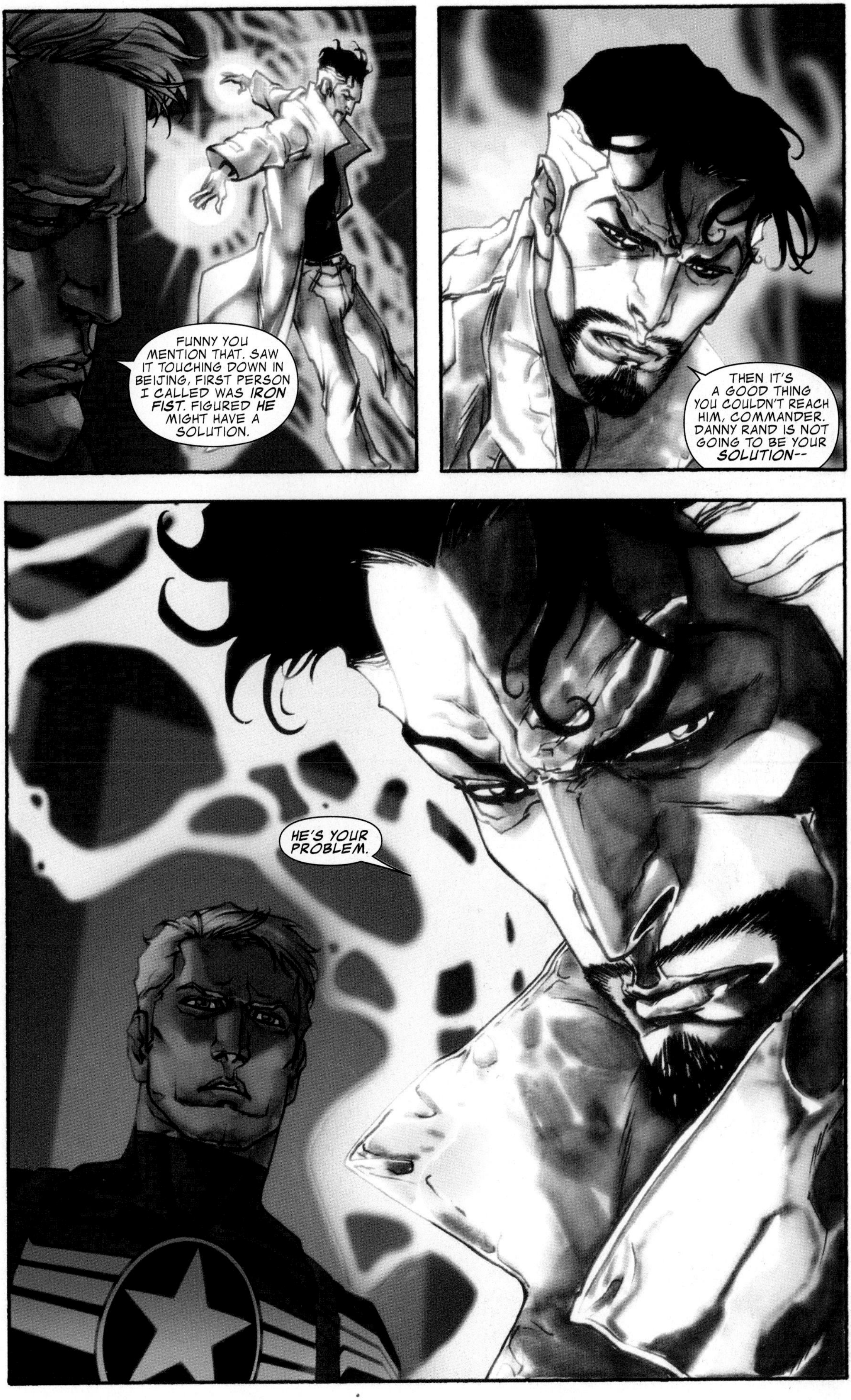
FUNNY YOU MENTION THAT. SAW IT TOUCHING DOWN IN BEIJING, FIRST PERSON I CALLED WAS IRON FIST. FIGURED HE MIGHT HAVE A SOLUTION.
THEN IT'S A GOOD THING YOU COULDN'T REACH HIM, COMMANDER. DANNY RAND IS NOT GOING TO BE YOUR SOLUTION--
HE'S YOUR PROBLEM.

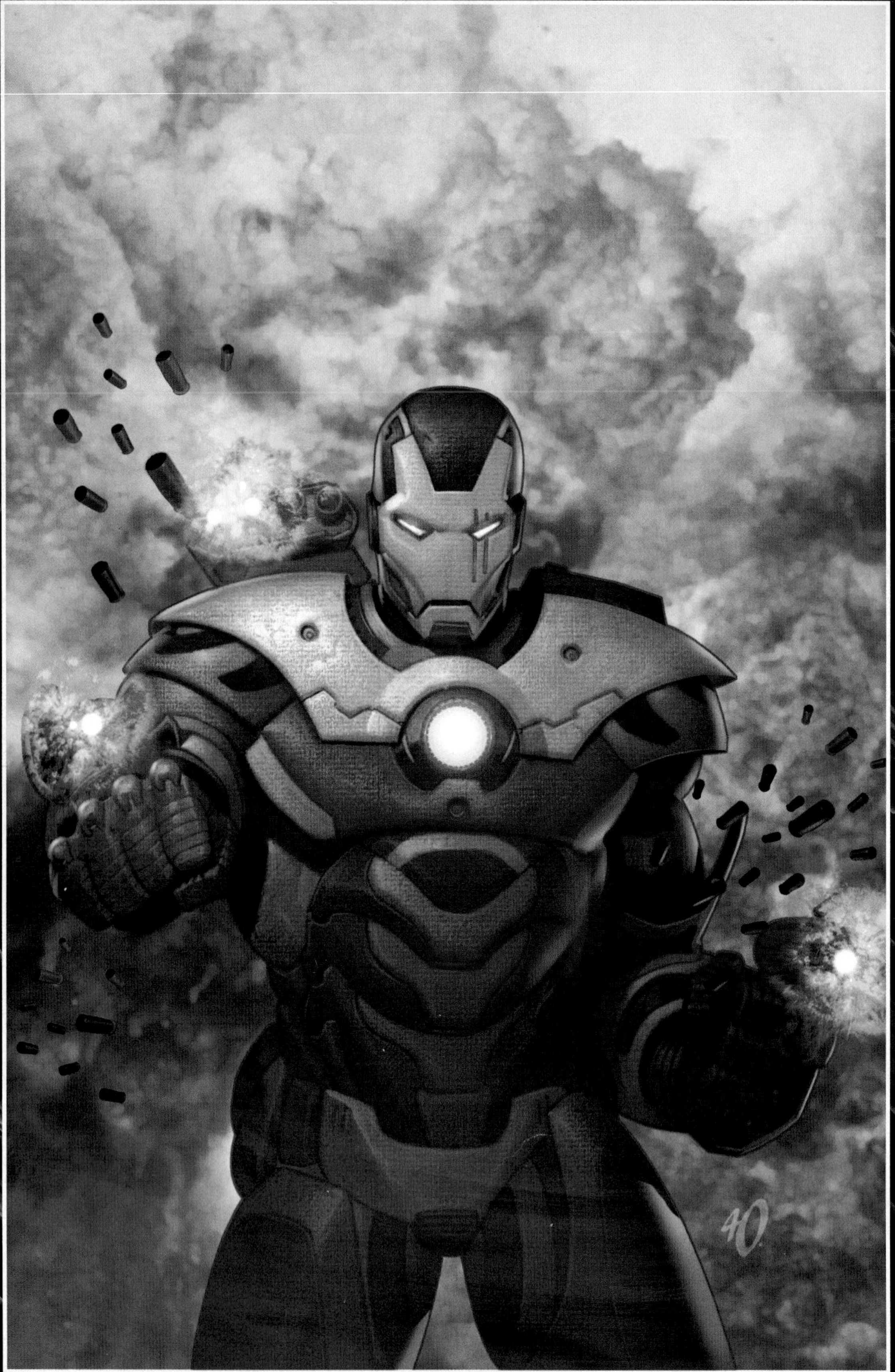

7

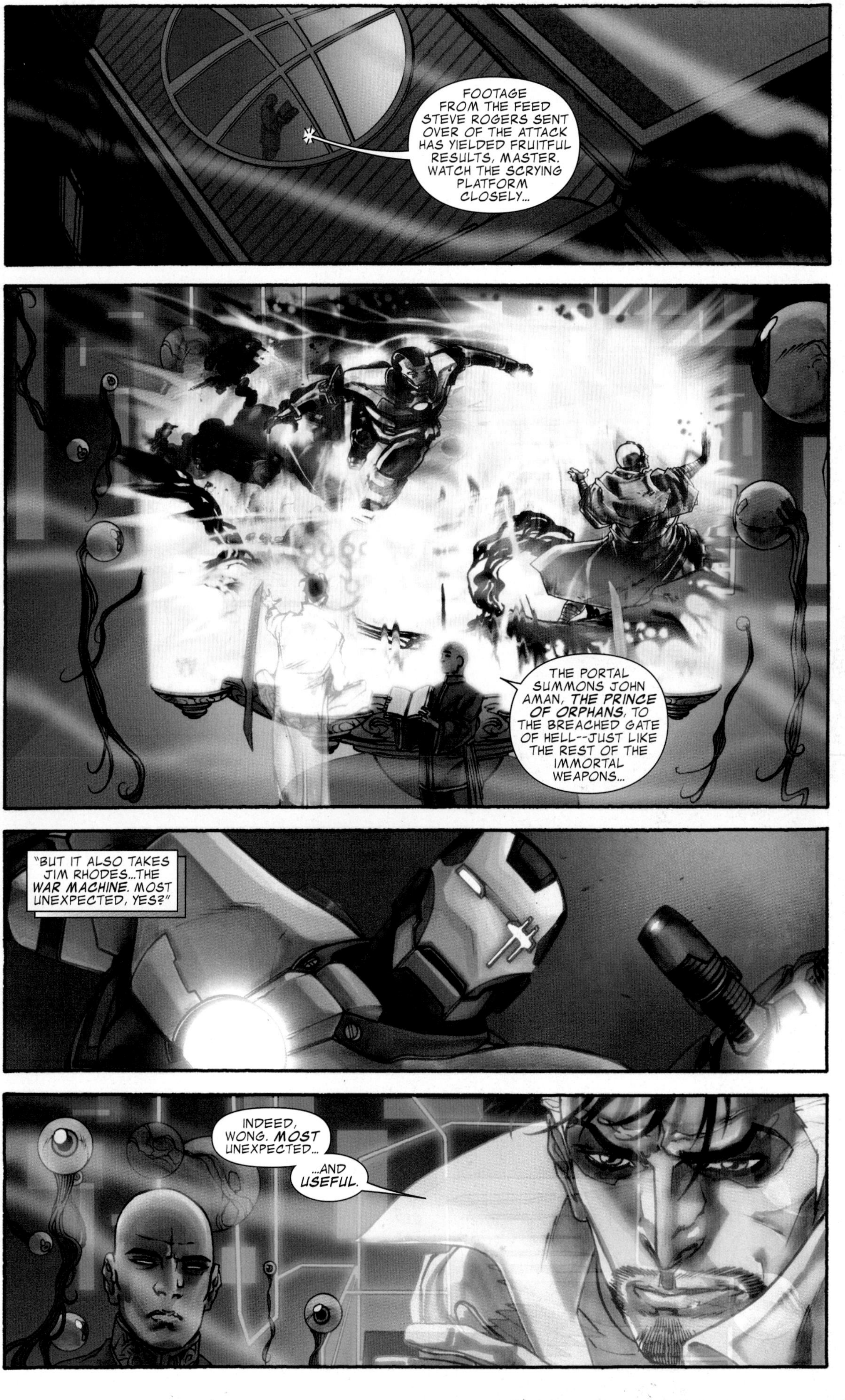
FOOTAGE FROM THE FEED STEVE ROGERS SENT OVER OF THE ATTACK HAS YIELDED FRUITFUL RESULTS, MASTER. WATCH THE SCRYING PLATFORM CLOSELY...
THE PORTAL SUMMONS JOHN AMAN, THE PRINCE OF ORPHANS, TO THE BREACHED GATE OF HELL--JUST LIKE THE REST OF THE IMMORTAL WEAPONS...
"BUT IT ALSO TAKES JIM RHODES...THE WAR MACHINE. MOST UNEXPECTED, YES?"
INDEED, WONG. MOST UNEXPECTED...
...AND USEFUL.

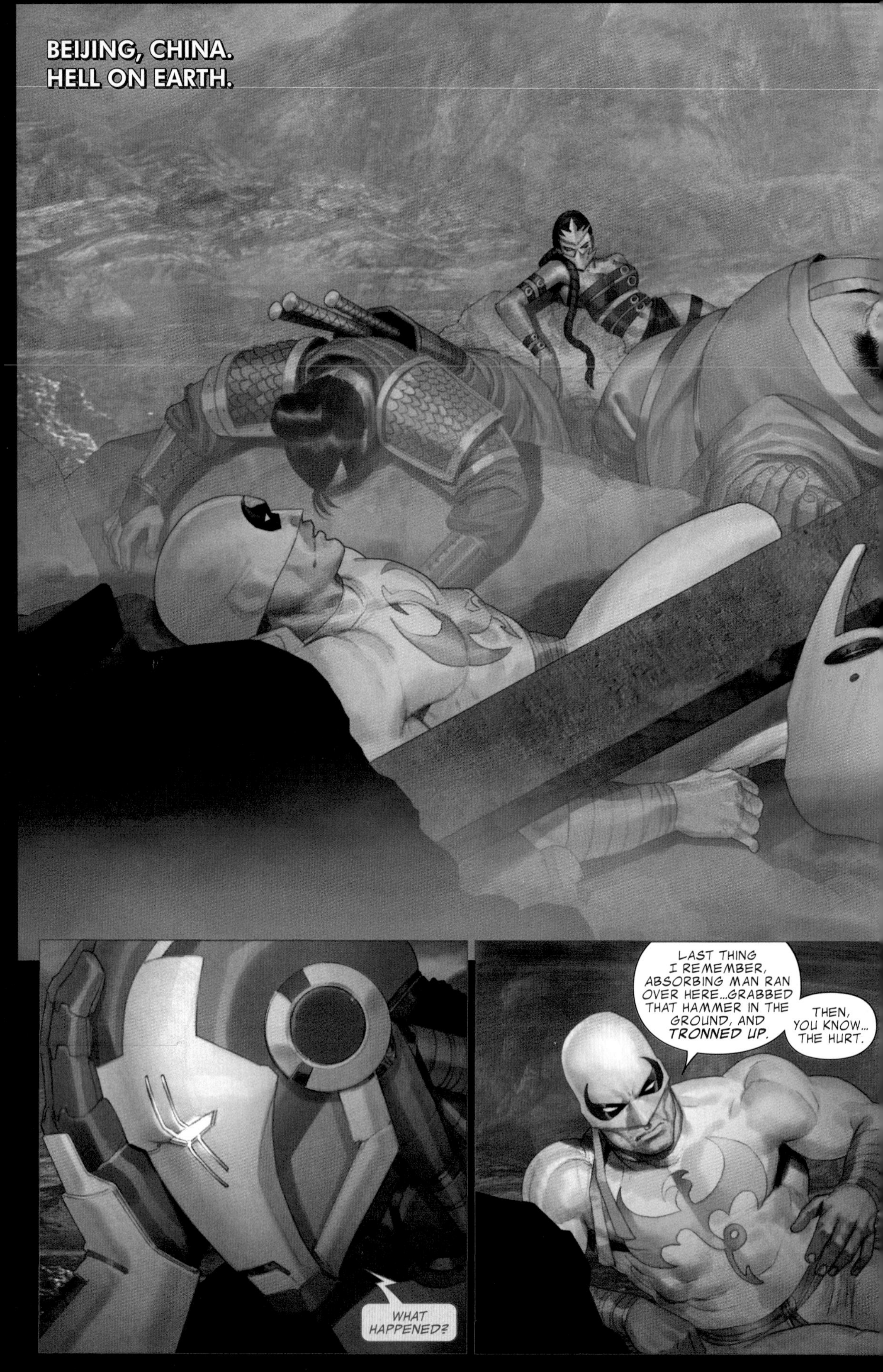
BEIJING, CHINA.
HELL ON EARTH.
WHAT HAPPENED?
LAST THING I REMEMBER, ABSORBING MAN RAN OVER HERE...GRABBED THAT HAMMER IN THE GROUND, AND TRONNED UP.
THEN, YOU KNOW... THE HURT.

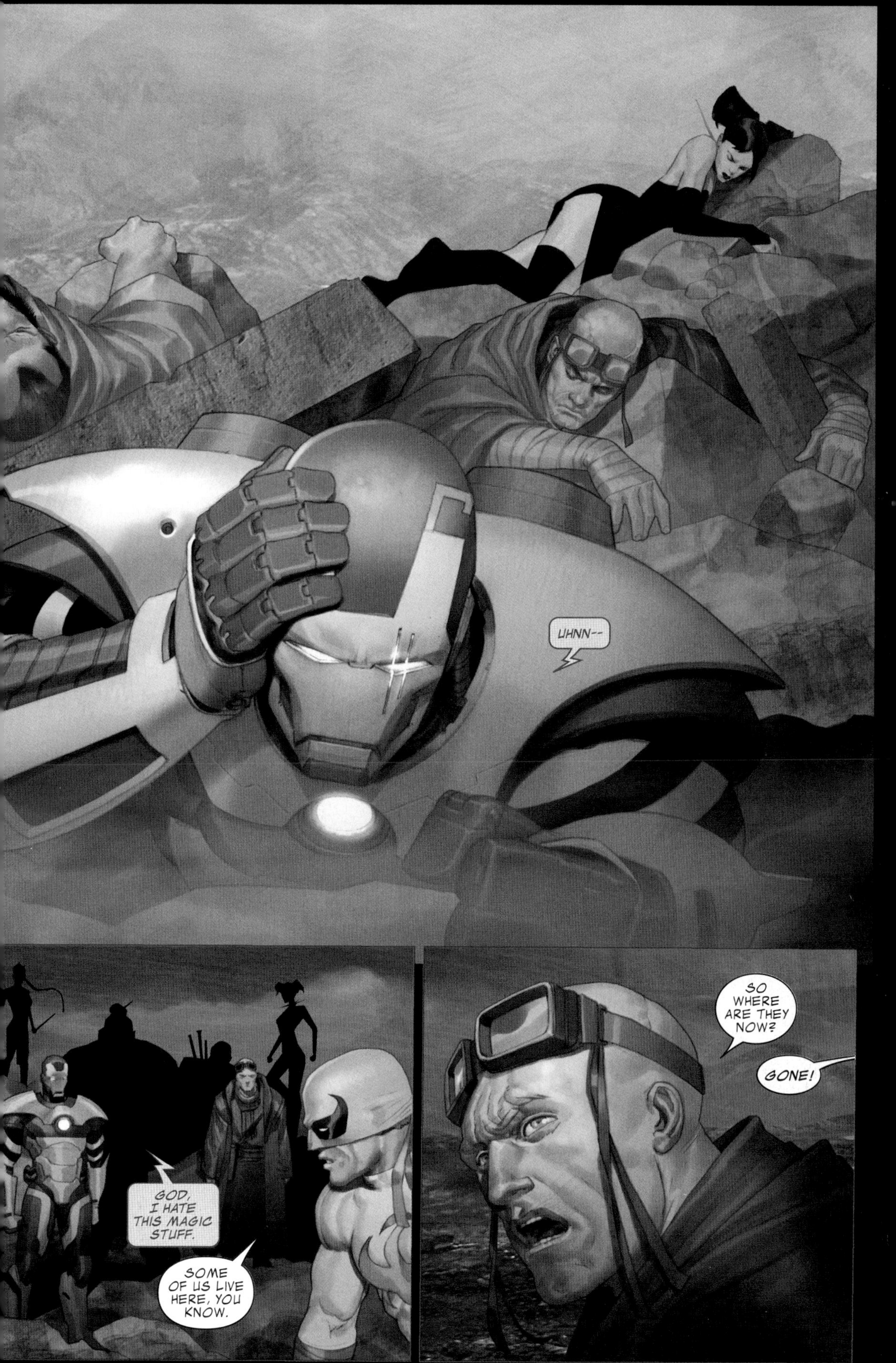
UHNN--
GOD, I HATE THIS MAGIC STUFF.
SOME OF US LIVE HERE, YOU KNOW.
SO WHERE ARE THEY NOW?
GONE!

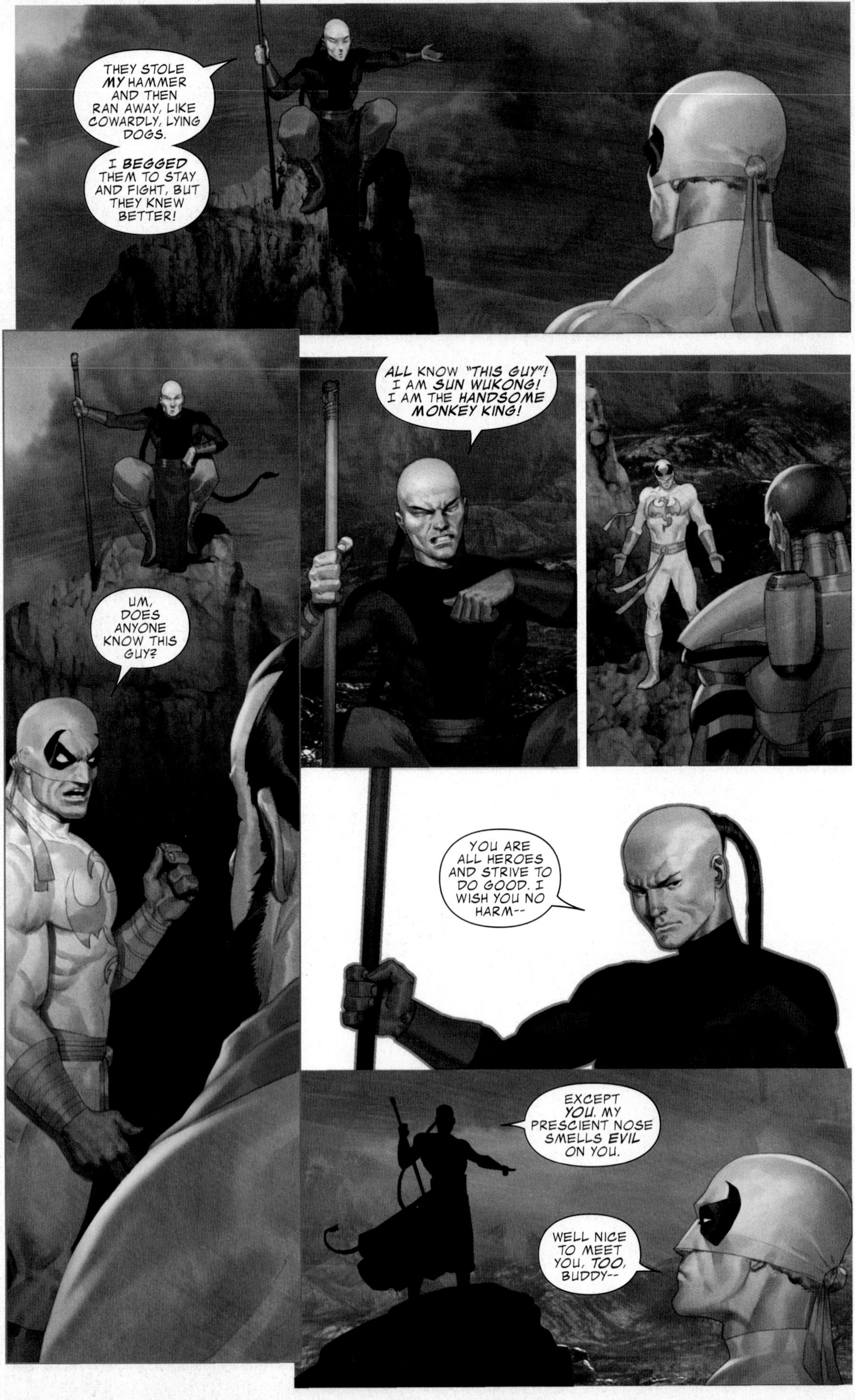
THEY STOLE MY HAMMER AND THEN RAN AWAY, LIKE COWARDLY, LYING DOGS.
I BEGGED THEM TO STAY AND FIGHT, BUT THEY KNEW BETTER!
UM, DOES ANYONE KNOW THIS GUY?
ALL KNOW "THIS GUY"! I AM SUN WUKONG! I AM THE HANDSOME MONKEY KING!
YOU ARE ALL HEROES AND STRIVE TO DO GOOD. I WISH YOU NO HARM--
EXCEPT YOU. MY PRESCIENT NOSE SMELLS EVIL ON YOU.
WELL NICE TO MEET YOU, TOO, BUDDY--

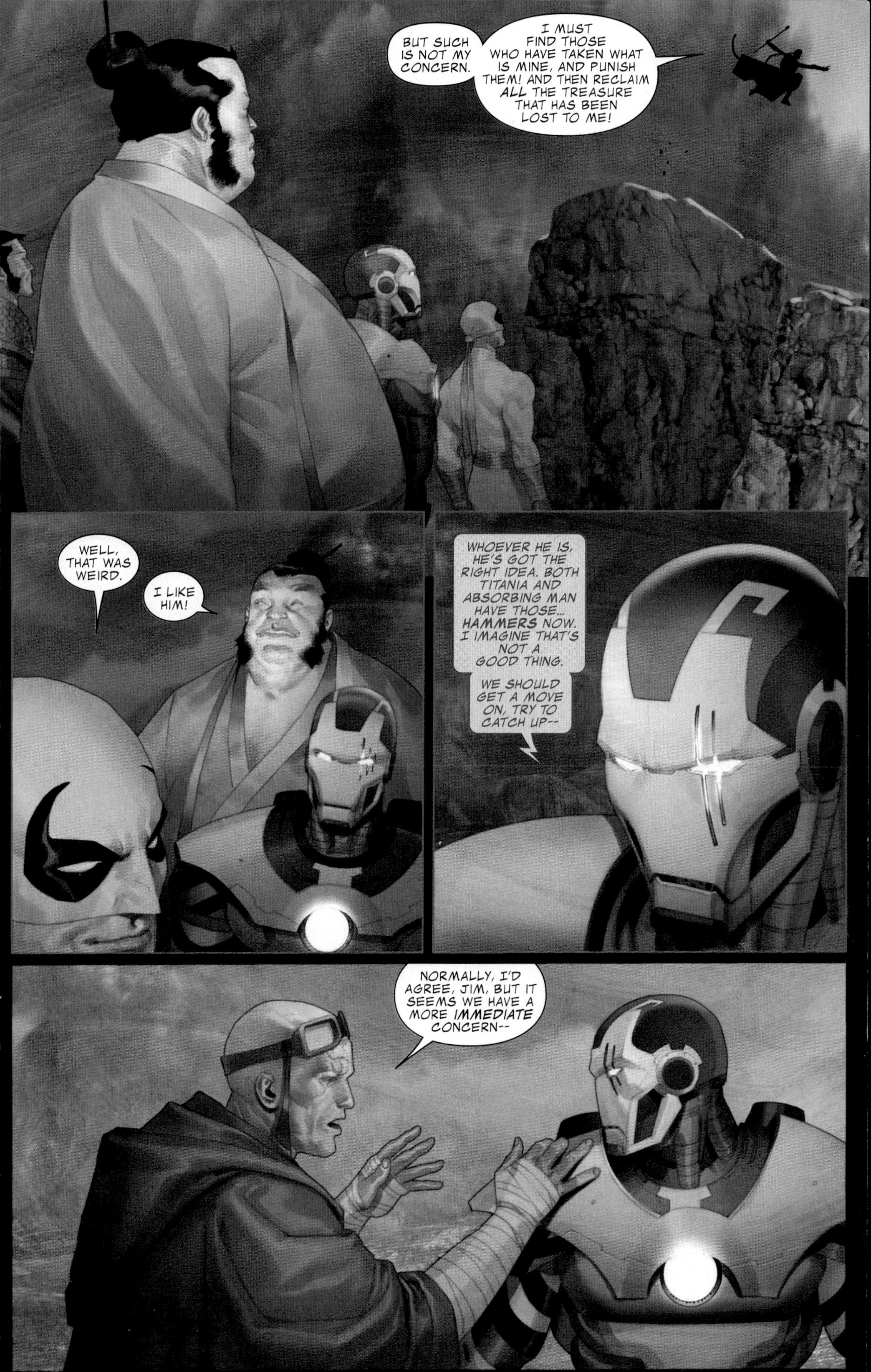
BUT SUCH IS NOT MY CONCERN.
I MUST FIND THOSE WHO HAVE TAKEN WHAT IS MINE, AND PUNISH THEM! AND THEN RECLAIM ALL THE TREASURE THAT HAS BEEN LOST TO ME!
WELL, THAT WAS WEIRD.
I LIKE HIM!
WHOEVER HE IS, HE'S GOT THE RIGHT IDEA. BOTH TITANIA AND ABSORBING MAN HAVE THOSE... HAMMERS NOW. I IMAGINE THAT'S NOT A GOOD THING.
WE SHOULD GET A MOVE ON, TRY TO CATCH UP--
NORMALLY, I'D AGREE, JIM, BUT IT SEEMS WE HAVE A MORE IMMEDIATE CONCERN--

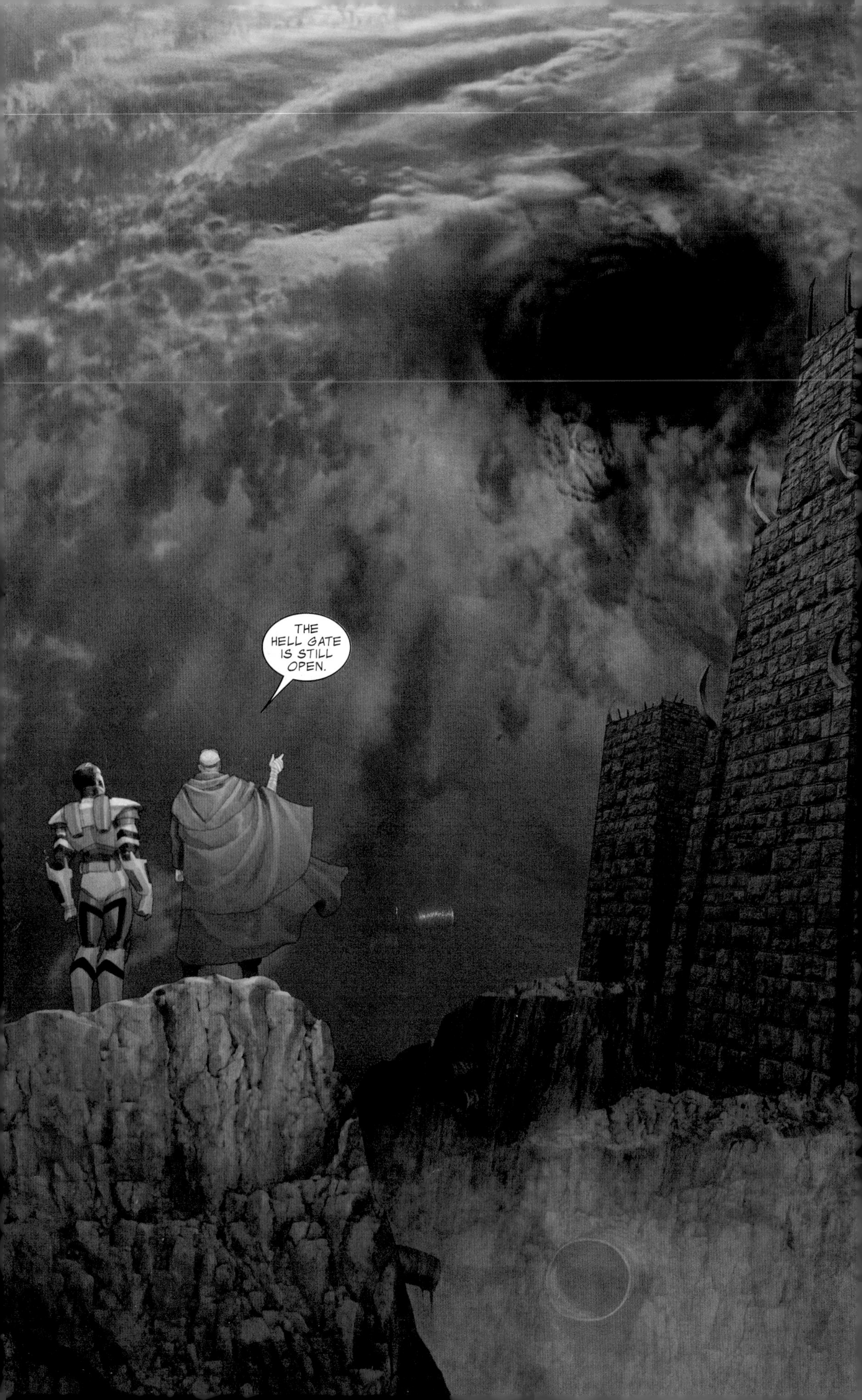
THE HELL GATE IS STILL OPEN.

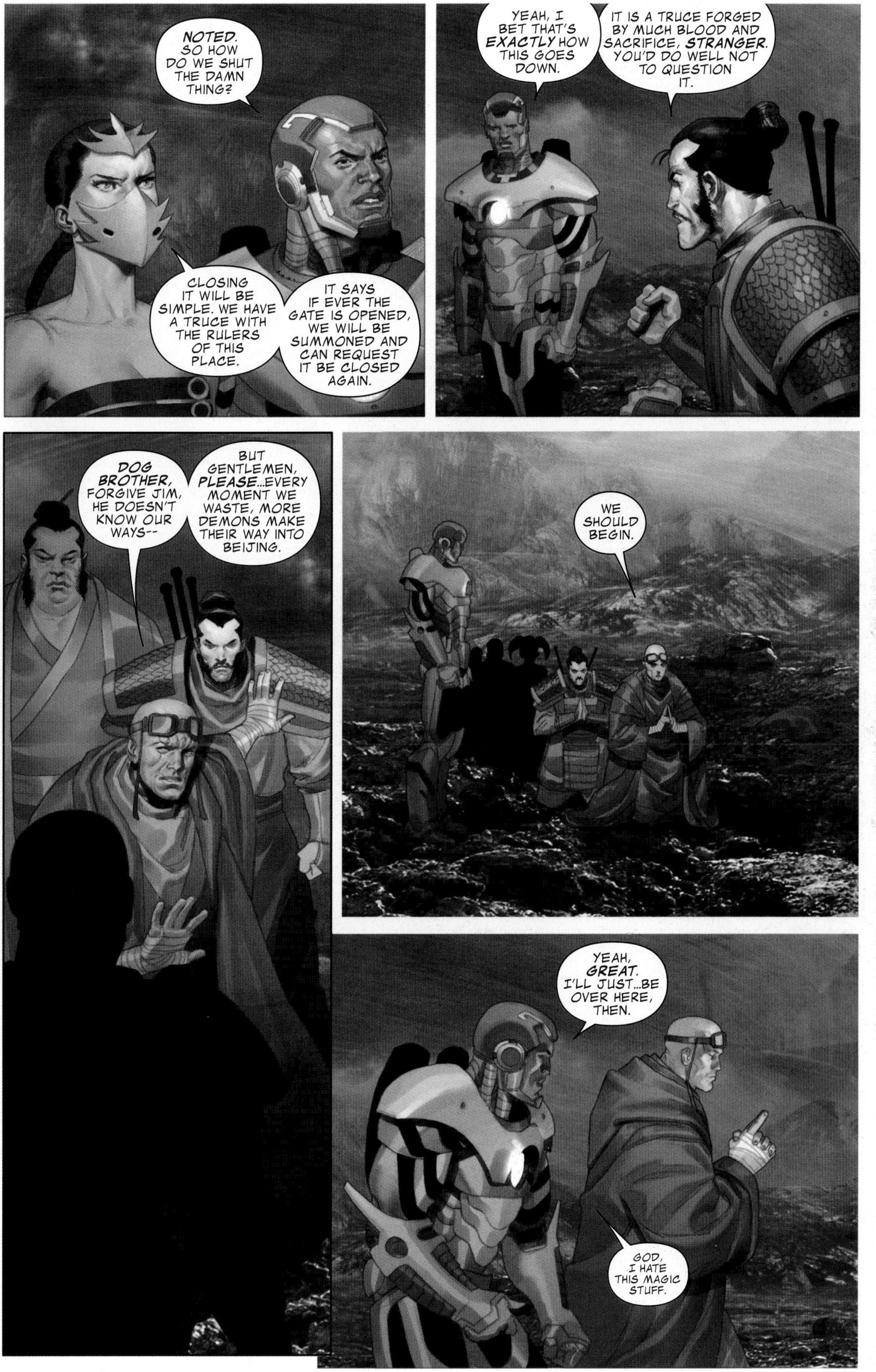
NOTED. SO HOW DO WE SHUT THE DAMN THING?
CLOSING IT WILL BE SIMPLE. WE HAVE A TRUCE WITH THE RULERS OF THIS PLACE.
IT SAYS IF EVER THE GATE IS OPENED, WE WILL BE SUMMONED AND CAN REQUEST IT BE CLOSED AGAIN.
YEAH, I BET THAT'S EXACTLY HOW THIS GOES DOWN.
IT IS A TRUCE FORGED BY MUCH BLOOD AND SACRIFICE, STRANGER. YOU'D DO WELL NOT TO QUESTION IT.
DOG BROTHER, FORGIVE JIM, HE DOESN'T KNOW OUR WAYS--
BUT GENTLEMEN, PLEASE...EVERY MOMENT WE WASTE, MORE DEMONS MAKE THEIR WAY INTO BEIJING.
WE SHOULD BEGIN.
YEAH, GREAT. I'LL JUST...BE OVER HERE, THEN.
GOD, I HATE THIS MAGIC STUFF.

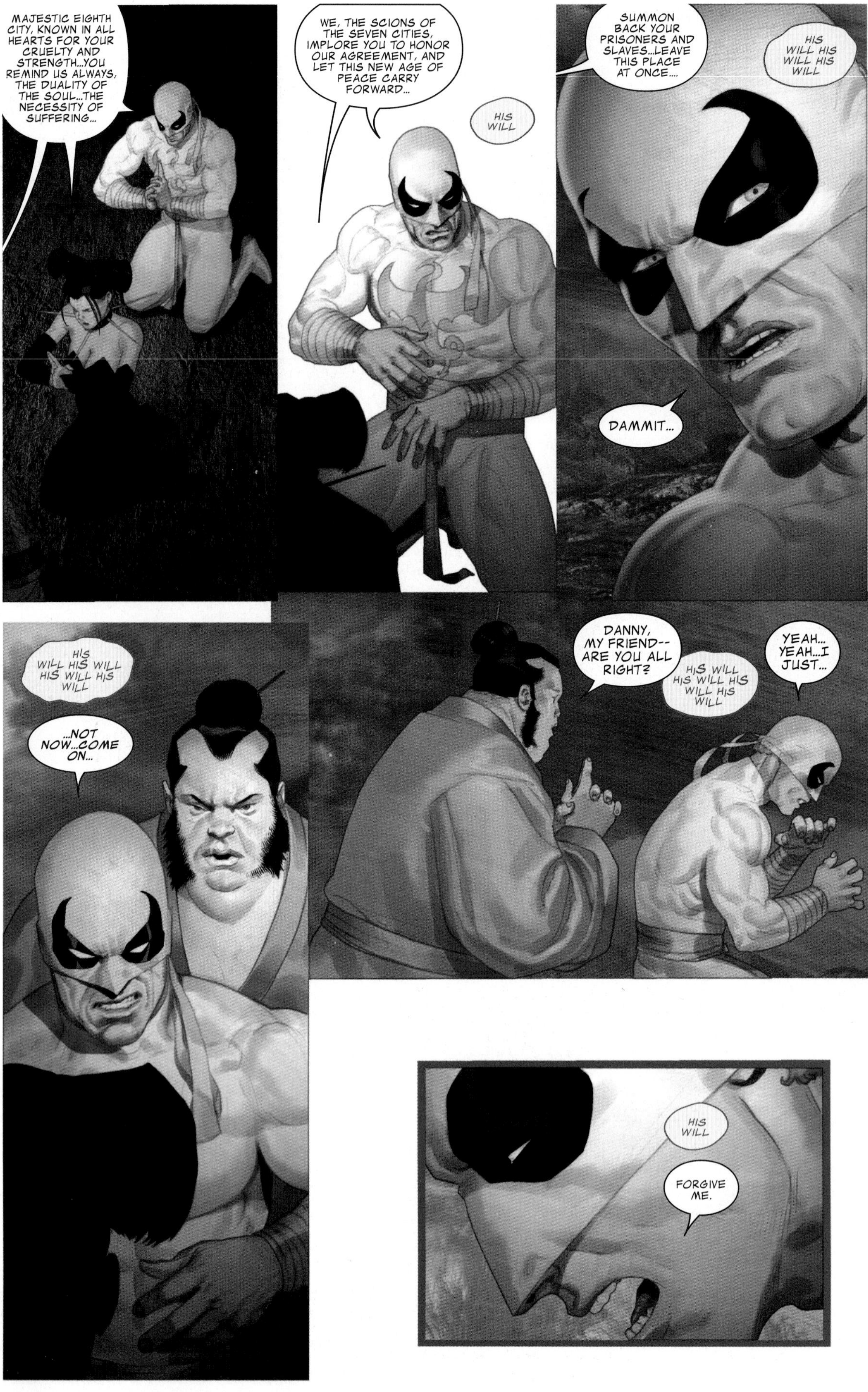
MAJESTIC EIGHTH CITY, KNOWN IN ALL HEARTS FOR YOUR CRUELTY AND STRENGTH...YOU REMIND US ALWAYS, THE DUALITY OF THE SOUL...THE NECESSITY OF SUFFERING...
WE, THE SCIONS OF THE SEVEN CITIES, IMPLORE YOU TO HONOR OUR AGREEMENT, AND LET THIS NEW AGE OF PEACE CARRY FORWARD...
HIS WILL
SUMMON BACK YOUR PRISONERS AND SLAVES...LEAVE THIS PLACE AT ONCE....
HIS WILL HIS WILL HIS WILL
DAMMIT...
HIS WILL HIS WILL HIS WILL HIS WILL
...NOT NOW...COME ON...
DANNY, MY FRIEND-- ARE YOU ALL RIGHT?
HIS WILL HIS WILL HIS WILL HIS WILL
YEAH... YEAH...I JUST...
HIS WILL
FORGIVE ME.

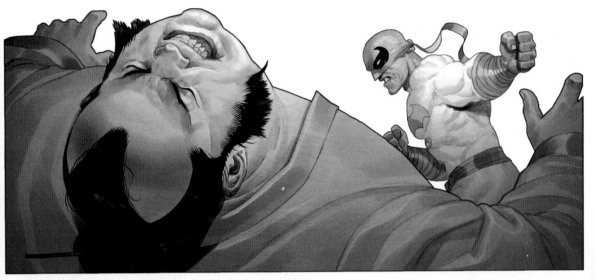

THE HELL?!

DANNY-- WHAT HAVE YOU DONE, BOY?

I'M SORRY... I CAN'T EXPLAIN RIGHT NOW, BUT-- THE GATE...WE CAN'T DO THIS.

PLEASE, I'M BEGGING YOU-- ALL OF YOU... GET BACK.

THE GATE MUST BE CLOSED, IRON FIST!

I WISH IT WERE THAT SIMPLE, DAUGHTER--I DO. BUT--

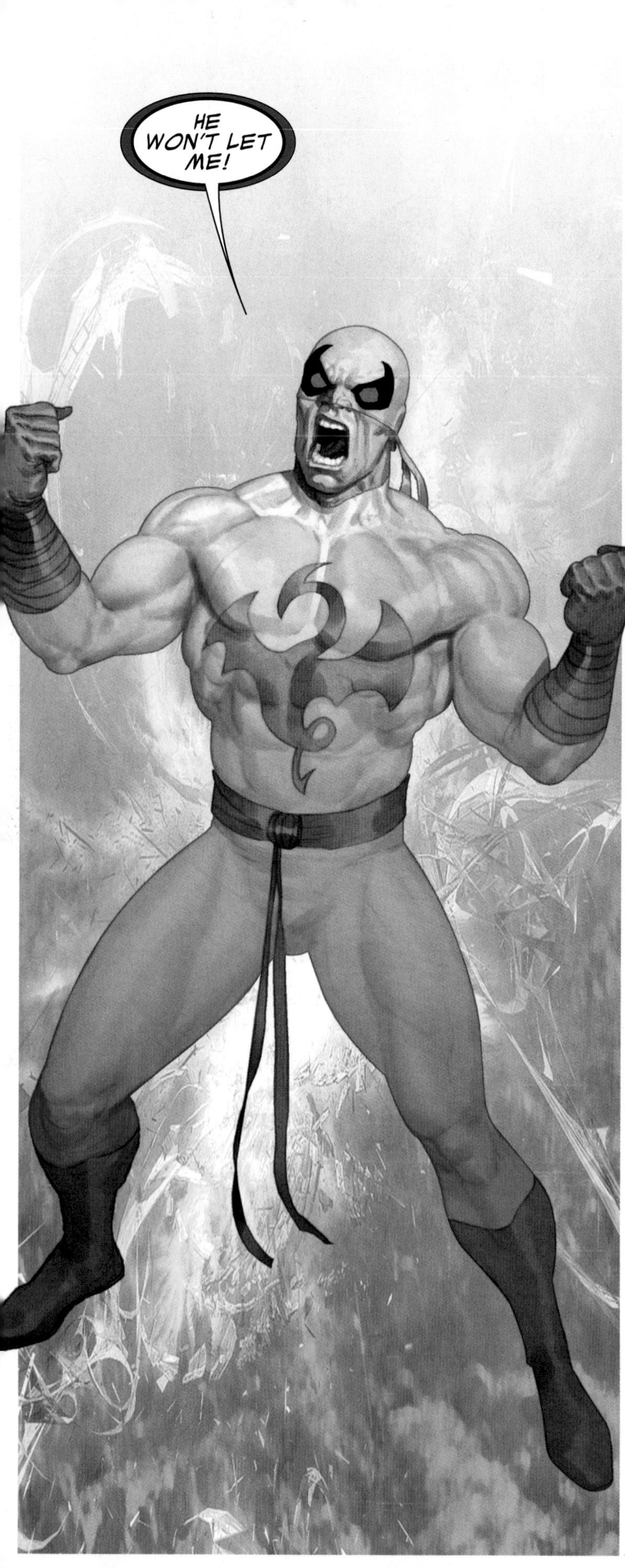
HE WON'T LET ME!

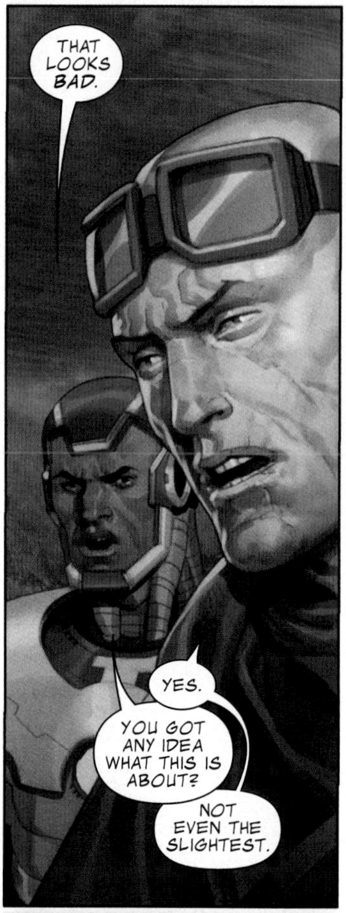
THAT LOOKS BAD.
YES.
YOU GOT ANY IDEA WHAT THIS IS ABOUT?
NOT EVEN THE SLIGHTEST.

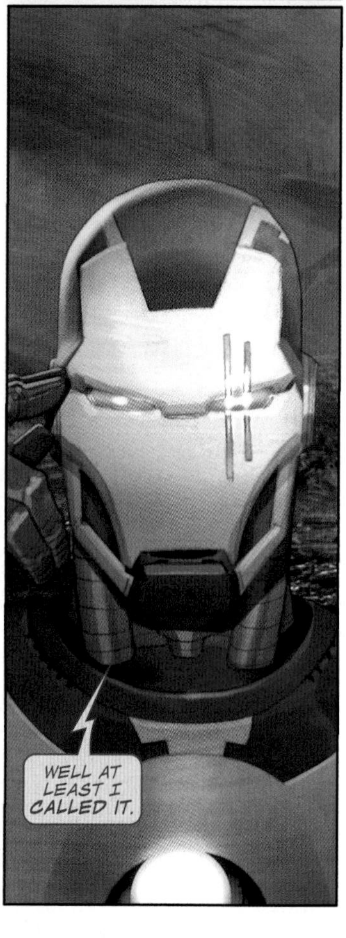
WELL AT LEAST I CALLED IT.

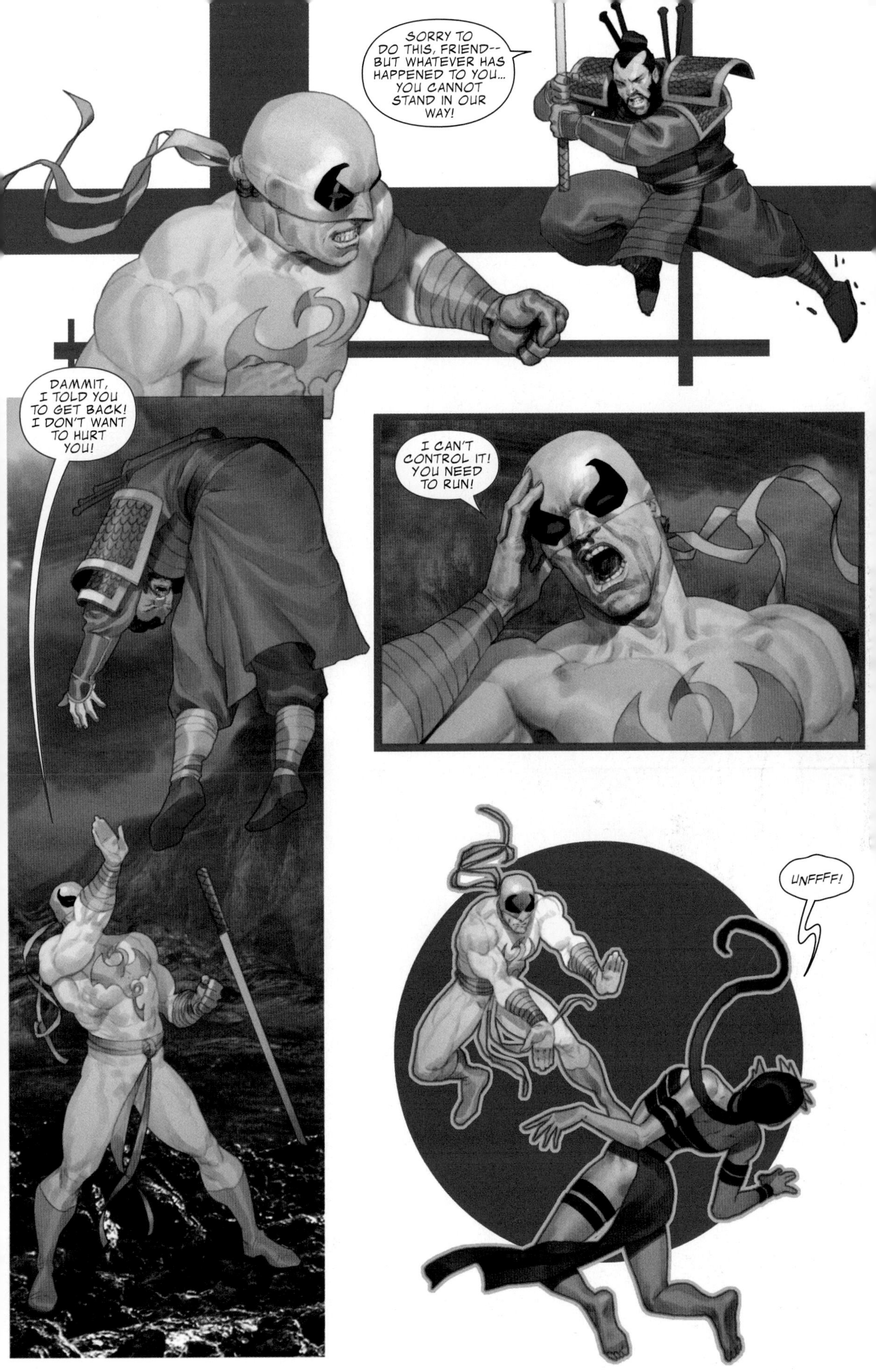
SORRY TO DO THIS, FRIEND-- BUT WHATEVER HAS HAPPENED TO YOU... YOU CANNOT STAND IN OUR WAY!
DAMMIT, I TOLD YOU TO GET BACK! I DON'T WANT TO HURT YOU!
I CAN'T CONTROL IT! YOU NEED TO RUN!
UNFFFF!

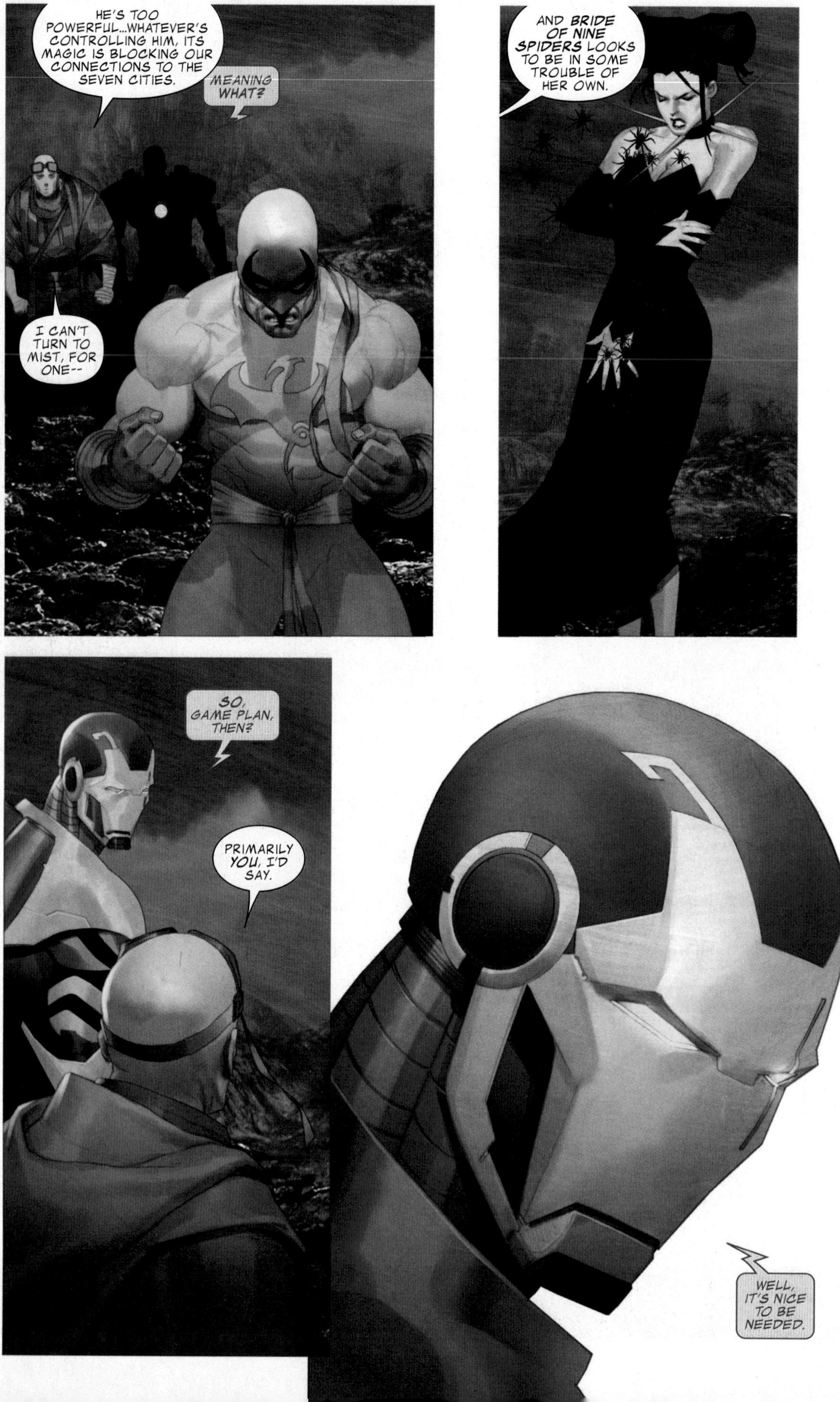
HE'S TOO POWERFUL...WHATEVER'S CONTROLLING HIM, ITS MAGIC IS BLOCKING OUR CONNECTIONS TO THE SEVEN CITIES.
MEANING WHAT?
I CAN'T TURN TO MIST, FOR ONE--
AND BRIDE OF NINE SPIDERS LOOKS TO BE IN SOME TROUBLE OF HER OWN.
SO, GAME PLAN, THEN?
PRIMARILY YOU, I'D SAY.
WELL, IT'S NICE TO BE NEEDED.

IRON FIST, MY FRIEND, YOU MUST FIGHT THIS DEMON INSIDE YOU! HELP US!

TOO LATE...TOO LATE FOR THAT...

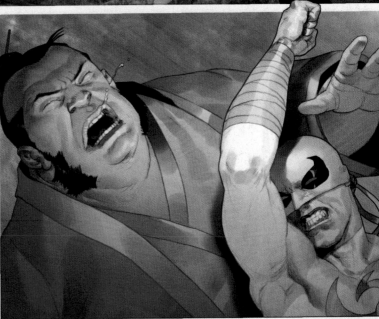

I'M SO SORRY...

I'M SORRY TOO, DANNY--

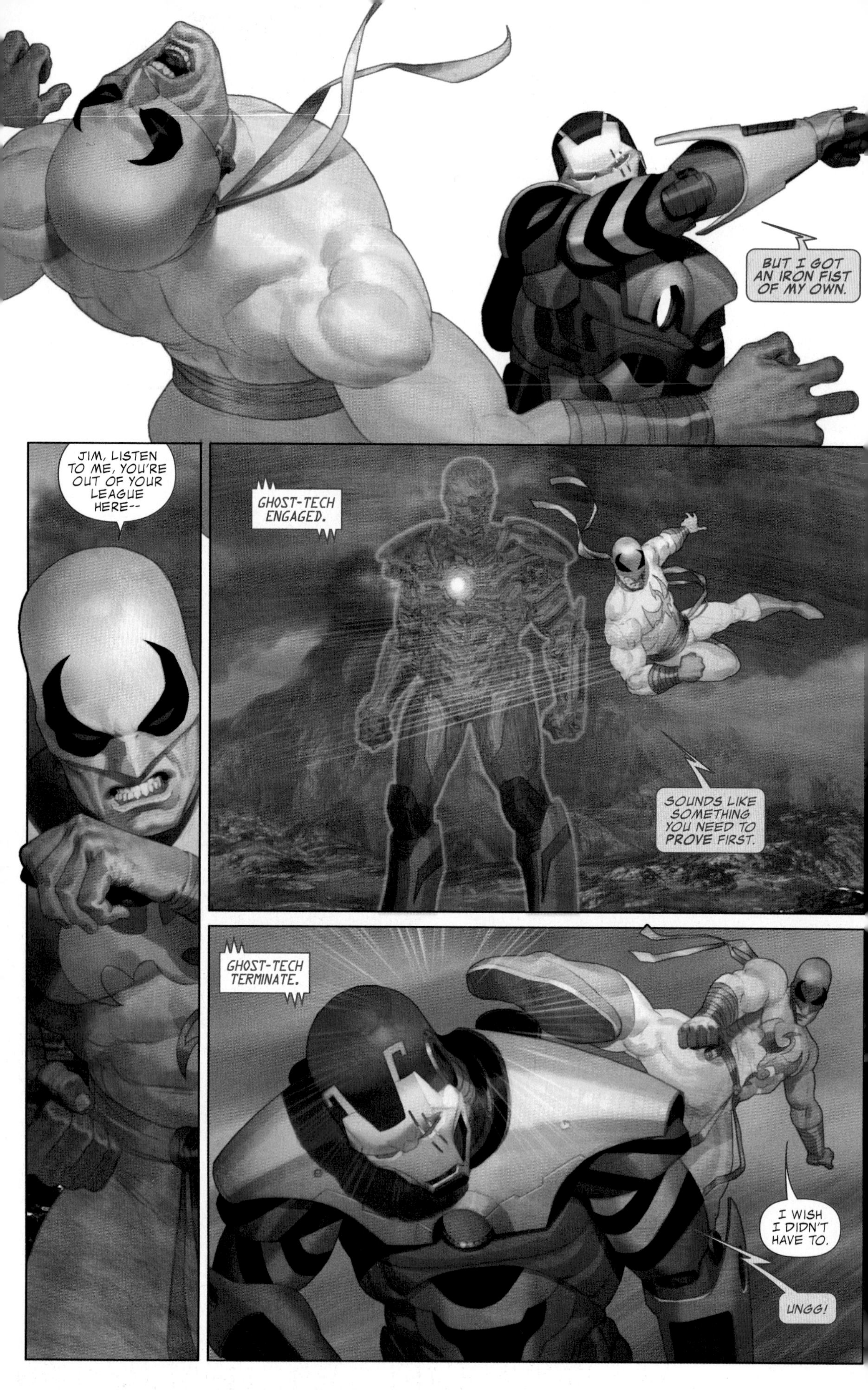
BUT I GOT AN IRON FIST OF MY OWN.
JIM, LISTEN TO ME, YOU'RE OUT OF YOUR LEAGUE HERE--
GHOST-TECH ENGAGED.
SOUNDS LIKE SOMETHING YOU NEED TO PROVE FIRST.
GHOST-TECH TERMINATE.
I WISH I DIDN'T HAVE TO.
UNGG!

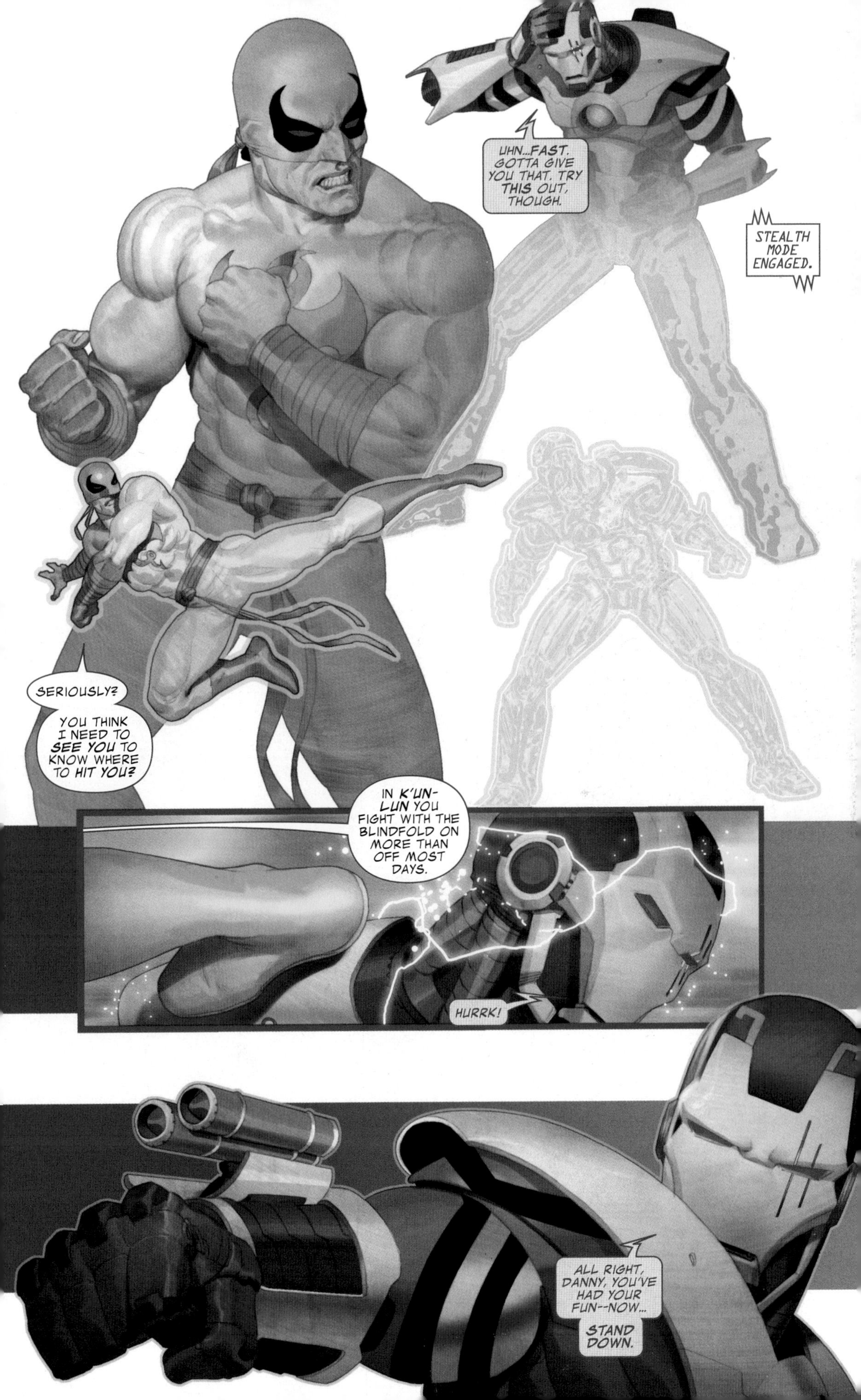
UHN...FAST. GOTTA GIVE YOU THAT. TRY THIS OUT, THOUGH.
STEALTH MODE ENGAGED.
SERIOUSLY?
YOU THINK I NEED TO SEE YOU TO KNOW WHERE TO HIT YOU?
IN K'UN-LUN YOU FIGHT WITH THE BLINDFOLD ON MORE THAN OFF MOST DAYS.
HURRK!
ALL RIGHT, DANNY, YOU'VE HAD YOUR FUN--NOW...
STAND DOWN.

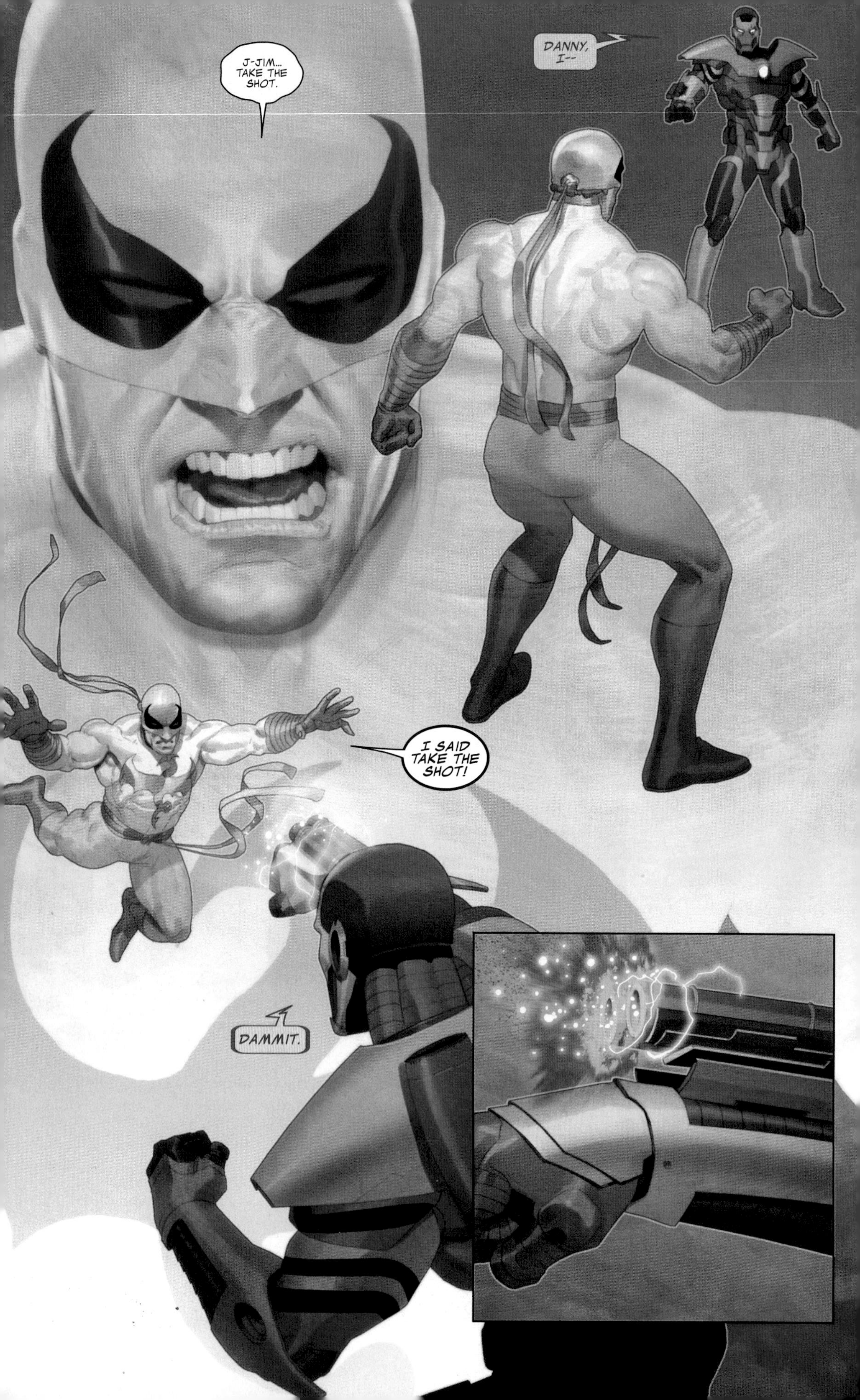
J-JIM... TAKE THE SHOT.
DANNY, I--
I SAID TAKE THE SHOT!
DAMMIT.

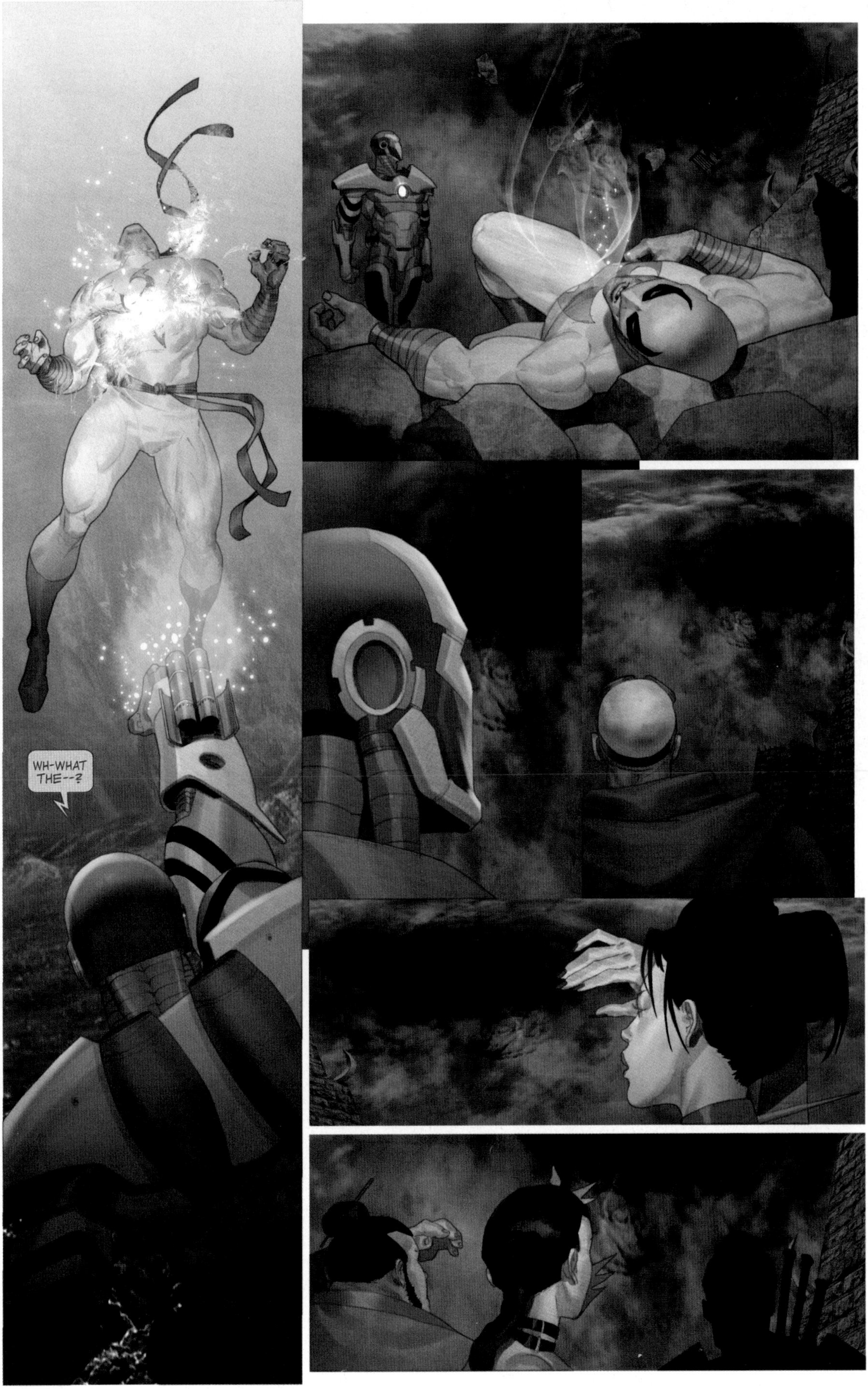
WH-WHAT THE--?

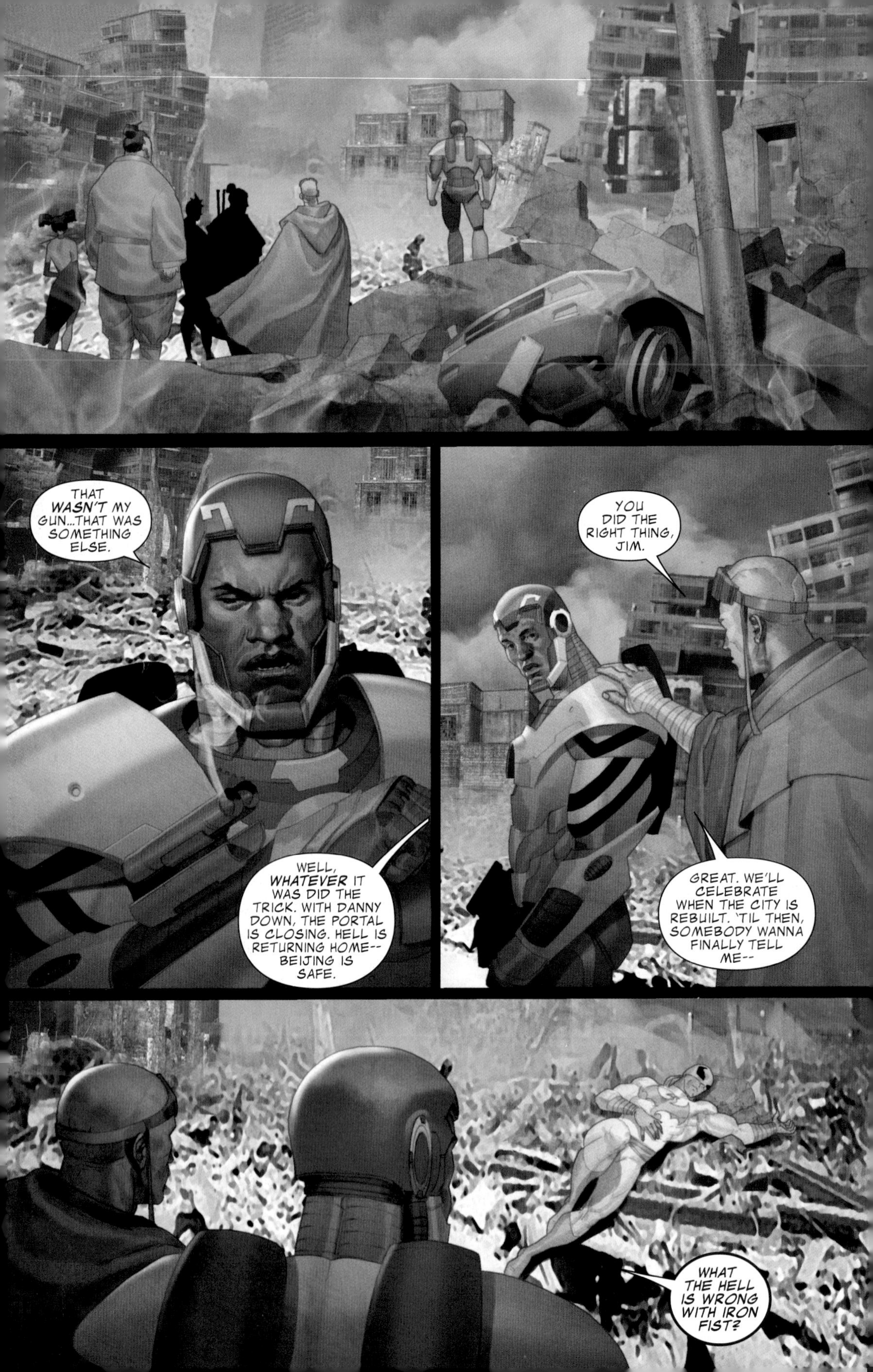
THAT WASN'T MY GUN...THAT WAS SOMETHING ELSE.
WELL, WHATEVER IT WAS DID THE TRICK. WITH DANNY DOWN, THE PORTAL IS CLOSING. HELL IS RETURNING HOME--BEIJING IS SAFE.
YOU DID THE RIGHT THING, JIM.
GREAT. WE'LL CELEBRATE WHEN THE CITY IS REBUILT. 'TIL THEN, SOMEBODY WANNA FINALLY TELL ME--
WHAT THE HELL IS WRONG WITH IRON FIST?

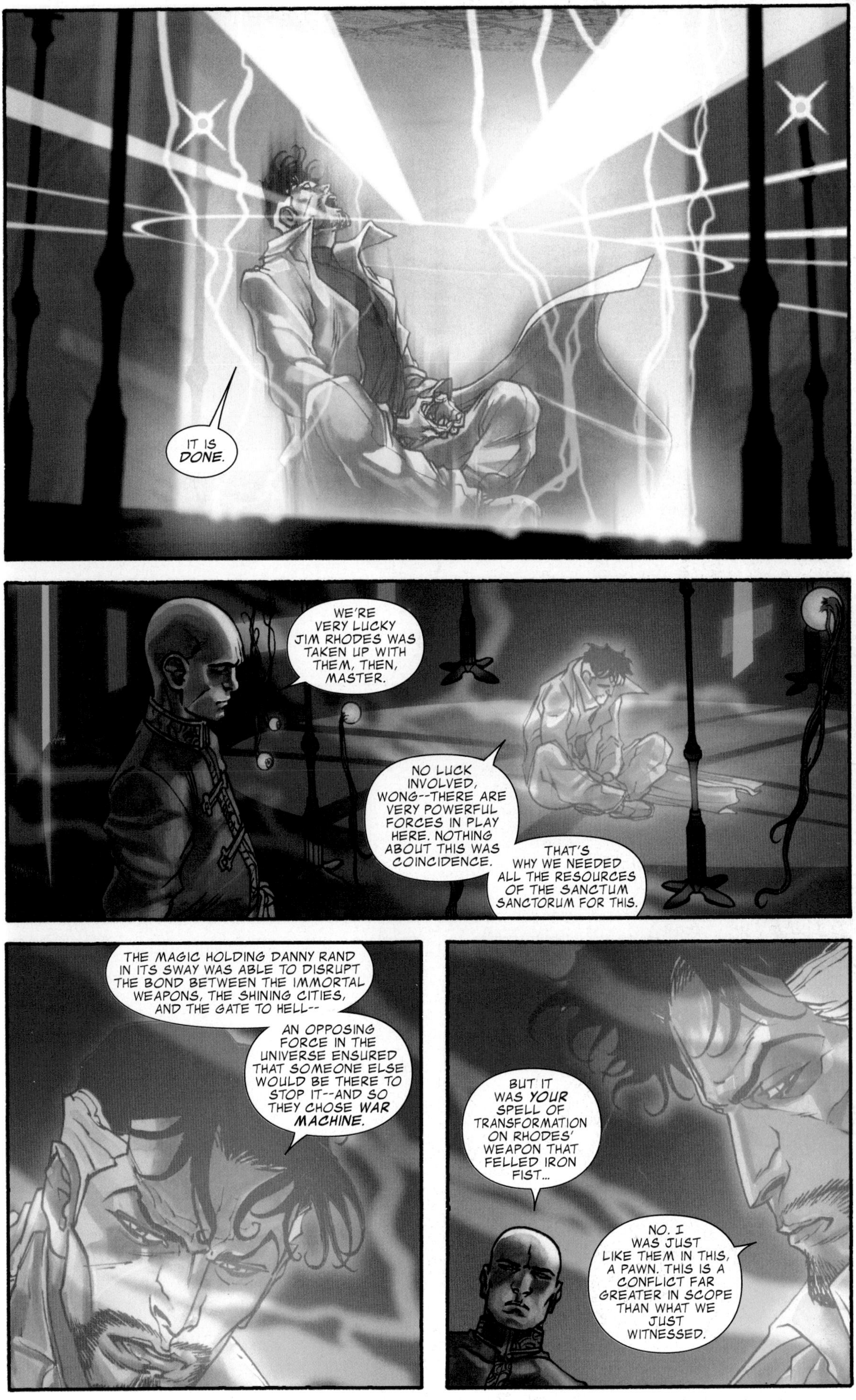

IT IS *DONE*.
WE'RE VERY LUCKY JIM RHODES WAS TAKEN UP WITH THEM, THEN, MASTER.
NO LUCK INVOLVED, WONG--THERE ARE VERY POWERFUL FORCES IN PLAY HERE. NOTHING ABOUT THIS WAS COINCIDENCE.
THAT'S WHY WE NEEDED ALL THE RESOURCES OF THE SANCTUM SANCTORUM FOR THIS.
THE MAGIC HOLDING DANNY RAND IN ITS SWAY WAS ABLE TO DISRUPT THE BOND BETWEEN THE IMMORTAL WEAPONS, THE SHINING CITIES, AND THE GATE TO HELL--
AN OPPOSING FORCE IN THE UNIVERSE ENSURED THAT SOMEONE ELSE WOULD BE THERE TO STOP IT--AND SO THEY CHOSE ***WAR MACHINE.***
BUT IT WAS *YOUR* SPELL OF TRANSFORMATION ON RHODES' WEAPON THAT FELLED IRON FIST...
NO. I WAS JUST LIKE THEM IN THIS, A PAWN. THIS IS A CONFLICT FAR GREATER IN SCOPE THAN WHAT WE JUST WITNESSED.

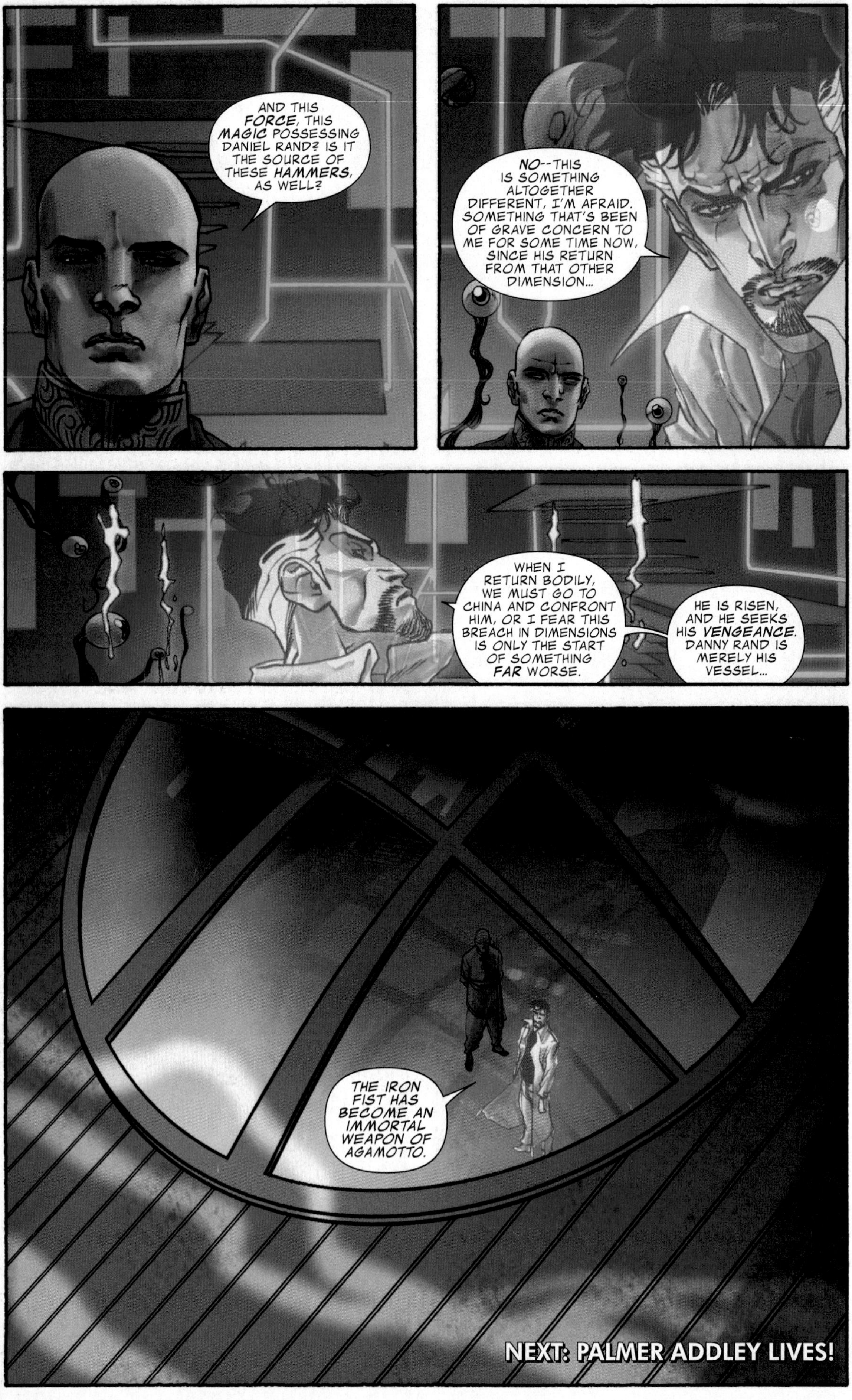
AND THIS FORCE, THIS MAGIC POSSESSING DANIEL RAND? IS IT THE SOURCE OF THESE HAMMERS, AS WELL?
NO--THIS IS SOMETHING ALTOGETHER DIFFERENT, I'M AFRAID. SOMETHING THAT'S BEEN OF GRAVE CONCERN TO ME FOR SOME TIME NOW, SINCE HIS RETURN FROM THAT OTHER DIMENSION...
WHEN I RETURN BODILY, WE MUST GO TO CHINA AND CONFRONT HIM, OR I FEAR THIS BREACH IN DIMENSIONS IS ONLY THE START OF SOMETHING FAR WORSE.
HE IS RISEN, AND HE SEEKS HIS VENGEANCE. DANNY RAND IS MERELY HIS VESSEL...
THE IRON FIST HAS BECOME AN IMMORTAL WEAPON OF AGAMOTTO.
NEXT: PALMER ADDLEY LIVES!

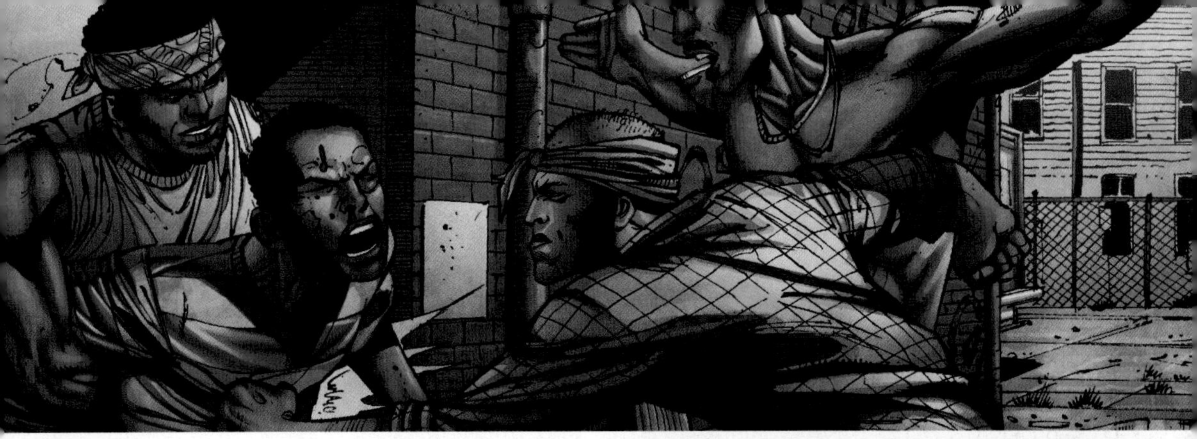

The story of War Machine begins on the streets of South Philly. James Rhodes was born poor — a loner bullied by whites for being black, and harassed by other neighborhood kids for trying to stay clean and make good grades. Despite his turbulent childhood, Rhodes was motivated enough to join the Marines. Pushed hard by his drill instructors, he took to the structured military culture.

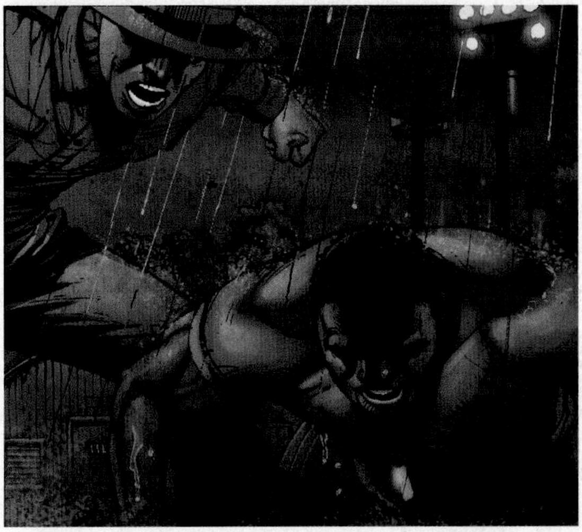

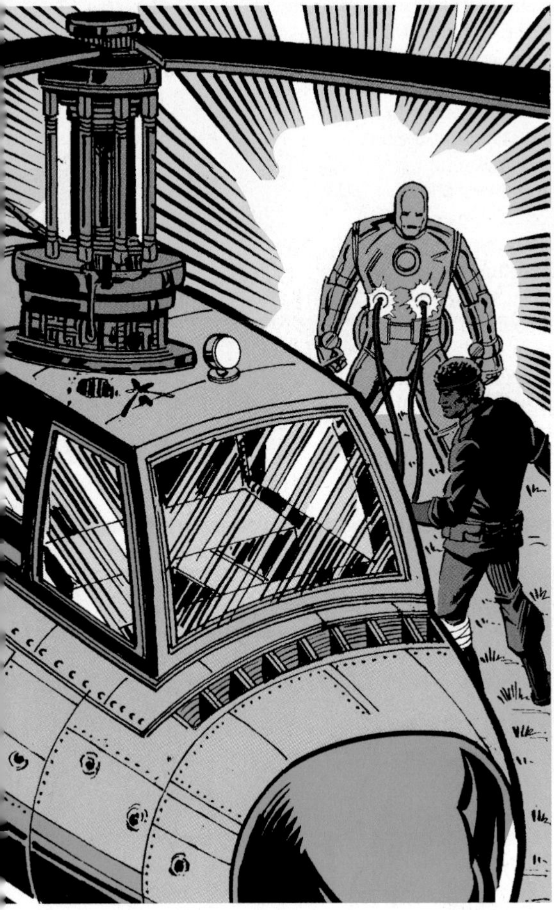

When the helicopter he piloted was shot down in hostile territory, Rhodes was rescued by Tony Stark, fresh out of his captor's cave and fleeing in his first suit of Iron Man armor. Together, they evaded sniper fire, booby traps and armed assaults. Despite not knowing Iron Man's secret identity, Rhodes formed a blood brotherhood with Stark. Stark offered the recovering Rhodes a job any time he wanted one. Years later, after his military career evolved into life as a mercenary, Rhodes would take him up on that offer.

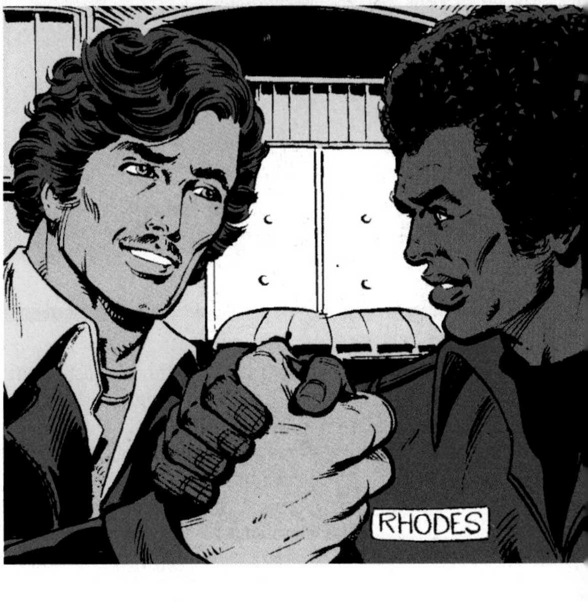
RHODES

Working for Stark meant being a private pilot and chief aviation engineer, but it also meant getting sucked into adventures alongside Stark's "bodyguard" Iron Man. A friendship born of mutual respect and trial by fire flourished between Stark and the pal he called "Rhodey."

That friendship was put to the test during Stark's initial slide into alcoholism. It was the first time Rhodes would have to stand by his best friend during his dark hours of addiction, but it wouldn't be the last. Even so, adventure was a life Rhodes was seemingly born for, and as Tony Stark's ace pilot, he got his fill: One day, it was a firefight with the crime syndicate the Maggia; the next, a helicopter dogfight against Spymaster. The job of Tony's "straight man" required it. But Jim Rhodes could never have imagined the day would come when his job would demand he don the Iron Man armor.

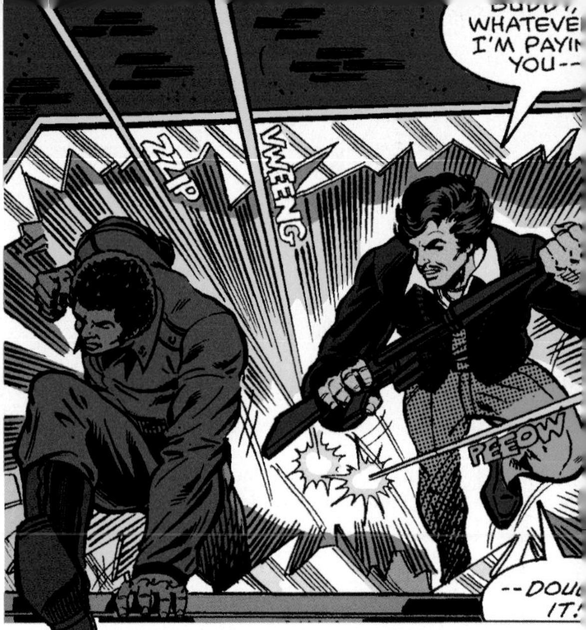
YOU--
ZZIP
VWEENG
PEEOW

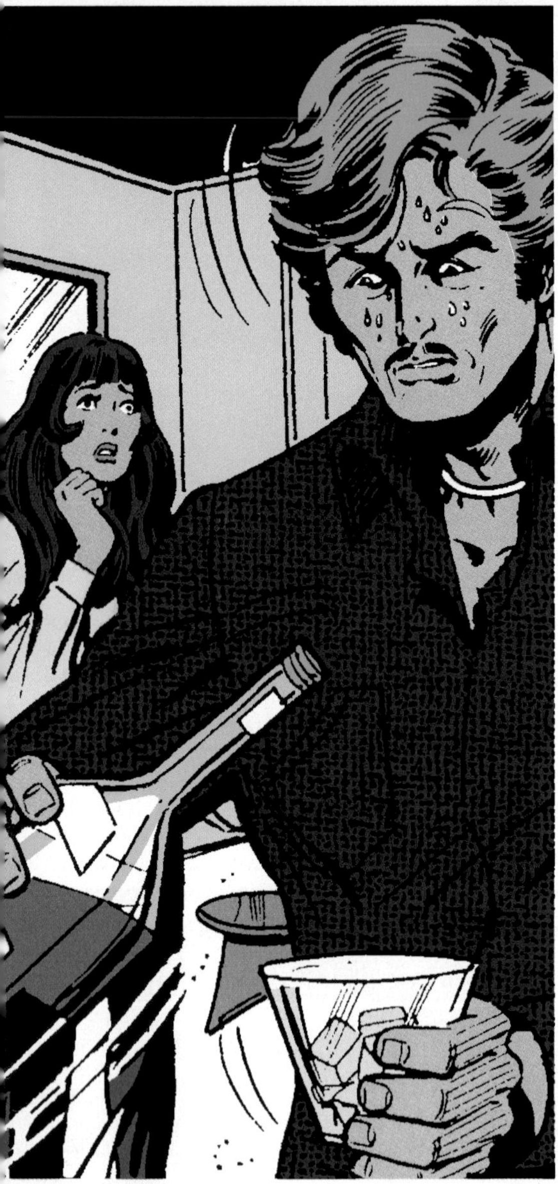

In the aftermath of a confrontation with rival industrialist Justin Hammer in Scotland, Tony fell off the wagon. After embarrassing confrontations with Machine Man and Magma, it became apparent he was unfit to fight as Iron Man. With Magma on a rampage, Rhodes' only option was to take him on as Iron Man. Though inexperienced, his natural abilities as a pilot enabled him to struggle his way to a victory against the villain. With Tony's urging, he took on the role of Iron Man full time.

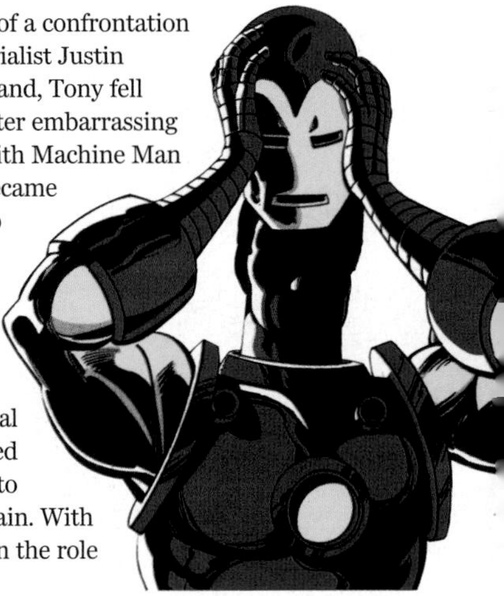

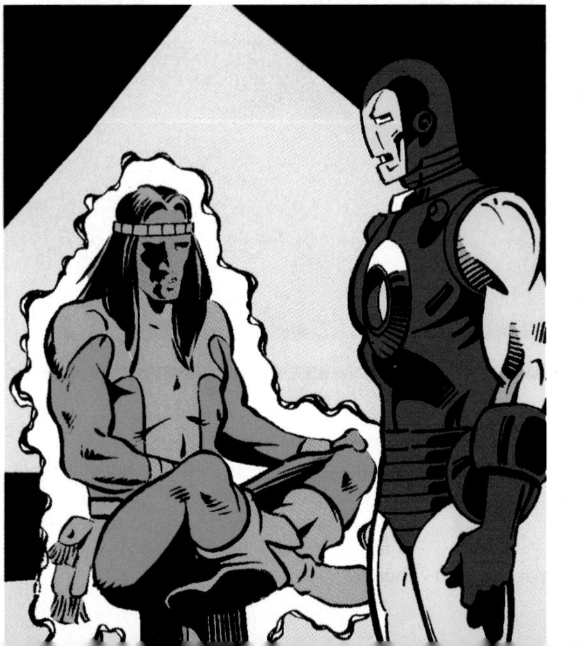

During his first run as Iron Man, Rhodes clashed with the likes of Thunderball, Obadiah Stane, the Zodiac and the Eternals. He also faced a crisis of faith in his own abilities, brought out by his brainwaves not meshing with the armor's cybernetic systems. This required a harrowing trip through his own soul, courtesy of Alpha Flight's Shaman, to reconcile his emotional issues with Tony and his armor.

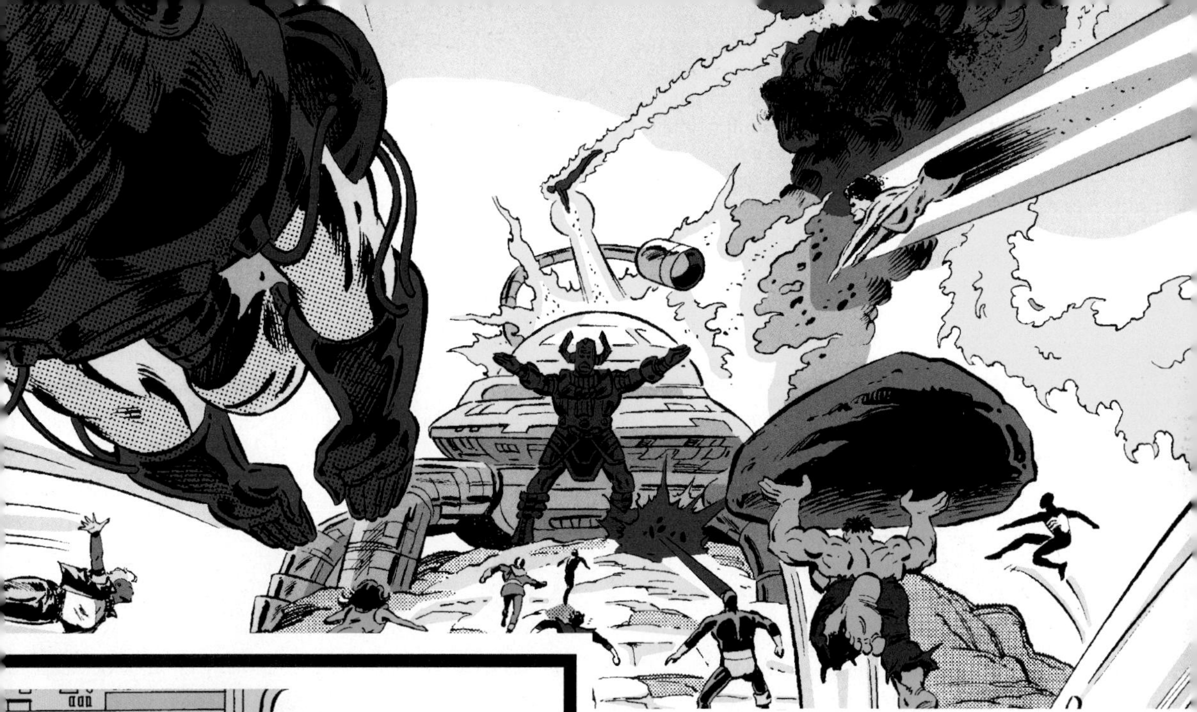

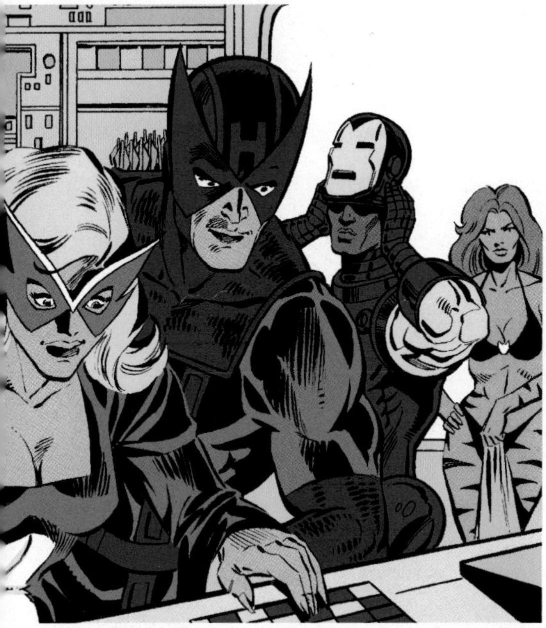

Rhodes didn't have long to dwell on his own inadequacies as he was transported with the heroes of Earth to Battleworld, the fabricated planet created by the godlike Beyonder. Rhodes fought alongside Captain America, the Hulk and Spider-Man as they turned trial into triumph and made it back to their home planet alive — and the universe still in one piece. It was a major test of Rhodes' fortitude as Iron Man, and one that prepared him for the next milestone in his burgeoning super-hero career.

When the Avengers saw fit to form a second regular team to complement the group in New York City, the West Coast Avengers invited Iron Man to be one of their heavy hitters. Settling into his new role led to several awkward situations for Rhodes, as his teammates assumed they were working alongside the Iron Man they had known for years. He fought gallantly against foes like Goliath, the Blank, Graviton and Maelstrom, eventually revealing his new identity to an understanding crew.

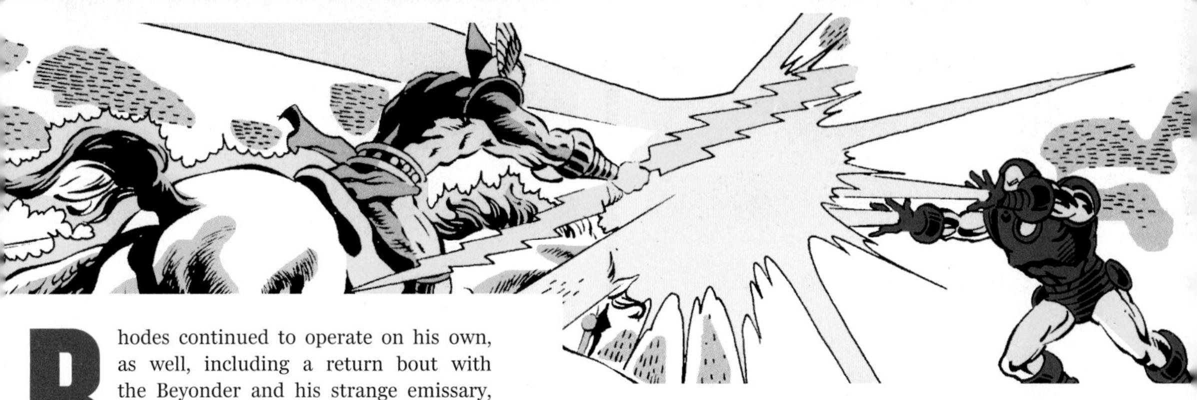

Rhodes continued to operate on his own, as well, including a return bout with the Beyonder and his strange emissary, Thundersword. Soon after, he helped Tony defend himself against the onslaught of Obadiah Stane's Iron Monger, eventually winding up in the hospital due to wounds sustained in a Stane bombing.

tark took back the Iron Man armor to defeat Stane, leaving Rhodes without a regular gig. He fell back into working as Stark's pilot, feelings of inferiority still haunting him. There would be time for team-ups, though, with both men wearing armor against such foes as the Living Laser and the Zodiac. On one adventure, the duo had to race back to Earth following an assault on Stark's orbiting space station by the terrorist group A.I.M. In one of the most horrific moments of his life, Rhodes' armor shielding gave in to the intense heat pressures of Earth's atmosphere, causing him to literally burn up on re-entry. It was a close call that kept Rhodes in recovery, and out of the armor, for quite some time.

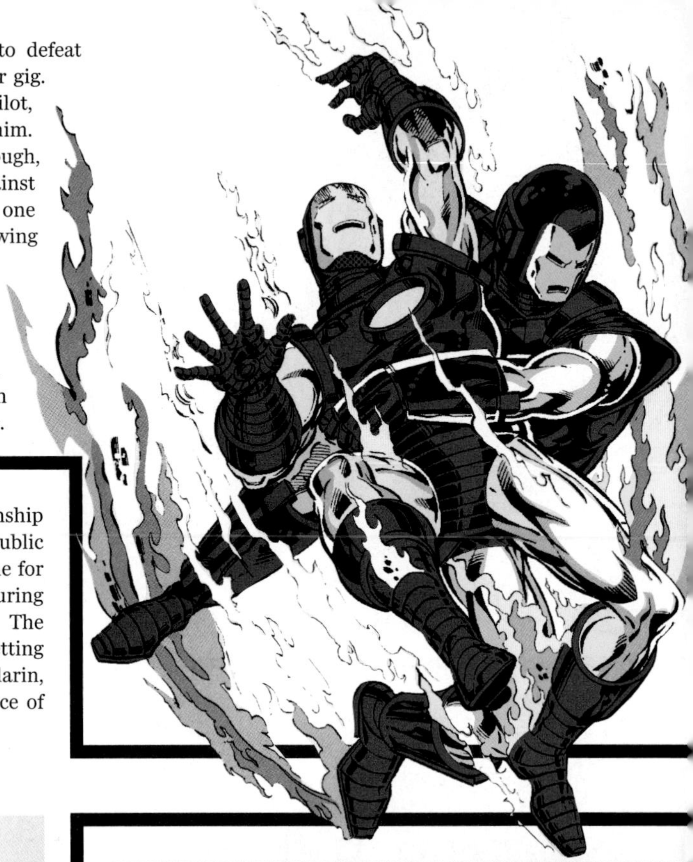

Rhodes developed a romantic relationship with Marcy Pearson, Stark's chief of public relations, which caused many a headache for him as he loyally stood by his boss during Iron Man's controversial Armor Wars. The two Iron Men teamed up again after getting embroiled in an internecine fight between the Mandarin, the Chinese Communists and Fin Fang Foom's race of alien dragons.

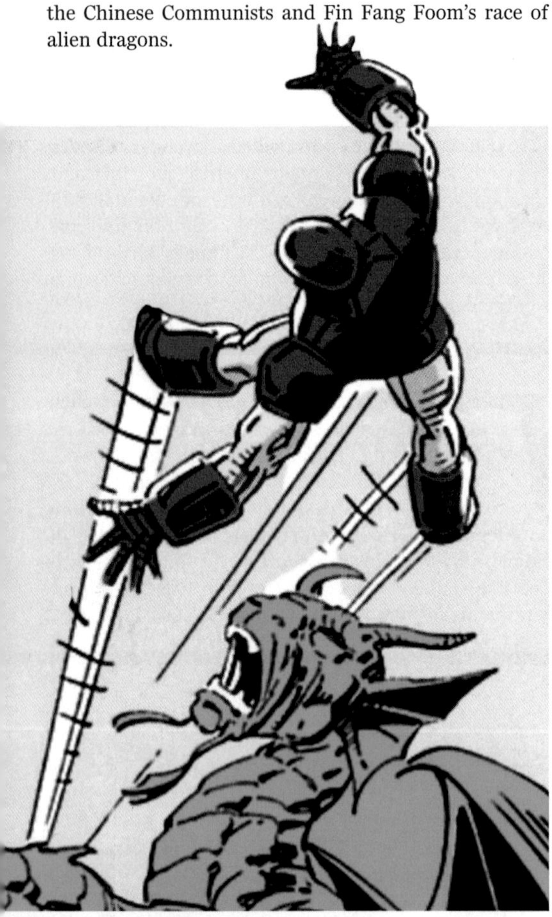

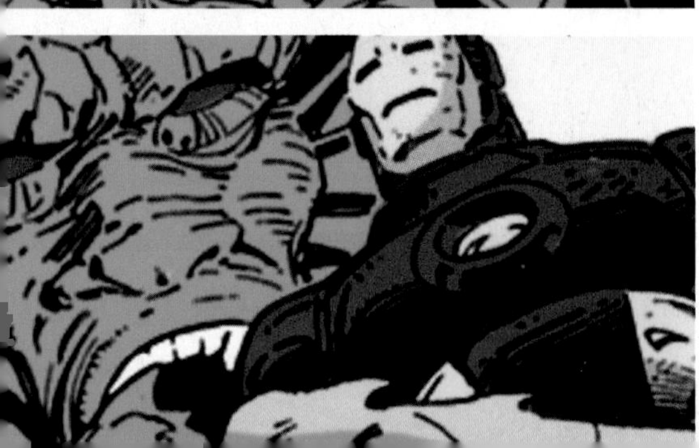

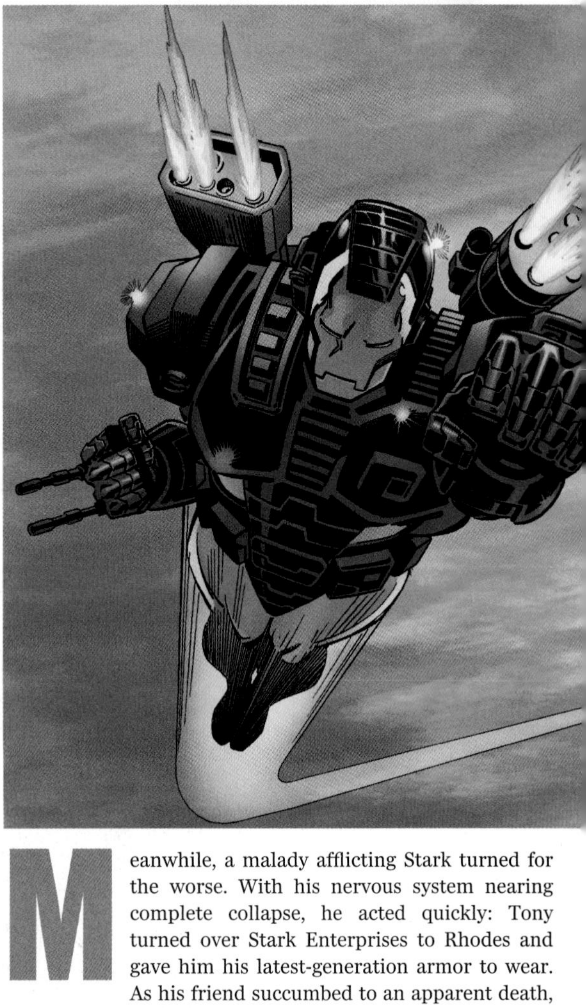

Meanwhile, a malady afflicting Stark turned for the worse. With his nervous system nearing complete collapse, he acted quickly: Tony turned over Stark Enterprises to Rhodes and gave him his latest-generation armor to wear. As his friend succumbed to an apparent death, Rhodes donned the War Machine armor, never to look back.

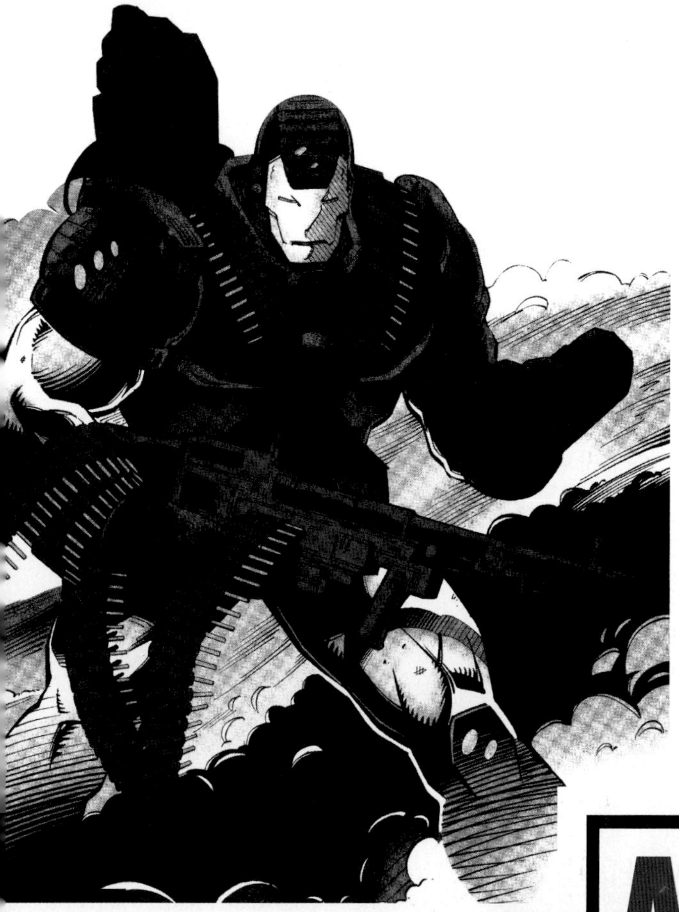

His relationship with Marcy on the rocks, Rhodes devoted his undivided attention to battling Justin Hammer; the villainous triumvirate of Beetle, Blacklash and Blizzard; Firepower; and the Living Laser. When Stark revealed he'd faked his death, Rhodes was furious with his friend for duping him, even with good intentions, and isolated himself from Tony. After a second stint with the West Coast Avengers, and the healing of time, Rhodes and Stark would eventually repair their relationship.

The raw power at War Machine's command, in many ways superior to Stark's own armor, was a perfect synthesis of super-hero flash and tactical military advantage. And Rhodes was ready to use it for the benefit of all. Opportunity came knocking when billionaire philanthropist Vincent Cetewayo offered him the job as CEO of the human-rights organization Worldwatch. Cetewayo's kidnapping and murder at Imayan dictator Eda Arul's hands sealed the deal for Rhodes. Knowing there were good people trying to make a difference in the world and getting paid back with death at the hands of despots convinced him he had a role to play as War Machine.

As Worldwatch's powerful exemplar, War Machine took on Deathtoll, mixed it up with Iron Man and the Mandarin, and even traveled back in time to World War II to unravel a Nazi plot and fight alongside Nick Fury and his Howling Commandos. Still, War Machine's exploits inevitably caused the diplomacy-minded Worldwatch much grief, and he and the organization amicably parted.

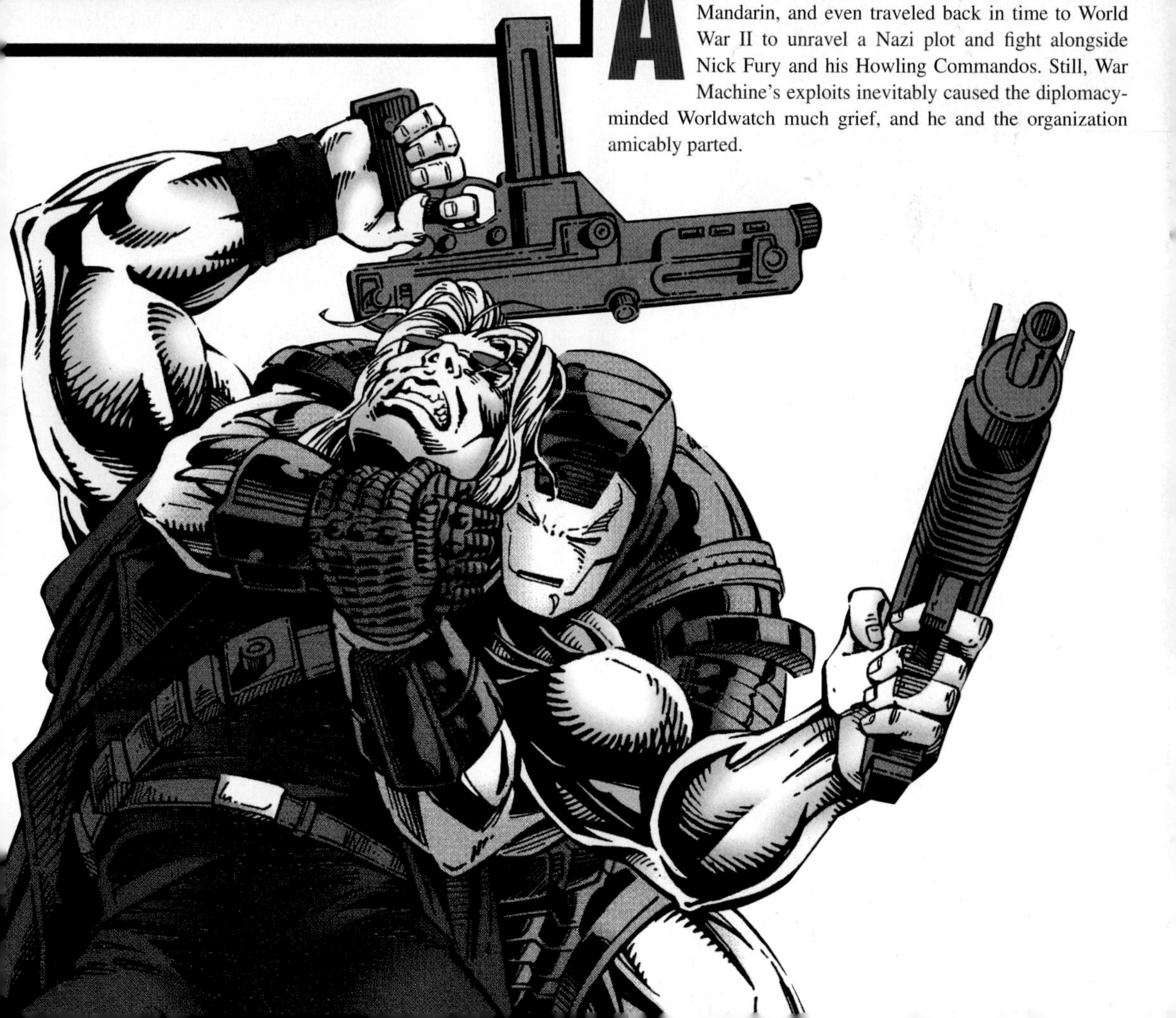

With Iron Man missing, along with the Avengers and Fantastic Four, Rhodes mothballed his War Machine armor and started up Rhodes Recovery, a marine-salvage business. After Iron Man's heroic return, Rhodes continued to become involved in the hero's adventures. Rhodes learned old friend and weapons dealer Parnell Jacobs had requisitioned the War Machine armor in his stead. He also helped Tony defeat Justin Hammer in a battle leading to the legendary foe's apparent death.

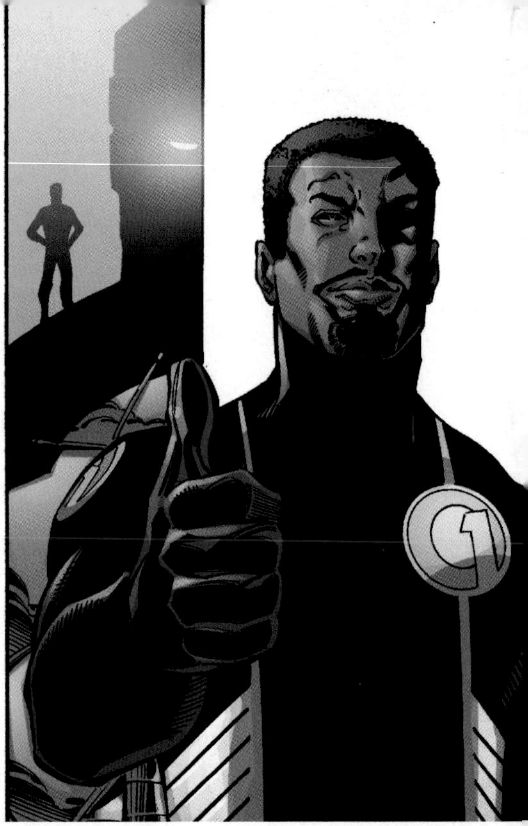

After a turn with White Tiger, Junta and Josiah X as the vigilante Crew, Rhodes was on hand at Avengers Mansion in the aftermath of the Scarlet Witch's deadly outburst of insanity. Soon after, he would don a new suit of armor for the Office of National Emergency (O*N*E). As the Sentinel Squad's drill instructor, and a pilot of personal Sentinel armor himself, he oversaw the implementation of Valerie Cooper's squad in the field after M-Day depowered millions of mutants. Later, he supported Stark's crusade to register all super-powered humans, recognizing the benefits of training heroes to harness their powers for the benefit of all.

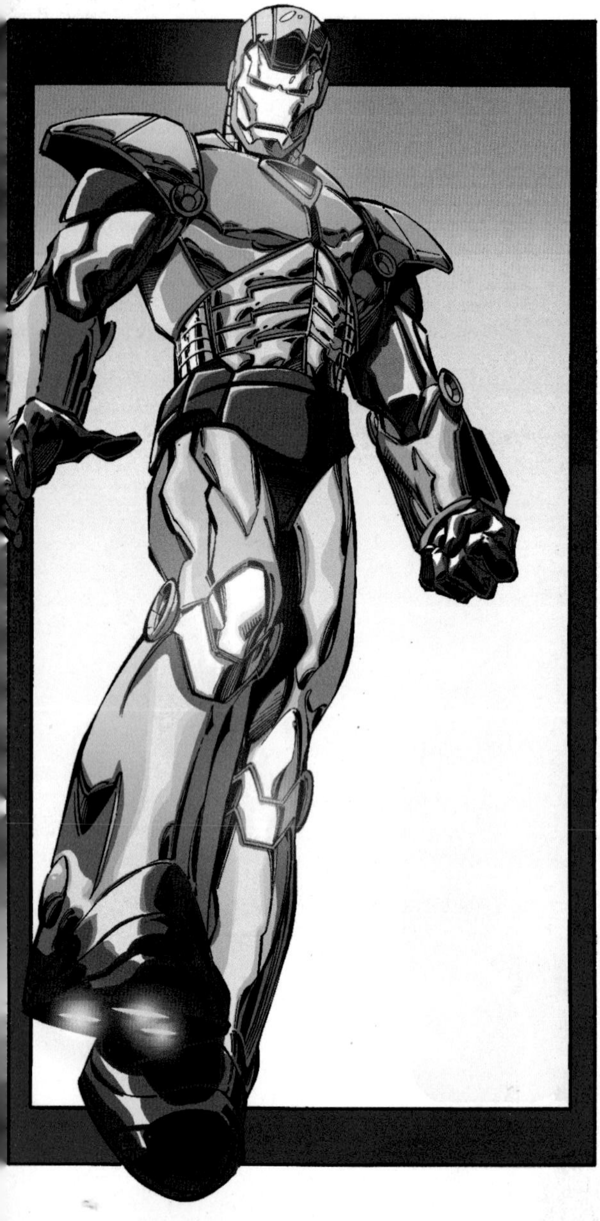

This support evolved into a job as director of Camp Hammond, the resultant Initiative's training ground. Back in his War Machine armor — and with the heroes Gauntlet, Justice and Yellowjacket working under him as drill instructor, counselor and chief scientist — Rhodes whipped newly registered superhumans into shape with training far beyond what they would have received operating on their own.

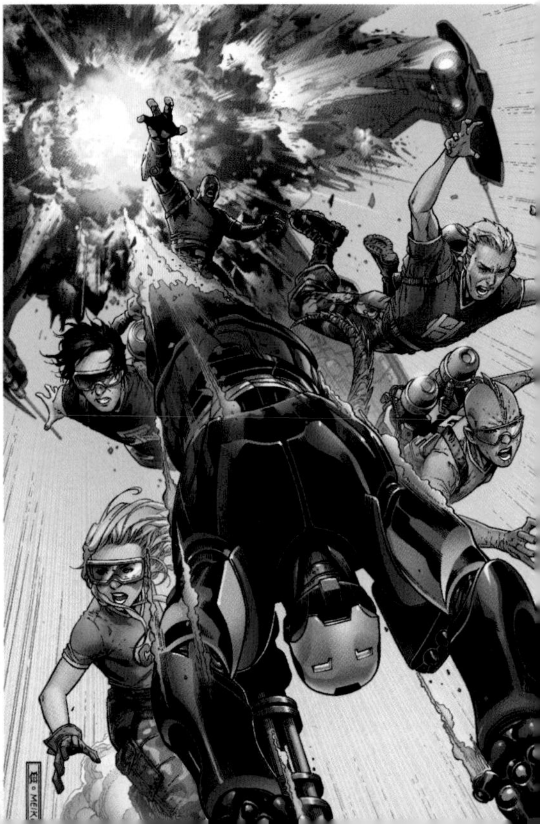

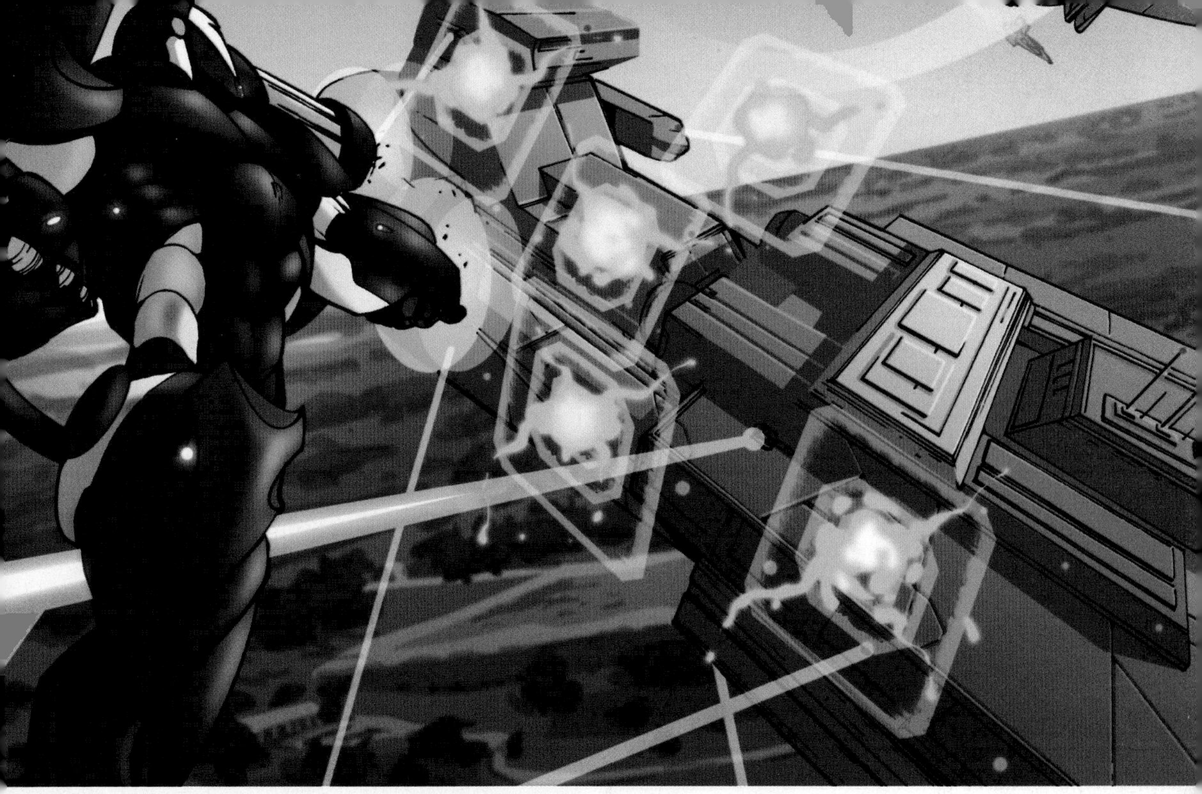

For his first Initiative sortie, War Machine led his recruits into battle alongside seasoned heroes like Wonder Man, Justice and the Texas Initiative team, the Rangers. They took out a massive Hydra terror-carrier on its way to assassinate the president.

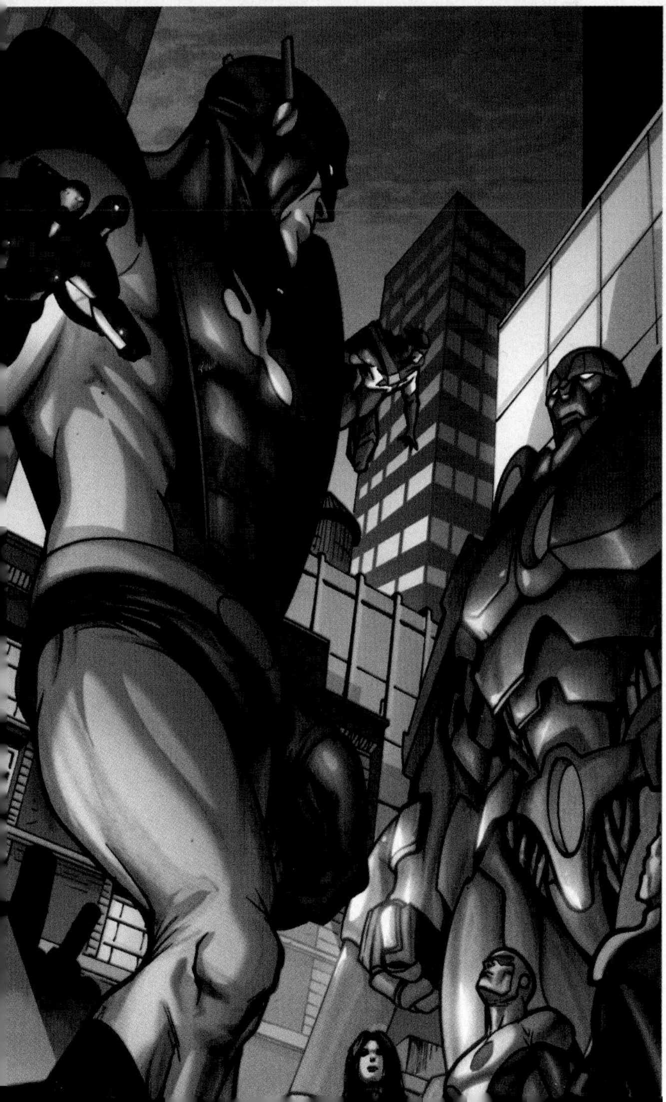

On another mission, War Machine and Komodo hunted down Spider-Man, attempting unsuccessfully to take his abilities from him with power-sapping S.P.I.N. Tech darts. Spider-Man got the upper hand on both of them. During a World War initiated by a vengeance-seeking Hulk, War Machine led virtually the entire 50 State Initiative network and his old Sentinel Squad teammates to provide a perimeter isolating the Hulk's rampage inside Manhattan.

Over time, the public began protesting Camp Hammond. And when Yellowjacket stood revealed as a Skrull impostor during the shapeshifting aliens' invasion of Earth, Rhodes left Camp Hammond on an urgent mission under direct orders from Tony Stark.

As the Skrulls marauded through the planet's defenses, War Machine headed to Stark's satellite. Assimilating his armor tech with the space station, he transformed into a giant robotic fighting form to take on the Skrulls in space and in Russia, supporting the Crimson Dynamo's Winter Guard.

But underneath his new armor, Rhodes kept a terrible secret. A year previous, while providing security consulting in Dubai, a terrorist bombing had taken both his arms and legs, and horribly burned his face. He survived with Stark marrying what was left of his corporeal self to his armor. In literal terms, Jim Rhodes was now a cyborg.

His new makeup allowed him to tap every database on the planet, with access to all war crimes committed during the past 70 years. Without the ability to turn this feature off, War Machine was driven like never before to bring justice to the guilty — and ever increasingly, this meant death. Whether confronting death squads in Santo Marco, taking on the bloodsuckers of Eaglestar International, stopping the spread of the Ultimo virus or rounding up the seemingly beyond retribution Bainsville Ten, War Machine brought quick and final justice to those who deserved it — which made him one of Norman Osborn's biggest targets.

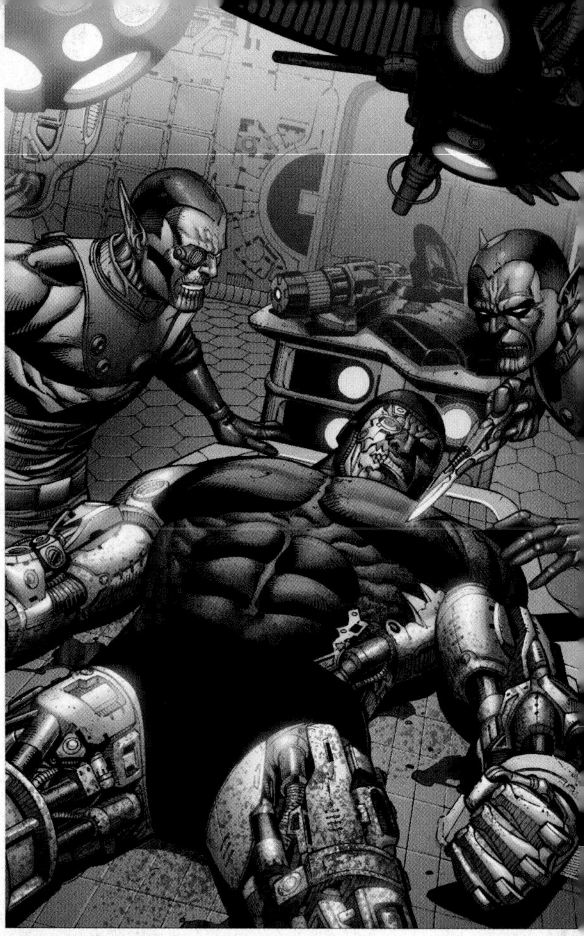

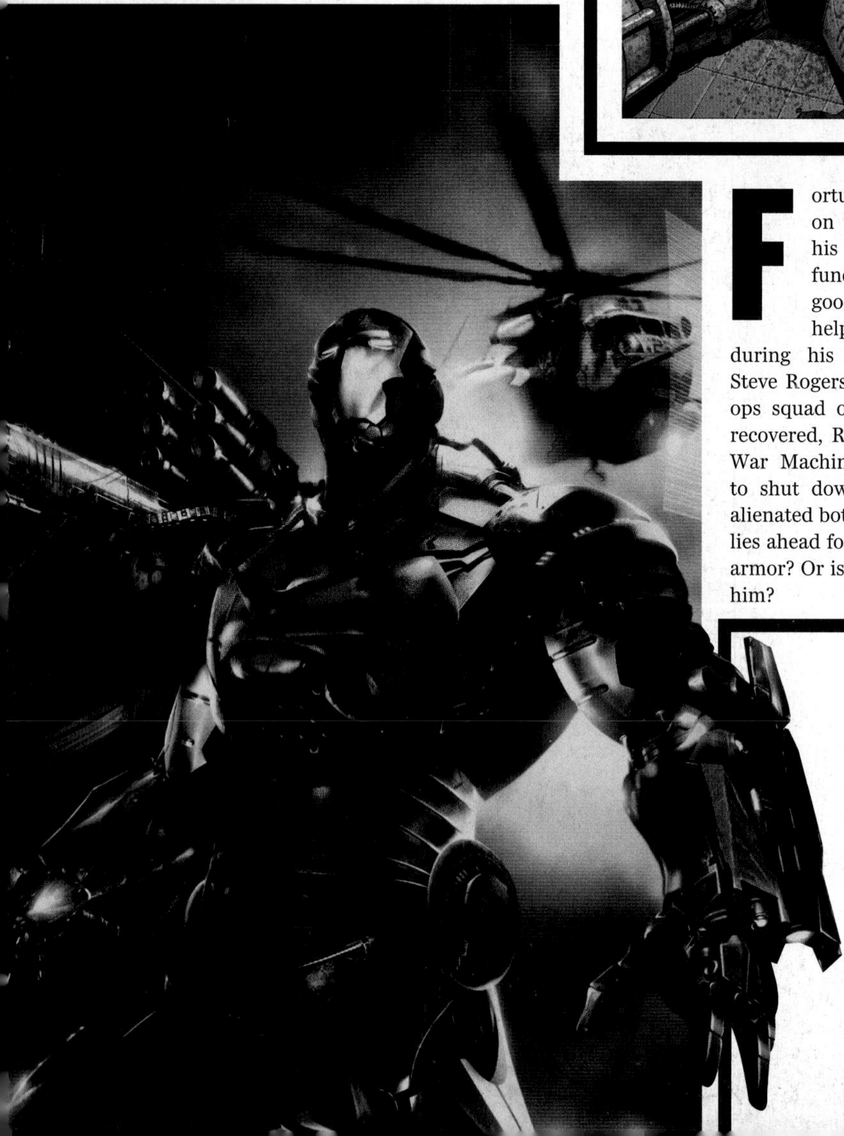

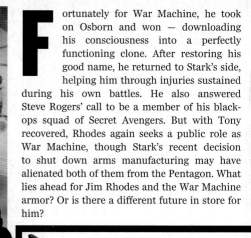

Fortunately for War Machine, he took on Osborn and won — downloading his consciousness into a perfectly functioning clone. After restoring his good name, he returned to Stark's side, helping him through injuries sustained during his own battles. He also answered Steve Rogers' call to be a member of his black-ops squad of Secret Avengers. But with Tony recovered, Rhodes again seeks a public role as War Machine, though Stark's recent decision to shut down arms manufacturing may have alienated both of them from the Pentagon. What lies ahead for Jim Rhodes and the War Machine armor? Or is there a different future in store for him?

WRITTEN BY: John Rhett Thomas
DESIGN BY: Travis Bonilla

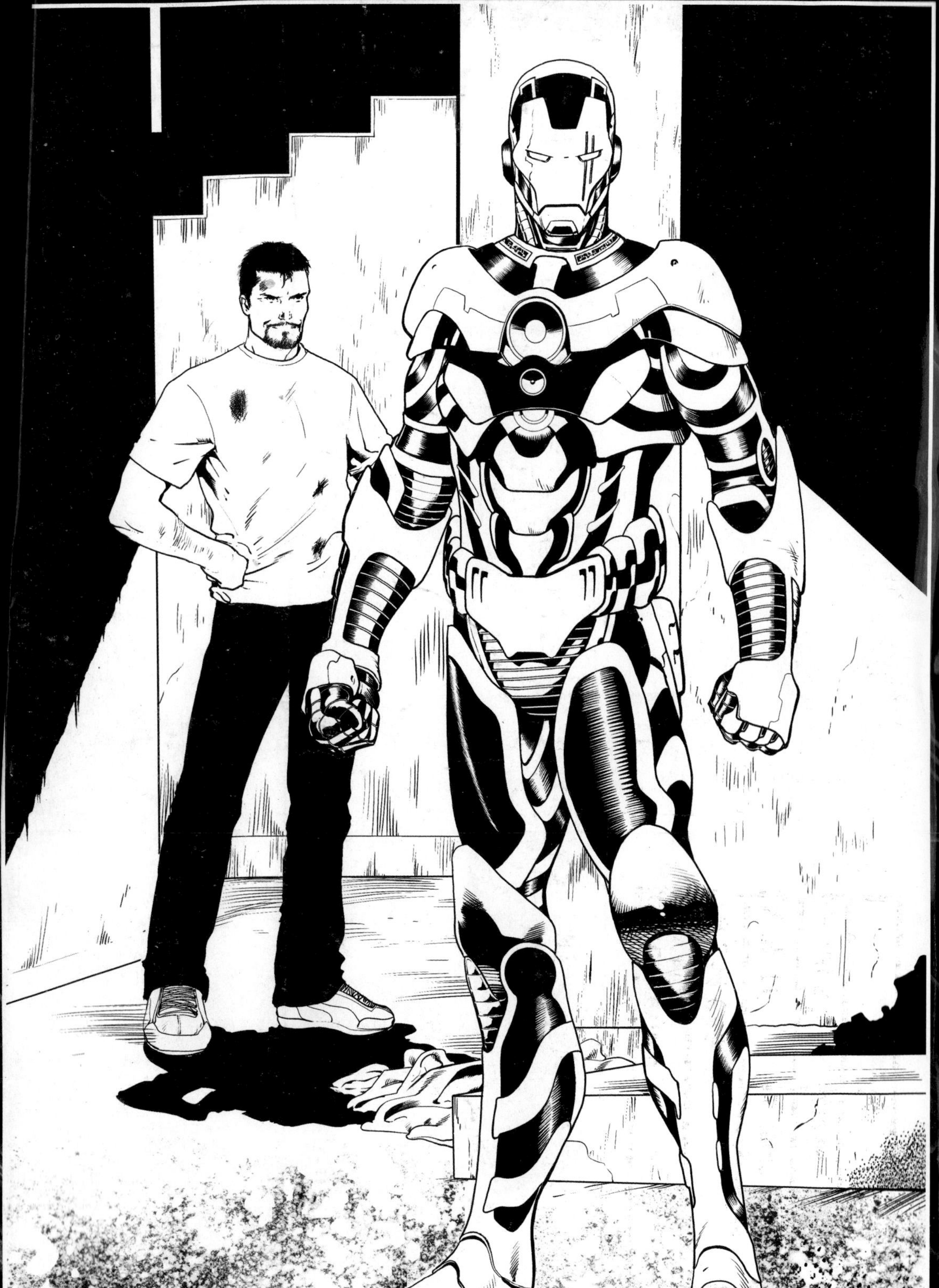

ISSUE #3, PAGE 20 INKS BY BARRY KITSON

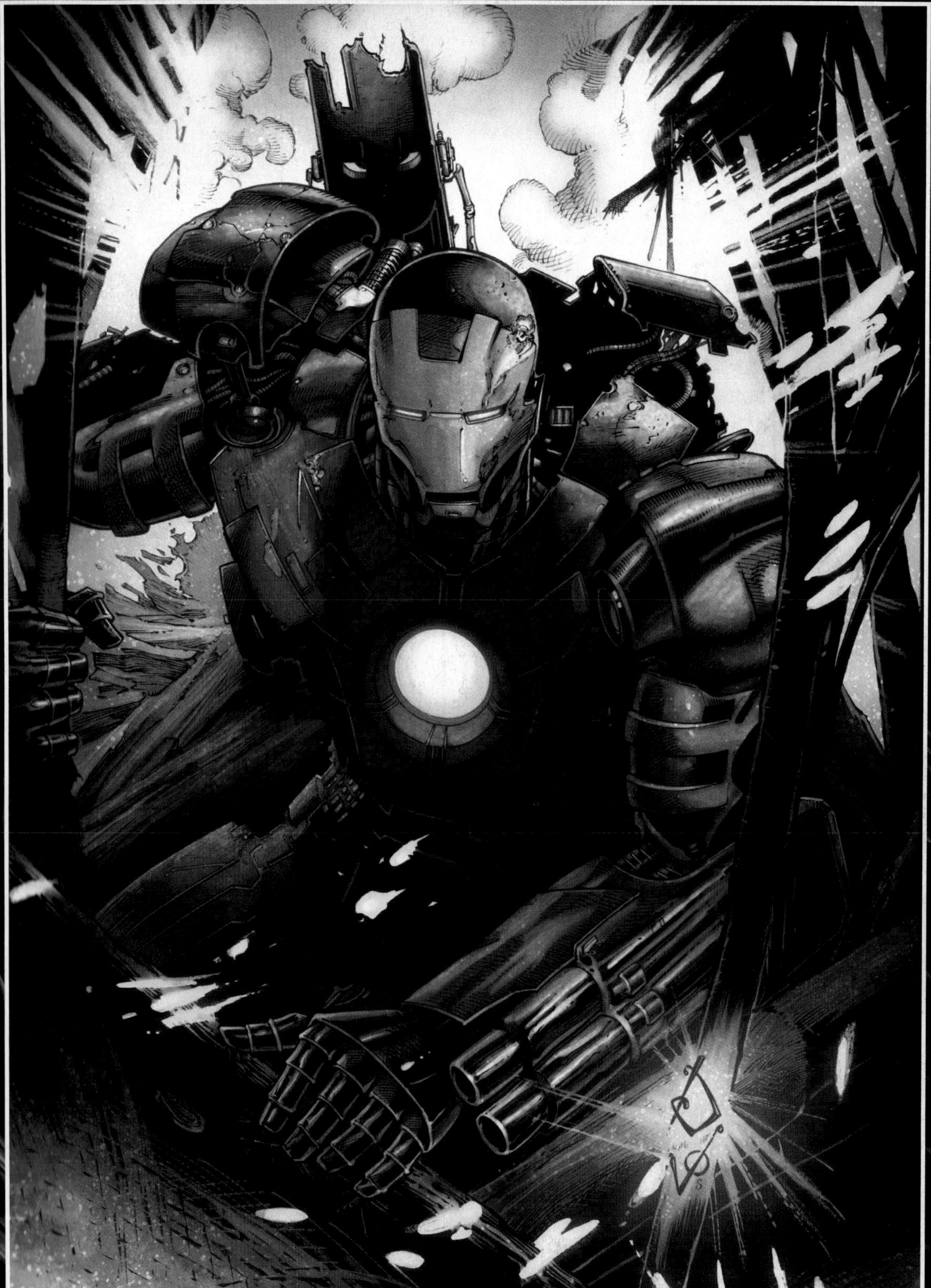

#1 VARIANT BY DHEERAJ BERMA, VICTOR OLAZABA & MORRY HOLLOWELL

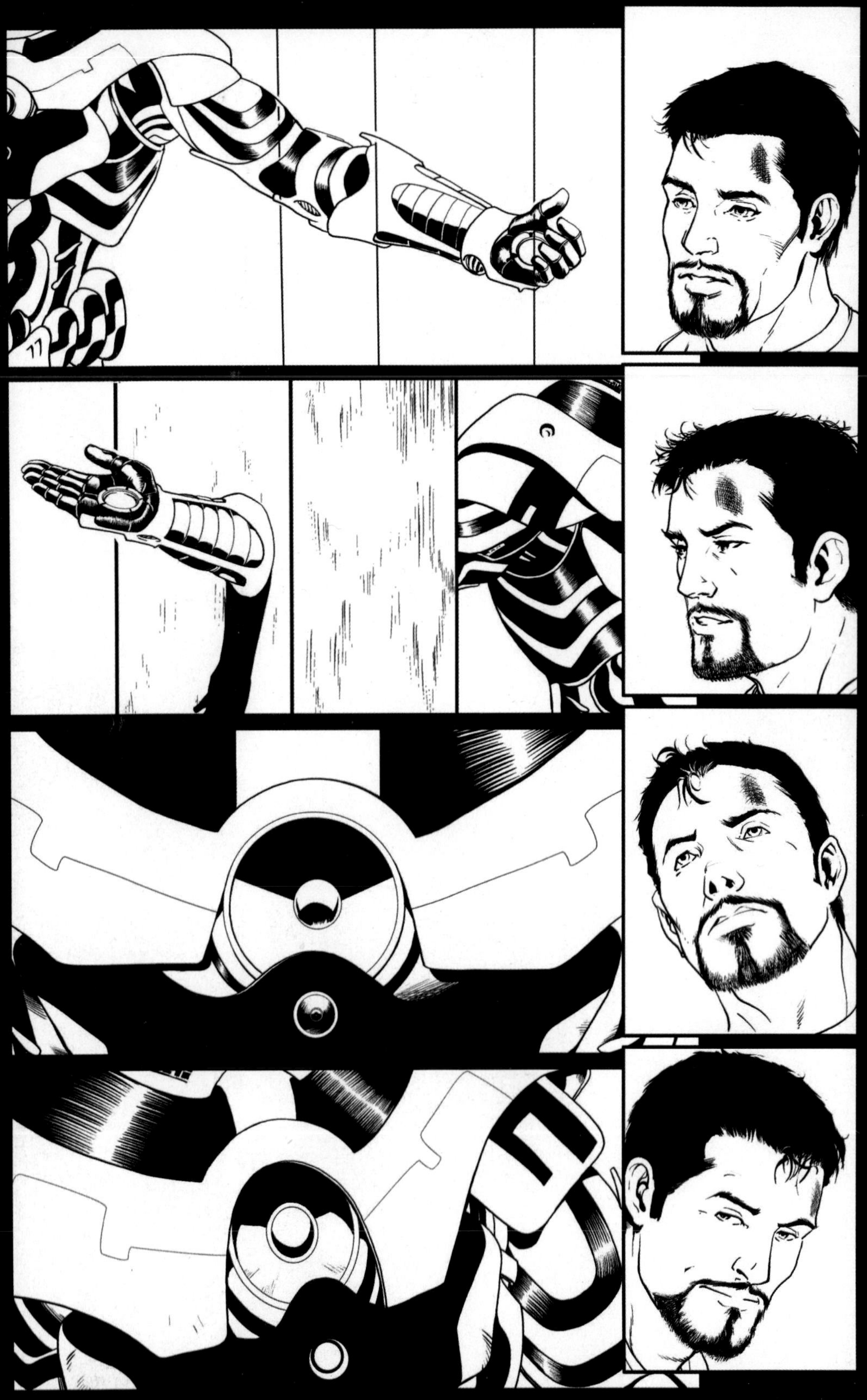

ISSUE #3, PAGE 18 INKS BY BARRY KITSON

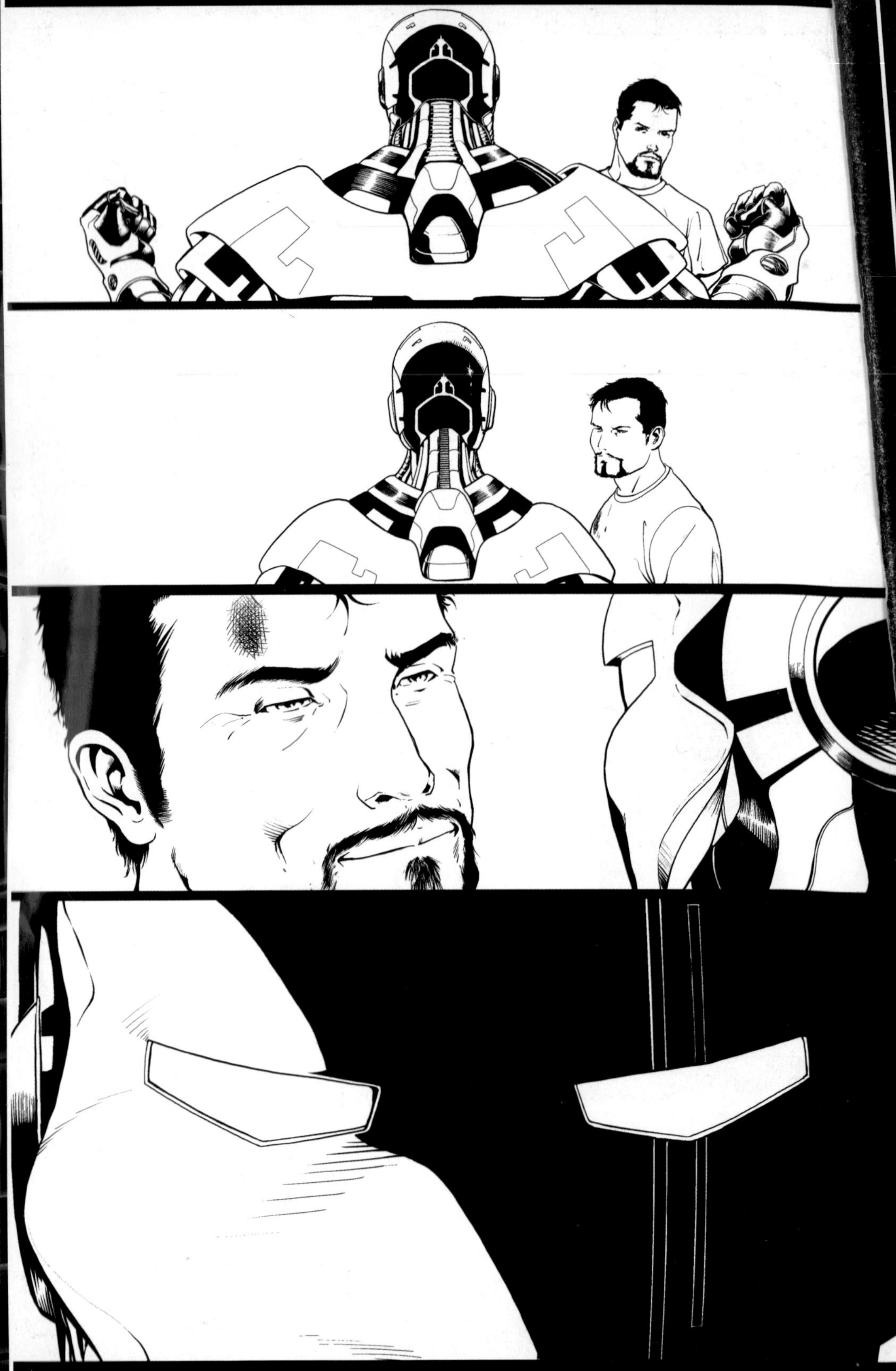

ISSUE #3, PAGE 19 INKS BY BARRY KITSON

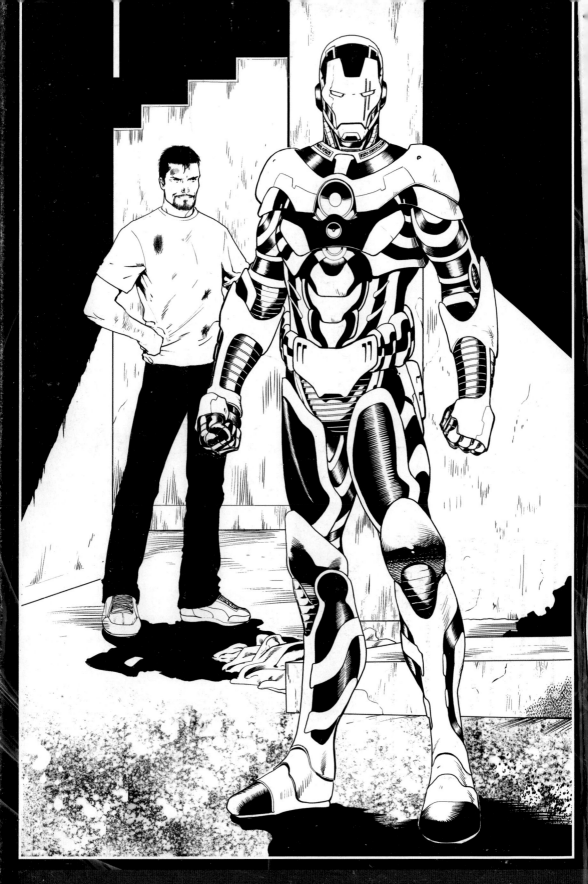

ISSUE #3, PAGE 20 INKS BY BARRY KITSON

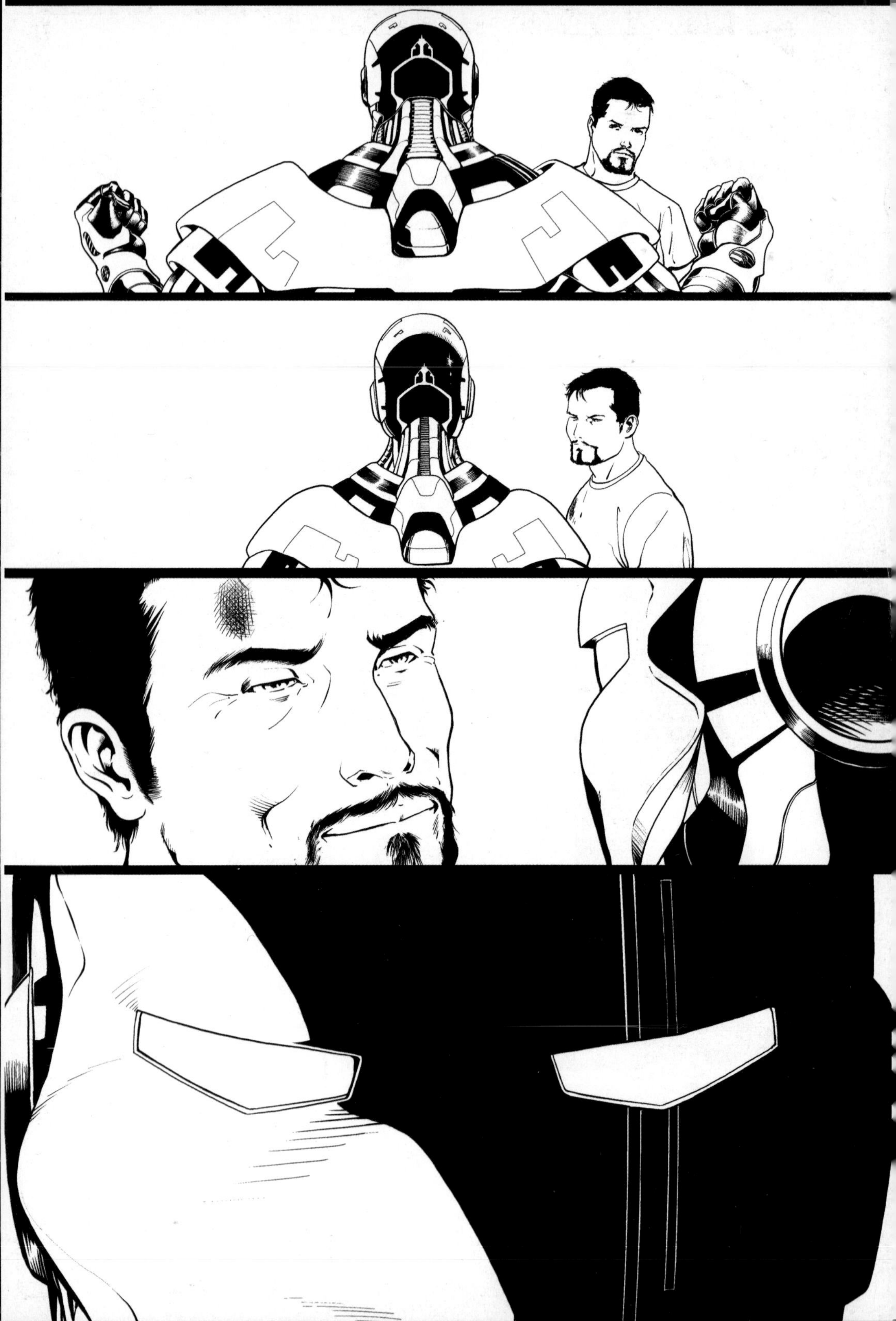

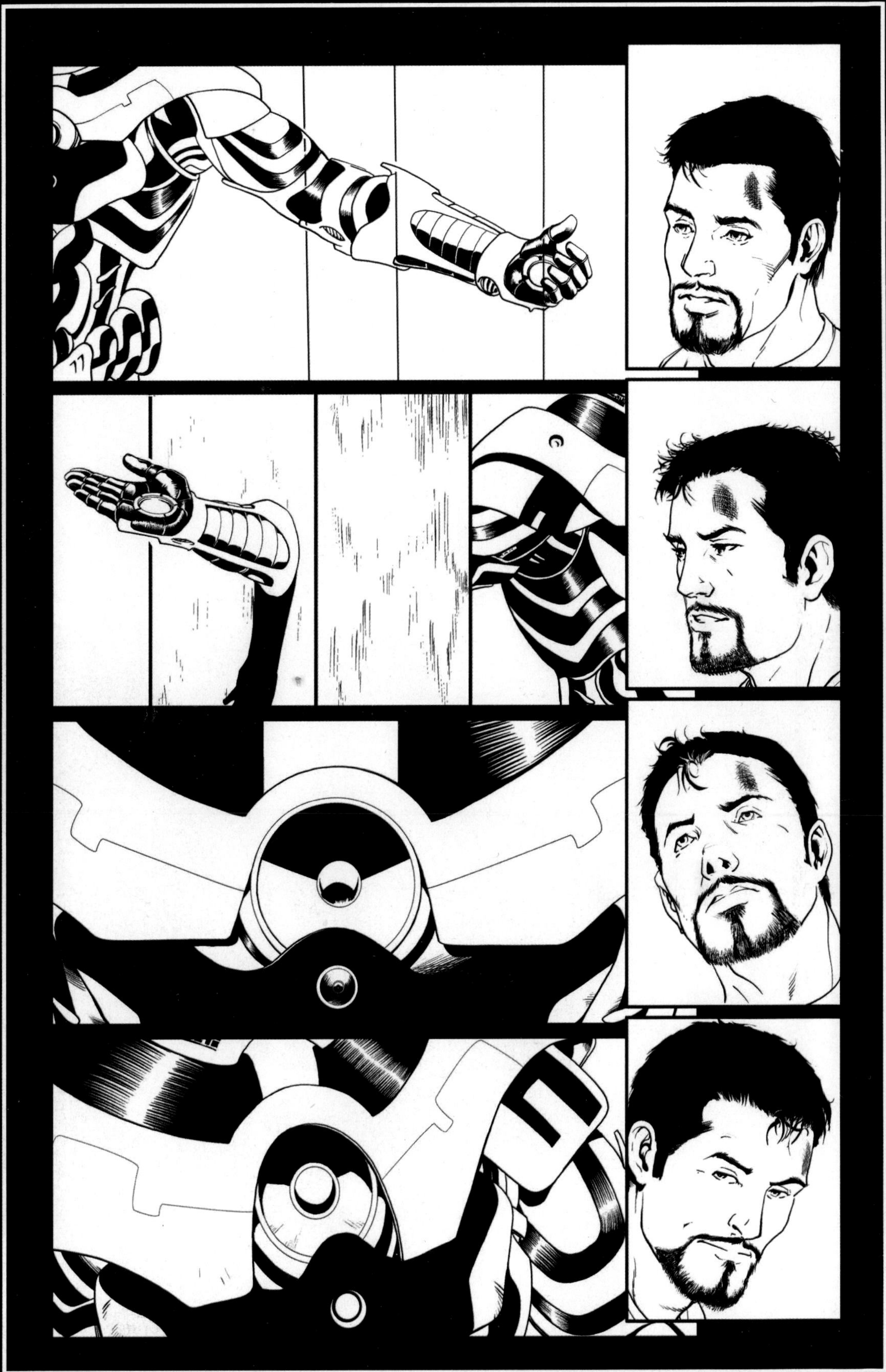

ISSUE #3, PAGE 18 INKS BY BARRY KITSON

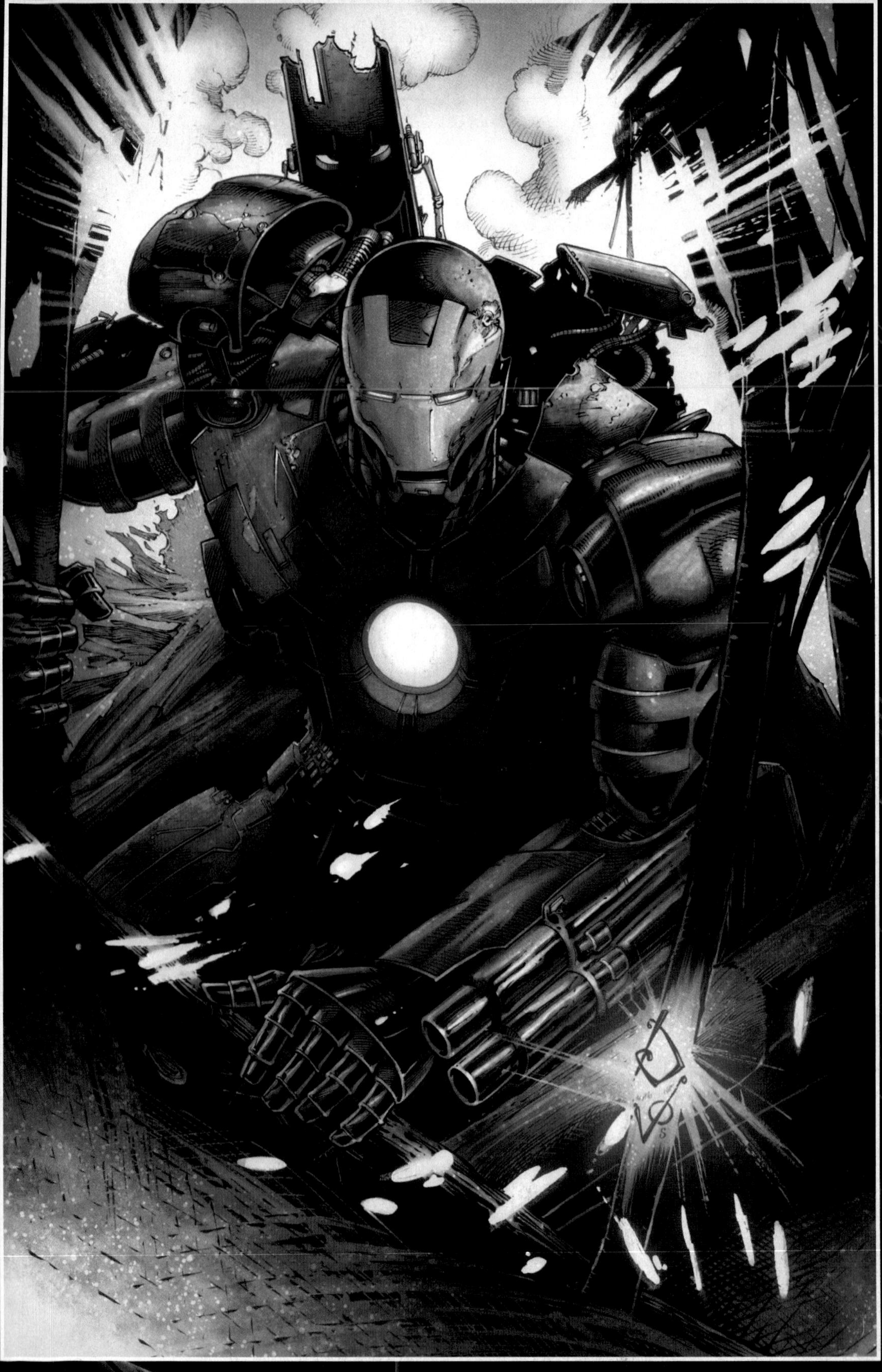

#1 VARIANT BY DHEERAJ BERMA,
VICTOR OLAZABA & MORRY HOLLOWELL